SHAKESPEARE AND WISDOM

Dedicated to the Beloved Community

care-centred activists working
for liveable communities and a liveable planet
child care providers and teachers
healthcare workers
frontline workers of all sectors
life-giving parents
sapient elders
sapient youth
striving for Life

SHAKESPEARE AND WISDOM

Ecumenical, Ecological and Ethical Horizons

◆ ◆ ◆

EDITED BY
UNHAE PARK LANGIS AND
JULIA REINHARD LUPTON

EDINBURGH
University Press

Edinburgh University Press is one of the leading university presses in the UK. We publish academic books and journals in our selected subject areas across the humanities and social sciences, combining cutting-edge scholarship with high editorial and production values to produce academic works of lasting importance. For more information visit our website: edinburghuniversitypress.com

© editorial matter and organisation Unhae Park Langis and Julia Reinhard Lupton, 2024
© the chapters their several authors, 2024

Edinburgh University Press Ltd
13 Infirmary Street
Edinburgh EH1 1LT

Typeset in 11/14 Adobe Sabon by
IDSUK (DataConnection) Ltd, and
printed and bound in Great Britain

A CIP record for this book is available from the British Library

ISBN 978 1 3995 1656 3 (hardback)
ISBN 978 1 3995 1658 7 (webready PDF)
ISBN 978 1 3995 1659 4 (epub)

The right of Unhae Park Langis and Julia Reinhard Lupton to be identified as the editors of this work has been asserted in accordance with the Copyright, Designs and Patents Act 1988, and the Copyright and Related Rights Regulations 2003 (SI No. 2498).

CONTENTS

List of Illustrations	vii
Acknowledgements	viii
Preface	ix

Introduction *Unhae Park Langis and Julia Reinhard Lupton*	1

PART I: Shakespeare and the *Oikumene*

1. Wisdom Ecology: Mapping the Ancient Wisdom World into the Future *Unhae Park Langis*	23
2. Sophia on the Cydnus: *Antony and Cleopatra* as Wisdom Literature *Julia Reinhard Lupton*	46
3. 'Like Prayers Divine': Shakespeare's Sonnets as Spiritual Exercise *Sean Keilen*	73
4. Morality on Stage: Free Will, Counsel and Self-Counsel in Shakespeare and Glissenti *Eugenio Refini*	95

PART II: *Oikeiôsis* and Ecology

5. Jaques the Pythagorean: Ecognosis and Pythagorean Wisdom Literature in *As You Like It* *Todd Andrew Borlik*	119

vi]   *Contents*

6. Sovereign Care and Natural Goodness: Stoic Wisdom
   in *The Winter's Tale*   146
   Benjamin Parris

PART III: A Kinaesthetic Ethics of the Heart-Mind

7. *Prajñāpāramitā* and the Buddhist Path of Wisdom in
   King Lear   171
   Marguerite A. Tassi

8. Loving 'Not Wisely But Too Well': Race, Religion and
   Sufi Theoeroticism in *Othello*   200
   Unhae Park Langis

9. No Magistrate, No Engine, No Oil: *Calvin's Case*
   (1608) and the Kinaesthetic Wisdom of *The Tempest*   237
   Carolyn Sale

PART IV: Grace-Notes of Creative Wisdom

10. Holding a Space for Possibility: A Conversation with
    Madeline Sayet   269

11. Wisdom and Welcome in Madeline Sayet's *Where
    We Belong*   285
    Robin Alfriend Kello

12. *wétos, vitus, vecchia, vita*   298
    Jos Charles

13. The Buddha and the Bard: On Shakespeare and
    Mindfulness   311
    Lauren Shufran

    Afterword: Shakespeare's Open O: Sounding Global
    Wisdoms into the Future   323
    Joan Pong Linton

Notes on Contributors   331
Works Cited   336
Index   369

ILLUSTRATIONS

Figures

3.1	Position of the pronouns in Sonnet 120 by William Shakespeare. Created by Sean Keilen.	90
9.1	*Magus goggled and tracking Nature through the night with staff and lamp* (by Theodor de Bry, in Michael Maier, *Atalanta fugiens, hoc est, Emblemata nova de secretis naturae chymica*, 1618). RB 600059, The Huntington Library, San Marino, California.	249
9.2	*Their danses vvhich they vse at their highe feastes* (by Theodor de Bry, in Thomas Hariot, *A briefe and true report of the new found land of Virginia*, 1590), right half. RB 5360, The Huntington Library, San Marino, California.	261
13.1	Quotation from *The Two Noble Kinsmen* II.ii by William Shakespeare. Created by Lauren Shufran.	317
13.2	Quotation from *The Winter's Tale* III.ii by William Shakespeare. Created by Lauren Shufran.	318

Table

3.1	Organisation of time in Sonnet 120 by William Shakespeare. Created by Sean Keilen.	89

ACKNOWLEDGEMENTS

We express gratitude to the Indra's Net of sages, thinkers and writers, ancient and modern, that has made it possible for us to make another offering to the 'string of pearls'.

We thank our life-partners for their love and generosity of time to enable this volume to come to fruition.

We thank Elizabeth Fraser at Edinburgh University Press for her support, Erin Hughes, Julia's former student and source sleuth, for assistance with manuscript preparation, Cathy Falconer for keen copy-editing and Samantha Clark for capacious indexing. The UCI New Swan Shakespeare Center, funded by our generous donors, has provided funding for editorial work.

PREFACE

Amicorum communia omnia (Friends hold all things in common).

> Proverb attributed to Pythagoras and cited by
> Erasmus, *Adagia* 1.1[1]

What's mine is yours, and what is yours is mine.

> *Measure for Measure*, 5.1.524

This project is the fruit of a friendship born two decades ago, out of our mutual recognition of the special wisdom of *All's Well That Ends Well* and the hidden power of virtue that animates Shakespeare's plays. Our friendship deepened during the pandemic, when social isolation and forced stillness led us to reconnect our hearts and minds through shared study and collaborative writing. The world struggled through COVID surges to settle back into its individualist, consumerist way of life, further enriching the corporate elite but also deepening the commitment of others to building a more thoughtful world together. Looking both inward at the sources of beauty, value and strength that motivate us from our different spiritual backgrounds and outward at the urgency of social transformation, we wanted to host this exploration of wisdom, approaching Shakespeare as he himself approached literature: as an immersive platform inviting readers to take stock of their lives, ponder the pearls of living and string them together in new patterns.

---

[1] *The Adages of Erasmus*, ed. William Barker (U of Toronto P, 2001), 28–30.

x] *Preface*

For scholar-citizen Unhae, a Korean immigrant, wisdom has been a slow arboreal layering since her undergrad days and teaching years later informed by Aristotelian and Stoic pursuits of *eudaimonia*, the Greek concept of well-being, or flourishing (literally, state of divine being). In managing sciatica, she joyfully stumbled upon Eastern expressions of *eudaimonia* in Buddhism, Daoism and Sufism. This ouroboric joining of East-West wisdom traditions was a spiritual and ethnic homecoming as she endeavoured to put study into practice for the well-being of all members of her trigenerational household during COVID lockdown. A half-century of hybrid living in the US, capped by the countless hours of contemplation that this volume afforded, has strengthened her identity and way of life as a cosmopolite—a citizen of the world and a joyful partaker of Earth and the cosmic dance.[2] For Unhae, living in Northern California, wisdom also means wondering at the beauty and variety of the natural world even as we bid many endangered species goodbye. It means sensing the sacredness of each organic and inorganic being and feeling down to the invisible, indivisible atoms of our bodies that each of us is literally made of stardust from 'the cosmic ingredients that sustain us and the starlight that powers it all'.[3]

For citizen-scholar Julia, living in Southern California, wisdom has taken shape in her concerted study of the Book of Psalms and other works of Hebrew wisdom literature with two online congregations and with her friend Sean Keilen, a contributor to this project. For Julia, wisdom is a body of images and ideas that exists through its sharing, a work of hospitality and friendship that unfolds in dialogue both with artists and sages of the past and with fellow travellers in the present. As she delved into the

---

[2] Lyanda Lynn Haupt, *Rooted: Life at the Crossroads of Science, Nature, and Spirit* (Little, Brown Spark, 2021), 62.

[3] Naomi Austin, Stephen Cooter and Alice Jones, dirs., *Our Universe*, Netflix Documentary Series, narr. Morgan Freeman (BBC Studios, 2022). In reaction to the ecological crisis, scientists, thinkers and activists from various disciplines—the sciences, history and religion—have come up with a coherent, unifying narrative of a living Earth as requisite common ground to galvanise collective will to combat the climate crisis. Going by many names—the Great Story, evolutionary epic, Big History—its common underlying theme is planetary interdependence. See 'One Epic Story, Many Epic Storytellers', *Epic of Evolution*, accessed October 2, 2023. https://epicofevolution.com/one-epic-story-many-epic-storytellers

Preface [xi

prehistory of the Hebrew wisdom books, she began to appreciate the antiquity of their conversation with neighbouring traditions as well as the impact of these works' translation into Greek for the Jews of Alexandria. She came to appreciate the interpenetration of Hellenistic and Near Eastern philosophy and mythopoesis in new thought formations that flowered in Sufism and Kabbalah as well as the Renaissance humanism practised by Christian, Jewish and a/ gnostic scholars of the human record, and she deepened her sense of the virtues beyond the Aristotelian tradition to encompass Platonic, Stoic and Persianate worldviews.

For both of us, wisdom is ultimately not the preserve of books but what is felt and practised joyfully and gratefully in connection with all beings in a shared enlivened world. Wisdom is not a matter of who has it or whether it's attainable. Instead, the heart of wisdom is at once simple and daunting: to live in a manner that hurts none and contributes to the flourishing of all. Our collaboration itself was part of this journey of experiential wisdom, offering lessons of joy, attentive listening, magnanimity, humility, forgiveness, impermanence, resilience and gratitude. On this journey it matters less that we don't measure up on a particular day, and matters more that we reflect regularly on our actions, and find joy in our efforts toward the common good as we 'dance at the brink of the world', to quote a line from an Ohlone song.

True to the Pythagorean ideal that friends hold all in common, this collection gathers together scholars beyond an intellectual endeavour to reflect on the ways we each love Shakespeare and pursue wisdom. In honouring this communal spirit in the Greco-Buddhist tradition, we have become a fellowship of seekers in a burgeoning branch of virtue and wisdom studies in Shakespeare. At the hub of this camaraderie is Julia Lupton, whose work in political theology had found its way via hospitality and the ethics of care into virtue criticism. Meanwhile, Unhae had all but left academia when, through a New Year's email exchange reconnecting her with Julia, she found herself, as an early author of Shakespeare and virtue, contributing to a flurry of projects around that topic even as they eventually evolved into a lively engagement with ancient and Indigenous wisdom traditions. Our collaborations connected and reconnected us with other travellers on this journey.

While working on this volume, we supported one another in love, death, sickness and marriage, in art exhibits and book launches. The time of writing saw members of our group affected by COVID, suffering debilitating back trouble and recovering from a catastrophic traffic accident. Unhae's mother and father and Julia's father passed. Ben Parris published his first book, *Vital Strife: Sleep, Insomnia, and the Early Modern Ethics of Care*, and poet Lauren Shufran, her first book outside of poetry, *The Buddha and the Bard: Where Shakespeare's Stage Meets Buddhist Scriptures*.[4] Julia and Sean taught community seminars on Shakespeare and wisdom. Julia met poet Jos Charles and graduate student Robin Kello in her graduate seminar on Shakespeare and wisdom, to which both Sean and Unhae contributed. Todd Borlik joined our group through his scholarship on Pythagoras and we discovered Eugenio Refini through an intriguing online lecture on Venetian morality plays. Carolyn Sale entered our circle through a companion project, *Shakespeare's Virtuous Theatre: Power, Capacity and the Good*.[5] Marguerite Tassi reached out to Unhae after reading her Buddhist essay on *King Lear*, in a collection to which Julia also contributed.[6] Since then, Lauren, Marguerite and Unhae have revelled in a rare shared interest in Shakespeare and Buddhism. Joan Pong Linton, a longtime fellow traveller, provided detailed feedback on all the chapters and graciously agreed to write an Afterword. Through the process of compiling this book, we shared resources and bonded through deep exchanges of thoughts and emails—all of which will continue and deepen in the months and years to come.

One recent experience of such bonding comes to mind. Unhae and Marguerite had the opportunity to meander in the enchanted woods of the Land of Medicine Buddha in Soquel, California, land originally of the Awaswas-speaking Uypi Tribe. It was sacred space lingering with the spirits of Indigenous hunting tribes who worshipped animal spirits as gods and sought animal powers in their dreams,

---

[4] Benjamin Parris, *Vital Strife: Sleep, Insomnia, and the Early Modern Ethics of Care* (Cornell UP, 2022); Lauren Shufran, *The Buddha and the Bard: Where Shakespeare's Stage Meets Buddhist Scriptures* (Mandala Publishing, 2022).

[5] Kent Lehnhof, Julia Reinhard Lupton and Carolyn Sale, eds., *Shakespeare's Virtuous Theatre: Power, Capacity and the Good* (Edinburgh UP, 2023).

[6] 'Humankindness: *King Lear* and the Suffering, Wisdom, and Compassion within Buddhist Interbeing', in *Literature and Religious Experience: Beyond Belief and Unbelief*, ed. Matthew J. Smith and Caleb D. Spencer (Bloomsbury, 2022), 209–26.

Preface [xiii

dream[ing] of you jumping.
Rabbit,
Jackrabbit,
Quail.[7]

It was where mushrooms of astonishing variety soundlessly broke ground, their faces poking into the light as if to greet their human visitors. The silence was so awe-ful that at times their conversation lowered to a whisper, which was privy only to the adjacent fairy rings of wise and sentient redwoods. Among the different strands of talk weaving in and out, they discovered to their delight that each wanted to write a (spiritual) practice book, one that will extend the work of this volume for a popular audience beyond Shakespeare: a book that would be a living body of global wisdom drawn from the storehouse of their lived practice. A book for the cultivation of humankindness and active compassion! They decided there and then to braid their efforts together. It was a classic instance of losing oneself in the wilderness to find oneself. It was in the age-old tradition of travel as the spiritual practice of seeking the Stranger: how meandering can lead to an amazing view, one that connects ourselves to the world in the most kindred way. May we abound in further acts of creative wisdom toward the deepening of shared traditions in the service of healing the Earth and knowing ourselves.

Unhae and Julia
Santa Cruz and Irvine, California

---

[7] Geoffrey Dunn, 'Spirit Weavers', *Good Times*, May 8, 2013. https://www.goodtimes.sc/spirit-weavers

INTRODUCTION

Unhae Park Langis and Julia Reinhard Lupton

Ecumenical and Ecological Shakespeare

What does it mean to call Shakespeare 'ecumenical'? Certainly, the word points to his search for ethical and spiritual understandings beyond the confessional divisions of his day. It also implies his receptivity to manifold phenomena of the social and natural world, expressed in John Keats's 'negative capability'. Although largely associated with unity among Christians, the word *oikumene* was first used by the ancient Greeks to describe the entirety and diversity of the inhabited world as they knew it, which included India to the east, the Celts to the west, the Ethiopians to the south and the Scythians to the north.[1] The Hellenistic and post-Hellenistic *oikumene* composed a heterogeneous imperial and cultural space that mixed Hellenic, Babylonian, Egyptian, Jewish and Indian traditions.[2] At once concurring with and broadening Michael Witmore's characterisation of Shakespeare as part of a 'wider wisdom culture' irreducible to any particular source of religious insight, we read Shakespeare's *oikumene* expansively, to encompass cosmopolitan Pythagorean, Orphic, Stoic, Abrahamic, Gnostic, Hindu, Buddhist and Indigenous formations of knowledge and understanding.[3] We address Shakespeare as the

---

[1] Klaus Geus, 'Oikoumene/Orbis Terrarum', in *Oxford Classical Dictionary*, published online December 22, 2016, https://doi.org/10.1093/acrefore/9780199381135.013.8008

[2] Ljuben Tevdovski, 'The Beauty of the *Oikumene* Has Two Edges: Nurturing Roman Imperialism in the "Glocalizing" Traditions of the East', in *Community and Identity at the Edges of the Classical World*, ed. Aaron W. Irvin (Wiley Blackwell, 2021), 7–28.

[3] Michael Witmore, 'Shakespeare and Wisdom Literature', in *Shakespeare and Early Modern Religion*, ed. David Loewenstein and Michael Witmore (Cambridge UP, 2015), 194.

ecumenical poet of an integrated thought- and lifeworld touched by many ancient spiritual teachings. These teachings are channelled both directly and indirectly in the stories, images, maxims and myths that enliven Shakespeare's plays and poems with the promise of a common truth in a shared world. Pythagorean ecology in *As You Like It*, Stoic cosmopolitanism in *The Winter's Tale*, Afro-Platonism and Abrahamic spirituality in *Othello* and *Antony and Cleopatra*, Buddhist interbeing in *King Lear* and the Mohegan theatre of welcoming in Madeline Sayet's *Where We Belong*—all bespeak an ethics of hospitality, responsibility and care. Acknowledging the breadth of ancient wisdom opens Shakespeare beyond Shakespeare, exposing his moral limits and then healing those breaches with the resources that an expansive mapping of tradition—itself invited by the imaginative reach of his plays—offers to those who seek wisdom today.

'Ecumenical' and 'ecological' share a common root in *oikos*, meaning household, understood as the dynamic hub of production and consumption in the service of life processes. Whereas the ecumenical ingathers shared habits of thought, the ecological emphasises interdependence among living beings and their environments. Different schools of wisdom, including Greek, Indian and Indigenous traditions, conceive of the cosmos as an ensouled world organised by reason, animated by shared breath, and hospitable to an ethics of stewardship, magnanimity, benevolence, sympathy, friendship and care. Since the Industrial Revolution, however, our thinking and grasping have been out of tune with the cosmic order governed by the various iterations of *Anima Mundi*, Brahman, Great Spirit and Nature. Yet the notion that 'we are all kin' was second nature to Shakespeare and his contemporaries, the heirs of ancient Greek philosophy, who lived before this eclipsing of Oneness in the West. The ecumenical and the ecological converge in a wisdom ecology that embraces various facets of experiential life—numinous, cognitive, emotional and prudential—in an enlivened world where thinking and living beings must find their way back to an ecological rather than ego-logical way of being. Wisdom in the world operates at the cognitive-affective-ethical interface as we practise protean skills in social and natural environments, where *oikos* intertwines the ecumenical, the ecological and the ethical.

From the perspectives of Greek and Buddhist-Daoist teleology as well as Native science and evolutionary biology, realising the 'sapiens'

Introduction

[3

in *homo sapiens* entails recovering our vibrant and joyful connection to the world. Thus enlivened, we must direct our powers to apprehend moral and spiritual truths toward compassionate, effective and equitable solutions to the gamut of physical, economic, political and emotional insecurities suffered by human beings and other vulnerable ecological co-habitants of our planet in crisis. In these pages, we enlist Shakespeare and his kinship with global wisdom traditions to mobilise world audiences in the service of restoring our common *oikos* called Earth.

As a dramatist-sage and seer into the world, Shakespeare surpasses the King James Bible in collections of English quotations, continuing the practice of Renaissance commonplacing that distilled wise sayings for individual and cultural use. Scholars in fields such as political science, philosophy and law still turn to Shakespeare as a guide to human motivation and psychology.[4] Shakespeare scholars, however, often avoid courting wisdom in his plays and poems, given centuries of co-option for capitalist and colonialist ends alongside discomfort with ethical education as a literary end. This volume recovers Shakespeare's participation in a *sensus communis* fed by world wisdom traditions. Contributing to the religious turn, the eudaimonic turn and the renewal of virtue ethics in literary studies, we interweave Shakespeare's wisdom with ancient spiritual practices and the insights of a post-secular age in order to create a transhistorical space of sapient knowing and living.[5] Within this ethical-aesthetic framework, we approach wisdom as a variegated, embodied and enlivened ensemble of mental qualities, habits, insights and teachings which take shape in specific forms of life and resonate across diverse cultures and discourses. Pursuing the delight of heart, soul and understanding in the synaesthetic experience of theatre and the meditative space of poetry, sapiential Shakespeare explores knowledge, love, beauty, nature, will and power in conversation with

---

[4] Julie Maxwell and Kate Rumbold, eds., *Shakespeare and Quotation* (Cambridge UP, 2018).

[5] See Ken Jackson and Arthur F. Marotti, eds., *Shakespeare and Religion: Early Modern and Postmodern Perspectives* (U of Notre Dame P, 2011); Unhae Park Langis, *Passion, Prudence, and Virtue in Shakespearean Drama* (Continuum, 2011); Julia Reinhard Lupton and Donovan Sherman, eds., *Shakespeare and Virtue: A Handbook* (Cambridge UP, 2023); Louis Tay and James O. Pawelski, eds., *The Oxford Handbook of the Positive Humanities* (Oxford UP, 2021).

multiple wisdom traditions. Shakespeare, his contemporaries and the premodern world also viscerally knew that human nature is one with Nature and that self-knowledge is one with knowledge of the world. It is in this primal insight into our lifeworld that the ecumenical, the ecological and the ethical converge.

This volume begins in the Mediterranean with classical, biblical and Egyptian wisdom, moves to the east to consider Sufi and Buddhist wisdom, and then turns to the west to reflect on Indigenous science and ways of knowing. Part I begins with 'Wisdom Ecology: Mapping the Ancient Wisdom World into the Future' (Unhae Langis), an introduction to the many tributaries and common themes of ancient wisdom and how they weave into the present and the future. *Antony and Cleopatra* braids Jewish, Egyptian and Hellenistic motifs in fashioning Cleopatra as a wisdom queen (Julia Lupton). The Sonnets belong to a long history of meditative verse anchored by the biblical Psalms and Proverbs and the Book of Common Prayer, which Shakespeare mixes freely with Ovidian and Pythagorean teaching (Sean Keilen). Post-Reformation morality plays pose questions around free will and counsel that take different shapes in Shakespeare and his Venetian contemporary Fabio Glissenti (Eugenio Refini).

Part II, '*Oikeiôsis* and Ecology', turns to Pythagorean and Stoic ideas around living in accord with nature. In *As You Like It*, the pre-Socratic sage Pythagoras contributes to ecological thinking by advocating vegetarianism, reincarnation, mutability and cosmic harmony (Todd Borlik). In *The Winter's Tale*, the Stoic concept of *oikeiôsis* describes the natural orientation of living beings toward their proper objects of care, beginning with themselves and expanding outward as circles of inclusion and mutual support (Benjamin Parris).

Part III, 'A Kinaesthetic Ethics of the Heart-Mind', orchestrates love, grace, dance and movement as the matrix of a whole-bodied ethics of social and environmental attunement. In *King Lear*, Cordelia embodies the Buddhist Sophia who, by cutting away illusion, guides her father to wisdom and nurtures him tenderly to visions of joyfully 'sing[ing] like birds', pondering 'the mystery of things' (*King Lear*, 5.3.16) (Marguerite Tassi). In *Othello*, the theoerotic practice of the Sufis frames the divine quest of two lovers whose ecumenical vision is undermined by racist and anti-Muslim hatred (Unhae Langis). In *The Tempest*, Indigenous wisdom, animal intelligence and labouring knowledge disclose a natural law tradition that diverges

Introduction [5

from the Lockean emphasis on private property and revels in the power of dance to tune bodies and breath with the cosmos (Carolyn Sale).

Finally, since creativity, in partnership with reason, directs life processes in search of wisdom, the collection ends with a suite of experimental pieces by artist-teachers. Mohegan playwright Madeline Sayet in conversation with Robin Kello plumbs the misuses of 'wisdom' in both the Shakespeare industry and cultural idealisations of Indigeneity in order to recover theatre as a space of genuine welcome. Poet Jos Charles explores the sonnet form as a medium of healing. Lauren Shufran reflects on Shakespeare and mindfulness in her own practices of writing, teaching and contemplation.[6] In the chapters ahead, we enlist Shakespeare as a dramatist-sage whose global origins and global audiences can help promote peace, understanding and benevolent action toward the healing of this shared *oikos* we know as Earth.

Shakespeare and Wisdom Literature

Biblical scholars in the nineteenth century coined the term 'wisdom literature' to refer to a group of books from the Hebrew Bible, including Proverbs, Job, Ecclesiastes and the Song of Songs, works that feature wisdom as a universal resource, lyric occasion and mythopoetic matrix.[7] The Hebrew wisdom literature received by Shakespeare was a many-layered phenomenon, stemming from the clay tablets of ancient Mesopotamia, the complex composition of Jewish and Christian scriptures over time, and medieval and Renaissance receptions of Greek philosophy by Muslim, Jewish and Christian philosophers. The works of Scripture reflect transactions, translations and rivalries with neighbouring Canaanite, Egyptian and Greek forms of thought, while Hellenic and Hellenistic philosophies interacted and overlapped with Zoroastrian and Buddhist teachings. The term 'wisdom literature' has in recent decades been extended to include

---

[6] Lauren Shufran, *The Buddha and the Bard: Where Shakespeare's Stage Meets Buddhist Scriptures* (Mandala, 2022).

[7] Leo G. Perdue, *Wisdom Literature: A Theological History* (Westminster John Knox, 2007).

traditions far beyond the Mediterranean, an inclusive approach pursued in this volume.[8]

Shakespeare, unlike Dante or Rumi, was not directly a wisdom writer; instead, he recovers wisdom in the shufflings and strivings of human actors, who 'with windlasses and with assays of bias / By indirections find directions out' (*Hamlet*, 2.1.63). Keats, depicting life as the 'vale of Soul-making', embedded Shakespeare's 'negative capability' in a large-souled vision of a nondual, interconnected lifeworld.[9] Shakespeare's grammar school training in *utramque partem* (double-sided argumentation), his 'myriad-minded' perspectivism and his love of role-playing made him a fitting seeker of the wisdom that hides in many layers of phenomena.[10] His receptiveness to the social and natural world as ceaselessly generous and generative required an open heart-mind, 'an organ of spiritual perception' in global wisdom traditions: as Reverend Cynthia Bourgeault explains, the heart looks beyond 'the boundaried surface of things . . . into a deeper reality, emerging from some unknown profundity, which plays lightly upon the surface of this life'.[11] Such a description resonates with Shakespeare's kenosis, his ease with existential uncertainty and insight into the workings of the lifeworld, as represented at the Wooden O, his theatrical Globe.

Although most appearances of the word 'wisdom' and its variants in the Shakespearean canon are formulaic epithets rather than meaningful moral expressions, Shakespeare repeatedly discloses wisdom's elusiveness and nonduality, the disciplined practice it demands, the dissonance between moral knowledge and moral conduct, and suffering as its cardinal illuminator. Prince Hal cites Proverbs 1:20 in

---

[8] Will Kynes, ed., *The Oxford Handbook of Wisdom and the Bible* (Oxford UP, 2021); Robert J. Sternberg and Jennifer Jordan, eds., *A Handbook of Wisdom: Psychological Perspectives* (Cambridge UP, 2005); Roger Walsh, ed., *The World's Great Wisdom: Timeless Teachings from Religions and Philosophies* (SUNY, 2014).

[9] John Keats, *The Letters of John Keats, 1814–1821*, ed. Hyder Edward Rollins, 2nd ed., 2 vols. (Harvard UP, 1965), 2:101–2; 1:193.

[10] Samuel Taylor Coleridge, *Biographia Literaria; or, Biographical Sketches of my Literary Life and Opinions* (Leavitt, Lord and Company, 1834), 181, borrowed the epithet ascribed to a patriarch of Constantinople by a Greek monk.

[11] Cynthia Bourgeault, *The Heart of Centering Prayer: Nondual Christianity in Theory and Practice* (Shambhala, 2016), 54.

Introduction

[7

his banter with Falstaff: 'wisdom cries out in the streets and no man regards it' (*1 Henry IV*, 1.2.72). Even if we are lucky enough to experience true insights into life, actualising these insights is difficult, as Portia quips: 'If to do were as easy as to know what were good to do, chapels had been churches and poor men's cottages princes' palaces' (*The Merchant of Venice*, 1.2.12). In *Measure for Measure*, Angelo's abuse of authority reveals the chasm between intellectual and experiential knowledge. Descending from Socrates and Erasmus, Shakespeare's Fools shuttle between wisdom and folly, a canny practice 'as full of labour as a wise man's art' (*Twelfth Night*, 3.1.54). In *King Lear*, the more an experience tries the heart, mind and body, the greater are the possibilities for transformative insight: in Rumi's words, 'The Wound is where the Light enters you'.[12]

Shakespeare often conveys wisdom through proverbs, enjoying their compactness while holding up their application for critical examination, as Keilen attests in his reading of the Sonnets for this volume. The monumental *Adagia* of Erasmus, William Baldwin's *A Treatise of Morall Philosophie* and Isabella Whitney's *A Sweet Nosegay* (1573) supplemented the many manuscript commonplace books kept by ordinary women and men for private meditation as well as inscription on walls and furnishings.[13] In *Hamlet* and *All's Well That Ends Well*, Polonius and the Countess of Roussillon bless their departing sons with collections of aphorisms, yet the tenor of their advice is substantially different. Polonius focuses on form and appearance, ambition rather than moral character; his lessons on tact and discretion inculcate civil and rational behaviour in the service of self-advancement. Unlike Polonius's social advice, the Countess's pithy counsel comes from the heart-mind:

> Be thou blest, Bertram and succeed thy father
> In manners, as in shape! thy blood and virtue
> Contend for empire in thee and thy goodness
> Share with thy birthright! (*All's Well*, 1.1.48–51)

---

[12] Rūmī, 'Where the Light Enters You', trans. Omid Safi, On Being Project, May 7, 2015. https://onbeing.org/blog/where-the-light-enters-you/

[13] John Considine, 'Wisdom-Literature in Early Modern England', *Renaissance Studies* 13.3 (1999): 325–42.

8]   *Unhae Park Langis and Julia Reinhard Lupton*

She prays that Bertram, still an 'unseasoned courtier' (1.1.58), fulfil his potential for 'goodness' by 'birthright', as in him 'blood and virtue / Contend for empire'. Despite the class conflict that later prompts Bertram to reject Helena, nobility, in Wisdom's eye, actualises the potential for excellence that resides in every being. Her advice affirms the power of love in human interactions:

> Love all, trust a few,
> Do wrong to none: be able for thine enemy
> Rather in power than use and keep thy friend
> Under thy own life's key . . . (1.1.51–4)

The saying 'Do wrong to none' echoes the Sanskrit dictum of *ahimsā*, 'cause no injury', the principle of non-violence that forms one of the cardinal virtues in Indian religions.[14] *Ahimsā* encourages eco-logic rather than ego-logic in a wisdom ecology composed of manifold life processes and the ethical comportments required to respect them. The contrast between Polonius and the Countess as teachers underscores the dissonance between the mere study of wisdom (in Polonius's case, a 'studied' semblance) and its embodied acquiring in the energetic forcefield of virtue and vitality. Here and elsewhere, Shakespeare approaches wisdom literature as a seed bank, a precious compendium of multiplex life stored in proverb, image, myth and hymn, ready to burst into new bloom under conditions of attention and care.

The Countess of Roussillon stands in a long line of wise women whose archetypes include the goddesses and sibyls of ancient Mesopotamia and Woman Wisdom in the Hebrew Book of Proverbs and the Greek Septuagint. In Plato's *Symposium*, Socrates, feminised as a midwife of truth, is the archetypal figure of *erōs*, defined as the love of wisdom (*sophia*), also figured as the pursuit of the beautiful and noble (*kalon*).[15] As suggested in Lupton's essay, the Jews of Alexandria rendered Woman Wisdom (*chokmah*) as Sophia, who was further enriched by her affiliations with Greek

---

[14] Brianne Donaldson, 'Bioethics and Jainism: From *Ahimsā* to an Applied Ethics of Carefulness', *Religions* 10.4 (2019): 1–19. https://doi.org/10.3390/rel10040243

[15] Plato, *Symposium*, in *Plato: Complete Works*, ed. John M. Cooper and D. S. Hutchinson (Hackett, 1997), 180d–185c, 206b–d.

Introduction [9

Athena, associated with *nous* and *gnosis*, and Egyptian Isis, who bore 'the epithets Phronesis (Intelligence) and Wisdom (Sophia)'.[16] Leo Perdue associates the fluidity of the Septuagint's Sophia with the fire and air of Stoic pneuma, while Johan Thom compares her to 'a second divine principle similar to what we encounter in Middle Platonism'.[17] The Afro-Platonism of *Othello* and *Antony and Cleopatra* translates the Proverbs' harmfully double-sided representation of woman as Wisdom and Stranger into what Howard Caygill calls the 'Alexandrian aesthetic', characterised by 'the processions between the many to the one, between dispersal and unification, between the senses and the intellect, between pleasure and abstinence, pollution and purity, between even perdition and redemption'.[18]

Shakespeare's plays suggest again and again that the wisdom embodied in female experience counterbalances the more visible forms of masculine activity in the military, political and commercial realms. In this volume, Julia Lupton recreates Cleopatra as an Egyptian wisdom queen and Marguerite Tassi presents Cordelia as the incarnation of Buddhist compassionate wisdom. Unhae Langis reads Desdemona as a figure of the Sophianic Feminine in the Sufi-Christian tradition, whose beauty and wisdom Othello mistakenly rejects in defence of ego weakened by anti-Muslim and racist enmity. Benjamin Parris presents Paulina as a Stoic sage and Perdita as a graceful choreographer of cosmic harmonies. Across Shakespeare, artful women such as Kate, Portia, Rosalind, Marina and Imogen heal, teach, suffer and learn. These sapiential seekers transcend their roles as guides to male enlightenment in order to become astute managers of their own virtues and capacities. Their other-oriented care

---

[16] Michael V. Fox, *Proverbs 1–9: A New Translation and Commentary*, Anchor Bible 18A (Doubleday, 2000), 366–8; Michael C. Legaspi, 'Wisdom in Dialogue with Greek Civilization', in *The Oxford Handbook of Wisdom and the Bible*, ed. Will Kynes (Oxford UP, 2021), 155–72.

[17] Perdue, *Wisdom Literature*, 296; Johan C. Thom, 'Sophia as Second Principle in Wisdom of Solomon', in *Toward a Theology of the Septuagint: Stellenbosch Congress on the Septuagint, 2018*, ed. Johann Cook and Martin Rösel (Society of Biblical Literature, 2020), 263–76 (264).

[18] Howard Caygill, 'The Alexandrian Aesthetic', in *The New Aestheticism*, ed. John J. Joughin and Simon Malpas (Manchester UP, 2003), 100.

10]   *Unhae Park Langis and Julia Reinhard Lupton*

is animated by their personal intelligence and charisma, exercised within and beyond the social norms that constrain women's practices of actualisation.

In *All's Well*, Helena embodies the gamut of mental habits (*techne, episteme, ennoia, epinoia*) practised in the healing arts, moral understanding, purposeful attention and 'country matters' (*Hamlet*, 3.2.99). A midwife of herself and others, Helena deftly mediates between *sophia* and *phronesis* to birth true nobility in Bertram through a noetic erotics. In his discussion of faith as 'the substance of things hoped for, the evidence of things not seen', St Paul alludes to 'a subtle seeing in the dark, a kind of spiritual night vision that allows one to see with inner certainty that the elusive golden thread glimpsed from within actually does lead somewhere'.[19] The vexed ending of *All's Well*, encapsulated in Bertram's elusive proposition, 'If she, my liege, can make me know this clearly, / I'll love her dearly, ever, ever dearly' (5.3.315–16), requires that we, as audience members, have faith that Helena has skilfully made him 'know [her] clearly' through her healing of the King and the assisted pregnancy of the bed trick—acts that take place in the darkened rooms of spiritual and tactile knowing. *Sophia* or *sapientia* (from Latin *sapere*, to taste) is wisdom increased by experiential tasting and testing. Shakespeare reveals wisdom as a way of life practised with whole-body mindfulness and engaging many protean skills in modulating the emotional-mental-physical interface in social and natural spaces.

A saying ascribed to Muhammad, 'Wisdom is the lost item of the believer, he recovers it wherever he finds it', highlights the gift of wisdom's renewal in acts of discovery and recovery.[20] The rhythm of wisdom lost and found reverberates throughout the sapiential *oikumene* reconstructed in this volume. Iranian philosopher Seyyed Hossein Nasr does well to remind us that

> [i]n Hinduism, that oldest of religions and the only echo of the 'primordial religion' to survive to this day, the sacred texts which serve

---

[19] Cynthia Bourgeault, 'The Way of the Heart', *Parabola*, January 31, 2017. https://parabola.org/2017/01/31/the-way-of-the-heart-cynthia-bourgeault/

[20] U. Isra Yazicioglu, 'Wisdom in the Qur'an and the Islamic Tradition', in *The Oxford Handbook of Wisdom and the Bible*, ed. Will Kynes (Oxford UP, 2021), 221–40 (232).

Introduction [11]

as the origin of the whole tradition, namely the Vedas, are related to knowledge. Etymologically *veda* and *vedanta* derive from the root *vid* which means 'seeing' and 'knowing' and which is related to the Latin *videre* 'to see' and the Greek *oida* 'to know'.[21]

Similarly, *Ayurveda*, the ancient Hindu knowledge of healing linked to a sacred way of life, seeks holistic health through a balance between body, mind, spirit and social well-being, the goal of Indigenous forms of knowing worldwide. Its literal meaning, 'knowledge of life', suggests the cardinal role of *gnosis* (Greek 'knowledge'), sapient knowing that unifies and sanctifies life. From this Greek word of Indo-European origin derives both the English word *know* and the Sanskrit word *jhana*, referring to meditational practice toward enlightenment.[22] *Gnosis* is the spiritual knowledge or awareness of a unitive, interpenetrating cosmos propelled and organised by creative energy—whether emanating from a divine source or the collective energy of interbeing.[23] In classical Indian Vedantic teaching, 'what is needed' 'is not to become *brahman* [One] but to come to know that one already *is*'.[24] Informed by the sun obscured by clouds, Buddhist practices are then about uncovering our buddha-nature, our natural human heartedness and innate capacities toward Good.[25] Indigenous

---

[21] Seyyed Hossein Nasr, *Knowledge and the Sacred* (SUNY, 1989), 6.

[22] Gilles Quispel, *Gnostica, Judaica, Catholica: Collected Essays of Gilles Quispel*, ed. Johannes van Oort (Brill, 2008), 182. 'know, v.', *OED* online.

[23] Nasr, *Knowledge and the Sacred*, 41; Frithjof Schuon, *The Essential Writings of Frithjof Schuon*, ed. Seyyed Hossein Nasr (Amity House, 1986). This primordial knowing is etymologically reflected in the Gnostic tradition, whose aspirants strive after divine knowledge, or *gnosis*. We are defining *gnosis* in a broad, nonsectarian way to disassociate from the particular persuasion 'Gnosticism' and its problematics, which include a negative view of the visible world. See Roelof van den Broek, *Gnostic Religion in Antiquity*, trans. Anthony Runia (Cambridge UP, 2013), ch. 1.

[24] Thomas McEvilley, *The Shape of Ancient Thought: Comparative Studies in Greek and Indian Philosophies* (Allworth, 2002), PDF, 558; emphasis in original.

[25] Gaylon Ferguson, 'Awakening Loving-Kindness and Compassion', talk presented at The Wisdom of Pema Chödrön: A Summit of Timeless Teachings to Awaken the Heart, April 7–11, 2022, https://learn.lionsroar.com/p/the-wisdom-of-pema-chodron-summit-upgrade; Dacher Keltner, 'The Compassionate Instinct', *Greater Good Magazine*, March 1, 2004. https://greatergood.berkeley.edu/article/item/the_compassionate_instinct

coming-to-know, similarly, is 'a precultural biological awareness' of the interdependence of all creation, entailing 'a physical, cognitive and emotional orientation like a map in the head'.[26]

These worldviews mesh with the ancient Greek notion of natural goodness, which Benjamin Parris explores through *The Winter's Tale* in this volume. In Aristotle's teleological account, the ultimate good for human beings is *eudaimonia*, the soul's flourishing, a flow-state attained by developing our natural capacities to their fullest potential.[27] Reason, as a defining human capacity, guides us to *eudaimonia* through evaluative goodness, the ability to self-reflect and direct the will and emotions toward whole-bodied well-being.[28] In a more sacred sense, *eudaimonia* is being homed in on divine being, one's portion (*daimon*) as part of the One, one's divine spark as part of the Cosmic Source. The two—naturalistic and divine—facets merge in ancient Stoic ethics, which features *oikeiôsis*, literally, 'making something one's own', a process of assimilating oneself to nature as one's home (*oikos*). These diverse wisdom traditions converge on the premise that sapient ways bring benefit and flourishing to our lives, which become congruent with cosmic well-being.

As the ecumenical treasure of cultures, wisdom was passed down orally through teaching, storytelling, performance, rituals and spiritual exercises. The emergence of writing facilitated the transmission of wisdom in scriptures, proverbs, sermons and dialogues. The dharmic *sūtra*, derived from Sanskrit *sīv*, 'to sew', is a 'thread' or 'rule', stringing not only sheets of palm leaf together but also thoughts and ideas, the collection of proverbs inscribed on those leaves,[29] which serves as a collective sapiential resource to aid in the suturing of the

---

[26] Gregory Cajete, 'Philosophy of Native Science', in *American Indian Thought: Philosophical Essays*, ed. Anne Waters (Blackwell, 2004), 45–57 (46); Waters, introduction to same volume, xxi.

[27] Aristotle, *Ethica Nicomachea* (*Nicomachean Ethics*), in *The Basic Works of Aristotle*, ed. Richard McKeon (Modern Library, 2001), VI.1144b3.

[28] Christine M. Korsgaard, 'Natural Goodness, Rightness, and the Intersubjectivity of Reason: Reply to Arroyo, Cummiskey, Moland, and Bird-Pollan', *Metaphilosophy* 42.4 (2011): 381–94 (382).

[29] 'sutra, n.', *OED* online; Stan Florek, 'Book and Sutra', *Australian Museum*, June 14, 2023. https://australian.museum/learn/cultures/international-collection/african/book-and-sutra/

Introduction [13]

divisive self and the healing of communal bodies. Similarly, the *tantra*, the esoteric traditions of Hinduism and Buddhism, as its original Sanskrit meaning suggests ('loom, weave, warp'), aims to weave text and practice into the texture and textile of life.

This volume, in *sūtra* fashion, aims to interweave Shakespeare's 'mingled yarn' (*All's Well*, 4.3.54) with global wisdom traditions and new perspectives of a post-secular age in a transhistorical space of sapiential knowing. While living in linear time (Greek *chronos*), ancient and Indigenous peoples were also attuned to what the Greeks called *aion*, time that is cyclical, unbounded and eternal. What Hamlet terms 'the mortal coil' (3.1.68) would be a grim vision of the human condition were it not for the awareness that we simultaneously participate in the miraculous mystery play of Life. In Nonnus's fifth-century CE epic poem *Dionysiaca*, Aion integrates with the Horae, or Hours, the goddesses of the seasons and the natural portions of time and 'changes the burden of old age like a snake who sloughs off the coils of the useless old scales, rejuvenescing while washing in the swells of the laws [of nature]'.[30] In the context of our climate crisis, the self-destructive futility of a serpent biting its tail can, given political and collective will, transmute into an ouroboric message of regeneration. Callous, egoic paradigms licensing megalomania have yielded the present nexus of interrelated crises—prolonged pandemic, climate catastrophes, polarising social and economic injustices, and enfeebled democracies combating resurgent authoritarian forces. Explorations of Shakespeare and Renaissance culture can wisely pivot backward and forward, like Janus and Prudence, to recover and rejuvenate ancient wisdoms and truths vital to our era of transition, upheaval and, hopefully, regeneration.

Chapter Overview

Part I, 'Shakespeare and the *Oikumene*', begins with Unhae Park Langis's essay, which outlines the many forms and themes of ancient wisdom and maps the interaction and transmission of wisdom traditions within Shakespeare's *oikumene* into the present and future.

---

[30] Nonnus, *Dionysiaca*, 41.180; qtd. in Doro Levi, 'Aion', *Hesperia* 13.4 (1944): 274, 306–8 ff.

14]　　*Unhae Park Langis and Julia Reinhard Lupton*

Exemplary is the fertile confluence of Mesopotamian, Egyptian, Greek and Hebrew wisdoms in several centuries before and after Jesus Christ in Alexandria, the setting of Julia Lupton's essay (Chapter 2). Pythagoras, detailed in Todd Borlik's essay (Chapter 5), looms large in further suggestive interactions with and between Indian and Buddhist wisdom traditions, the hermeneutic framework of Marguerite Tassi's essay (Chapter 7). If tantalising similarities cannot be proven definitively, given the orality of ancient wisdom traditions and dearth of written documentation, a rich trove of metaphors and motifs shared within the *oikumene* and beyond might be more soulstirring and evidentially suasive, suggesting how the Afro-Eurasian thoughtworld may converse with Indigenous understandings through a global *sensus communis* rooted in energetic knowing-with. Such sapiential globetrotting on the horizontal plane works jointly with a transhistorical transmission on a vertical plane. Of utmost existential relevance—literally, a rising again—to our present and future being is the 'unforgetting' of ancient and Indigenous wisdom traditions for our sapient evolving toward a liveable planet.[31] Sharing a common root in *oikos*, meaning home, the ecumenical and the ecological converge in an embodied ethics and politics of care, transforming an ego-logical into an ecological way of being.

Julia Reinhard Lupton's essay depicts Cleopatra as a wisdom queen, who in composing her greatest speeches and spectacles as wisdom poems in the style of Solomon, Orpheus and Pythagoras also incarnates the Greco-Egyptian-Hebraic wisdom tradition and library at Alexandria. Like her Wisdom sisters Desdemona, Cordelia and others, Cleopatra is presented as a harmoniser of the secular and the divine, this time, in an international sphere of governance. Managing the challenges of sustaining her sovereignty in a gynophobic world dominated by male rulers, this wisdom queen integrates prudential politics with a hermeneutics and diplomatics of hospitality in the gorgeous scene on the Cydnus.

Resisting the convention of treating Shakespeare's Sonnets as exclusively secular poems about sexual love, Sean Keilen in the next

---

[31] Patty Krawec, *Becoming Kin: An Indigenous Call to Unforgetting the Past and Reimagining our Future* (Broadleaf Books, 2022), 18. This is a term that Krawec borrows from historian Roxanne Dunbar-Ortiz.

Introduction [15

piece reads Sonnets 108, 60 and 120 in conversation with biblical texts and Ovidian and Pythagorean teaching, meditating on concepts of time, being and change; the value of another human life; and the possibility of forgiveness. Sonnet 108 becomes a spiritual exercise connecting speaker, beloved and reader in a transhistorical pneumatic world of shared vitality. Sonnet 120 'boldly recasts our shared fallibility as the basis for the self-transcendence we achieve through mercy'. Anchored in a long-standing wisdom tradition, the Sonnets, like the Psalter, are 'fitted to the ways we live, love, die and hope to survive through time'.

In the next piece, Eugenio Refini examines spiritual practice in the deep-rooted morality play tradition by placing Shakespeare in conversation with the Baroque Italian dramatist Fabio Glissenti. Shakespeare's more submerged expression of the morality tradition in the context of a concertedly public theatre in a Reformed space contrasts with Glissenti's explicitly didactic post-Tridentine method of staging morality internally and externally, through the struggles of conscience and the dynamics of moral education. Linking Iago's philosophy on will to Glissenti's moralities, Refini's comparative study focusing on counsel, self-counsel and will ultimately sheds light on how two distinct approaches toward self-cultivation mutually inform one another, with an eye on the pan-European reach of allegorical and spiritual theatre.

Part II, '*Oikeiôsis* and Ecology', begins with Todd Borlik's ecocritical exploration of *As You Like It*, which mounts a compelling case for Jaques as a Pythagorean initiate who practises a philosophical way of life, further illuminated by Timothy Morton's concept of ecognosis. Borlik freshly assesses the play's ecocosmopolitan possibilities within a Global Shakespeare that 'might harness his cultural prestige to broadcast non-Western wisdom traditions and Indigenous knowledge systems, overcome Nimbyism, and foster collective solutions to environmental problems unfolding on local, regional and global levels'.

Next, by examining 'natural goodness' in *The Winter's Tale* through the lens of Stoic *oikeiôsis*, Benjamin Parris explores the intertwined relationship between norms and nature upon which wisdom depends. Stoic *oikeiôsis* describes the natural orientation of living beings toward their proper objects of care, beginning with themselves and expanding outward as circles of inclusion and mutual support. Leontes's egoic appeal to a sovereign 'natural goodness' serves as a foil to other kinds of goodness grounded in nature as divine being and developed through interconnected and mutually sustaining relations of care—from the cultivation of flora to the nurturing of children to the benefits of friendship to the flourishing of kingdoms.

Part III, 'A Kinaesthetic Ethics of the Heart-Mind', begins with Marguerite A. Tassi's essay, which showcases Cordelia as a 'Buddhist Sophia' who guides her father toward wisdom. Tassi displays how Buddhist hermeneutics can illuminate Shakespeare in ways unavailable to Western perspectives. Buddhism reveals Cordelia's special moral and spiritual force as *Prajñāpāramitā*, the Mother of Perfect Wisdom and the instantiation of the *Heart Sūtra*—its wisdom of nothing—combined with active compassion, the manifest heart of Buddhism. Tassi incisively explains the 'nothing' dialogue as a Buddhist koan, a teaching moment for Cordelia to impart her lesson on the emptiness of the ego-self and to point to compassion as its antidote. In her role as compassionate nurturer, Cordelia moreover offers the antidote to Lear's misogyny, and when left with a lifeless Cordelia in his arms, Lear, as a chastened Pietà figure, shows the radical upside to the play's heart-wrenching ending 'as an allegory of awakening to wisdom'.

In Unhae Park Langis's second essay, Woman Wisdom shifts from the role of daughter to that of wife in *Othello*. By reimagining Othello as a spiritual traveller in the Sufi tradition of his native North Africa, following a path of love, we come to see Desdemona and Othello's courtship and marriage in theoerotic terms of a divine union—if briefly—of two lovers, who mutually regard each other as visible emblems of the divine. This Sufi reading, further infused with Audre Lorde's expansive understanding of eros, highlights its sapient, transformative possibilities then and now, on stage and beyond. Since his deviation from love is circumstantial rather than substantial, Othello rights his path instantly upon disabusal, and his self-immolation can be seen as a Sufi's return to God, revising the racist, anti-Muslim trope of 'turning Turk'. An understanding of eros as creative energy spurring excellence, humanity and 'natural democracy' undergirds present care-centred efforts to address an intersectionality of racial, religious, economic and environmental injustices faced by marginalised communities.[32]

---

[32] Cajete, 'Philosophy of Native Science', 46.

Introduction   [17

Lastly in this section, Carolyn Sale's essay on *The Tempest* situates it in relation to the jurisprudence of *Calvin's Case* (1608), the wisdom attributed to Indigenous cultures of the Americas, and the theory of kinaesthetic resonance. Sale shows how the play models a 'gentle-kindness' via 'kinaesthetic resonance' from dancers on stage to spectators in the audience. Such kinaesthetic performance may be viewed as the most direct expression of embodied wisdom, human freedom and creative life energy.

Since the activity of wisdom intimately involves generation, intuition and syn- and kinaesthetic creativity, the collection ends with a suite of experimental pieces by artist-teachers. Mohegan playwright Madeline Sayet in conversation with Robin Kello explores the generational trauma of colonialism, Shakespeare's vexed relationship with Indigeneity, the unitive Mohegan worldview, and the challenges of being an Indigenous artist and of hybrid living. Although Sayet emphasises Shakespeare's deployment as a symbol of European imperialism and settler colonialism, what is heartening here is how much of her animist, communal Indigenous perspective is attuned to the spiritual keynote of our volume, resonating with so many of the readings here. The ethics of care, the themes of harming/healing and of welcoming are indeed central practices of the ecological rather than ego-logical perspective that the volume bodies forth. Kello's interview of Sayet is followed by his analysis of her work.

Writers Jos Charles and Lauren Shufran use public forms of poetry and contemplation towards healing and transformation. Poet Jos Charles explores grief as a human experience transcending ethnic, racial and cultural divides. In her poetic essay, the sonnet form, conversing with Arabic poetic forms, becomes a vital, lyrical and organic medium of healing. Employing 'the proverbial as hermeneutic', her piece reveals 'how co-production translates wisdom through the life experiences readers bring to the sonnet, and what we make of that largely unrecorded dissemination of wisdom that is part of ongoing living'.[33] Shufran reflects in a personal essay on their spiritual journey from poet/PhD student to yoga practitioner and teacher of Shakespeare to mindfulness blogger to author of *The Buddha and the Bard*. Through this journey, Shufran, like Charles,

---

[33] Joan Pong Linton, reader's report on *Shakespeare and Wisdom*.

comes to model contemplation in public, inviting us to connect inner experience to vibrant life. Revealing candidly 'how fresh and how messy and how fumbling I often feel on this path', they affirm that 'mindfulness—even in its convoluted, commodified, despiritualised forms—is as important as ever; and I'm up for the ongoing humility of expressing out loud what I'm discovering in those listening spaces'.

Finally, Joan Pong Linton offers closing words in the form of an Afterword that reflects her deep engagement with every essay in this volume. Termed in different ways, the varied versions of ecumenical vision explored here—Alexandrian confluence of wisdom traditions, Pythagorean Oneness and ecognosis, Stoic cosmopolitanism, Sufi-Greek-Christian interspirituality, Buddhist interbeing, Indigenous kinship—all bespeak an ethics of responsibility, care and welcome.

Wisdom is key to 'human edification, which equips and informs human agency for the challenging, all-encompassing task of living'.[34] Diverging from ancient life-giving wisdom cultures, the West for the past three centuries has subscribed to a mechanised understanding of the world revering private property. This path led to the Industrial Revolution and the anthropogenic climate crisis in which we find ourselves, amidst a stew of correlated challenges globally—disorder, displacement, disaster profiteering, democracies threatened by autocracy, to name a few. Ironically in this post-truth era, even science so touted by the Newtonian-Cartesian paradigm has been unable to galvanise unified action toward a liveable planet. Luckily, more and more people in the West are looking to Eastern and Indigenous wisdom traditions for more wholesome ways of being. These sapient ways of life, complementing modern science with its predecessor *scientia* (Greek *gnosis*), effectively recover and rejoin with their Western cousins, Greek and biblical wisdom traditions. This more expansive form of knowing includes the faith that what we hold in common is far greater than what divides us as families, communities, as a species, within 'a natural democracy'.[35] Collectively, it is high time to

---

[34] William P. Brown, 'Virtue and its Limits in the Wisdom Corpus: Character Formation, Disruption, and Transformation', in *The Oxford Handbook of Wisdom and the Bible*, ed. Will Kynes (Oxford UP, 2021), 45–64 (46).

[35] Cajete, 'Philosophy of Native Science', 46.

Introduction [19

'unforget' that each of us beholds in our bodies, brains and hearts the 13.8-billion-year story of life; that each of us—brother, sister, mother, father, plant, animal, mycelium and mineral—is a walking or standing holograph of this marvel of our marbled planet. As Shakespeare reminds us, what wisdom we might learn if only we, as homo sapiens-to-be, might truly attend to 'tongues in trees, books in the running brooks, / Sermons in stones' and seek to find and do 'good in every thing' (*As You Like It*, 2.1.16–17)! 'For never any thing can be amiss / When simpleness and duty tender it' (*A Midsummer Night's Dream*, 5.1.82) as we seek to restore order to nature inside and outside us. We tender this *sūtra* of healing, Shakespeare's 'mingled yarn' interwoven with global wisdom traditions, with hopes of awakening insight, compassion and courage to act for the common good.

Part I:

Shakespeare and the *Oikumene*

CHAPTER 1

WISDOM ECOLOGY: MAPPING THE ANCIENT WISDOM WORLD INTO THE FUTURE

Unhae Park Langis

Ecumenical Shakespeare calls for a historical and phenomenological mapping of the global wisdom traditions in which he vibrantly participates. This synthesis traces in broad strokes the faint and intricate lines of cultural cross-fertilisation between wisdom traditions in Shakespeare's Afro-Eurasian *oikumene*. His wisdom world also widens to converse with Indigenous understandings through a global *sensus communis* rooted in animate knowing-with. Let me begin with a brief anatomy of wisdom's parts. Despite its complexity, profundity and variety, wisdom in the ancient traditions appears in two distinct forms.[1] The first is practical advice, recorded in the Hindu Vedas, the Tamil Kural, Tibetan *lojong* texts, and the proverb collections of Mesopotamian, Egyptian and Hebrew teacher-scribes.[2] The other form, found in the later revealed traditions like the Abrahamic religions, is wisdom 'unveiled as a divine gift and . . . cultivated by pondering and aligning one's life with it'.[3] Mesopotamian and Hebrew wisdom literatures exhibit both positive wisdom, rooted in traditional normative values, and negative wisdom, with its critical

---

[1]   Roger Walsh, 'What Is Wisdom? Cross-Cultural and Cross-Disciplinary Syntheses', *Review of General Psychology* 19.3 (2015): 278–93 (279–80).
This essay is in remembrance of my father Patrick Byunghwa Park, who passed during the work on this volume. I am grateful for the name he gave me, meaning 'sea of grace'. A lodestar for my life, the name, for me, expands universally to mean that each one of us is a wave riding this animate ocean that holds quiet depths of joy.

[2]   James L. Crenshaw, *Old Testament Wisdom: An Introduction*, 3rd ed. (Westminster John Knox, 2010); Roger Walsh, 'The World's Great Wisdom: An Integral Overview', in *The World's Great Wisdom: Timeless Teachings from Religions and Philosophies*, ed. Roger Walsh (SUNY, 2014), 214.

[3]   Walsh, 'World's Great Wisdom', 214–15.

and existential perspective on the human condition.[4] While the Book of Proverbs offers advice for achieving material and ethical success in life, Kohelet or Ecclesiastes meditates on the illusions and inequities in the world and the vanity of human pursuits. Kohelet's *carpe diem* theme, 'Vanity of vanities, saith the Preacher: vanity of vanities, all is vanity', echoes Old Babylonian Sumerian compositions.[5] The tension between positive and negative wisdom also shapes *The Epic of Gilgamesh*, which moves from a hero's glorification to ruminations on the futility of human striving.[6] In Shakespeare, Hamlet and Lear plumb the existential depths of Ecclesiastes and Job, while Caliban and Ariel compose psalms of hope and transformation at the edges of exegesis.

The semantic breadth of wisdom is composed of a number of core capabilities. In the Hebrew wisdom writings, *chokmah* could mean skill, learning, perceptiveness, cleverness, prudence and sagacity.[7] Maimonides (1138–1204 BCE), the Jewish philosopher of Andalusia, understood *chokmah* in several ways: as the apprehension of true realities, the cultivation of arts and moral virtues, and the aptitude for stratagems and ruses.[8] Islamic wisdom (*hikma*) comes from the same root as judgement (Arabic *hukm*), the ability to discern the difference between truth and falsehood in the metaphysical as well as practical realms.[9] In the Qur'an, wisdom refers to divine revelation (*kitab*) in half of its twenty references; elsewhere, it is metonymically

---

[4] Michael V. Fox, *Proverbs 1–9: A New Translation with Introduction and Commentary*, Anchor Bible 18A (Doubleday, 2000), 336–8; Yoram Cohen and Nathan Wasserman, 'Mesopotamian Wisdom Literature', in *The Oxford Handbook of Wisdom and the Bible*, ed. Will Kynes (Oxford UP, 2021), 121–40 (135).

[5] Ecclesiastes 1:1 (Geneva Bible); Fox, *Proverbs*, 6; Yoram Cohen, *Wisdom from the Late Bronze Age*, Writings from the Ancient World, vol. 34 (Society of Biblical Literature, 2013), 15; Bendt Alster, *Wisdom of Ancient Sumer* (CDL, 2005).

[6] Cohen, *Wisdom from the Late Bronze Age*, 16.

[7] Fox, *Proverbs*, 33.

[8] Jonathan Schofer, 'Wisdom in Jewish Theology', in *The Oxford Handbook of Wisdom and the Bible*, ed. Will Kynes (Oxford UP, 2021), 241–54.

[9] U. Isra Yazicioglu, 'Wisdom in the Qur'an and the Islamic Tradition', in *The Oxford Handbook of Wisdom and the Bible*, ed. Will Kynes (Oxford UP, 2021), 221–40 (226). See also Dimitri Gutas, 'Classical Arabic Wisdom Literature: Nature and Scope', *Journal of the American Oriental Society* 101.1 (January–March 1981): 49–86.

Wisdom Ecology

[25

associated with sovereignty, counsel, goodness and signs—themes that Benjamin Parris and Eugenio Refini explore in different sapiential traditions in their respective chapters of this volume.[10] Because wisdom is relational and developmental, one must open oneself to God/Good to receive it, and after the initial revelatory experience, one must then work hard to live by this revealed goodness. As both knowledge and skill, wisdom entails the salvific *gnosis* of primal reality, followed by applied sapience in the lived world. This marriage of noetic and practical wisdom lies at the heart of many wisdom traditions. In Aristotelian philosophy, for instance, *nous*, intuitive reason or the heart-mind, and *phronesis*, practical wisdom, combine to form *sophia*, or wisdom *tout court*.[11] Spiritually and morally guided by this noetic beacon, wisdom's beneficence is directed by *phronesis*, which prudentially marshals capacities, virtues and energies to achieve worldly ends.[12]

In the contemplative Christian tradition informed by ancient Greek *theoria* (contemplation), participants aspire to a 'divine union' of spirituality and praxis, as modelled, for instance, in the *Philokalia*, a group of Eastern Orthodox texts collected between the fourth and fifteenth centuries. In Cynthia Bourgeault's gloss, repeated urgings to 'Put the mind in the heart' teach the participant 'how to align spontaneously with Jesus's own continuously creative and enfolding presence through emulating his kenotic practice in all life situations'.[13] A similar unitive awakening lies at the core of ancient Buddhist moral conduct (*sīla*), manifested in actions embedded in lovingkindness, discipline and karmic understanding that each ethical action is the seed for a future one. Wisdom was understood by the ancients as the self-sufficient perfection of human life, but in practice, as Richard Trowbridge notes, 'the Confucian sage, the Bodhisattva, . . . the Platonic philosopher', not to mention the philanthropic Stoic cosmopolite, were 'all dedicated

---

[10] Yazicioglu, 'Wisdom in the Qur'an', 223–4.

[11] Aristotle, *Ethica Nicomachea (Nicomachean Ethics)*, in *The Basic Works of Aristotle*, ed. Richard McKeon (Modern Library, 2001), VI.7.1141a18–9, 1141b3–4.

[12] Aristotle, *Nicomachean Ethics*, VI.12.1144a6–9.

[13] *Philokalia*, qtd. in Cynthia Bourgeault, *The Heart of Centering Prayer: Nondual Christianity in Theory and Practice* (Shambhala, 2016), 53; also, Bourgeault, 'Centering Prayer and Attention of the Heart', *CrossCurrents* 59.1 (March 2009): 15–27 (17).

to a life of service to others, that is, helping others attain the *sophian* perspective'.[14] Sapiential traditions of the East and West idealise wisdom as 'the perfect integration of mind and character for the greater good'.[15] Such integration at the individual and collective level is perhaps intimated in the Orphic-Pythagorean Masque of Hymen at the end of *As You Like It*:

> Then is there mirth in heaven
> When earthly things made even
> Atone together. (5.4.90–2)[16]

'Atone' here means to become one, hearkening not only to the reconciliation of brothers and the wedding of lovers, but also to a more primal *attuning*,[17] an ability to listen with open ear and full heart to the true music of a self-reflective universe, a noosphere. Mind is the last frontier, bringing self-consciousness home to Consciousness (literally, 'knowing with'), unifying 'nature and human nature'—the inner and outer ecology of ego and *oikos*—within our thinking and living.[18] As an inward-outward homecoming, a 'presencing ourselves alongside self, other and world', it is a religature of what is 'out of joint' (*Hamlet*, 1.5.186), an interweaving of the text and textile of

---

[14] Richard Hawley Trowbridge, 'Waiting for Sophia: 30 Years of Conceptualizing Wisdom in Empirical Psychology', *Research in Human Development* 8.2 (2011): 149–64 (157).

[15] Ursula M. Staudinger and Judith Glück, qtd. in Walsh, 'What Is Wisdom?', 280.

[16] All citations of Shakespeare in this chapter are from *The New Oxford Shakespeare: The Complete Works, Modern Critical Edition*, ed. Gary Taylor, John Jowett, Terri Bourus and Gabriel Egan (Oxford UP, 2016). Oxford Scholarly Editions Online. doi:10.1093/actrade/9780199591152.book.1

[17] Julia Reinhard Lupton, '"Good in Every Thing": Erasmus and Communal Virtue in *As You Like It*', *Journal of Medieval and Early Modern Studies* 52.3 (2022): 567–91.

[18] In exploring the Mind-World relation, the essence of 'becoming animal', through the body's animate experience in nature, David Abram, *Becoming Animal: An Earthly Cosmology* (Pantheon, 2010), 107–9, draws on Baruch Spinoza's (1632–77) revision of the Cartesian mind-body dualism through a 'unitary substance', 'which he called Deus, sive Natura, "God, or Nature"', the 'creative dynamism and intelligence of Nature itself'.

Wisdom Ecology [27

Life through countless assays, or tests, that further interbraid the
ethical, ecumenical and ecological.[19]

The Afro-Eurasian Oikumene: *A Historical Mapping*

William Baldwin's multiply reprinted *A Treatise of Morall Philosophie* (first printed 1547) attests to wisdom's broad diffusion after the
Hellenistic model of Diogenes Laertius:

> There is great diversity among Writers, some attributing it to one
> and some to another: as the Thracians to Orpheus, the Grecians to
> Linus, the Libyans to Atlas, the Phoenicians to Ocechus, the Per-
> sians to their Magi, the Assyrians to their Chaldees, the Indians to
> their Gymnosophists, of which Buddha was chief, the Italians to
> Pythagoras and the Frenchmen to their Druids.[20]

Baldwin's commonplace book, like countless other Renaissance
texts, posits a common Hebrew origin of *sophia* to accommodate
the 'diversity' of spiritual exercise among the nations of the world.
Far from being an origin, Hebrew wisdom literature itself reflects
the influence of Mesopotamian, North African and Greek and even
Indian sages.[21] The Book of Exodus acknowledges active cultural
exchange when it depicts the Israelites taking gold from their Egyptian neighbours, a motif later used to justify Christian use of pagan
philosophy, first by the Church Fathers and later by Renaissance
humanists like Erasmus.[22] Historically, the Persian Empire founded
by Cyrus the Great and later conquered by Alexander the Great

---

[19] Stephen Jenkinson, *Come of Age: The Case for Elderhood in a Time of Trouble* (North Atlantic Books, 2018), 133, 240; Douglas Lockhart, 'The McEvilley
Bombshell', accessed October 3, 2023. http://www.douglaslockhart.com/wp-
content/uploads/The-McEvilley-Bombshell.pdf

[20] William Baldwin, *A treatise of Morall Phylosophie, contayning the sayinges of the
wyse* (Edward Whitchurch, 1547), ed. Robert Hood Bowers (Scholars' Facsimiles
and Reprints, 1967). This passage (cited with modernised spelling) is reminiscent
of the beginning lines of Diogenes Laertius' (*fl.* third century CE) *Lives and Opinions of the Eminent Philosophers.*

[21] Leo G. Perdue, *Wisdom Literature: A Theological History* (Westminster John
Knox, 2007).

[22] Kathy Eden, *Friends Hold All Things in Common: Tradition, Intellectual Property,
and the 'Adages' of Erasmus* (Yale UP, 2001).

was 'a single, interactive cultural sphere' enriched by an exchange of ideas and goods along ancient trade routes.[23] The Achaemenid Empire (550–330 BCE), founded by Cyrus and expanded by Darius I, brought 'the most advanced parts of Greece and India', not to mention Mesopotamia (the Neo-Babylonian or Chaldean Empire) and Egypt, under a cosmopolitan Persian rule, known for its religious toleration, fair treatment toward foreigners and asylum for their statesmen.[24] Especially for the first hundred years, 'Greek and Indian functionaries of various types sat down together at the Persian court, where there was a growing multicultural milieu that promoted diffusion contacts'.[25] During this same period, the pre-Socratic philosophers of Asia Minor and nearby islands became active, while the annexed Central Asian regions of Bactria and Gandhara (today, Pakistan, Afghanistan, Tajikistan and Uzbekistan) were settled by Greeks (including citizens of Miletus, relocated after the unsuccessful Ionian Revolution), paving the way for later interaction of Hellenic and Hellenistic philosophies with Buddhist teachings in what some have called a Greco-Buddhism in the Greater Gandhara region from 200 BCE through to the ninth century CE, and in Bactria from the fourth through to the eighth centuries CE.[26]

---

[23] Thomas McEvilley, *The Shape of Ancient Thought: Comparative Studies in Greek and Indian Philosophies* (Allworth, 2002), PDF, ch. 1; Stephen Batchelor, 'Greek Buddha: Pyrrho's Encounter with Early Buddhism in Central Asia', Review of *Greek Buddha: Pyrrho's Encounter with Early Buddhism in Central Asia*, by Christopher I. Beckwith, *Contemporary Buddhism* 17.1 (2016): 195–215 (212). For a review of scholarship on the East-West historical interaction, see Ethan Mills, 'Skepticism and Religious Practice in Sextus and Nāgārjuna', in *Ethics without Self, Dharma without Atman: Western and Buddhist Philosophical Traditions in Dialogue*, ed. Gordon F. Davis (Springer, 2018), 91–106 (92). See also Sheiba Kian Kaufman, 'Persian Virtues: Hospitality, Tolerance, and Peacebuilding in the Age of Shakespeare', in *Shakespeare and Virtue: A Handbook*, ed. Julia Reinhard Lupton and Donovan Sherman (Cambridge UP, 2023), 300–5. For an account of Buddhist ethical interaction with ancient Greek Scepticism and Stoicism, see Unhae Park Langis, 'Buddhist Virtues: Equanimity, Mindfulness, and Compassion in *Hamlet*', in the same volume.

[24] McEvilley, *Shape of Ancient Thought*, ch. 1.

[25] McEvilley, 41, 143.

[26] Kurt A. Behrendt, *The Art of Gandhara in the Metropolitan Museum of Art* (Metropolitan Museum of Art, 2007), ix; Olga Kubica, *Greco-Buddhist Relations in the Hellenistic Far East: Sources and Contexts* (Routledge, 2023).

The enigmatic personage of Pythagoras (c. 581–500 BCE), as Todd Borlik explores in this volume, is prominent among the many figures who served as possible mediators between Orient and Occident. In Florentine Neoplatonist Marsilio Ficino's view, 'Plato learned Pythagorean wisdom (which emanated from Zoroaster) from Archytas, Eurytos and Philolaus', and Socrates was a medium of Pythagorean wisdom.[27] According to later writers of Platonic and Aristotelian lineage, Pythagoras was 'the interlocutor of Zarathustra, . . . pupil of the Chaldeans, Brahmans and Druids', and 'a cultural hero who united Egyptian and Babylonian mathematics with Indian metempsychosis'.[28] In the absence of clear evidence of borrowing, what should satisfy the historian of 'influences between early Greek and Indian thought', Paolo Magnone suggests, 'is merely to establish that the historical conditions were actually there which could have made cross-cultural contacts possible'.[29] If the emphasis is on plausibility rather than irrefutability, Pythagoras stands as a possible 'transmitter of a borrowed doctrine, an Egyptian doctrine, in the ancient view, or an Indian one in the modern view',[30] to which some scholars add another alternative: Indian doctrine learned from yogi living in Egypt under cosmopolitan Persian rule.[31] Along these lines, Magnone believes the chariot metaphor common in Indian scripture and Greek writings, especially Plato, is more plausibly an example of westward diffusion from India to Greece.

Indo-Greek interaction was clearly more evident after Alexander's conquest of the Achaemenid Empire in 331 BCE, such that despite their varied ethnic origins, religions and languages, Buddha (c. 563–c. 483 BCE), Democritus (c. 460–370 BCE) and Pyrrho (360–270 BCE), not to

---

[27] Michael J. B. Allen, 'Marsilio Ficino on Plato's Pythagorean Eye', *Modern Language Notes* 97.1 (January 1982): 171–82 (175).

[28] Leonid Zhmud, *Pythagoras and the Early Pythagoreans*, trans. Kevin Windle and Rosh Ireland (Oxford UP, 2012), 24; Walter Burkert, *Greek Religion*, trans. John Raffan (Harvard UP, 1985), 445; Christoph Riedweg, *Pythagoras: His Life, Teaching, and Influence*, trans. Steven Rendall (Cornell UP, 2008), 7–8.

[29] Paolo Magnone, 'Soul Chariots in Indian and Greek Thought: Polygenesis or Diffusion?', in *Universe and Inner Self in Early Indian and Early Greek Thought*, ed. Richard Seaford (Edinburgh UP, 2016), 149–67 (151).

[30] Zhmud, *Pythagoras*, 228.

[31] McEvilley, *Shape of Ancient Thought*, 170–1; Batchelor, 'Greek Buddha', 212.

mention the legendary figure of Pythagoras, inhabited the same sapiential thoughtworld.[32] In Diogenes Laertius' account, Pyrrho, accompanying Anaxarchus (c. 380–c. 320 BCE) with Alexander's entourage, is known to have met with 'Indian gymnosophists'. His association with Anaxarchus, his exposure to Indian philosophy, or both, according to Ascanius of Abdera, prompted him to embrace 'agnosticism (*akatalêpsia*) and suspension of judgement (*epochê*)', denying that 'anything was honourable or dishonourable, just or unjust . . . ; for no single thing is in itself any more this than that'.[33] The first two verses of the *Dhammapada*, the Buddha's teachings in aphoristic verse, claim emphatically and repeatedly that 'Mind is the forerunner' of all good and evil states. 'Mind is chief; mind-made are they': 'If one speaks or acts with wicked mind, because of that, suffering follows one, even as the wheel follows the hoof of the draught-ox . . . If one speaks or acts with pure mind, because of that, happiness follows one, even as one's shadow that never leaves.'[34] The phrase 'because of that' underscores the strict causal chain between thought, speech and action, hence the theory of ethical karma. This concept that evil begets evil, good begets good, thereby reinforcing good or bad conduct, is profoundly important in mindful ethical conduct, beyond the popular understanding of karma as external punishments and rewards. Greek historian Megasthenes (c. 350–c. 290 BCE), conversing with Indian 'Brachmanes' (Brahmins), recounts that they 'discourse much on death, for it is their opinion . . . that death to philosophers is birth to a real and a happy life. They therefore discipline themselves much to prepare for death'—both the physical and the psychic death of self. Within this salvific and eudaimonic framework, the Brahmins allude to the sceptical tenet opening the *Dhammapada* ('it's the mind, just

---

[32] Batchelor, 'Greek Buddha', 211–13.

[33] Diogenes Laertius, *Lives of Eminent Philosophers*, trans. R. D. Hicks, 2 vols., Loeb Classical Library (Harvard UP, 1925, 1972), vol. 2, IX.61, p. 475; Perseus Digital Library, accessed October 3, 2023. https://www.perseus.tufts.edu/hopper/

[34] These two verses are translated by Ven. Nārada Thera in 'Parallel Reading (paragraph granularity) of The Buddha's Path of Wisdom—Dhammapada (Dhp.)—Fulltext', Fucheng Buddhism Network, updated October 9, 2016. http://nanda. online-dhamma.net/tipitaka/sutta/khuddaka/dhammapada/dhp-contrast-reading/ dhp-contrast-reading-en/

Wisdom Ecology   [31

the mind, it's all in the mind'): 'nothing which happens to man is bad or good'.[35]

A version of this sceptical gnome appears in Shakespeare, cluing us to a wealth of Indo-Greek interaction, when Hamlet states: 'There's nothing either good or bad but thinking makes it so' (*Hamlet*, 2.2.247–8).[36] This aphorism, as mediated through the works of Epictetus, Marcus Aurelius and others, became widely diffused in the West among early modern writers including Montaigne and Shakespeare.[37] Indeed, Buddhist and Greek scepticism share systemic affinities in concepts such as the non-substantiality of persons and things, non-reactivity or suspension of judgement (*epochē*) and mindfulness as key to equanimity and virtue.[38] Upon thorough examination of the tetralemma, the fourfold sceptical negation, Everard Flintoff reasonably concludes that Pyrrho, 'adopt[ing] his sceptical and "epochic" philosophy' as a consequence of his encounters with Indian gymnosophists, is the likely agent of transmission from India to Greece of the use of 'epochic' philosophy toward tranquility.[39] We must rest content with reconstructions of plausible historical conditions of diffusion in the prevailing absence of verifiable, documented evidence, given the primacy of oral teaching in ancient global wisdom traditions.

Pyrrho's possible encounter with Indian/Buddhist scepticism precedes by a half-century Mauryan emperor Ashoka's great expansion

---

[35] Megasthenes, in *The Geography of Strabo*, trans. H. C. Hamilton and W. Falconer, 3 vols. (George Bell, 1903), XV.I.59 and 65; Perseus Digital Library, accessed October 3, 2023. https://www.perseus.tufts.edu/hopper/
It was common during the time of the Buddha for major spiritual teachers to debate in public halls among ascetics and philosophers of various stripes, who for all their differences in metaphysics and methodology held similar views about human potentiality and ethical conduct of human beings to each other and to nature.

[36] *Hamlet*, ed. G. R. Hibbard (Oxford UP, 1987). See Langis, 'Buddhist Virtues'.

[37] Other variants appear in Epictetus, *Discourses, Fragments, Handbook*, trans. Robin Hard, intro. Christopher Gill (Oxford UP, 2014), *Handbook* 5; Marcus Aurelius, *Meditations*, trans. and intro. Gregory Hays (Modern Library, 2003), 8.47, 2.15, 2.11, 4.3.

[38] Everard Flintoff, 'Pyrrho and India', *Phronesis* 25.1–2 (1980): 88–108 (88); McEvilley, *Shape of Ancient Thought*, ch. 17, 439–40; Langis, 'Buddhist Virtues', 306–16 (307), within a Buddhist-Sceptic-Stoic reading of *Hamlet*.

[39] Flintoff, 89; Adrian Kuzminski, 'Pyrrhonism and the Mādhyamaka', *Philosophy East and West* 57.4 (October 2007): 489–90.

of Buddhism during his rule of 268–232 BCE. According to Buddhist tradition, Ashoka, ruing the carnage of an expansionist war he waged against the state of Kalinga, converted to Buddhism and became its active patron, promoting its spread northeast through Asia and northwest to the eastern Mediterranean. Ashoka's stone edict thirteen, out of thirty, expressly proclaims the success of the Buddhist missions to four Hellenistic kingdoms in the eastern Mediterranean, in establishing *dhamma* (Pāli; Sanskrit *dharma*), or Buddhist teaching, there.[40] These missions fuelled the great circling of Buddhism south to Sri Lanka, north to Central Asia, and east to China, Korea, Japan, Vietnam and Indonesia. As with the story of human migration, the process entails much interaction and interbreeding. Chan/Zen Buddhism is a cross-fertilisation between Mahayana Buddhism and indigenous Daoism. Buddhist influence upon the Islamic world, especially during the Abbasid period (750–1258 CE), is broadly reflected in science, literature, medicine and architecture. During the reign of Caliph Mansur (753–774 CE), embassies from Sind to Baghdad included Buddhist scholars, who interacted with Manichaean scholars at court. Mansur also promoted intellectual exchange by embarking on an extensive translation project at Baghdad's 'House of Wisdom' (*bayt al-ḥikma*), during which many scientific, philosophical and cultural texts—Indian, Greek, Persian—were translated into Arabic in the eighth century.[41] Through such developments, Islamic *ḥikma*, as U. Isra Yazicioglu explains, accrued 'insights from other traditions and cultures that did not necessarily link to revelation or any transcendent reality' and also became a philosophical term in the contexts of Peripatetic-Platonic philosophy and natural philosophy.[42]

The port city of Alexandria, founded by Alexander in 331 BCE, became the cultural centre of the ancient Mediterranean until the Arab conquest of Egypt in 641 CE. The city's sapiential pluralism,

---

[40] U. R. Kleinhempel, 'Traces of Buddhist Presence in Alexandria: Philo and the "Therapeutae"', *Aliter* 11 (2019): 3–31 (5); McEvilley, *Shape of Ancient Thought*, ch. 14.

[41] Yazicioglu, 'Wisdom in the Qur'an', 231; Alexander Berzin, 'Historical Survey of the Buddhist and Muslim Worlds' Knowledge of Each Other's Customs and Teachings', *The Muslim World* 100.2–3 (2010): 187–203. See also Johan Elverskog, *Buddhism and Islam on the Silk Road* (U of Pennsylvania P, 2011).

[42] Yazicioglu, 232.

Wisdom Ecology [33

as Julia Reinhard Lupton explores in her essay in this volume, is reflected in Shakespeare's *Antony and Cleopatra*, where Platonic, Lucretian, Gnostic and Egyptian themes feed the play's erudite spectacles and cosmic musings. The centre of Hellenism under the Macedonian Ptolemies (305–30 BCE), Alexandria was also home to a sizable Greek-speaking Jewish community (established since the Persian and Alexandrian conquests of Egypt in the fourth century BCE). The convergence of Greek philosophy and the Hebrew Bible in the Septuagint, said to have been commissioned by the Ptolemies, resonates through this volume. After the destruction of the philosophical schools of Athens in the 80s BCE, 'pagan philosophy and Semitic religions coexist[ed] and inform[ed] one another without any obvious contradiction', producing 'brilliant and enigmatic . . . eclecticism' in vibrant intellectual exchange.[43] The Egyptian priest and scholar Manetho composed works in Greek on Egyptian history and religion. Egyptian, Ethiopian, Indian, Persian, Elamite, Babylonian, Assyrian, Chaldaean, Phoenician, Syrian and Latin masterpieces were probably translated and preserved in Greek as well. In Ullrich Kleinhempel's view, Philo of Alexandria's documentary on the ascetic community of the 'Therapeutae' at Lake Mareotis attests to Buddhist reception in Egypt.[44] The Neoplatonist Plotinus (204/5–270 CE) would also study in Alexandria, near Thebes, where he may have met Greeks, Jews, Egyptians and even Indian 'naked philosophers'. King Lear's greeting of Edgar as a 'learnèd Theban' 'philosopher' (*King Lear*, 3.4.125, 140, 144) may be a nod to Egypt, where so many Greek philosophers—Thales, Pythagoras, Hippocrates, Plato—sojourned, and also to possible Indo-Greek interactions by Greek philosophers and historians such as Democritus, Pyrrho, Megasthenes and Onesicritus, reported to have encountered gymnosophists in India or in Egypt.[45]

---

[43] Phillip Sidney Horky, 'Cosmic Spiritualism among the Pythagoreans, Stoics, Jews and Early Christians', in *Cosmos in the Ancient World*, ed. Phillip Sidney Horky (Cambridge UP, 2019), 270–94 (280).

[44] Kleinhempel, 'Traces of Buddhist Presence', 3–31.

[45] The legendary Indian origin of Dionysus is reported in Philostratus, *The Life of Apollonius of Tyana*, Vol. I: Books 1–5, trans. F. C. Conybeare, Loeb Classical Library (Heinemann, 1912), II.2. See also Flintoff, 'Pyrrho and India', 89; McEvilley, *Shape of Ancient Thought*, chs. 9, 13 and 22 on Diogenes, Pyrrho and Plotinus respectively. William Woodthorpe Tarn, *The Greeks in Bactria and India* (Cambridge UP, 1938, 2010), 370, notes Sir F. Petrie's discovery of a Buddhist gravestone in Alexandria.

34] *Unhae Park Langis*

Neoplatonism also serves as possible common ground for Hindu Advaita Vedantism, Christianity and Islam—all built on monistic systems. Advaita, a nondual path of spirituality, is the most influential school of Vedanta, one of six philosophical systems of Indian philosophy. Michal Just rightly finds striking elements of correspondence between the Indian and the Neoplatonic philosophies regarding notions of the dynamic absolute, mutual interdependence and the interpenetration of everything with everything else.[46] This resemblance, according to Just, might be explained by 'the nature of the mind as it appears under a focused and systematic introspection', or by parallel responses to a common opponent, or by cross-cultural exchange.[47] Up through the Islamic Golden Age (roughly 900–1300 CE) and the Renaissance in the West, Neoplatonism also became a point of convergence among Christian, Kabbalistic and Sufi thinkers, who all engaged with Plotinian ideas, including the doctrine of the One, absolute consciousness called *Nous* and the subtle shuttling between the sensible and divine worlds.[48] Broadly understood as the 'belief in the possibility of union with or absorption into God by means of contemplation and self surrender',[49] mysticism was a common element in the religious traditions arising from Mesopotamia and Egypt, including Neoplatonism, Hermeticism, Gnosticism, Judaism, Christianity, Islam and the *prisca theologia* of the Renaissance humanists, yielding an esoteric ecumenicism. Classicist John Burnet has likened Pyrrho to a 'Buddhist *arhat*' even as several modern Muslim scholars have viewed Hellenic sages such as Plato, Plotinus, Proclus and Pyrrho 'as metaphysicians and seers like the *rsis* of India rather than as profane philosophers'.[50] Such

---

[46] Michal Just, 'Neoplatonism and Paramadvaita', *Comparative Philosophy* 4.2 (2013): 1–28 (22–3). https://doi.org/10.31979/2151-6014(2013).040206. See also McEvilley, *Shape of Ancient Thought*, ch. 22.

[47] Just, 23.

[48] Algis Uždavinys, 'At-Tasawwuf and Neoplatonic Philosophy', *Acta Orientalia Vilnensia* 2 (2001): 73–8.

[49] 'mysticism, n., 2', *OED* online.

[50] Seyyed Hossein Nasr, *Knowledge and the Sacred* (SUNY, 1989), 29. John Burnet, 'Sceptics', in *Encyclopædia of Religion and Ethics*, ed. James Hastings et al., vol. 11 (T & T Clark, 1921), 228–31 (229), observes: 'We see that those who knew Pyrrho well describe him as a sort of Buddhist *arhat* and that is doubtless how we should regard him. He is not so much a sceptic as an ascetic and quietist.'

are the intriguing ghostly traces of cultural cross-fertilisation between wisdom traditions in Shakespeare's *oikumene*.

Sensus Communis: *Wisdom of the World*

What stands out beyond these tantalising yet ultimately inconclusive lineages is a broadly inclusive wisdom culture grounded in a creative energy that not only propels a self-organising universe but also undergirds the love and dignity sought by all participants, organic and inorganic members of the world and, implicitly, the care and stewardship required by the most valuable and vulnerable of these. Such nature-centred formations of wisdom are grounded in perceptual phenomenology. As Tewa Pueblan Greg Cajete explains in his writing on Native science, phenomenology 'roots the entire tree of knowledge in the soil of direct physical and perceptual experience of the earth'.[51] Whole-body perception is more circular than linear, reflected in the cycles of the day and the seasons, the patterns of birth, growth and death, and rhythms in our economic and emotional lives from boom to bust, from joy to grief. The heart-mind-body experience in this swirling lifeworld is reflected in ancient and Indigenous systems of knowledge. The holographic notion of part in whole and whole in part was fundamental to ancient wisdom traditions as diverse as the Pachakúti Mesa (Peru), Hopi, Celtic, Chinese, Arabic, Hindu and Greek worldviews.[52] Within this common sharing of holographic wisdom, the Husserlian lifeworld is, at the same time, 'culturally relative, diverse and different for each culture and each person because it is based on the experienced world of distinct peoples'.[53] As Yoram Cohen and Nathan Wasserman point out, wisdom literatures from diverse places were nonetheless 'susceptible to transmission east and west' because they 'voic[ed] inclusive human

---

[51] Gregory Cajete, 'Philosophy of Native Science', in *American Indian Thought: Philosophical Essays*, ed. Anne Waters (Blackwell, 2004), 45–57 (45).

[52] Joseph Selbie, *The Physics of God: Unifying Quantum Physics, Consciousness, M-Theory, Heaven, Neuroscience and Transcendence* (New Page, 2017), ch. 5, 67–84. Renee A. Levi, 'Holographic Theory and Groups', *Collective Wisdom Initiative*, December 16, 2001.

[53] Cajete, 'Philosophy', 45.

issues', producing a *sensus communis*—that sane and sublime wisdom for thriving and healing that runs through global traditions of knowing.[54] This noetic wisdom subsumes reason, which, comparatively, Aristotle identified as an indispensable but imperfect rudder for human beings toward personal and collective flourishing—an idea that Shakespeare echoes: 'But shall you on your knowledge find this way?' (*Measure for Measure*, 4.1.34).[55] 'When Empedocles referred to his quartet [of the elements] as *rhizomata* ("roots")', Nick Allen writes, 'he and his predecessors were surely aware that roots spread out from a central trunk or stem'[56] of the Tree of Life: of humusy, humoural and human *gnosis*. The Renaissance humanists professed a similar conviction in their pursuit of a *prisca theologia* while current academic approaches turn to cognitive science, evolutionary biology and quantum physics to explain these commonalities in global wisdom traditions.[57]

This *sensus communis* manifests itself further in the various global cosmogonies that feature the concept of a World Soul. Hindu Brahman, Hellenic *Anima Mundi*, Christian Holy Spirit, Native American Great Spirit—all strive to integrate the physical and ethical dimensions of being. In his *Timaeus*, Plato presents the world as a living organism following a tradition from Pythagoras, who may well have been influenced by Indian yogis.[58] According to later

---

[54] Cohen and Wasserman, 'Mesopotamian Wisdom Literature', 135. For a practical, common-sense manifestation of *sensus communis* in urban planning grounded in 'everyday life and lived society-nature relations', see Richard Bärnthaler, 'Towards Eco-Social Politics: A Case Study of Transformative Strategies to Overcome Forms-of-Life Crises', *Environmental Politics* (2023): 1–22. PDF. https://www.tandfonline.com/doi/full/10.1080/09644016.2023.2180910

[55] Aristotle, *Nicomachean Ethics*, VI.1144a22, 29.

[56] Nick Allen, 'The Common Origin Approach to Comparing Indian and Greek Philosophy', in *Universe and Inner Self in Early Indian and Early Greek Thought*, ed. Richard Seaford (Edinburgh UP, 2016), 12–27 (26).

[57] Donald Wehrs, 'Cognitive Virtue and Global Ecosociability', in *Shakespeare and Virtue: A Handbook*, ed. Julia Reinhard Lupton and Donovan Sherman (Cambridge UP, 2023), 244–56; Selbie, *Physics of God*; Robert J. Sternberg and Jennifer Jordan, eds., *A Handbook of Wisdom: Psychological Perspectives* (Cambridge UP, 2005).

[58] Alberto Bernabé and Julia Mendoza, 'Pythagorean Cosmogony and Vedic Cosmogony (RV 10.129). Analogies and Differences', *Phronesis* 58.1 (2013): 32–51.

commentators, the Pythagoreans believed that the cosmos was an animal being, inhaling and exhaling '"breath" from the infinity that surrounds it'. This 'regular respiration' differentiates 'the universe and its constituents . . . from what is chaotic and disorderly', evincing what may be the first usage of the Greek word *kosmos* to mean 'order'.[59] In Genesis 2:7, God blew the breath of life into Adam; the Septuagint rendered 'breath' (Hebrew *neshamah*) as 'spirit' or 'wind' (Greek *pneuma*), since the Alexandrian Jews, versed in Greek philosophy, knew that the Orphics, Plato and the Stoics believed the human soul was composed of the same *pneuma*, or spirit, as the divine God. In ecologist-philosopher David Abram's words, 'the affinity between the mind and wind is one of the oldest and most common intuitions, as though the air itself was aware'.[60] This idea resembles the Hindu *atman*, literally, 'breath', meaning the soul as a divine essence, within the same humoural system, which circulated through the entire Indo-European continent and further into Asia.[61] Pervading everything, even time, as 'life's universal witness', *prana* (breath, life energy, equivalent to Chinese *qi*) 'was equated with, contained in and associated with all elements which produced and maintained life'.[62] At the juncture of the ethical, the ecumenical and the ecological, both the Vedic mantra *So'ham* ('That am I') and the Hebraic-Christian God's 'I am that I am' (Exodus 3:14) illustrate the pneumatic concept of breath as divine energy, equating the self with the Absolute whether through divine grace or the contemplative exercise of stillness.[63] A major influence on Shakespeare and his contemporaries, Seneca's tragedies show improper *cura sui* writ large with cataclysmic consequences. As such, they prefigure the reckless breathing of humanity, especially the greedy, self-interested

---

[59] Horky, 'Cosmic Spiritualism', 273.

[60] *Becoming Animal*, directed by Emma Davie, Peter Mettler. With David Abram, Peter Mettler. Maximage and SDI Productions, 2018.

[61] Gilles Quispel, *Gnostica, Judaica, Catholica: Collected Essays of Gilles Quispel*, ed. Johannes van Oort (Brill, 2008), 162; McEvilley, *Shape of Ancient Thought*, 49.

[62] Kenneth G. Zysk, 'The Science of Respiration and the Doctrine of the Bodily Winds in Ancient India', *Journal of the American Oriental Society* 113.2 (April–June 1993): 198–213 (200).

[63] Sally Kempton, *Meditation for the Love of It: Enjoying Your Own Deepest Experience* (Sounds True, 2011), 107, 128, 138.

38]   *Unhae Park Langis*

fossil fuel industry, upsetting the carbon balance in our atmosphere as well as our moral balance and equilibrium with the natural ways of life.

Despite the prominent intellectual focus of Platonic scholarship, spiritual practice enters the Hellenic tradition through 'the practice of stillness, a widespread Pythagorean mental discipline', by prominent fifth-century philosophers such as Empedocles (c. 483–423 BCE), Parmenides (515–450 BCE) and Socrates (470–399 BCE), who were known for their exercises of 'withdrawing consciousness from sense-objects through introspective concentration', resembling Indian meditative practices.[64] Such practices resemble the *Vedānta*, literally, the end of the Hindu Vedas ('end' meaning both 'part' and 'purpose'): to investigate the nature of *atman* (soul) and to 'direct the enquirer toward it',[65] as *telos*, as an ultimate end. In the words of Socrates, 'When the soul investigates by itself it passes into the realm of what is pure, ever-existing, immortal and unchanging . . . its experience then is what is called wisdom'.[66] Such spiritual practices of one's empirical ego dying into the cosmic Self before physical death were familiar to Shakespeare, who was acquainted with Michel de Montaigne's *Essays* (1580; Englished 1603), notably the essay 'That to Philosophise Is to Learn to Die'.[67]

The practices of attunement/at-Onement translated into more worldly settings suggest that wisdom is living fully, living a graceful, compassionate life, turning ego- to ecology. This compassionate conviviality, or coexistence, as part of wisdom, is reflected in Western ethical ideas such as the Pythagorean maxim beloved by Erasmus, 'All is common between friends' (*koina ta philôn*), Socrates' notion of ignorance as operating in service of the good, Aristotle's theories

---

[64] John Bussanich, 'Plato and Yoga', in *Universe and Inner Self in Early Indian and Early Greek Thought*, ed. Richard Seaford (Edinburgh UP, 2016), 87–103 (98); Diogenes Laertius, *Lives of Eminent Philosophers*, vol. 2, IX.61, p. 475.

[65] F. Max Müller, trans., *The Upanishads*, Part 1, The Sacred Books of the East, vol. 1 (Clarendon, 1879), lxxxvi; Poolla Tirupati Raju, *Structural Depths of Indian Thought* (SUNY, 1985), 35.

[66] Plato, *Phaedo*, in *Plato: Complete Works*, ed. John M. Cooper and D. S. Hutchinson (Hackett, 1997), 79d1–7.

[67] Michel de Montaigne, *The essayes or morall, politike and millitarie discourses of Lo: Michaell de Montaigne*, trans. John Florio (Edward Blount, 1603).

Wisdom Ecology

[39

of virtuous friendship and true aristocracy grounded in virtue (*aretē*), the Stoic ideals of philanthropy and the concurrence of personal and public good, and even the medieval ideal of 'noblesse oblige', which provided a countermeasure of protection and care within a hierarchical order. These ethical concepts pervaded Shakespeare's society, in which the guild system and the corporate life of cities managed the daily welfare of the community. Indeed, notions of the community, commons and the common good were arguably stronger in the pre- and early modern periods than in the privatised, rights-based and neoliberal social orders of today. But community leaders and activists are recovering a 'solidarity economy' implementing 'cooperative economics that promote social solidarity, mutual aid, reciprocity and generosity'.[68]

Like Hindu and Pythagorean-Platonic philosophies, Native American wisdom traditions harbour concepts about the four elements and the relatedness of life forms through breath and air. In Diné (Navajo) thought, for instance, as Indigenous scholar Anne Waters explains, the breath of life 'constantly being exchanged in the universe, from the cosmos and to the earth', grounds a 'complementary metaphysical thought' in which both sky-reaching smoke and 'words when spoken or sung' may have incantatory power.[69] Breath, as a medium of physical exchange in this Indigenous view, underscores the reciprocity that humans share with nature and the deep responsibilities of care involved therein.[70] As Robin Wall Kimmerer points out, Native cultures of gratitude are necessarily cultures of exchange, in which each person or creature pledges 'reciprocity with the living world': 'If an animal gives its life to feed me, I am in turn bound to support its life. If I receive a stream's gift of pure water, then I am responsible for returning a gift in kind.'[71] A similar natural reciprocity fuels Seneca's

---

[68] Kali Akuno and Ajamu Nangwaya, eds., *Jackson Rising: The Struggle for Economic Democracy and Black Self-Determination in Jackson, Mississippi* (Daraja, 2017), ch. 4.

[69] Anne Waters, ed. and intro, *American Indian Thought: Philosophical Essays* (Blackwell, 2004), 103–4.

[70] Waters, 104.

[71] Robin Wall Kimmerer, *Braiding Sweetgrass: Indigenous Wisdom, Scientific Knowledge, and the Teachings of Plants* (Milkweed, 2013, 2015), 115–16.

circle of gifts, which does not bind but rather inspires one to return a gift.[72]

Despite geographic, historical and cultural differences, Native customs and processes of 'coming-to-know', indeed, share features with ancient Stoic wisdom, not to mention Ayurvedic knowing. The etymological links between the words *science, consciousness* and *conscience* attest to their roots in a holistic worldview. The word *science* comes from the Latin verb *scīre*, to know, as translated from ancient Greek συνείδησις (*syneidesis*), meaning 'knowledge, consciousness, conscience'.[73] Conscience here means not guilt for sin but 'joint-knowing, i.e. *conscience* which joins moral and spiritual consciousness as part of being created in the divine image', thus resembling eudaimonic well-being.[74] In so far as *syneidesis* joins moral and spiritual consciousness with knowing nature around us, Native coming-to-know resembles Stoic *oikeiôsis*, defined by Chrysippus (279–206 BCE) as 'living in accordance with experience of what happens by nature'.[75] At the heart of the Stoic way of life is conspiration through breath (*pneuma*), endowed with tensile properties within a pneumatic hierarchy that accounts for the integrity of a rock as well as the moral integrity of a sage.[76] While the rock possesses tenor, the 'internal breath' that holds its physical entity together, the Stoic sage skilfully manages 'animal breath' to maintain the virtue of his soul in response to all phenomena as tensile movements between

---

[72] Seneca, 32 ff., in Edgar Wind, *Pagan Mysteries in the Renaissance*, rev. ed. (Norton, 1968).

[73] 'science, n.', *OED* online; Strong's Concordance, suneidésis. https://biblehub.com/greek/4893.htm

[74] See discussion of *eudaimonia* in the introduction of this volume.

[75] Gregory Cajete, *Native Science: Natural Laws of Interdependence* (Clear Light, 2000), 72–3, 80–1. See also Jacob Klein, 'The Stoic Argument from Oikeiôsis', in *Oxford Studies in Ancient Philosophy*, ed. Victor Caston, vol. 50 (Oxford UP, 2016), 143–200. On the Axial Age of sages, the eighth to third century BCE flourishing in speculative thought and ethics, occurring simultaneously and independently in India, Persia, East Asia and the Greco-Roman world, see Christopher Peet, *Practicing Transcendence: Axial Age Spiritualities for a World in Crisis* (Palgrave Macmillan, 2019), 6, 63.

[76] Phillip Sidney Horky, 'Our Common Breath: "Conspiration" from the Stoics to the Church Fathers', in *The Life of Breath in Literature, Culture and Medicine: Classical to Contemporary*, ed. David Fuller, Corinne Saunders and Jane Macnaughton (Springer Nature, 2021), 55–68; Horky, 'Cosmic Spiritualism', 279–81.

Wisdom Ecology

[41

bodies within the macrocosm—psychomaterial conspiration that translates into Stoic *contentment*. Such tensile control *within* best equips a person to confront the enormous challenges of effecting harmony in the world—within and beyond the household. Breath was the key medium of exchange in these holographic systems, which revealed the cosmos as an organic Whole.[77] While the Stoic hierarchy of breath offers graduated access to the World Soul among animate beings, Indigenous animate philosophies, much like Pythagorean views of cosmic harmony and sattvic Hindu and Buddhist respect for all sentient beings, extend 'personhood', or beingness, to all members of the natural world within 'a natural democracy'.[78] In such a view, mind and sentience can be better understood less as properties of bodies and more as relational events of bodies participating within the animate, elemental field that is the Mind-World.

Similarly, practitioners of Chinese shamanic wisdom, dating back to the first millennium BCE, cultivated holistic (medical, martial and 'spirited') *daoyin* exercises to assist the 'bio-connectivity of our innate life vitality into the Dao', the unalterable intelligent order of heaven and earth, as witnessed in the organic rhythms and patterns in nature.[79] This art of nourishing life (*yang sheng shu*) is known today as *qigong*, loosely translated as cultivating life energy in the interaction of our self-organising body with that of the world. Like Native coming-to-know, *qigong* is founded on 'close, systematic and inspired observation of the rhythms and cycles of nature, and the movements and innate characteristics of animals in the wild'.[80] In Shakespeare's words, 'One touch of nature makes the whole world kin' (*Troilus and Cressida*, 3.3.169). As in Indigenous practices of living harmoniously with nature, the radiance of the human spirit as

---

[77] For global accounts of the world as a cosmic being, see Michael A. Rappenglück, 'The World as a Living Entity: Essentials of a Cosmic Metaphor', *Mediterranean Archaeology and Archaeometry* 18.4 (2018): 323–31.

[78] Cajete, 'Philosophy', 46.

[79] Roy Jenzen, 'Thoughts on the Relevance of Qigong to the Understanding and Practice of Chinese Medicine', *The Journal of Chinese Medicine* 87 (June 2008): 10–13 (11); Livia Kohn, *Daoism: A Contemporary Philosophical Investigation* (Routledge, 2019), 16–19. At present, Shakespeare and Daoism, through similar if different systems of humoural/elemental medicine, is a lightly mined field of research that deserves more study.

[80] Jenzen, 10.

'inherent-vitality' (*shen ming*)[81] is aligned with our rootedness in the perpetual rhythms of nature. Our present climate crisis reveals how much we have veered from an enlivened world in which plants, animals, stones and the elements, according to their particular virtues, mutually support and coexist with each other, an interconnectedness that Indigenous cultures worldwide revere. As David Abram suggests, a view to how 'our body politic breathes' within 'this broader commonwealth' forges 'new forms of place based community and planetary solidarity, along with a commitment to justice and the often exasperating work of politics'.[82]

Indra's Net

The kaleidoscopic patterns cast by a *sensus communis* ground the appositions of Shakespeare with various wisdom traditions mounted in this volume. More than any definitive historical proof, the clues to our shared humanity manifestly lie in the motifs and metaphors that poets and sages including Shakespeare bountifully use—ones resonating across manifold spiritual disciplines and human quests. An ancient Buddhist *sūtra* known as Indra's Net, referring to one cluster of these motifs, brings us back to India, the possible origin of many Platonic and Neoplatonic ideas. Originating in the Athara Veda, Indra's Net was further developed by the Mahayana school in the third century. According to one description, there lies in the heaven of the goddess Indra 'a network of pearls so arranged that if you look at one you see all the others reflected in it'.[83] This metaphor intertwining light, mirror and pearl—staple tropes in Afro-Eurasian wisdom traditions—superbly highlights certain ideas about the nature of truth and about the interaction between the various traditions of wisdom. The scintillating metaphor reveals that the nature of reality and truth is as infinitely multifaceted as the multiplicity of these mirror-like pearls simultaneously reflecting each other. This hall of mirrors recalls epistemologically, if not tonally, the Socratic *elenchus*,

---

[81] Jenzen, 11.

[82] Abram, *Becoming Animal* (2010), 9.

[83] Sir Charles Eliot, *Japanese Buddhism* (Routledge & Kegan Paul, 1935, 2018), EPUB. See also Francis H. Cook, *Hua-yen Buddhism: The Jewel Net of Indra* (Penn State UP, 2010); Alan Watts, *The Way of Zen* (Vintage, 1999), PDF, 86, 138.

Wisdom Ecology

[43

by which the 'refutation of each false belief empties the mind of one thought after another, inducing successive non-conceptual states, ending in numbness and shame'.[84] Socrates' apophatic knowing, that is, by negation, suggests that reality lies not in forms themselves but in the empty spaces between them and the totality of interbeing, to use the late Buddhist monk and activist Thich Nhat Hanh's term for the Buddhist concepts of interdependence and the co-dependent arising of all things. According to the *sūtra* of Indra's Net, 'each object in the world is not merely itself but involves every other object and in fact is every other object'.[85] The word *sūtra* itself embodies the nondual interwovenness of Buddhist *dharma*, which multivalently means doctrine, nature, truth and norm.[86] Like the Daoist Way, as well as Stoic and Indigenous forms of naturalistic being, *dharma*, as natural law, comprehends human norms of good conduct. This 'conform[ing] to what one is' entails a marbled ecology of wisdom and phenomena.[87] An acute sense of relatedness lies at the core of this livened knowing and seeing deep into the heart of things. When Juliet envisions Romeo 'cut out in little stars' in a new constellation of love, Shakespeare alludes to such an embodied sense of relatedness and its practised forms of love, caring and stewardship.

Since the emergence of a mechanical paradigm leading eventually to the Industrial Revolution, the wisdom traditions of Shakespeare's *oikumene* have sadly been 'eclipse[d] for the last three centuries', emphatically 'a deviation from two millennia of Western natural philosophy', not to mention our deeper species history of having spent over 99.99 per cent of our time living in the natural environment.[88]

---

[84] Plato, *Apology*, in *Plato: Complete Works*, 23b.

[85] Eliot, *Japanese Buddhism*, EPUB.

[86] 'Dhamma, Dhammā: 12 definitions', Wisdom Library, accessed October 4, 2023. https://www.wisdomlib.org/definition/dhamma

[87] Alain Daniélou, *Gods of Love and Ecstasy: The Traditions of Shiva and Dionysus* (Inner Traditions, 1992), EPUB.

[88] Bruce Scofield, 'Gaia: The Living Earth—2,500 Years of Precedents in Natural Science and Philosophy', in *Scientists Debate Gaia: The Next Century*, ed. Stephen H. Schneider, James R. Miller, Eileen Crist and Penelope J. Boston (MIT, 2004), 151–60 (157); Chorong Song, Harumi Ikei and Yoshifumi Miyazaki, 'Physiological Effects of Nature Therapy: A Review of the Research in Japan', *International Journal of Environmental Research and Public Health* 13.8 (2016): 781–98 (781). https://doi.org/10.3390/ijerph13080781

In response, people in the West over the recent decades have turned increasingly to Eastern, Indigenous, Black, feminist and environmental philosophies to retrieve a post-secular sense of holographic wisdom in the aim of healing Earth and its most vulnerable beings. But what is noteworthy here is that the unitive visions of Shakespeare's *oikumene*—Pythagorean *koinonia*, Platonic One and Many, and Stoic cosmopolitanism—are in many ways cousins of Buddhist interbeing, Indigenous kinship, ecosophy, not to mention other vibrant hybridisations resonating in the popular consciousness. Like the ouroboros, this kaleidoscope of diverse wisdom traditions knitting the past with the present within a common evolutionary *sūtra* of homo sapiens-to-be forms a wisdom ecology for the future within which conscientious beings may ply whole-body skills to save our *oikos*, our home, in ways engaging the ecumenical, the ecological and the ethical. It is the imaginary for a post-growth era where economic integrates with ecological, organic and spiritual growth aimed at the thriving of whole societies rather than their top 1 per cent. According to activists such as Margaret Wheatley, Grace Lee Boggs, Dean Spade and adrienne maree brown, we must to this end 'tap into the most ancient systems and patterns for wisdom as we build tomorrow'.[89] Advocating mutual aid to transform our political economies into 'systems of care and generosity' instead of personal profit, Spade speaks of the 'false separation of politics and injustice from ordinary life' and how activism should not be a kind of 'lifestyle accessory' but rather an enlivened way of life 'in alignment with our hopes for the world and with our passions'.[90] Paul Hawken's *Blessed Unrest* spotlights more than a million self-healing civic groups around the globe, weaving spiritual growth and awakening with practical actions in our daily lives.[91]

---

[89] Margaret J. Wheatley, *Leadership and the New Science: Discovering Order in a Chaotic World*, 2nd ed. (Berrett-Koehler, 1999); Grace Lee Boggs and Scott Kurashige, *The Next American Revolution: Sustainable Activism for the Twenty-First Century* (U of California P, 2012), 42–5; Dean Spade, *Mutual Aid: Building Solidarity during This Crisis (and the Next)* (Verso, 2020), 16; adrienne maree brown, *Emergent Strategy: Shaping Change, Changing Worlds* (AK, 2017), PDF, 7.

[90] Spade, 10, 27; Boggs and Kurashige, 39.

[91] Paul Hawken, *Blessed Unrest: How the Largest Movement in the World Came into Being, and Why No One Saw It Coming* (Penguin, 2007). As one example, Citizens' Climate Lobby, of which the author is a member, has burgeoned from twenty-seven to over 500 chapters worldwide since 2011.

Wisdom Ecology

[45

Such is the Beloved Community that transhistorically has inspired mystics, poets, healers and activists from Buddha and Pythagoras of the Axial Age to Martin Luther King Jr and Thich Nhat Hanh to our young activists and leaders Greta Thunberg, Vanessa Nakate, Helena Gualingua, Autumn Peltier, David Hogg, US Representative Alexandria Ocasio-Cortez, Tennessee State Representative Justin Jones, among countless others.[92] Call it what you will—Beloved Community, interbeing, entanglement or 'indigenising'—we must 'build on the wisdom of our ancestors and try to make the world not perfect but just a bit more kind'.[93] May ecumenical, ecological and ethical Shakespeare bolster this blessed unrest in these times that try our souls, times that must 'grow our souls', bringing forth a Second Axial Age.[94]

---

[92] Marc Andrus, *Brothers in the Beloved Community: The Friendship of Thich Nhat Hanh and Martin Luther King Jr.* (Parallax, 2021), PDF.

[93] Kimmerer, *Braiding Sweetgrass*, 210–13; William F. Schulz, *Reversing the Rivers: A Memoir of History, Hope, and Human Rights* (U of Pennsylvania P, 2023), 225.

[94] Boggs and Kurashige, *Next American Revolution*, 38; William Keepin, *Belonging to God: Spirituality, Science and a Universal Path of Divine Love* (SkyLight Paths, 2016), xviii.

CHAPTER 2

SOPHIA ON THE CYDNUS: *ANTONY AND CLEOPATRA* AS WISDOM LITERATURE

Julia Reinhard Lupton

Cleopatra's entry into Tarsus on the Cydnus River in 41 BCE, recollected by Shakespeare in both *Antony and Cleopatra* and *Cymbeline*, was designed by Cleopatra VII herself out of Greek and Egyptian traditions and then delivered to Shakespeare via Plutarch.[1] The appearance of the episode on Imogen's walls acknowledges Cleopatra's association with female wisdom and virtue, a recurrent counterstrain to more negative depictions of the queen's wiles. Like Imogen, Bess of Hardwick included a portrait of Cleopatra flanked by Fortitude and Justice in her textile gallery of famous women at Hardwick Hall, announcing Cleopatra as an exemplar of heroic values and capacities.[2] The scene on the Cydnus is a visual wisdom poem, a learned spectacle that assembles mythological motifs, philosophical ideas and prudential strategies, unfurling a hermeneutics and diplomatics of hospitality. This wisdom work, executed as part of a public communications plan at Cydnus, becomes newly urgent and freshly embodied in Cleopatra's elegy for Antony and her heroic suicide. The historical Cleopatra participated in a Hellenistic *oikumene* shaped by the Fertile Crescent and Silk Road and managed by the interdependence of imperial dynasties that hailed from Alexander and incorporated local deities in their royal

---

[1] All citations from *Antony and Cleopatra* are from the Oxford edition, ed. Michael Neill (Oxford UP, 1994). Citations from other works by Shakespeare are from *The New Oxford Shakespeare: The Complete Works, Modern Critical Edition*, ed. Gary Taylor, John Jowett, Terri Bourus and Gabriel Egan (Oxford UP, 2016). Oxford Scholarly Editions Online. doi:10.1093/actrade/9780199591152.book.1

[2] Susan Frye, *Pens and Needles: Women's Textualities in Early Modern England* (U of Pennsylvania P, 2011), 30–73.

cults.[3] A female sovereign mediating between gynocratic Egypt and gynophobic Rome, Cleopatra integrates political know-how, sexual knowledge and iconographic erudition in a dexterous handling of the eudaemonistic, erotic and contemplative facets of *sophia* in the mixed Hellenistic space of Alexandria.[4]

Rich scholarship attests to the play's deployment of Venus and Isis iconography.[5] I interweave this body of material with a neighbouring tradition, Hebrew wisdom literature, including the Book of Proverbs, the Song of Songs, the philosophical romance of Solomon and Sheba, and the deuterocanonical wisdom writings, some translated or composed in Alexandria itself. I begin with the Egyptian sources and afterlives of Hebrew wisdom literature, an international genre of writing whose Hebrew articulations often express both attraction and hostility towards neighbouring sources. Although the North African and Near Eastern presence in Hebrew wisdom literature was not fully disclosed until the advent of modern biblical scholarship, these findings were anticipated in the idea, familiar in the patristic period and revived by humanists and syncretists like Pico della Mirandola and Giordano Bruno, that Moses studied philosophy in Egypt and that Egyptian wisdom and the revelation at Sinai share common insights.[6] At the end of the play, Cleopatra's efforts to retain her wealth and secure her legacy reverse Augustine's typological defences of Christian humanism as the Egyptian gold of

---

[3] Ljuben Tevdovski, 'The Beauty of the *Oikumene* Has Two Edges: Nurturing Roman Imperialism in the "Glocalizing" Traditions of the East', in *Community and Identity at the Edges of the Classical World*, ed. Aaron W. Irvin (Wiley Blackwell, 2021), 7–28.

[4] In Egypt, for example, women could inherit and own property, and a woman could be Pharoah as long as she had a consort. Jane Rowlandson and Ryosuke Takahashi, 'Brother-Sister Marriage and Inheritance Strategies in Greco-Roman Egypt', *The Journal of Roman Studies* 99 (2009): 104–39 (105).

[5] See Michael Lloyd, 'Cleopatra as Isis', *Shakespeare Survey* 12 (1959): 88–94; Janet Adelman, *The Common Liar: An Essay on Antony and Cleopatra* (Yale UP, 1973); Barbara J. Bono, *Literary Transvaluation: From Vergilian Epic to Shakespearean Tragicomedy* (U of California P, 1984); and Peggy Muñoz Simonds, *Myth, Emblem, and Music in Shakespeare's 'Cymbeline': An Iconographic Reconstruction* (U of Delaware P, 1992), 95–101.

[6] Frances A. Yates, *Giordano Bruno and the Hermetic Tradition* (Routledge & Kegan Paul, 1964).

48]   *Julia Reinhard Lupton*

Exodus and the captive woman of Deuteronomy 21. *Anti-Augustan* on the political terrain and *anti-Augustinian* on the hermeneutic plane, the stratagems of Shakespeare's Cleopatra effectively de-typologise the treasures of ancient wisdom as the properly Judeo-Egyptian legacy of Alexandria.[7]

Isis figures in my readings of Cleopatra as an ancient source and analogue of Woman Wisdom and as the Hellenised goddess of goddesses whose virtues Cleopatra fostered in her royal cult. My approach emphasises Hebrew wisdom's own entanglement with Egypt and the echoes of that conversation in Shakespeare's Alexandrian composition. Partially assimilated to Christian typology, this discourse becomes erotically charged and racially expansive when women of wisdom appear as strange, dark, Jewish or foreign in overlapping scenes of erotic union, political diplomacy and royal hospitality. Woman Wisdom's origins in Near Eastern nature divinities lean her toward animism, feathering the line drawn by monotheism between Creator and creation for Renaissance humanist readers of these myths. The wisdom distilled in *Antony and Cleopatra* is distinctively 'Alexandrian': born in Egypt, fed by Greek sources and illuminated by the Septuagint. Wisdom literature is built on intercultural acts of entertainment, hospitality, diplomacy, worship and romance along with the aggressive and defensive attitudes that these actions manage, including theft, rape, seduction, conquest, enslavement and exile. Like the creator God and his consort Wisdom, or Solomon and his foreign guests and brides, Shakespeare the dramatist and Cleopatra the savvy and learned political actor orchestrate human diversity and cosmic order in response to the realities of imperial ambition.

Out of Egypt: Woman Wisdom

The Book of Proverbs was compiled over a series of centuries, beginning in the monarchical period and concluding as late as the early

---

[7] On Cleopatra's prudence and her challenges as a virtuous virago, see Unhae Park Langis, *Passion, Prudence, and Virtue in Shakespearean Drama* (Continuum, 2011), 98–119. On Augustine's typological defences of Christian humanism, see Kathy Eden, *Friends Hold All Things in Common: Tradition, Intellectual Property, and the 'Adages' of Erasmus* (Yale UP, 2001).

Sophia on the Cydnus

[49

Hellenistic era.[8] Female figures of wisdom frame the book: Woman Wisdom graces the collection's prologue (Prov. 1–9), while the advice of the mother of King Lemuel to her son and the encomium of the woman of valour end the book (Prov. 31). Egypt leaves its traces throughout the Book of Proverbs. The book's oldest layer, Proverbs 22:17–23, transmits the Wisdom of Amenemope, an Egyptian collection that probably entered the Hebrew canon via a Canaanite translation when the region was part of the Egyptian empire (late sixteenth to late twelfth centuries BCE).[9] Egypt may have also shaped the Book of Proverbs' most recent layer, its poetic prologue, including the passages that feature Woman Wisdom. Michael V. Fox inventories a range of models for this hypostasis of God's creative powers, including the Canaanite goddess Ishtar and the Egyptian goddesses Ma'at and Isis; of these, he finds Isis the closest to Chokmah, 'not so much in her native Egyptian form . . . as in the universalistic, international persona that she acquired in Hellenistic times . . . As the consummately wise goddess, she had the epithets Phronesis (Intelligence) and Wisdom (Sophia).'[10] Writing in North Africa, Augustine identified ancient wisdom with the Egyptian gold borrowed or stolen by the Israelites in Exodus 21, providing the rationale for Christian humanism.[11] In the Renaissance, Isis and Sophia (Chokmah's name in the Septuagint) merged with the Virgin Mary in the art of Donatello and Pinturicchio, while Bruno, Fico and Pico asserted the antiquity of Egyptian wisdom as the core of a *prisca theologia*.[12] Sophia presides over a sapiential *oikumene* that bridges eudaemonistic ethics and noetic wisdom across diverse traditions.

Greek aretalogies of Isis were inscribed in temples across the Mediterranean from the late second century BCE onwards and most likely

---

[8] Michael V. Fox, *Proverbs 1–9: A New Translation with Introduction and Commentary*, Anchor Bible 18A (Doubleday, 2000), 6, 48–9.

[9] For the full text of 'The Instruction of Amen-Em-Opet', see James B. Pritchard, ed., *Ancient Near Eastern Texts Relating to the Old Testament*, 3rd ed. (Princeton UP, 1969), 447–50. Fox notes that 'Israel was never out of contact with Egypt' and that 'translation of Egyptian literature may have taken place in the period of the monarchy as well'. *Proverbs*, 19.

[10] Fox, 336–8.

[11] Eden, *Friends Hold All Things*, 14–16.

[12] Yates, *Giordano Bruno*, 114–16; Regina Stefaniak, 'Isis Rising: The Ancient Theology of Donatello's "Virgin" in the Santo', *Artibus et Historiae* 27.53 (2006): 89–110.

50]   *Julia Reinhard Lupton*

built on earlier Egyptian hymns to the goddess.[13] Shakespeare knew the aretalogy in *The Golden Ass*, written by the North African Platonist Apuleius and translated into English by William Adlington in 1566:

> Behold Lucius I am come, thy weeping and prayers hath moved me to succor thee, I am she that is the natural mother of all things, mistress and governess of all the Elements, the initial progeny of worlds, chief of the powers divine, Queen of heaven, the principal of the Gods celestial, the light of the Goddesses, at my will the Planets of the air, the wholesome winds of the Seas, and the silences of Hell be disposed, my name, my divinity, is adored throughout all the world, in divers manners, in variable customs, and in many names, for the Phrygians call me the mother of the Gods: The Athenians, Minerva: the Cyprians, Venus: the Candians, Diana: the Sicilians, Proserpina: the Eleusians, Ceres: some Juno, other Bellona, other Hecate: and principally the Ethiopians which dwell in the Orient, and the Egyptians which are excellent in all kind of ancient doctrine, and by their proper ceremonies accustom to worship me, do call me Queen Isis. (XI.47)[14]

The phrase 'initial progeny of worlds [*saeculorum progenies initialis*]' identifies Isis with *natura naturans* and may be picked up by Titania in Shakespeare's most Apuleian text, *A Midsummer Night's Dream*.[15] Appearing 'in divers manners, in variable customs, and in many names', Isis Myrionymos receives her proper habitation and name in Ethiopia and Egypt, where she is called 'Queen Isis'.[16] Apuleius's exaltation of

---

[13] Paraskevi Martzavou, 'Isis Aretalogies, Initiations, and Emotions: The Isis Aretalogies as a Source for the Study of Emotions', in *Unveiling Emotions: Sources and Methods for the Study of Emotions in the Greek World*, ed. Angelos Chaniotis (Franz Steiner, 2012), 269–72.

[14] Lucius Apuleius Africanus, *The Golden Asse*, trans. William Adlington (H. Wykes, 1566), Kindle, rpt. from the 1639 edition.

[15] James A. S. McPeek, 'The Psyche Myth and *A Midsummer Night's Dream*', *Shakespeare Quarterly* 23.1 (Winter 1972): 69–79. I develop the Isis-Titania connection in 'The Titania Translation: *A Midsummer Night's Dream* and the Two *Metamorphoses*', in *Ovid's 'Metamorphoses' and the Environmental Imagination*, ed. Francesca Martelli and Giulia Sissa (Bloomsbury, 2023), 145–62. Latin citation is from Apuleius Madaurensis, *Metamorphoses, Book XI: The Isis Book*, ed. Wytse Hette Keulen and Ulrike Egelhaaf-Gaiser (Brill, 2015), XI.5.1, 72.

[16] On the names of Isis, see Laurent Bricault, *Isis Pelagia: Images, Names and Cults of a Goddess of the Seas*, Religions in the Graeco-Roman World, vol. 190, trans. Gil H. Renberg (Brill, 2020), 4.

Isis as an international goddess bespeaks his own cosmopolitanism as a North African who spoke Greek and wrote in Latin, and whose mother tongue may have been Punic.[17] Apuleius was writing in a setting where Isis presided as both a neighbouring local deity and a universal principle of natural becoming, and she reflects his own identity as a Romanised and Hellenised North African.

Chokmah, like Isis, is associated with the generativity of the natural world, though allied with a singular God who stands outside creation rather than identified with processes immanent within nature. She delivers her own aretalogy in Proverbs 8:

> The Lord hath possessed me in the beginning of his way: *I was* before his works of old.
>
> I was set up from everlasting, from the beginning, *and* before the earth.
>
> When there were no depths, was I begotten, when there were no fountains abounding with water.
>
> Before the mountains were settled: *and* before the hills, was I begotten.
>
> [. . .]
>
> Then was I with him *as* a nourisher, and I was daily *his* delight, rejoicing always before him,
>
> And took my solace in the compass of his earth: and my delight *is* with the children of men. (Prov. 8:22–31; Geneva)[18]

Wisdom precedes the creation of the world because wisdom concerns its designing, its conceptualisation and composition—Apuleius's 'initial progeny of worlds'. Working with wisdom as both capacity and partner, God organises the primal chaos marshalled by ancient creation myths, an unbounded sea of forces and energies, into something beautiful and bearable. The highly rare Hebrew אָמוֹן (amon), translated in the Geneva Bible as 'nourisher', may also mean artificer/architect or ward/nursling; it also appears as the transliteration of the Egyptian god Amon or Amun (Jer. 56:25).[19] Although the passage as a

---

[17] Benjamin Todd Lee, Ellen Finkelpearl and Luca Graverini, eds., *Apuleius and Africa* (Routledge, 2014), 5.

[18] Citations from the Bible and KJV 1611 are from BibleGateway.com. Citations from the Hebrew Bible are from Sefaria.org.

[19] R. B. Y. Scott, 'Wisdom in Creation: The āmôn of Proverbs VIII 30', *Vetus Testamentum* 10.2 (April 1960): 213–23; Fox, *Proverbs*, 285–7.

52]   *Julia Reinhard Lupton*

whole emphasises God's sublime activity as creator, this word implies some contributory agency on Chokmah's part. Woman Wisdom, no longer the independent goddess of ancient cults yet still bearing traces of those divinities' creative capacities, is born from a translation process by which monotheism arises out of and responds to polytheistic understandings of the cosmos.

Wisdom appears as both a consort present with God at creation and a daughter sporting before him, leading to her identification with Mary (as sapiential queen mother) and Jesus (as the living logos). Proverbs 8, joined by Isis aretalogies and Orphic, Platonic and neo-Pythagorean mythmaking, informs Paul's sublime hymn to Christ as 'the image of the invisible God, the first begotten of every creature, / For by him were all things created, which are in heaven, and which are in earth' (1 Col. 1:15–16; Geneva).[20] In rabbinic Judaism, Wisdom becomes the Shekinah, God's indwelling presence, from *shakan*, to dwell. The Shekinah was identified with the pillar of cloud that descended over the tabernacle in Exodus and Leviticus. In the late Middle Ages, the Shekinah would become the feminine principle of God, the lowest and most worldly of the ten sephirot or emanations of God in the Kabbalah.[21] Relatedly in Islam, wisdom is figured as Bilqis, the Queen of Sheba, often taken as the type of a rich and intelligent sovereign. Bilqis, for the mystic Ibn 'Arabi (d. 1240), becomes a figure for divine wisdom, the daughter of theory and praxis.[22]

According to Fox, God's pleasure in the playfulness of Wisdom resembles his delight in the sporting of the Leviathan in Psalms 104:26: 'There go the ships, *yea* that Leviathan, whom thou hast made to play therein' (Geneva).[23] The frisky leviathan of Psalms 104 most likely refers to dolphins following boats and leaping in their wake,

---

[20] Matthew E. Gordley, *The Colossian Hymn in Context: An Exegesis in Light of Jewish and Greco-Roman Hymnic and Epistolary Conventions* (Mohr Siebeck, 2007).

[21] Linda Munk, 'His Dazzling Absence: The Shekinah in Jonathan Edwards', *Early American Literature* 27.1 (1992): 1–30; Peter Schäfer, 'Mirror of His Beauty: The Femininity of God in Jewish Mysticism and in Christianity', *Irish Theological Quarterly* 70.1 (March 2005): 45–59.

[22] Annemarie Schimmel, *My Soul Is a Woman: The Feminine in Islam*, trans. Susan H. Ray (Continuum, 1997), 58–9.

[23] Fox, *Proverbs*, 287.

miniature incarnations of the chaos monster who glides through the deep waters shared by Hebrew and Canaanite creation stories. Modern commentators associate the Leviathan of Job 41:5–26 with the crocodile.[24] Beautiful Wisdom and sublime Leviathan are conjectural beings that emerge from the metamorphic depths of polytheism and become identified not only with God's power but also with God's love, pleasure and amusement. This element of play yields an aesthetic dimension that rebounds in Neoplatonism. In *The Two Gentlemen of Verona*, Orpheus is a Thracian David, 'Whose golden touch could soften steel and stones, / Make tigers tame and huge leviathans / Forsake unsounded deeps to dance on sands' (3.2.78–80). Sounding that deep is itself a dance: the mixed choreography of sapiential pluralism.

In Proverbs 9, Chokmah becomes an architect and a hostess:

> Wisdom hath built her house, *and* hewn out her seven pillars.
> She hath killed her victuals, drawn her wine, and prepared her table. (Prov. 9:1–2; Geneva)

In her house of wisdom, Chokmah hosts a Hellenistic symposium that combines serious study with the real pleasures of food and wine.[25] Wisdom's vibrant feast is contrasted with the pale offerings of Lady Folly, who serves 'stolen waters' and invites death (Prov. 9:17–18). Woman Wisdom is also contrasted with the Strange Woman or *ishah zarah*, who has 'decked [her] bed with ornaments, carpets and laces of Egypt' and 'perfumed [her] bed with myrrh, aloes, and cinnamon' (Prov. 7:16–17). Inhabiting an exotic softscape, her strangeness blends her status as another man's wife with intimations of foreign cults. When Othello laments that 'the fountain from which my current runs' has become a 'cistern for foul toads', he is probably alluding to Proverbs 5:15–18, which exhorts young men to 'drink the water of thy cistern' and avoid 'the strangers with thee'. Othello is representing Desdemona as the *ishah zarah*, perhaps projecting his heightened sense of his own foreignness onto his bride. The cistern

---

[24] Robert Alter, *The Art of Biblical Poetry*, revised and updated edition (Basic Books, 2011), 135–8. The notes in the Geneva Bible identify the beast as a whale. Marvin H. Pope calls it a dragon, in *Job: A New Translation with Introduction and Commentary*, Anchor Bible 15 (Doubleday, 1965), 339–41.

[25] Fox, *Proverbs*, 305–6.

itself, like the chalice, is a multivalent image, a welling up and concentration of physical and social flows whose roundness hearkens back to the curvilinear forms of prehistorical goddesses.[26] Meanwhile, the Egyptian Sibyl who wove the fateful handkerchief belongs to a pluralistic tradition memorialised by Michelangelo and other artists who assemble pagan priestesses alongside Hebrew prophets.[27] As Unhae Park Langis argues in this volume, Othello hails from a wider wisdom landscape whose resources he fatally misuses.

In 1 Kings 10, the Queen of Sheba, who visits the international court of Solomon as a fellow lover of wisdom, combines elements of the Strange Woman and Woman Wisdom. Sheba also merges with the dark-skinned Shulamite in the Song of Songs, another Solomonic wisdom book. Aemilia Lanyer retells the story of Sheba in terms that recall the love lyrics of the Song of Songs: 'Here Majestie did meete, / Wisdome to Wisdome yeelded true content, / One beauty did another Beauty greet, / Bounty to Bountie never could repent'.[28] James I advised his son to entertain his guests in Solomonic fashion, 'that when strangers shall visite your Court, they may with the Queen of Sheba, admire your wisedome in the glorie of your house', and a masque of Solomon and Sheba was performed at his court in 1606, shortly before the composition of *Antony and Cleopatra*.[29] In *Henry VIII*, Archbishop Cranmer blesses the infant Elizabeth by placing her in the line of Sheba (Saba): 'Saba was never / More covetous of wisdom and fair virtue / Than this pure soul shall be' (5.4.23–5). The story celebrated the learning of a foreign queen alongside the intellectual, mercantile and missionary ambitions of the philosopher-king.[30] Chokmah assumes a more human shape at the end of Proverbs, when the mother of King Lemuel chastises her son for womanising and drinking too much (31:3–7). If King Lemuel is Solomon,

---

[26] Thomas Nail, *Being and Motion* (Oxford UP, 2019), 192.

[27] Ariane Helou, 'Sibylline Voices: Prophecy and Power at the Medici Theater', *The Sixteenth Century Journal* 50.3 (Autumn 2019): 679–704.

[28] *The Poems of Aemilia Lanyer: Salve Deus Rex Judaeorum*, ed. Susanne Woods (Oxford UP, 1993), ll. 1,569–1,600.

[29] *Basilikon Doron*, cited in William Tate, 'King James I and the Queen of Sheba', *English Literary Renaissance* 26.3 (Autumn 1996): 561–85 (562). Tate discusses the masque, 564–76.

[30] Tate, 564–76.

as some commentators believed, this would make the speaker his mother Bathsheba, a woman with her own complicated marital history. The maternal speaker caps her harangue with an encomium of the woman of valour (31:10–31), who actualises noetic wisdom in the world of the *oikos*.

The Book of Proverbs is not itself an Alexandrian text, but its cosmopolitan origins and poetic prologue point the way to wisdom's Alexandrian expansions. Ben Sira, also called Ecclesiasticus, was written in Hebrew and heavily revised in its Greek translation; part etiquette manual and part call to study, the text includes directions for how to behave at a philosophical symposium (Ben Sira 23 [35]:1–13). Judith Newman argues that the Alexandrian translator of the text modelled the praise of Sophia on Isis aretalogies:

> I dwelt in high places, and my throne is in a cloudy pillar.
> I alone compassed the circuit of heaven, and walked in the bottom of the deep.
> In the waves of the sea and in all the earth, and in every people and nation, I got a possession.
> [. . .]
> I gave a sweet smell like cinnamon and aspalathus, and I yielded a pleasant odour like the best myrrh, as galbanum, and onyx, and sweet storax, and as the fume of frankincense in the tabernacle. (Ben Sira 24:4–6; 15 [KJV])[31]

Ben Sira compares the wisdom of the Torah to the waters that flow from the six great rivers of the region, including the Euphrates, the Jordan and the Nile ('Gihon') (24:23–4). This elemental and aromatic Sophia shares the international and cosmic reach of Isis while also merging with the Shekinah of Exodus, marking Israel's complex relationship with Egypt.

---

[31] Judith H. Newman, 'Hybridity, Hydrology, and Hidden Transcript: Sirach 24 and the Judean Encounter with Ptolemaic Isis Worship', in *Jewish Cultural Encounters in the Ancient Mediterranean and Near Eastern World*, ed. Mladen Popović, Myles Schoonover and Marijn Vandenberghe (Brill, 2017), 157–76. See also Kivatsi Jonathan Kavusa, 'The Torah Likened with Nurturing Water of Rivers in Sirach 24:23–24: Eco-Theological Significance', in *Pharos Journal of Theology* 99 (2018): 1–12.

56] *Julia Reinhard Lupton*

The Wisdom of Solomon, also called the Book of Wisdom, was, like the Septuagint itself, probably composed in Alexandria, whose large, vibrant Jewish community spoke Greek, not Hebrew. Composed in the period directly following the death of Cleopatra, when the Jews of Alexandria began losing rights and privileges under the Romans, the Wisdom of Solomon draws out commonalities among Hebrew, Greek and Hellenised Egyptian theology while asserting the distinctiveness of the Torah. According to John Kloppenborg, the pseudo-Solomonic author modelled Sophia on the goddess Isis, including her royal attributes, creative capacities and role as the protector and saviour of her initiates.[32] In his encomium of Sophia, which like Ben Sira may borrow from the Isis aretalogies, the Solomonic author writes:

> For in her is an understanding spirit holy, one only, manifold, subtil, lively, clear . . . For wisdom is more moving than any motion: she passeth and goeth through all things. (KJV 1611: 22–4)

Sophia's spiritedness participates in what Phillip Sidney Horky has described as a 'pneumatic cosmology' shared by Pythagoreans, Stoics and the Jews of Alexandria.[33] Greek Plutarch, African Apuleius and Jewish Philo were all Platonists in this Alexandrian vein. Richard Fletcher styles Apuleius as an 'Afro-Platonist', a moniker derived from Augustine's characterisation of his countryman as both *Afer* and *Platonicus*.[34] Plutarch visited Egypt and devoted considerable study to Egyptian religion. Philo and the wisdom writers of the Septuagint used Sophia to keep polytheism at bay while

---

[32] John S. Kloppenborg, 'Isis and Sophia in the Book of Wisdom', *Harvard Theological Review* 75.1 (January 1982): 57–84. Johann Cook notes that the Sophia of this Greek text takes a more active role in creation than the Chokmah of Proverbs 8, reflecting the influence of Stoicising Platonism. *The Septuagint of Proverbs— Jewish and/or Hellenistic Proverbs? Concerning the Hellenistic Colouring of LXX Proverbs*, supplements to *Vestus Testamentum*, vol. 69 (Brill, 1997), 239.

[33] Phillip Sidney Horky, 'Cosmic Spiritualism among the Pythagoreans, Stoics, Jews and Early Christians', in *Cosmos in the Ancient World*, ed. Phillip Sidney Horky (Cambridge UP, 2019), 270–94.

[34] Richard Fletcher, 'Prosthetic Origins: Apuleius the Afro-Platonist', in *Apuleius and Africa*, 297–312.

Sophia on the Cydnus

[57

acknowledging the feminine dynamism of the natural world.[35] The Hellenistic sages in turn understood the Jews as 'a people of philosophers'; they also associated Jewish wisdom with 'the Brahmans of India' thanks to the sublime singularity of their deity.[36] This Afro-Eurasian wisdom shines forth in Spenser's 'An Hymn of Heavenly Beauty', which presents Sapience as 'the sovereign darling of the Deity, / Clad like a queen in royal robes'. Spenser's Sapience exceeds paintings of Venus because she glows with energies within and beyond Greece, including Isaic and Hebraic presences.[37] And she shares this 'o'er-picturing' with Cleopatra.

On the Water, from the Desert: Nativity

Antony and Cleopatra takes place shortly before the birth of Jesus, prompting Shakespeare to imagine habits of thought before Christ and to test the wider landscape of sapience from which Christianity drew its early sustenance. As Hannibal Hamlin, William Junker and Gilberto Sacerdoti have noted, *Antony and Cleopatra* is pregnant with references to advent, nativity and epiphany as well as apocalypse, ascension and transfiguration. These motifs allude to a New Testament yet to come while signalling the wider traditions that fed those theophanic events.[38] Charmian jokes with the Soothsayer in the harem of the palace,

> Good now, some excellent fortune! Let me be married to three kings in a forenoon, and widow them all; let me have a child at fifty, to

---

[35] Johan C. Thom, 'Sophia as Second Principle in Wisdom of Solomon', in *Toward a Theology of the Septuagint: Stellenbosch Congress on the Septuagint, 2018*, ed. Johann Cook and Martin Rösel (Society of Biblical Literature, 2020), 263–76 (263).

[36] Joseph Meleze Modrzejewski, 'How to Be a Jew in Hellenistic Egypt?', in *Diasporas in Antiquity*, ed. Shaye J. D. Cohen and Ernest S. Frerichs, Brown Judaic Studies, vol. 288 (Scholars, 2020), 65–92 (89).

[37] Edmund Spenser, 'An Hymne of Heavenly Beautie', ll. 183–9, 211–14, Bartleby, accessed December 20, 2023. https://www.bartleby.com/261/5.html

[38] Hannibal Hamlin, *The Bible in Shakespeare* (Oxford UP, 2013), 221; William Junker, 'The Image of Both Theaters: Empire and Revelation in Shakespeare's "Antony and Cleopatra"', *Shakespeare Quarterly* 66.2 (Summer 2015): 167–87; Gilberto Sacerdoti, *Nuovo cielo, nuova terra: la rivelazione copernicana di 'Antonio e Cleopatra' di Shakespeare* (Il Mulino, 1990).

58]   *Julia Reinhard Lupton*

whom Herod of Jewry may do homage; find me to marry me with
Octavius Caesar, and companion me with my mistress. (1.2.26–30)

Charmian's allusive ribaldry offsets the 'universal peace' that Octavian
announces in Act 4 with a counter-messianism anchored by the power
couples Octavian-Charmian and Antony-Cleopatra and sealed by the
supplication of Jewry's mixed-birth king.[39] This is a *pax Judeo-Egypta*
in which the Nile shares power with the Tiber and the Temple in Jerusalem probably still stands. Charmian is sketching what archaeologist
Ljuben Tevdovski calls the Hellenistic and post-Hellenistic *oikumene*,
the region stretching from Egypt to Punjab and ruled by divine kings
in Greco-Eastern garb. The *oikumene* was shaped by the rivalry and
interdependence of the Macedonian dynasties, including the Ptolemies,
Seleucids and Achaemenids, who integrated and elevated local elites
like Herod in Judea into a 'global dynastic system' that became increasingly hybridised. Cleopatra VII was the queen of this *oikumene*; fluent
in many languages, including Hebrew, she used her Alexandrian lineage and the iconography of Isis and Venus to administer her portion
of the 'globalized Hellenistic world'.[40]

Whereas Charmian bastardises the birth of Jesus in a Hellenistic-
Herodian frame, Cleopatra's arrival in Tarsus on the Cydnus River
is modelled on the nativity and *adventus* of another divinity, Venus:

> The barge she sat in, like a burnished throne
> Burned on the water. The poop was beaten gold;
> Purple the sails, and so perfumèd that
> The winds were love-sick with them. The oars were silver,
> Which to the tune of flutes kept stroke, and made
> The water which they beat to follow faster,
> As amorous of their strokes. For her own person,
> It beggared all description. She did lie
> In her pavilion—cloth of gold, of tissue—
> O'er-picturing that Venus where we see
> The fancy outwork nature. On each side her

---

[39] Cf. Gilberto Sacerdoti, 'Three Kings, Herod of Jewry, and a Child: Apocalypse
and Infinity of the World in *Antony and Cleopatra*', in *Italian Studies in Shakespeare and his Contemporaries*, ed. Michele Marrapodi and Giorgio Melchiori (U
of Delaware P, 1999), 165–84.

[40] Tevdovski, 'The Beauty of the *Oikumene*', 17.

Stood pretty dimpled boys, like smiling Cupids,
With divers-coloured fans whose wind did seem
To glow the delicate cheeks which they did cool,
And what they undid did. (2.2.190–204)

Shakespeare, following Plutarch, models the scene on the Venus Anadyomene or Venus emerging from the sea. The conch that carries the newborn goddess ashore in ancient iconography becomes a festival barge, and the flowing hair and billowing garments of the divinity and her attendants morph into purple sails, glittering pavilion and silken tackle in a softscape composed of fabrics, sounds, smells and the impressionistic play of light.[41] The historical Cleopatra as well as Plutarch and Shakespeare also probably had Isis in mind. Apuleius models Isis emerging from the sea at Corinth on Venus Anadyomene.[42] The Hellenistic type of Isis Pelagia, reborn as the Marina-like St Pelagia in the Middle Ages, shares features with the marine Venus, including sails and sail-like garments.[43] Frederick Brenk reads Plutarch's life of Marc Antony and his Platonising essay 'Of Isis and Osiris', translated into English in 1603, as parallel romance texts.[44] In *Antony and Cleopatra*, Shakespeare pursues a similar kind of mythographic life-writing, impelled by both Plutarch's example and the political-theological aspirations of the historical couple themselves.

W. S. Heckscher emphasises the religious character of the original pageant, including its wisdom claims.[45] G. Wilson Knight argues that Shakespeare's Cleopatra melds imperial, erotic and elemental

---

[41] On Cydnus as softscape, see Colby Gordon, 'Candied Cleopatra: The Cute Aesthetics of Shakespeare's Political Theology', *Journal for Early Modern Cultural Studies* 16.3 (Summer 2016): 30–45.

[42] Apuleius Madaurensis, *Metamorphoses, Book XI*, ed. Keulen and Egelhaaf-Gaiser, 124–5.

[43] W. S. Heckscher, 'The "Anadyomene" in the Medieval Tradition: (Pelagia–Cleopatra–Aphrodite) A Prelude to Botticelli's "Birth of Venus"', *Nederlands Kunsthistorisch Jaarboek (NKJ)/Netherlands Yearbook for History of Art* 7 (1956): 1–38. Simonds develops the connection to *Cymbeline* and *Pericles* in *Myth, Emblem, and Music*, 126–9.

[44] Frederick E. Brenk, SJ, 'Antony-Osiris, Cleopatra-Isis: The End of Plutarch's *Antony*', in *Plutarch and the Historical Tradition*, ed. Philip A. Stadter (Routledge, 1992), 159–82.

[45] Heckscher, 'The "Anadyomene"', 19.

60] *Julia Reinhard Lupton*

symbols into a 'transcendental humanism'.[46] Barbara Bono proposes that Cleopatra's entry 'draws all the levels of elemental reality toward an inexpressible new plane of desire'.[47] As these views suggest, Cleopatra, like Apuleius, is an 'Afro-Platonist', an erudite and savvy Egyptian queen who cannily plays the philosophical tradition at Alexandria. Enobarbus begrudgingly acknowledges the sacred character of the scene when he reports that 'the holy priests / Bless her when she is riggish' (2.2.237–8). Appearing just once in Shakespeare, 'riggish', of 'uncertain origin', evokes 'rig' or wanton woman and 'wrig', or sinuous movement (*OED*), like the 'bends / Adornings' of her handmaids; the word also belongs to the assemblage of sails and tackles that drape Cleopatra's barge. Knight places 'riggish' in a sonic cloud of short i-sounds along with 'dragonish', 'discandying' and 'dislimns', an effect he deems feminine in 'its apparent weakness, yet intense buried energy'.[48] The variegated colours of the fans in Shakespeare may reflect the rainbow robes of Isis. According to Plutarch, the 'habiliments' of the goddess (a word that appears later in the play) are 'of different tinctures and colours: for her whole power consisteth and is employed in matter which receiveth all forms, and becometh all manner of things, to wit, light, darkness, day, night, fire, water, life, death, beginning and end'.[49] Fanning cools skin but feeds fire—contrary effects that give her radiance a transient quality, like the indeterminate blush of a Cézanne apple where red vibrates against green. Aerated by this moving pleat of references, Cleopatra skilfully navigates a mythographic network whose global dispersion, cosmic aspirations and phenomenological penumbra cannot be reduced to political expedience.

The wisdom literature of the Hebrew Bible and the Greek Septuagint contribute to the play's Alexandrian aesthetics. Cleopatra's embassy to meet Marc Antony at Tarsus recalls Sheba's visit to the court of Solomon, recently acted out at the court of James and a possible prompt for Shakespeare's play. The bride of the Song of

---

[46] G. Wilson Knight, *The Imperial Theme: Further Interpretations of Shakespeare's Tragedies, Including the Roman Plays*, 3rd ed. (Methuen, 1951), 210, 222.

[47] Bono, *Literary Transvaluation*, 172.

[48] Knight, *Imperial Theme*, 208.

[49] Plutarch, 'Of Isis and Osiris', in *The philosophie, commonlie called, the morals*, trans. Philemon Holland (Arnold Hatfield, 1603), 1,289. Spelling modernised.

Songs describes herself as 'black . . . but comely' (1:4), a topos that beckons to Shakespeare across his works, but especially in *Antony and Cleopatra*, as Camilla Caporicci argues.[50] However historians understand the racial identity of the historical Cleopatra, for Shakespeare, she was clearly a Black woman, in the tradition of Sheba and the Shulamite. In both the Sheba and the Cleopatra scenarios, a male ruler, associated with the core cultural values of the stories' narrators, receives the politically lesser but more splendid monarch of a foreign realm. 1 Kings 10 emphasises Sheba's fragrant entrance bearing sumptuous gifts: 'And she came to Jerusalem with a very great train, *and* camels that bare sweet odors, and gold exceeding much, and precious stones . . . There came no more such abundance of sweet odors, as the queen of Sheba gave to king Solomon' (1 Kings 10:2, 10). In the Song of Songs, Sheba's aromatic *adventus* becomes the arrival from the desert of the bride of Solomon, sometimes identified with the 'Egyptian princess' of 1 Kings 3: 'Who is she that cometh up out of the wilderness like pillars of smoke perfumed with myrrh and incense, *and* with all the spices of the merchant?' (Song of Songs 3:6). The approach of the bride resembles the Shekinah that settles on the ark of the covenant, a sapiential redolence that helped secure the Song of Songs in the canon of wisdom writing.

Like Sheba's arrival in Jerusalem, Cleopatra's journey is depicted as a royal entry. Like the Song of Songs' perspectivism, Enobarbus is entranced by the moving picture choreographed by the approaching queen, whose ambient presence overflows her picturing. In *Cymbeline*, this impressionism is heightened in Iachimo's elliptical ecphrasis, which skitters across the reflective affordances of tapestry, water and the shimmering 'silk and silver' of Shakespeare's verse. The hanging of Imogen's tapestry in what is clearly a wisdom space, on a par with Bess of Hardwick's learned galleries, asserts the sapiential aspirations of one line of feminine Cleopatrising while also tapping the phenomenology of apparition and approach nascent in these ancient texts. Enobarbus's retelling occurs within its own scene of hospitality: 'Welcome from Egypt, sir,' Maecenas says when the Triumvirate has departed. The Cydnus story, already known to Agrippa, surges out of

---

[50] Camilla Caporicci, 'Black But Yet Fair: The *Topos* of the Black Beloved from Song of Songs in Shakespeare's Work', *Shakespeare* 14.4 (2018): 360–73.

62] *Julia Reinhard Lupton*

the men's boozy, newsy gossip with the force of revelation, countering their old-boy repartee with a welcome of another order.

Images of Solomon and Sheba usually depict the queen as a suppliant kneeling before the king on his dais; in one iconic rendering, Holbein placed Henry VIII as Solomon high upon his chair of state while Sheba approaches from below.[51] Another compositional type, however, sets the two rulers on more equal footing, standing and conversing or perhaps shaking hands, as seen on the East Door of the Florence Baptistery by Lorenzo Ghiberti. Like Holbein's Solomonic Henry, Antony, 'enthroned i'th'market-place', attempts to use the spatial advantages of the receiving monarch to heighten his own sovereignty (2.2.214). Cleopatra, however, manages to rescript the scene. The spectacle of her entry leaves Antony alone in the marketplace, and when he invites her to supper, 'She replied / It should be better he became her guest' (2.2.219–20). Cleopatra works the dynamics of hospitality to reorganise the flow of power and authority, a move that Antony will appropriate for his own purposes when he insists that Octavian take his seat before Antony does (2.2.30–1). Like Venus with Adonis and Isolde with Tristan, Cleopatra instructs her partner in political pragmatics, sensual love and the unity of the cosmos. Cleopatra uses received social scripts and new theatrical designs to broker power in an unstable geopolitical space, demonstrating her prudential 'cunning past men's thought' (1.2.44). At the same time, her political-theological efforts map a cosmos in which masculine and feminine principles as well as eastward and westward worldviews counterbalance and suffuse each other in a shared wisdom ecology. She channels the feminine dynamism of the natural world, which can attract simple air (Shekinah) toward her, even as she orients Antony from a Roman egologic to an Alexandrian eco-logic.

Already at Cydnus, Cleopatra's pragmatic know-how and her cosmic-sublime aspirations participate in the play's relational forcefield of dialectical differences and minded gaps, projecting the universe itself as one great *stichomythia*. Whereas Antony may desire to found a 'new heaven, new earth' for a love beyond reckoning, Cleopatra dryly promises to 'set a bourn how far to be beloved' (1.1.15–16). Her ironic management of his romantic exuberance mirrors the play's

---

[51] Tate, 'King James I', 569–70.

Sophia on the Cydnus

[63

universe of oppositions dancing with each other. Michael Lloyd argues that Antony, unlike Cleopatra, 'wavers between trust and distrust, fidelity and infidelity' and that her ultimate achievement is to heal the division in him between soldier and lover.[52] Lloyd misses the extent to which Cleopatra herself works with the volatile uncertainties created by distrust, cynicism and divided loyalties. Upon hearing of Fulvia's death, she tells him,

> I prithee turn aside, and weep for her;
> Then bid adieu to me, and say the tears
> Belong to Egypt. Good now, play one scene
> Of excellent dissembling, and let it look
> Like perfect honour. (1.3.76–80)

She gives Fulvia her due as wife and calls Antony to his obligations as widower while conscripting these emotional debts into an imagined scene of loving farewell that simulates the singularity of attachment that Antony only pretends to avow. Here and elsewhere, Cleopatra speaks with the wisdom of the author of the Sonnets, who, in Sean Keilen's formulation, demonstrates 'how one might love another person, given the inconstancy of human behaviour and the certainty of death in a changing world'.[53] In this, as in so much else, Cleopatra resembles Juliet, who, in Paul Kottman's words, makes parting into a project, so that the lovers can 'make their separateness' into a creative interval that is 'actively accomplished, not passively suffered'.[54] In *Antony and Cleopatra*, two wisdoms, both alike in dignity, meet in a palmers' kiss in which unitive understanding joins hands with ironic consciousness.

The historical Cleopatra was indeed a learned queen; like Queen Elizabeth I, she mastered many languages for diplomatic purposes. Hers included Hebrew, for conversing with the court of 'Herod of Jewry' (the plentiful Jews of Alexandria spoke Greek).[55] Cleopatra would have studied philosophy with scholars affiliated with the famous

---

[52] Lloyd, 'Cleopatra as Isis', 88–9.

[53] Sean Keilen, Chapter 3 of this volume.

[54] Paul A. Kottman, 'Defying the Stars: Tragic Love as the Struggle for Freedom in "Romeo and Juliet"', *Shakespeare Quarterly* 63.1 (Spring 2012): 1–38 (28).

[55] Plutarch, 'The Life of Marcus Antonius', in Appendix A to *Antony and Cleopatra*, ed. Neill, 333; Stacey Schiff, *Cleopatra: A Life* (Little, Brown, 2011).

64]   *Julia Reinhard Lupton*

Mouseion or Library attached to the palace. The Arab world lauded her as 'the Virtuous Scholar' who contributed substantially to alchemy, medicine and mathematics. The historian Al-Masudi (d. 956) described her as 'a sage, a philosopher, who elevated the ranks of scholars and enjoyed their company'.[56] Among the works attributed to her is a 'Dialogue of the Philosophers', which supposedly translated Egyptian sources into Greek.[57] These Arab historians may have merged the last Ptolemy with another scientific Cleopatra, 'Cleopatra the Alchemist', also called 'Chrysopoiea Cleopatra' (Cleopatra, transmuter of gold), who lived in Alexandria in the third century CE. Represented in an unusual painting featuring Persian motifs by Lavinia Fontana (1605), this other Cleopatra may have been educated by Mary the Jewess, an Alexandrian alchemist who shows up in Gnostic texts as the composer of wisdom maxims.[58] Hebrew, Greek, Egyptian, Arabic and Persian learning are sublimated in the sapiential alchemy described by Langis: 'a finely wrought commingling of divine and sensual striving, channelled in both metaphorical and physical ways within a greater Mediterranean thoughtworld that comprehends Greek, Sufi and Abrahamic traditions'.[59] Multilingual Cleopatra is Isis and Venus, great goddess of Greece, Rome and Egypt; she is also the Queen of Sheba, the Shulamite, and the Pharoah's daughter, African lovers of wisdom in the Hebrew Bible. And she remains a savvy *gubernator* unafraid to bend and turn her riggishness to direct the ship of state. On the water and out of the desert, Cleopatra erects the iridescent pavilions of her erotic-aesthetic Egypt out of the same soft goods (fabric, myth, music, perfume) with which she governs her dominions.

With the Body, into Air: Ascension

The wisdom displayed in the scene on the Cydnus is learned but not yet lived. The queen is with the spectacle, but the spectacle is not yet with the queen. As the play gallops apace towards its glorious end,

---

[56] Okasha El Daly, *Egyptology: The Missing Millennium: Ancient Egypt in Medieval Arabic Writings* (Routledge, 2016), 133.

[57] El Daly, 130.

[58] Liana de Girolami Cheney, 'Lavinia Fontana's *Cleopatra the Alchemist*', *Journal of Literature and Art Studies* 8.8 (August 2018): 1,159–80.

[59] Langis, Chapter 8 of this volume.

Sophia on the Cydnus
[65

Cleopatra willingly takes on the more chthonic and transcendental aspects of the wisdom persona within her suffering, yearning and deliberative person. In Act 5, the Alexandrian queen retreats to her final house of wisdom, her monument abutting the Temple of Isis.[60] There this woman of valour delivers two great wisdom canticles, beginning with her elegy for Antony:

Cleopatra	I dreamt there was an Emperor Antony.
	O, such another sleep, that I might see
	But such another man!
Dolabella	If it might please ye—
Cleopatra	His face was as the heav'ns, and therein stuck
	A sun and moon, which kept their course and lighted
	The little O o'th'earth.
Dolabella	Most sovereign creature—
Cleopatra	His legs bestrid the ocean; his reared arm
	Crested the world. His voice was propertied
	As all the tunèd spheres, and that to friends;
	But when he meant to quail and shake the orb,
	He was as rattling thunder. For his bounty,
	There was no winter in't; an Antony it was,
	That grew the more by reaping. His delights
	Were dolphin-like; they showed his back above
	The element they lived in. In his livery
	Walked crowns and crownets. Realms and islands were
	As plates dropped from his pocket. (5.2.75–91)

The tuning of Antony's voice to the spheres evokes the philosopher Pythagoras, who, as Todd Borlik notes in this volume, was said to have 'visited the Aegiptians, Arabians, and Chaldeans, and went also into Iury [Jewry]'.[61] At once cosmic in its reach and global in its sources, her dream vision merges the Colossus of Rhodes with the Book of Revelation in order to spreadeagle an enormous Antony across the heavens themselves.[62] Dressing her dead lover in the attri-

---

[60] Plutarch, 'Life of Marcus Antonius', 353.

[61] Borlik, citing Robert Allot, *Wits theater of the little world* (Nicholas Ling, 1599), in Chapter 5 of this volume.

[62] James K. Aitken, 'Apocalyptic, Revelation and Early Jewish Wisdom Literature', in *New Heaven and New Earth: Prophecy and the Millennium, Essays in Honour of Anthony Gelston*, ed. Peter J. Harland and Robert Hayward, supplements to Vetus Testamentum, vol. 77 (Brill, 1999), 181–93.

butes of the Apocalyptic Woman, 'clothed with the Sun, and the Moon . . . under her feet' (Rev. 12:1), Cleopatra hoists Antony's broken body into the heavens by wrapping him in a feminine archetype of wisdom and splendour. The Apocalyptic Woman of the Book of Revelation (Rev. 19:7–9; 21:2) in turn participates in the wisdom visions of Proverbs and Psalms, where God 'covereth himself with light, as with a garment', 'walketh upon the wings of the wind' and 'appointed the moon for certain seasons' (Ps. 104:2, 3, 19). Cleopatra's blazon also recalls the Shulamite's praise of her lover's body in the Song of Songs: 'His legs are as pillars of marble set upon sockets of fine gold' (5:15). Antony's autumnal plenty recalls the Wisdom of Sirach, 'who maketh understanding abound as the Euphrates, who multiplieth it as the Jordan in the time of harvest' (Sirach 24:36 [Douay-Rheims]).[63] The 'reared arm' of Antony 'crest[ing] the world' is echoed in the dolphin that flashes above the waters; a flourish of pure movement, the sea creature's crescent curve recalls the dancing leviathans of Psalms 104 and *The Two Gentlemen of Verona*, where 'huge leviathans / Forsake unsounded deeps to dance on sands' (3.2.78–9). Cleopatra's dream vision nourishes a global classicism where pillars, limbs and dolphins surge in a hermaphroditic fantasy of self-renewing bounty and delight that harmonises sovereign ambition, sexual desire and natural reason. In the process, she achieves imperial sovereignty, if not in a worldly sense then sublimely in a mytho-ethical sense.

Cleopatra's elegy yields a portrait of magnanimity that overflows the measures of aristocratic excellence (generous to friends, fearsome to enemies) to touch upon the abounding order of the cosmos. Like the 'o'er-picturing' that Cleopatra shares with Spenser's Sapience, art and nature exchange places in the kind of dizzying exchange that Richard Strier associates with Plotinus, for whom 'the whole cosmos, with all of its creatures, is "the expression of Reason teeming with intellectual variety"'.[64] At the same time, the colossal portrait of Antony remains profoundly political. Islands dropping from his pockets like plates of gold, Antony glitters and

---

[63] Compare *The Tempest*: 'Spring come to you at the farthest, / In the very end of harvest' (4.1.114–15).

[64] Richard Strier (citing Plotinus), *The Unrepentant Renaissance: From Petrarch to Shakespeare to Milton* (U of Chicago P, 2011), 119.

Sophia on the Cydnus

[67

clangs with the weight of extracted wealth, trumpeting the couple's own imperial dreams and grounding the queen's transcendental self-stagings in the realpolitik of her contest with Octavian. Dolabella gamely tries to interject his own ambassadorial messaging, but he is overwhelmed by the sheer poetic energy of this 'most sovereign creature'.

Approaching her own death, Cleopatra declares, 'Bring me my robes, I am again for Cydnus'. If at Cydnus eros overshadowed cosmos, here cosmos absorbs eros as Cleopatra ascends into the wisdom tradition as its acolyte and priestess. Her garments are robes of mourning, recalling the black cloak draped over the iridescent gown of the bereft Isis in Apuleius and Plutarch. They are also marriage robes: as Caporicci argues, Cleopatra is 'now more than ever, the black and beautiful Bride of the Song of Songs, longing to be reunited with her Bridegroom'.[65] Her gossamer veils of sublunar life soar aloft into the ether of divine union when she dedicates her own person to 'fire and air'. Leo Perdue describes the Greco-Jewish Sophia of the Septuagint as channelling Stoic pneuma, the creative energy of the higher elements.[66] Cleopatra's melting into air also evokes the atmospheric advent of the Shekinah from the desert in Exodus and the Song of Songs. The apocalyptic imagery launched at the beginning of the play and collected in the elegy for Antony climaxes in Shakespeare's identification of Cleopatra with the Apocalyptic Woman, who merges Mary, Sophia and the Shulamite and is often pictured overcoming a dragon or serpent.[67] William Junker compares the scene to 'the Jewish Torah and the Pauline letters' in its summoning of a messianic temporality that is both layered and universal in its ingathering of transcendental motifs.[68]

By killing herself, Cleopatra refuses to become the captive woman from Deuteronomy 21, another *ishah zarah*. The trimming of the captive woman's hair and nails and the month delay before marriage

---

[65] Caporicci, 'Black But Yet Fair', 368.

[66] Leo G. Perdue, *Wisdom Literature: A Theological History* (Westminster John Knox, 2007), 296.

[67] Rebecca S. Beal, 'Bonaventure, Dante and the Apocalyptic Woman Clothed with the Sun', *Dante Studies, with the Annual Report of the Dante Society* 114 (1996): 209–28 (212).

[68] Junker, 'Image of Both Theatres', 186–7.

are designed to dull the passion of her captor and allow the foreign bride to mourn her past life. Christian humanists from Origen and Augustine to Erasmus used these rules to conceptualise the preparation of pagan texts for Christian use.[69] In refusing capture but claiming the rights of mourning, Cleopatra, to quote the Psalmist, 'takes captivity captive' (68:18), assuming authorship of her own legacy within a situation of radical constraint. Both mourning and desire fill the garments that bear Cleopatra upwards, out of the sea of becoming and into the empyrean of ideation, whose Platonic imaginings and Scriptural remixes hover over the pressing realities of geopolitical conflict that continue to shape them.

Mourning runs through Hebrew wisdom literature, most prominently in Job and Ecclesiastes, and a feminine hermeneutics of mourning permeates ancient wisdom myths, epitomised by Psyche's quest for Cupid, Venus's lamentation for Adonis, and Isis's reassembly of Osiris.[70] Juliet, Cleopatra and Isolde all briefly survive their lovers, whose abortive deaths and broken bodies become the material for cosmic stellification projects. Cleopatra's elegy for Antony takes him apart in order to reassemble him on a higher plane of being, while her ritual staging of her own death draws on wisdom literature as a sublime body drawn from many traditions.

Milton traces such a narrative in the *Areopagitica*:

> Truth indeed came once into the world with her divine master, and was a perfect shape most glorious to look on: but when he ascended, and his apostles after him were laid asleep, then strait arose a wicked race of deceivers, who as that story goes of the Egyptian Typhon with his conspirators, how they dealt with the good Osiris, took the virgin truth, hewed her lovely form into a thousand pieces, and scattered them to the four winds. From that time ever since, the sad friends of truth, such as durst appear, imitating the careful search that Isis made for the mangled body of Osiris, went up and down gathering up limb by limb still as they could find them. We have not yet found them all,

---

[69] Eden, *Friends Hold All Things*, 14–16.

[70] Ilit Ferber and Paula Schwebel, eds., *Lament in Jewish Thought: Philosophical, Theological, and Literary Perspectives* (De Gruyter, 2014); William Kolbrener, 'The Hermeneutics of Mourning: Multiplicity and Authority in Jewish Law', *College Literature* 30.4 (Fall 2003): 114–39.

Lords and Commons, nor ever shall do, till her master's second coming; he shall bring together every joint and member, and shall mould them into an immortal feature of loveliness and perfection.[71]

Milton builds the image of a broken Christian truth from the Egyptian myth transmitted by Platonising Plutarch and shared with syncretic humanists like Bruno. The resulting body of Truth is multiple in its sources, does not belong to Christianity alone, and gleams with a feminine 'loveliness and perfection' borrowed from Isis and Sophia. A few pages later, Milton cites Dionysius Alexandrinus, an Egyptian Church Father who argued for an uncensored curriculum, in the spirit of his city's famous Library: "'Read any books whatever come to thy hands, for thou art sufficient to judge aright, and to examine each matter.'"[72] Antony, a self-styled 'Dionysus Alexandrinus' of another sort, is transfigured by Cleopatra into a sublime corpus of motifs alive with plural origins and destinies.

Conclusion: Cleopatra's Egyptian Gold

The Church Fathers and Renaissance humanists used the Israelites' purloining of Egyptian gold to fund their exodus (Ex. 2:21; 12:35–6) in order to distinguish the right uses of pagan literature from borrowings that might lead to idolatry or licentiousness.[73] Read typologically, the trope of Egyptian gold pays little attention to the integrity, survival and interdependence of Egypt and Israel in the ongoing interpretive dialectics of Christian humanism. When, at the end of *Antony and Cleopatra*, the Egyptian queen withholds treasure and refuses to become a captive, she is also arguably pushing back against the assimilative impulses of the Augustan and Augustinian tradition.

In a strangely bathetic moment between Antony's death and her own, Cleopatra hands Octavius a document inventorying the wealth that she is transferring to him. Her treasurer Seleucus, however, reveals that she has 'kept back / Enough to purchase what you have made known' (5.2.143–4). Cleopatra admits to having 'reserved'

---

[71] John Milton, *Areopagitica and Other Writings*, ed. William Poole (Penguin, 2014), 130.

[72] Milton, 109.

[73] Eden, *Friends Hold All Things*, 8–32.

'some lady trifles', 'immoment toys' that she plans to give to Livia and Octavia to 'induce / Their mediation' (5.2.164–70). Embarrassed, Caesar tries to save the situation: 'Nay, blush not, Cleopatra, I approve / Your wisdom in the deed' (5.2.145–6). But what wisdom is it that hides in this deed? Like Jessica grabbing ducats on her way out of Shylock's house, Cleopatra reserves gold and other valuables for her own use: in this scenario, she is both the Israelite matron and the Egyptian neighbour, keeping back goods that no longer fully belong to her as she prepares for a forced exodus. These treasures index the layered traditions on display in the sublime compositions that Cleopatra choreographed at Cydnus, performed over the body of Antony, and will soon summon in her own death scene. Plutarch reports that Cleopatra has filled the monument with 'all the treasure and precious things she had of the ancient kings her predecessors: as gold, silver, emeralds, pearls, ebony, ivory, and cinnamon, and besides all that, a marvellous number of torches, faggots, and flax'.[74] Holding her own heritage hostage, she presides over an embattled precinct overflowing with wealth whose destructibility is her only insurance. When Cleopatra fills her monument—her mausoleum but also her Mouseion, her museum and library—with treasure, she is laying claim to the bibliographical enterprises, curatorial efforts and syncretic integrations that the Ptolemies have overseen, including the commissioning of the Septuagint itself. When she threatens to burn that treasure, she points to the vulnerability of human wisdom and the tenuousness of the hospitable liaisons that shelter its sharing. Cleopatra's Egyptian gold is a wisdom born in the laughter of creation, burnished by the blood and tears of conquest, and stewarded with canny prudence, irony and a sense of theatre.

In the revisionary narrative put forward by Ljuben Tevdovski, Cleopatra VII really did preserve her Egyptian legacy from Augustan capture and Augustinian typology. Although the historical Cleopatra lost the battle (at Actium), she won the symbolic war, understood as integrating Rome into the Hellenistic *oikumene* by using myth and cult to create divinised rulers in a mixed space at once unified by a shared political theology and distinguished by a diversity of dialects. Antony's daughter Antonia Minor, Antony

---

[74] Plutarch, 'Life of Marcus Antonius', 359.

and Cleopatra's daughter Cleopatra Selene and their descendants continued to shape the Hellenistic *oikumene* as the heirs of Cleopatra VII's masterful management of sovereign symbols. Berenice, the Jewish Herodian bride of Vespasian, was a 'new Cleopatra', marrying Rome and the Near East in the same dynastic fashion initiated by Antony-Dionysius and Cleopatra-Isis in the Donations of Alexandria (*AC*, 3.6.1–19).[75] Berenice's spiritual dowry is Jewish and Egyptian as well as Greek and Roman. Tevdovksi speculates that the success of so-called 'oriental cults', including the worship of Isis and the rise of diasporic Judaism and early Christianity, reflects the enduring power of the Hellenistic and post-Hellenistic *oikumene*.[76]

The doubling of Woman Wisdom and the Strange Woman of the Book of Proverbs figure the richly ambivalent sourcing of Hebrew wisdom literature in Israelite, Canaanite, Egyptian, Ethiopian, Greek and Persian traditions. In its 'infinite variety' and 'infinite virtue', the ecumenical pluralism of wisdom literature allowed Shakespeare to entertain the mutual enrichment of traditions beyond the operations of biblical typology and the Pax Romana. Tracking the mysteries of creation, wisdom literature assembles a *prisca sapientia* where strangers can meet, talk, feast, study and make love without rescinding the cautious reserve that accompanies the lovers' knowledge of each other's sexual baggage. Alexandrian translation projects, Hellenistic art forms, Hebrew poetry, and the monuments and memories of Egyptian wisdom converge under the dazzling direction of a female curator and stage designer who wills her own becoming-idea. When Pompey tells his guests aboard the galley, 'This is not yet an Alexandrian feast' (2.7.89), he gestures toward the play's utopian horizon, where the Greek symposium in its Platonic, Epicurean and Solomonic provenances is managed by a knowing hostess who wraps her splendid person in the rainbow weave of global knowledge practices. From Cleopatra's marine birth as a new Venus-Isis-Sophia at Cydnus to her sunsetting at Alexandria as an apocalyptic wisdom queen, the soft power of culture provides the billowing bridge between utopia and realpolitik.[77] In *Antony and Cleopatra*, the library of Alexandria

---

[75] Tevdovski, 'The Beauty of the *Oikumene*', 28.

[76] Tevdovski, 21.

[77] On Cleopatra, utopianism and soft power, see Hugh Grady, *Shakespeare's Dialectic of Hope: From the Political to the Utopian* (Cambridge UP, 2022), 111–50.

houses the politics of culture and the realism of prudence alongside Egyptian mythopoesis, the world soul of the philosophers, and the dream of a unitive consciousness that gestures beyond the Mediterranean to the Indigenous and Eastern nondualisms addressed in this volume.

CHAPTER 3

'LIKE PRAYERS DIVINE': SHAKESPEARE'S SONNETS AS SPIRITUAL EXERCISE

Sean Keilen

Would you have a love song, or a song of good life?
Twelfth Night, 2.3.33

'Herein lives wisdom, beauty, and increase,' writes Shakespeare of his verses; '[w]ithout this, folly, age, and cold decay' (11.5–6).[1] The Sonnets say they hope to make us wise, but few readers take them at their word. Francis Meres, the author of the first recorded comment about the Sonnets, praises them for sweetness, not for wisdom, and compares Shakespeare to the Roman writer Ovid, the author of three collections of sexually explicit love poems. For Meres, the sonnets are like candy: '[T]he sweet witty soul of Ovid lives in mellifluous and honey-tongued Shakespeare, witness his *Venus and Adonis*, his *Lucrece*, his sugared *Sonnets* among his private friends, etc.'[2] The sonnets' sweetness does not prevent them from being wise. It could be evidence they are ripe and fruitful, like the teachings of the Lord in Psalm 119:103: 'O how swete are thy wordes unto my throte? Yee more the hony unto my mouth.'[3] By the same token, while 'sugared' might mean 'sugary', it might also mean 'sweetened': like bitter pills

---

[1] All quotations from the Sonnets are taken from *Shakespeare's Sonnets and Poems*, ed. Barbara A. Mowat and Paul Werstine (Simon & Schuster, 2009).

[2] See Francis Meres, *Palladis Tamia. Wits Treasury Being the Second part of Wits Common wealth* (Cuthbert Burbie, 1598), STC 17834, 281ᵛ–82ʳ.

[3] Myles Coverdale, *The Psalter or Boke of Psalmes both in Latyn and Englyshe* (Richard Grafton, 1540), STC 2368. Unless noted, all quotations from the Psalter are from this edition. See also Psalm 19: 10: '[The judgements of the Lord] are to be desired above golde and muche precyous stone, and sweter then hony and the honyecombe.' In Coverdale's edition, Psalm 19 appears as Psalm 18, Psalm 119 as Psalm 118, because Psalms 9 and 10 are printed as a single text.

74]   *Sean Keilen*

we do not want to swallow even when we know they are good for us. And yet the claim that Shakespeare is the reincarnation of Ovid suggests that if the Sonnets have anything to teach us, it is unlikely to be practical guidance for living a good life. Renaissance readers called Ovid *doctor amoris* (the love doctor) not because he was wise or virtuous but because he claimed to know how to seduce, manipulate and abandon lovers as desire waxed and waned.

Meres's comment is one point of departure for criticism that reads the Sonnets for pleasure rather than wisdom. Another is the distinction between sacred and profane poetry that translators of the Psalter made during the English Reformation. For these writers, the pleasure sonnets give is inherently carnal. Therefore sonnets—unlike psalms— cannot be bearers of wisdom, because wisdom is contrary to their nature, like spirit to flesh. The sonnet corrupts, but the Psalter edifies. In *Goostly psalmes and spirituall songes* (1535), for example, an early and incomplete translation of the Psalter, Myles Coverdale separates the wisdom of psalms from the wantonness of secular lyrics when he charges the youth of England 'not to pass their time in naughty songs of fleshly love and wantonness, but with singing of Psalms and such songs as edify and corrupt not men's conversation'.[4] Matthew Parker, the Archbishop of Canterbury, echoes Coverdale in his own translation of the Psalter (1567), which opens with an exorcism of sonnets and other 'songs lascivious' from the instruments that symbolise his office as a sacred poet:

> Depart ye songs lascivious,
>   from lute, from harp depart:
> Give place to Psalms: most virtuous,
>   and solace there your heart.
>
> Ye songs so nice: ye sonnets all,
>   of lothly lovers lays:
> Ye work men's minds: but bitter gall,
>   By fancy's peevish plays.[5]

---

[4] Myles Coverdale, *Goostly psalmes and spirituall songes drawen out of the holy Scripture* (John Gough, 1535), STC 5892, +iii^r–+iii^v.

[5] Matthew Parker, *The Whole Psalter Translated into English Metre* (John Daye, 1567), STC 2729, Bii^r. It might be adequate to paraphrase the second, more ambiguous quatrain thus: 'You subtle songs, all you sonnets dealing with a loathly

'Like Prayers Divine'

[75

To reach the pages of the translated Psalter from the starting point of these prefatory verses, Parker's reader must travel through passages from the writings of the early church that commend the psalms not for their beauty as lyrics but for their usefulness as wisdom. Shakespeare's era embraced the Psalms as a resource for knowing oneself and living virtuously. To read them was to engage in spiritual exercises that internalised the practical wisdom of the scriptures through repeated acts of reflection and imitation—in effect, to learn an ethic.[6] In this context, the era followed in the footsteps of Saint Basil, who argued that the Psalter 'showeth law for the governance of life [and] teacheth what ought to be done'; Saint Athanasius, who extolled it as 'a mirror' in which 'the movements of our own souls are reflected . . . and the words are our own, given us to serve both as a reminder of our changes of condition and as a pattern and model for the amendment of our lives'; and Jean Calvin, who described it as 'an Anatomy of all the partes of the Soule' that 'call[s] or drawe[s] every one of us to the peculiar examination of himself'.[7] John Donne preached in the same vein that King David 'foretells what I, and what any [person,] shall doe, and suffer, and say'. Thus do 'the Psalmes minister Instruction, and satisfaction, to every man, in every emergency and occasion'.[8] This perception of the Psalter and its purpose would have been entirely familiar to Shakespeare—who, as a boy at school, almost certainly imitated the Coverdale Psalter, translating it into and out of Latin until

---

kind of love, you arouse the mind; but you also vex it bitterly with scenes of perversity in love'. For this sense of 'peevish', as an attribute of the unobtainable female object of male desire, see *Two Gentlemen of Verona*, 5.2.52–3: 'Why, this it is to be a peevish girl, / That flies her fortune when it follows her'.

[6] On the origins of psalm reading as a discipline of self-formation, see Gordon J. Wenham, *Psalms as Torah: Reading Biblical Song Ethically* (Baker Academic, 2012), and Paul R. Kolbet, 'Athanasius, the Psalms, and the Reformation of the Self', *Harvard Theological Review* 99.1 (January 2006): 85–101.

[7] For Basil, see Parker, *Whole Psalter Translated*, Eii[r]. For Athanasius, see 'The Letter to Marcellinus on the Interpretation of the Psalms', in the Appendix to *On the Incarnation: New Edition*, trans. and ed. Penelope Lawson (St Vladimir's Seminary, 1998), 106. For Calvin, see *The Psalmes of Dauid and others, with M. Iohn Caluins commentaries*, trans. Arthur Golding (1571), STC 4395, *6r.

[8] John Donne, '*Psalms* 63.7. The Second Prebend Sermon preached at St. Paul's, January 29, 1625/6', in *John Donne's Sermons on the Psalms and Gospels, with a Selection of Prayers and Meditations*, ed. Evelyn M. Simpson (U of California P, 1963), 94. I am grateful to Shaina Trapedo for calling my attention to this passage.

Sean Keilen

its teachings, along with its cadences, became second nature to him.[9] In addition to the Psalms, Elizabethan schoolboys often worked with English translations of Proverbs, Ecclesiastes and Ecclesiasticus (also known as Sirach), a practice that underscored the status of the Psalter as a wisdom book offering practical guidance for life.[10]

The publication of an English Psalter for daily use in conjunction with the Book of Common Prayer influenced the development of sonnet writing in England in profound ways, and Shakespeare, as a writer of sonnets, was shaped by that influence.[11] The first sonnet sequence in English, by Anne Locke, is a pious meditation on Psalm 51. Edmund Spenser meticulously organised his Petrarchan sonnet sequence, the *Amoretti*, according to the liturgical calendar and biblical lessons and psalms that appear in the Book of Common Prayer for 1594.[12] Donne and George Herbert, both Anglican divines, wrote sonnets that drew upon the Psalter's vision of human experience. Because Shakespeare's sonnets are often bawdy, however, it seems to follow that Shakespeare himself is naturally ironic and profane. In 1765, Samuel Johnson argued that the poet's 'first defect is that to which may be imputed the most evil in books or in men. He sacrifices virtue to convenience and is so much more careful to please than to instruct that he seems to write without any moral purpose.'[13] George Bernard Shaw took up that theme in the twentieth century, complaining that Shakespeare's 'characters have no religion, no politics, no conscience, no hope, no convictions of any sort'.[14] Since then, it

---

[9] T. W. Baldwin, *William Shakespeare's Small Latine & Lesse Greeke*, 2 vols. (U of Illinois P, 1944), 1:144.

[10] See, for example, *The bokes of Salomon* (Wylliam Bonham, 1546), STC 2755.

[11] See, for example, Hannibal Hamlin, *Psalm Culture and Early Modern English Literature* (Cambridge UP, 2004), and Deirdre Serjeantson, 'The Book of Psalms and the Early Modern Sonnet', *Renaissance Studies* 29.4 (September 2015): 632–49.

[12] See *Edmund Spenser's 'Amoretti' and 'Epithalamion': A Critical Edition*, ed. Kenneth J. Larsen, vol. 146 (Medieval & Renaissance Texts & Studies, 1997).

[13] 'Preface to the Plays of William Shakespeare', in *Samuel Johnson: Selected Poetry and Prose*, ed. Frank Brady and W. K. Wimsatt (U of California P, 1977), 299–336 (307).

[14] George Bernard Shaw, *Shaw on Shakespeare: An Anthology of Bernard Shaw's Writings on the Plays and Production of Shakespeare*, ed. and intro. Edwin Wilson (Applause Books, 1961), 3; qtd. in Paul Edmondson, *Shakespeare: Ideas in Profile* (Profile Books, 2015), 160.

has grown commonplace to say that religious language in the Sonnets proves that the sequence is impious by design.[15] Departures from this critical consensus are rare—for example, J. B. Leishman's reflections on the frame of mind that Shakespeare's sequence models and commends. To compare 'the life of faith' in Donne's and Herbert's poems and Shakespeare's sonnets, Leishman argues, is to become aware of 'a distinction, not merely between religion and what might be called religiousness, but also between religion and the tragic view of life, in one or other of which man's profoundest attempts to make sense of living have always ended and, it may be, will always end'.[16]

There is no doubt that the pleasures criticism seeks in the Sonnets are there to be found. It is also true that the Sonnets, like the Psalter, have no illusions about the ephemerality of pleasure and of all living things. The sequence unfolds under the sway of 'sad mortality' (65.2). In this context, it has something in common with Shakespeare's dramatic works: the melancholy frame of mind that heralds the capacity for wise insight into human experience. The Sonnets look back to the fall of Adam and Eve (93) and forward to Judgement Day (55). They take place between the sullen earth, from which the lark arises, and the gate of heaven, at which the lark's ascent is stopped (29). As they unfold within these boundaries, there is nothing otherworldly about them. But they do not need to be otherworldly to be wise. Because the Sonnets are determined to make sense of living in the world, they go beyond both religiousness and a tragic view of life, to speak wisely about the topics they have in common with the Psalter: the predicament of mortality, the inconstancy of human nature, and the difficulty of forming enduring bonds of love and trust with other people, given who and what we are. And yet they do not despair of living a good life.

---

[15] According to A. D. Cousins, '[t]he speaker's sexual use of religious language . . . emphasises how very worldly the *Sonnets* are'. See 'Shakespeare's Sonnets', in *The Cambridge Companion to the Sonnet*, ed. A. D. Cousins and Peter Howarth (Cambridge UP, 2011), 125–44.

[16] J. B. Leishman, *Themes and Variations in Shakespeare's Sonnets* (Hutchinson, 1961), 230. For another notable departure from the critical tradition, see Lisa Freinkel, 'The Name of the Rose: Christian Figurality and Shakespeare's Sonnets', in *Shakespeare's Sonnets: Critical Essays*, ed. James Schiffer (Garland, 2000), 241–61.

78]   *Sean Keilen*

What it might mean to speak of the wisdom of the Sonnets, I will try to show in readings of three of my favourite poems from the sequence. In the first of them, Shakespeare makes the case that his sonnets are a kind of spiritual exercise, like prayer: a practice meant to conserve and perpetuate something of great value through time. In the second, he juxtaposes two different ways of thinking about the time of a human life, drawn from Ovid's portrait of Pythagoras in *Metamorphoses* and from the Book of Common Prayer. The third sonnet considers the nature of forgiveness under the rule of time, using Psalms and Proverbs to suggest, in a lesson worth repeating, that our natural propensity for doing the wrong thing is the reason why we can, and should, forgive each other.

*   *   *

The word 'wisdom' occurs only once in the Sonnets, in an exhortation to a young man to marry and produce an heir (11.5). In Sonnet 108, Shakespeare suggests what it would mean to approach the whole sequence as songs of good life:

> What's in the brain that ink may character
> Which hath not figured to thee my true spirit?
> What's new to speak, what now to register,
> That may express my love or thy dear merit?
> Nothing, sweet boy; but yet, like prayers divine,   5
> I must each day say o'er the very same,
> Counting no old thing old, thou mine, I thine,
> Even as when first I hallowed thy fair name.
> So that eternal love in love's fresh case
> Weighs not the dust and injury of age,   10
> Nor gives to necessary wrinkles place,
> But makes antiquity for aye his page,
> Finding the first conceit of love there bred,
> Where time and outward form would show it dead.

In this poem, 'I' (the speaker) reflects on the challenge of finding the right words to describe 'you' (the 'sweet boy' to whom the poem is addressed). Word play in line 3 suggests why this task is difficult: because I am talking about the present, rather than the past. In this context, you and my feelings about you are always *new* and happening *now* (l. 3). As the second quatrain begins, I acknowledge that the only words I have at my disposal are the words I used earlier, in other poems. However, I also imply that when I use the same words to express my love and praise your merit, I am creating something new, for I count 'no old thing old' (l. 7). What that means, I show you later in this line, the sonnet's turning point. There, I make a rhyming couplet: 'thou mine, I thine'. The couplet is reminiscent of the verses that early modern couples engraved in the posy rings they exchanged when they married.

While the speaker in 108 says he has no option but repeating the same old words, the sonnet shows how the repetition of familiar words can generate something new of great value. As the possessive pronouns 'thine' and 'mine' exchange the nominative pronouns with which they are associated grammatically—'thou' and 'I'—the couplet in line 7 seems to profess, or to renew, wedding vows. In the second quatrain, I also compare my songs to 'prayers divine'—unless 'prayers divine' refers not to the kind of composition I am singing but to the kind of singer I am becoming. Perhaps 'prayers divine' means members of the clergy or, more broadly, people who pray. In that case, I would be saying that I am like a priest or a monk who is bound by his vows to say the Daily Office and sing the Psalter every day. In an earlier sonnet, I called myself an 'unletter'd clerk [who cries] "Amen"' (85.6).

I also compare myself to people who pray when I gesture to the time when 'first I hallowed thy fair name'. This line invokes a key phrase from the Lord's Prayer: 'Our father, which art in heaven, hallowed be thy name' (Matthew 6:9). Commentators have noticed that just before Jesus teaches his followers this prayer in the Gospel of Matthew, he instructs them, 'when ye pray, use no vain repetitions as the Heathen: for they think to be heard for their much babbling' (Matthew 6:7). For Stephen Booth, the speaker's apparent ignorance of this gospel exhortation is reason to conclude that 'the wit of [the second quatrain] derives from the speaker's self-betrayal in presenting evidence of sacrilege'.[17] Helen Vendler argues that '[S]onnet 108 . . . finds its wit in blasphemy'.[18]

Imagine, however, that by evoking the Lord's Prayer in a sonnet that acknowledges the necessity of having to repeat oneself, the

---

[17] *Shakespeare's Sonnets*, ed. Stephen Booth (Yale UP, 1977), 349n5–8.
[18] Helen Vendler, *The Art of Shakespeare's Sonnets* (Harvard UP, 1997), 462.

Sean Keilen

speaker does not become the clueless butt of an irreligious joke or a deliberate blasphemer. Suppose instead he finds himself engaged in a spiritual exercise: performing an act of humility by confessing an awareness of his limitations—like prayers divine, who contemplate, recite and internalise the Psalter's teachings about human frailty every time they pray the Daily Office. That is the subject position the Sonnets invites every reader to inhabit and perform through the speaker's first-person pronouns. Such reading is more than a vicarious experience.[19] It is an answer to the Sonnets' call to imitate another person, and in that context, it has more in common with reverence than impiety: specifically, with reverence for the capacity of old words to generate new life when repeated in the spirit that this poem associates with the ritual of fervent prayer. At the end of the third quatrain, 'antiquity' is described as the servant of 'eternal love' (l. 12), and afterwards it becomes the place where love itself is bred. Colin Burrow, who discerns a pun on *page*, as a young servant, and *page*, as a sheet of paper, suggests that the word 'antiquity' in line 12 also means the writings of the ancients.[20] The answer to the questions the speaker poses in the first quatrain is the discovery, in the final couplet, that the way to make your merit and my spirit new again is, paradoxically, to keep repeating words as familiar as the contents of an old prayerbook, and to adapt oneself to the life forms these words preserve and extend.

Thus, Sonnet 108 demonstrates a way of conserving life under the authority of time. To approach the Sonnets as a prayerbook is to devote oneself to discerning what is beautiful and good in a human life and, in that way, to perpetuating it, like the maker of the Sonnets himself, through what we say and how we live. 'Truly as we love, so sing we,' writes Coverdale of the Psalter.[21] Perhaps in Shakespeare's Sonnets, the reverse is true: what we sing becomes, through practice, the way we

---

[19] In passing, Vendler compares the sequence to other 'private literary genres—such as the Psalms, or prayers printed in prayer books, or secular lyrics': 'One is to utter them as one's own words, not as the words of another' (18). On vicarious experience in the Sonnets, see William Flesch, 'Personal Identity and Vicarious Experience in Shakespeare's Sonnets', in *A Companion to Shakespeare's Sonnets*, ed. Michael Schoenfeldt (Blackwell, 2007), 383–401.

[20] William Shakespeare, *The Complete Sonnets and Poems*, ed. Colin Burrow (Oxford UP, 2002), 596n12.

[21] *Goostly psalmes and spirituall songes*, +ii^v.

'Like Prayers Divine'   [81

love and by extension who we are. Sonnet reading takes its place along-side sonnet writing and sexual reproduction as a strategy for coping with the melancholy awareness of our 'inconstant stay'—of which Sonnet 15 takes the full measure when it steps back from the fleeting nature of the young man's youth to the truth of our mortality in general (l. 9). '[E]verything that grows, / Holds in perfection but a little moment,' writes Shakespeare in one of the more overtly philosophical poems in the sequence—the same poem where he asserts, for the first time, that poetry has the power to extend life: 'And all in war with Time for love of you, / As he takes from you, I engraft you new' (ll. 1–2, 13–14).

In these lines, I prolong the presence of the pronoun 'you' by using it three times. First, I draw the rhyming word from line 13 into the middle of the next line and sound it again. Then I repeat 'you' a second time as the sonnet's penultimate word. Finally, I turn 'you' into something new: in fact, into the word 'new' itself. 'New' points back to you as it perpetuates the vowel sound of your personal pronoun. It also opens a path toward the future where you will be changed but continue to exist, just as the word 'new' sounds very like 'you' but is spelt quite differently. What is represented here is more than one man's consolation for his knowledge of mortality, however. This is a revival of something precious from the past, and an effort to transmit and diversify its meaning through the future as shared experience. For the life into which I engraft you is the collective vitality of reading itself, to which the speaker gestures in Sonnet 81. There he describes the Sonnets as a monument '[w]hich eyes not yet created shall o'er read' while 'tongues to be your being shall rehearse / When all the breathers of this world are dead' (ll. 9–12). You and I must stop breathing at some point, he says, but breath continues, and your being 'shall live . . . / Where breath most breathes, even in the mouths of men' (ll. 13–14). Henry David Thoreau might have been thinking about this passage in Shakespeare's sequence when he argued that the written word 'is the work of art nearest to life itself', because it may 'not only be read but actually breathed from all human lips'—that is to say, 'carved out of the breath of life itself', as old symbols become new speech.[22] That would make the Sonnets

---

[22] Henry David Thoreau, *Walden; or, Life in the Woods*, in *Walden, The Maine Woods, Collected Essays and Poems*, ed. Robert F. Sayre and Elizabeth Hall Witherell (Library of America, 2007), 84.

inspirational texts in more than one sense. Every reading endows your fleeting existence (*hevel* or 'vapour' in the Hebrew scriptures) with life-giving breath (*ruach*), and every reader stands to be incorporated and changed by the 'true spirit' of the text that new readings bring to life. 'So long as men can breathe or eyes can see,' writes Shakespeare in Sonnet 18, '[s]o long lives this and this gives life to thee' (ll. 13–14). 'This' is both the text that we are reading now and our encounter with the text that revitalises its spirit in the present moment. The Sonnets invite both once and future readers to participate not only in a tradition of praising beauty in spite of time, but also in a shared existence that we might describe as *pneuma* ('breath'): the name Stoic philosophers gave to the life-giving spirit of individual souls and the cosmos itself.

* * *

Focusing on the way that Shakespeare handles language has the advantage of reminding us that it is always fruitful to pay attention not only to what the Sonnets say but also to what they do. I agree with Paul Edmondson that Shakespeare is not a moral writer in the ordinary sense of that term.[23] He does not state how we ought to live. Instead, he shows us forms of life that might call our lives into question—forms that we inhabit through the speaker's first-person pronouns when we read the sequence. The Sonnets often use language with the aim of demonstrating how one might love another person, given the inconstancy of human behaviour and the certainty of death. To the extent we imitate the sequence as we learn to live and love, by so much could we claim to fulfil the Sonnets' stated purpose: to bring back to life what time alters and consumes.

Consider number 60, the second poem I want to explore. Events in this sonnet unfold according to the pattern in number 15. Sonnet 60 opens with philosophical observations about the nature of time, then it describes the impact of time on youth. Like Sonnet 15, it also ends in a couplet that evokes a future in which, the poet hopes, the young man's 'worth' will endure in and through the sequence.

---

[23] Edmondson, *Shakespeare*, 160.

'Like Prayers Divine' [83

Like as the waves make towards the pebbl'd shore,
So do our minutes hasten to their end;
Each changing place with that which goes before,
In sequent toil all forwards do contend.
Nativity, once in the main of light,   5
Crawls to maturity, wherewith being crown'd,
Crooked eclipses 'gainst his glory fight,
And Time that gave doth now his gift confound.
Time doth transfix the flourish set on youth
And delves the parallels in beauty's brow,   10
Feeds on the rarities of nature's truth,
And nothing stands but for his scythe to mow:
And yet to times in hope my verse shall stand,
Praising thy worth, despite his cruel hand.

The first quatrain of Sonnet 60 compares the movement of time to waves crashing on the shore. The second adopts a different perspective on time and focuses on the movement from birth to old age. The repetition of the double consonant 'cr' in 'Crawls', 'crowned' and 'Crooked' is acoustically equivalent to that movement: we hear the kind of motion the speaker describes. The first syllable of the final rhyme word in the second quatrain ('confound') echoes the first syllable of the final rhyme word of the first quatrain ('contend')—suggesting, again in the ear, something stretching forward and moving backward, like waves falling on the shore. The words 'gave' and 'gift' in line 8 work that way too. By the end of the second quatrain, time has become Time, and the third quatrain reflects on the damage this character inflicts on beauty's face with his scythe. In line 12, the rhyme word 'mow' is just different enough from its counterpart in line 10 ('brow') to suggest that as the sonnet moves from its beginning to its end, something has been disfigured, lopped off or changed: the sound that the diphthong makes in 'brow'. The concluding couplet contradicts the conclusions about time the other lines draw. To emphasise that point, the couplet picks up the words 'Time' (l. 8) and 'stands' (l. 12) and changes their meaning by changing their number and tense to 'times' and 'shall stand' (l. 13).

Such wisdom as this sonnet offers derives, in part, from the teachings of the philosopher Pythagoras, who argues—in Ovid's portrait of him in the *Metamorphoses*—that the essence of existence is change.[24] In

---

[24] See Borlik, Chapter 5 of this volume.

84]   *Sean Keilen*

Sonnet 60, Shakespeare evokes the following lines from Arthur Golding's 1565 translation of Pythagoras' speech (15.197–206):

> In all the world there is not that standeth at a stay.
> Things ebb and flow, and every shape is made to pass away,
> The time itself continually is fleeting like a brook,
> For neither brook nor lightsome time can tarry still. But look
> As every wave drives other forth, and that that comes behind
> Both thrusteth and is thrust itself; even so the times by kind
> Do fly and follow both at once and evermore renew.
> For that that was before is left, and straight there doth ensue
> Another that was never erst. Each twinkling of an eye
> Doth change.[25]

Golding's variation on the verb 'to thrust'—first using 'thrusteth', then 'is thrust'—is an effort to replicate in English a marvellous effect that Ovid achieves in Latin (15.181–3):

> sed ut unda inpellitur unda
> *urgeturque prior* veniente *urgetque priorem,*
> tempora sic fugiunt *pariter pariterque* sequuntur . . .[26]

> But look
> As every wave drives other forth, and that that comes behind
> Both *thrusteth* and is *thrust* itself; even so the times by kind
> Do fly and follow both at once . . .

In the second line of these Latin verses, Ovid creates the effect of waves moving by taking advantage of the fact that Latin adjectives (*prior, priorem*) and verbs (*urgetur, urget*) have different endings, related to the different kinds of work they do grammatically. Even without knowing that the line means 'the preceding [wave] is pushed along by the coming [wave] and pushes the wave that precedes it', we can hear it in the variations of the phrases on either

---

[25] Ovid, *Metamorphoses*, trans. Arthur Golding, ed. Madeleine Forey (Penguin, 2002). Line numbers for English verses are drawn from this edition.

[26] Ovid, *Metamorphoses*, trans. Frank Justus Miller, rev. by G. P. Goold, Loeb Classical Library, 2nd ed. (Harvard UP, 1994). Line numbers for Latin verses are drawn from this edition.

'Like Prayers Divine' [85

side of *veniente. Urgetur*, the verb in the first part of the line, loses a syllable and becomes *urget*, while the lost syllable seems to attach itself to the adjective *prior*, which becomes *priorem* in the second part of the line. To a lesser extent the repetition of *pariter*—which means equal or equally—achieves the same effect in the next line. Shakespeare demonstrates his awareness of these techniques and pays tribute to both Ovid and Golding in Sonnet 60. The fourth line of his first quatrain picks up Ovid's verb *sequuntur* and turns it into the unusual English adjective 'sequent'; according to the *Oxford English Dictionary*, this sonnet is the earliest recorded use of 'sequent' to mean 'forming an unbroken series or course; [or] consecutive'.[27] Like Golding, Shakespeare tries his hand at making English perform the feats of Ovid's Latin. After three lines of mostly one-syllable words, the fourth line swells with two-syllable words ('sequent toil . . . forwards . . . contend')—using the line's stress pattern, rather than its word endings, to create the impression of tidal movement.

Sonnet 60 also draws from a second wisdom tradition. Ovid's Pythagoras refers to time as 'the eater up of things', who 'leisurely by lingering death consumes [all things] every whit' (15.258–60), but when he comes to explain the doctrine of metempsychosis, or transmigration of souls, he is clear that while everything changes, and the new inevitably takes the place of the old, nothing truly dies.[28] In Sonnet 60, a different thought begins to take shape with the arrival of Time at the poem's midpoint in the guise of a reaper. This figure exposes a rich vein of wisdom leading to the Book of Common Prayer and the Bible, specifically to the Psalter.[29] In line 8 ('And Time that gave doth now his gift confound') there is an echo of Job 1:21, which opens 'The Order for the Burial of the Dead' in the 1559 Book of Common Prayer: 'We brought nothing into this world, neither may we carry anything out of this world. *The Lord giveth and the*

---

[27] 'sequent, adj. and n.', *OED* online.

[28] 'And though that variably, / Things pass perchance from place to place, yet all, from whence they came / Returning do unperished continue still the same' (15.282–4).

[29] For Shakespeare's relationship to the Book of Common Prayer, see Daniel Swift, *Shakespeare's Common Prayers: The Book of Common Prayer and the Elizabethan Age* (Oxford UP, 2012).

86]   *Sean Keilen*

Lord taketh away' (my italics). Four lines on from there, the sweep of
Time's 'scythe' points to the burial service a second time: 'Man that is
born of a woman hath but a short time to live, and is full of misery.
He cometh up and is cut down like a flower; he flieth as it were a
shadow, and never continueth in one stay.'[30] The path of these allusions in Sonnet 60 leads to the heart of the Psalter's wisdom about
the human condition: our lives are finite, they pass quickly and they
might be utterly extinguished in death (even in Coverdale's version,
the Psalter does not clearly and consistently demonstrate belief in an
afterlife). In Psalm 90, for example, our 'years shalbe things which
are esteemed for nothynge. In the mornyng let it fade away *like the
herbe*, let *it floryshe early and be gone*' (90:5–6; my italics). The
brevity of our lives is only one reason why they are pitiable. According to Psalm 103, to which Time's scythe in Shakespeare's sonnet
also gestures through the Book of Common Prayer, another reason
is that, despite being short, they may be judged to be wise or unwise,
worthy or unworthy of praise. 'Like as a father pytyeth his children,
so hathe the LORDE had compassion on them that fear hym', says
Psalm 103, 'for he knoweth whereof we be made' and 'He remembe-
reth that we are but dust: *a man is even grasse; his daye shal floryshe
as the floure of the field*. For the brethe shall go thorowe him, and
he shall vansyhe away, and know his place no more' (103:13–16; my
italics).

   Why does Shakespeare juxtapose Ovid's Pythagoras with the Book
of Common Prayer and the Psalter in Sonnet 60? Is it simply to restate
diverse teachings about the nature of existence; or to assert the superiority of one teaching to the other; or to underscore their harmony for
readers who were no less familiar with translated classics and collections of ancient proverbs than with the Psalter itself? I do not discount
those possibilities, but as I read the sonnet, it seems to be informed by
a different aspiration: not to instruct the reader but to demonstrate
how one could use time wisely should either Pythagoras' teachings
or the Psalter turn out to be true. The wisdom traditions that Shakespeare evokes in Sonnet 60 discern the truth of our circumstances as
mortal creatures and model ways of living with death and change that

---

[30] *The Book of Common Prayer, 1559: The Elizabethan Prayer Book*, ed. John E.
   Booty (U of Virginia P, 2005), 309, my italics.

'Like Prayers Divine' [87

endow brief life with enduring meaning. In this sense, the first quatrain not only imitates Ovid's poem. Like Sonnet 108, it also shows that art revives old forms of life, conserving their essence even as it alters the way they look and sound. The second and third quatrains are more pessimistic about life's resilience to time. However, as often happens in the Sonnets, an unhappy awareness of the end of human life becomes the ground on which the speaker builds his 'hope' (l. 13). In this case, it is hope that in the future his verses will show that the young man's life, long since ended by death, not only was valuable to the speaker but also continues to have 'worth' (l. 14) for us: a value that we honour when we read the Sonnets, stand in the speaker's position and conform ourselves to his point of view.

* * *

Sonnet 120 is the final poem from the sequence I want to consider as wisdom writing. In it, Shakespeare reframes the general predicament of living a mortal life in a meaningful way as the specific task of reconciling with another person after a breach of trust. Sonnet 120, like Sonnet 60, focuses on the concept of human worth. But where the earlier poem sets itself the task of imagining how our temporary existence may be given lasting value through poetic imitation, translation and courageous hope, Sonnet 120 focuses on the suffering that 'I' cause 'you', asks what it would mean for me to be worthy of your forgiveness, and develops an approach to reconciliation that aims at restoring both of us to positions of equal value on the basis of our shared humanity.

Sonnet 120 has something in common with Sonnet 60 in addition to its concern with the worth or worthiness of human beings: the presentation of time as the backdrop against which the poet's meditation on human worth plays out. In number 60, time appears as the movement of oceanic waters with the tide, then as a reaper, as we have seen. In 120, time takes the form of three different moments in a relationship between 'I' and 'you'. The sonnet distinguishes these moments from each other with adverbs and the phrase 'our night of woe' and moves among them, before gesturing toward the future in the final line:

That you were once unkind befriends me now,
And for that sorrow which I then did feel
Needs must I under my transgression bow,

Unless my nerves were brass or hammered steel.
For if you were by my unkindness shaken   5
As I by yours, you've passed a hell of time,
And I, a tyrant, have no leisure taken
To weigh how once I suffered in your crime.
O, that our night of woe might have remembered
My deepest sense how hard true sorrow hits,   10
And soon to you as you to me then tendered
The humble salve which wounded bosoms fits!
But that your trespass now becomes a fee;
Mine ransoms yours, and yours must ransom me.

The adverbs *once* and *then* at the start of the poem indicate the earliest moment in time in Sonnet 120 (ll. 1–2). Let us call it the distant past. What happened then? You wronged me, and I suffered. Then you sought my forgiveness, and I forgave you. The phrase *our night of woe* in line 9 points to the second moment in time with which the sonnet is concerned. At that time, I wronged you, and you suffered. I, however, having forgotten about the events in the distant past, did not seek forgiveness from you. Therefore, you did not forgive me, and that brings us to the occasion when I write this sonnet. In the present moment, indicated by the adverb *now* at the beginning and the end of the poem (ll. 1, 13), I remember the distant past, when you apologised to me, and regret not only what I did to make you suffer during the recent past, but also that I did not apologise to you at that time. As I compare our different experiences over time, with a willingness to scrutinise myself and my choices, I discern that an apology is 'the humble salve which wounded bosoms fits' (l. 12). By writing the sonnet, I seek your forgiveness and expect that we will ransom each other after you have read the poem. (Table 3.1 summarises the organisation of time in Sonnet 120.)

Pronouns, like time, are an important dimension of the poem's form and meaning. There are 117 words in Sonnet 120, approximately 20 per cent of which are either the first- or the second-person singular pronoun: no surprise, given Shakespeare's focus on forgiveness and reconciliation. The second-person pronoun consistently appears as 'you' rather than 'thou'. Only thirty-four of the sonnets in the sequence are addressed to 'you', and to Renaissance ears, this distinction was significant. In general, one used 'thou' when speaking to social inferiors or to express intimacy, but 'you' when speaking to

'Like Prayers Divine'   [89

Table 3.1 Organisation of time in Sonnet 120 by William Shakespeare. Created by Sean Keilen.

Distant Past	Recent Past	Present
once, then	*our night of woe*	*now*
You wronged me.	I wronged you.	I remember the distant past.
I suffered.	You suffered.	I suffer regret twice over.
You sought forgiveness.	I forgot the distant past.	I seek forgiveness.
I forgave you.	I did not seek forgiveness, became a tyrant, and you did not forgive me.	We 'ransom' each other.

people in superior positions or to be formal and respectful. So the use of 'you' in this sonnet might suggest both the esteem in which I hold you and the fact that there is a breach between us. I stand in an inferior moral position to you, because unlike you, I did not confess my fault and seek forgiveness in the recent past, when I could have done so. That is the reason why I call myself a 'tyrant' (l. 7).

There are a total of ten places where the speaker uses 'you', in contrast to thirteen places where he uses the first-person singular pronoun. If we look at first and second pronouns together something interesting comes to light. Whereas the first-person pronoun often stands alone in a line (ll. 2–4, 7, 10), the second-person pronoun stands alone only once (l. 13). 'I' and 'you' appear in the same line six times (ll. 1, 5, 6, 8, 11, 14).

Now consider the relationship between 'I' and 'you' when all of the other words in Sonnet 120 are removed but the position of the pronouns is preserved.

A picture emerges of the wisdom that the sonnet models. In the upper half of the text block, where the sonnet's octave is, there are approximately twice as many first-person pronouns as there are second-person pronouns. The sonnet's first line puts you and me at a wide distance from each other, and four of the first eight lines isolate the first-person pronoun. In the lower half of the text block, where the sestet unfolds, there are almost equal numbers of first- and second-person pronouns. The second-person pronouns are gathered together near the centre of the lines in which they occur

90]   *Sean Keilen*

That **you** were once unkind befriends **me** now,

And for that sorrow which **I** then did feel

Needs must **I** under **my** transgression bow,

Unless **my** nerves were brass or hammered steel.

For if **you** were by **my** unkindness shaken

As **I** by **yours, you've** passed a hell of time,

And **I**, a tyrant, have no leisure taken

To weigh how once **I** suffered in **your** crime.   8

O, that **our night of woe** might have remembered   9

My deepest sense how hard true sorrow hits,   10

And soon to **you** as **you** to **me** then tendered

The humble salve which wounded bosoms fits!

But that **your** trespass now becomes a fee;

Mine ransoms **yours**, and **yours** must ransom **me**.   14

Figure 3.1 Position of the pronouns in Sonnet 120 by William Shakespeare. Created by Sean Keilen.

and seem to be embraced by the first-person pronouns which frame lines 10 through to 14 ('My' and 'me'). The final line of the poem reiterates in its own form the transformation of perspective and relationship that is occurring in those five lines. I embrace you, and gradually we come to stand on equal footing. For a moment, in the presence of the speaker's new humility, personal pronouns vanish from the sonnet altogether. In line 12, we are no longer 'you' and 'I', divided from each other by the question of fault, but 'wounded bosoms' both alike. The pivotal moment in the movement of pronouns from alienation and self-absorption to concern for another person and new relationship comes at the start of the sestet in line 9, where the only first-person plural pronoun in the poem occurs. Along with the speaker's use of the subjunctive mood in line 5 ('if you were'), the phrase 'our night of woe' in line 9 marks a change in the imagination that clears the way for mutual forgiveness, in which each person's trespass becomes the other's 'ransom' from suffering and punishment (l. 14).

What does 'ransom' mean in Sonnet 120? According to the *OED*, the primary definition of 'ransom' as a noun is 'a sum of money', given in payment for an offence; as a verb, it means to atone for or redeem another person from sin or damnation, 'especially with reference to the Passion of Christ'.[31] Within Shakespeare's sequence, 'ransom' in Sonnet 120 hearkens back to Sonnet 34, a more light-hearted treatment of forgiveness (in fact, Sonnet 34 may be the distant past to which Sonnet 120 refers in its opening quatrain). In that poem, you encourage me to believe that the weather will be nicer than it turns out to be, so I go outside without a cloak and get soaked in the rain. Although you apologise to me, I am initially reluctant to forgive you, reasoning that 'Th'offenders sorrow lends but weak relief / To him that bears strong offense's cross', and that 'Though thou repent, yet I have still the loss' (ll. 10–12). But sure enough, your tears of contrition make things right, for 'they are rich and ransom all ill deeds' (l. 14). Described in this way, your tears become the currency that compensates me for my 'loss' (wet clothing, broken trust) and restores the trust between us.

In Sonnet 34, the words 'wound' (l. 8), 'repent' (l. 10), 'cross' (l. 12) and 'ransom' (l. 14) feel ironic or hyperbolic in the context of the trivial incident the poem relates. However, they also set the stage for Sonnet 120's more sober meditation on forgiveness and reconciliation as transformative events requiring the self-knowledge and self-sacrifice that the sonnet enacts. The speaker makes no mention of getting caught in the rain but refers to the past in vaguer terms that lend gravity to what he is saying. He also augments the three words the two sonnets share—wound, salve and ransom—with other words that evoke the Christian mystery of salvation: 'transgression' (l. 3), 'hell' (l. 6), 'tendered' (l. 11) and 'fee' (l. 13).[32] Of

---

[31] 'ransom, n. and v.', *OED* online.

[32] The word 'ransom' occurs only three times in Shakespeare's Sonnets: once in the last line of 34, twice more in the last line of 120. Further back in 34, Shakespeare uses the words 'salve' and 'wound'. These words also connect the two sonnets. In 34, the poet complains about the young man's sunny expression, which does not make him any drier, that 'no man well of such a salve can speak / That heals the wound and cures not the disgrace' (ll. 7–8). 'Wound' appears in several sonnets, including 120, but 'salve' occurs only in 34 and 120.

92] Sean Keilen

the seven modern commentaries that I consulted while writing this chapter, only two entertain the possibility that Sonnet 120 is at all influenced by the moral and religious narrative to which this core vocabulary points, and neither one of them puts much stock in it. Booth concedes that the phrase 'humble salve' (l. 12) '*can be* colored by a suggestion of "means of salvation" and in turn heighten the vague suggestion of Adam's sin and Christ's sacrifice inherent in the diction of lines 13–14', but states more confidently that it '*is* colored by the sense [of] . . . simple household remedy'.[33] Vendler writes that '[c]ommentators have sometimes seen a Christian allusion in *ransom*' and allows that 'there is play on the economic and religious meanings' of the word, but she will go no further.[34] And yet the words that Shakespeare uses in Sonnet 120 arguably reflect an engagement with biblical wisdom pertaining to human nature, justice and the question of why anyone would be worthy of mercy. In the Geneva Bible that Shakespeare knew well, the only time that 'ransom' and 'transgression'—two of Sonnet 120's key words—appear in the same passage is Proverbs 21:18, which is annotated in the following way:

> The* wicked shall be a ransom for the just, and the transgressor for the righteous.
>
> *God shall cause that to fall on their own heads, which they [the wicked] intended against the just, by delivering the just and putting the wicked in their places.[35]

I would hesitate to argue that Shakespeare is concerned to distinguish between 'the just' and 'the wicked' in Sonnet 120. More likely, his starting point for this poem's meditation on forgiveness is the perception that everyone is flawed. 'Use every man after his desert', says Hamlet, 'and who shall scape whipping?' (*Hamlet*, 2.2.469–70).[36] Perhaps, however, the gloss on Proverbs 21:18 led him to the thought that putting oneself in the place of another person is the essence of

---

[33] *Shakespeare's Sonnets*, ed. Booth, 406n12, my italics.

[34] Vendler, *Art of Shakespeare's Sonnets*, 510.

[35] See *The Geneva Bible: A Facsimile of the 1560 Edition*, intro. Lloyd E Berry (Hendrickson, 2007), for this and other quotations from this text.

[36] William Shakespeare, *Hamlet*, ed. A. R. Braunmuller (Penguin, 2001).

'Like Prayers Divine' [93

forgiving and being forgiven.[37] When the speaker in Sonnet 120 makes this effort, he remembers what it was like to suffer at the hands of his friend and he learns to see his own behaviour wisely.

In Shakespeare's most famous lines about mercy, from *The Merchant of Venice*, Portia argues that it is 'an attribute of God himself' (4.1.193).[38] And so it is, from the perspective of a Christian theology that teaches God's only son redeemed humanity by freely becoming one of our kind and paying a debt he did not owe. In Sonnet 120, the speaker, unlike the Messiah, is not blameless, and forgiveness is depicted in an altogether less exalted manner. The power to forgive in this poem resides in *you* and *me*: transient and peccant life forms who not only suffer but also cause suffering. Shakespeare acknowledges in Sonnet 35 that '[a]ll men make faults' (l. 5), but in Sonnet 120 his account of human fallibility seems to have absorbed the wisdom of the Geneva Bible's gloss on Psalm 103:15: *'man hath nothing in himself to move God to mercy, but only the confession of his infirmity and misery'*. The fact that you and I are 'wounded bosoms' turns out to be the ground of our compassion for each other and thus of our godlike capacity to be merciful even when we are aggrieved.

* * *

The agnostic temper of modern scholarship, combined with an enduring appetite for sonnets that celebrate the follies of desire, makes it difficult to believe that the Sonnets engage the wisdom traditions of the ancient world without irony, or that Shakespeare himself regarded his poems as counsel for living or vehicles of moral transformation. But in the nineteenth century Thomas Carlyle could appeal without embarrassment to the 'harmony' between Shakespeare's works and the Judeo-Christian scriptures. He praised the Shakespearean canon as 'a Revelation, so far as it goes' and 'a kind of universal Psalm' because Shakespeare's insight into human nature and experience is

---

[37] Beatrice Groves considers other examples of the influence of the Geneva Bible glosses on the Sonnets in 'Shakespeare's Sonnets and the Genevan Marginalia', *Essays in Criticism* 57.2 (April 2007): 114–28.

[38] William Shakespeare, *The Merchant of Venice*, ed. A. R. Braunmuller (Penguin, 2000).

complex, non-dogmatic and humane.[39] Like the wisdom traditions on which Shakespeare draws, and especially like the Psalter, the Sonnets are fitted to the ways we live, love, die and hope to survive through time. Sonnet 108 describes the writing of the sequence as a spiritual exercise that breathes new life into old language, by enlisting the reader's living breath in praising the merits of another person repeatedly, so that he and the way that the speaker feels about him may be incarnated and live again in a world of shared vitality. Sonnet 60 first appeals to Pythagorean and biblical teachings about mortality and change to question whether any fleeting life has merit; then it uses techniques such as allusion, imitation and translation to demonstrate why we may hope that future readers will conserve and proliferate what is beautiful and good under Time's unyielding dominion. Sonnet 120 poses the question of human merit and our value to each other in a different way. This poem, which evokes biblical wisdom about mortality and justice, boldly recasts our shared fallibility as the basis for the self-transcendence we achieve through mercy. The spirit of Shakespeare's Sonnets is open to many interpretations, and among them is the possibility that these poems, like prayers divine, are words awaiting readers to make their wisdom flesh.

---

[39] See Thomas Carlyle, *On Heroes, Hero-Worship, and the Heroic in History*, ed. David R. Sorensen and E. Brent Kinser (Yale UP, 2013), 100–1.

CHAPTER 4

MORALITY ON STAGE: FREE WILL, COUNSEL AND SELF-COUNSEL IN SHAKESPEARE AND GLISSENTI

Eugenio Refini

Morality plays are nowadays out of fashion. Yet, the allegorical principle according to which abstract notions of moral significance may be personified and brought on stage is a trope that continues to successfully inhabit Western culture. The annual performances of Hugo von Hofmannsthal's *Jedermann* at the Salzburg Festival are normally sold out; the 2015 animated film *Inside Out* did very well at the box office worldwide; the unusual allegorical flair of Terence Blanchard's 2019 opera *Fire Shut Up in My Bones*, in which the personifications of Destiny and Loneliness conveyed the moral of the narrative, was met with enthusiasm by the audience. While these modern 'moralities' are very different from the dramatic genre that, popular in late medieval and early modern Europe, aimed at inculcating moral or spiritual teachings by personifying abstract qualities, they bear witness to an ongoing fascination with a kind of moral discourse that merges moral knowledge and behaviour—a kind of discourse central to the scope of this volume emphasising experiential wisdom. In the morality play tradition, not only do the allegorical *dramatis personae* enact what they represent, but also their words and actions aim to increase moral knowledge while also disciplining and cultivating virtuous conduct. What makes the merger of knowledge and behaviour possible is the performative framework in which the homonymic equivalence of *staging a morality* and *staging morality* offers us a useful window into the significant role of theatrical performance in the broader field of wisdom literature and its practical aim of cultivating spiritual practice.

To this end, I will consider two seemingly different experiences in a time period—Shakespeare's lifetime—usually associated with the secularisation of drama, the decline of morality plays and the birth of modern theatre. A salient remnant of the morality play tradition appears in Shakespeare's presentation of Iago as a Vice figure in *Othello*. I will explore this morality figure alongside the meta-theatrical revival of allegorical drama as illustrated by the moral interlude *The Marriage of Wit and Wisdom* in the play *Sir Thomas More*. Together, they bear witness, as Ivan Lupić has recently suggested, to the interconnections of moral drama and the theme of counsel, central to my discussion.[1] I then move from Iago's fictive Venice to historical Venice, where morality plays were still frequently staged in the early years of the seventeenth century, particularly as school dramas within educational contexts. In this latter section of the chapter, I will consider a corpus of moralities authored by the physician and playwright Fabio Glissenti, who wrote them to be performed by the orphan girls based at the local hospitals.

Shakespeare's plays and Glissenti's moralities are undoubtedly very different. In the former, moral dilemmas are built around the characters' ambiguous handling of slippery notions of good and evil. In the latter, moral assessments are supposedly adamantine, with no doubts about what is good and what is evil. Yet, as I endeavour to show, these works share similar preoccupations with theatre's ability to provide a space for the staging and performance of moral conundrums, especially concerning the struggle of reason against the senses and whether it may be understood as devoid of moral implications. I explore these issues through the interplay of will, counsel and, importantly, self-counsel that informs these works. For Glissenti, the two-pronged phenomenon of counsel (*consiglio*) designates both the relational process by which one considers what to do, seeking advice internally or externally, and the ability to decide one's destiny as *libero consiglio* merges with free will proper.

Through this comparative study, I aim to shed light on the longevity of the morality play tradition as a productive link between wisdom literature and secular drama. More pointedly, I argue that Glissenti, building on the tradition of moralities, turns it into a tool for spiritual practice that exposes the twofold nature of the genre: while a

---

[1] Ivan Lupić, *Subjects of Advice: Drama and Counsel from More to Shakespeare* (U of Pennsylvania P, 2019), 30–55.

Morality on Stage [97

morality, generically speaking, is a play that stages a discourse about morals and how to behave according to virtue, ethically speaking, the morality is daily performed beyond the stage, both internally and externally, through the workings of conscience and the dynamics of moral education.

Self-Serving Counsel in Shakespeare's Iago

In Shakespeare's *Othello*, Iago's deceptive nature and his knack for dissimulation—in other words, his acting skills—coincide with a kind of pervasive agency that gradually undermines the title character's own ability to act. Accordingly, Iago is given plenty of textual and performative space to unveil his intentions and showcase his skills as stage director. As scholars have duly noted, the very characterisation of Iago inherits the 'negative qualities normally associated with vice figures' in the morality play tradition.[2] The transformation of an allegorical personage into a 'real' one—whereby 'real' refers to the notion of a human individual, historically grounded and psychologically credible—increases the complexity of the character, thus paving the way for the moral ambiguity that makes 'real' characters relatable, even when they are villains.

Iago's destructive drive has been—and still is—hard to explain and digest for readers and spectators.[3] What becomes overt in Giuseppe Verdi's romantic adaptation of the play—Iago's nihilism—remains implicit in Shakespeare's play.[4] Of particular interest from this entry point is Iago's remark in Act 1, when in a compelling dialogue with Roderigo he claims the centrality of will in human life. Responding

---

[2] D. M. Cohen, 'The Jew and Shylock', *Shakespeare Quarterly* 31.1 (Spring 1980): 53–63 (61); cf. Bernard Spivack, *Shakespeare and the Allegory of Evil: The History of a Metaphor in Relation to his Major Villains* (Columbia UP, 1964); Unhae Park Langis, *Passion, Prudence, and Virtue in Shakespearean Drama* (Continuum, 2011), 13–14. On the broader question of Vice figures in the theatre of the time, see Nan Morelli-White, 'The Evolution of the Vice Character from Medieval Through Restoration Drama', PhD diss., Florida State U, 1990; Katharine Eisaman Maus, *Inwardness and Theater in the English Renaissance* (U of Chicago P, 1995), 35–71.

[3] Peter Kishore Saval, *Shakespeare in Hate: Emotions, Passions, Selfhood* (Routledge, 2015), 52–77.

[4] Solveig Höchst, '*Son scellerato perché son uomo*'. *Das Motiv des Bösen in Arrigo Boitos Libretto 'Otello'* (GRIN Verlag, 2013).

98]   *Eugenio Refini*

to Roderigo's alleged intention to commit suicide because of Desdemona's unresponsiveness to his love, Iago sings the praises of the ability to determine one's own fate. As he contends, if 'our bodies are our gardens', then 'our wills are gardeners'. Emphatically—and ironically, since Iago subverts the well-established humanist metaphor associating gardening with education—it is up to us to take care of our garden: 'either to have it sterile with idleness or manured with industry, why the power and corrigible authority of this lies in our wills' (1.3.362–8).[5] What follows is one of those dramatic nodes in Shakespeare's theatre that offer piercing meta-theatrical insight into moral action on the stage of the world. In expatiating thus on the question of moral action in counsel to Roderigo, Iago presents himself as a false Wisdom figure, whereby wisdom is understood here and throughout this play as moral prudence. Iago's discourse on the power of the will (disguising his own will to power) performs a kind of deconstruction of human life, or 'anatomy of the soul', a term I also use later to describe the work of Fabio Glissenti's Venetian moralities:[6]

> If the balance of our lives had not one scale of reason to poise another of sensuality, the blood and baseness of our natures would conduct us to most prepost'rous conclusions. But we have reason to cool our raging motions, our carnal stings, our unbitted lusts—whereof I take this that you call love to be a sect or scion. (1.3.368–75)

Iago presents the standard Renaissance argument for the rule of reason: if it were not for reason, which is able to 'cool our raging motions, our carnal stings, our unbitted lusts', we would not stand a chance of overcoming the threats posed by the senses. As such, he offers a précis of moral education regarding the fight between sense

---

[5] William Shakespeare, *The Tragedy of Othello, the Moor of Venice*, ed. Barbara A. Mowat and Paul Werstine (Simon & Schuster, 2017). On the relevance of the gardening metaphor to humanist education, see Mary Thomas Crane, *Framing Authority: Sayings, Self, and Society in Sixteenth-Century England* (Princeton UP, 1993); Rebecca W. Bushnell, *A Culture of Teaching: Early Modern Humanism in Theory and Practice* (Cornell UP, 1996), 73–143.

[6] For the notion of 'anatomy of the soul', see Eugenio Refini, *Staging the Soul: Allegorical Drama as Spiritual Practice in Baroque Italy* (Legenda, 2023), 135–208.

and reason, body and soul, virtues and vices—the same psychomachia at the core of the morality play tradition.[7]

Despite the irony of wisdom spouting from the mouth of a villain, Iago's celebration of will and his praise of reason as the most powerful antidote against the excesses of the senses is consistent with two main strands that informed Renaissance morals. One strand involves the debate about human agency regarding ethical conduct that eventually leads to either salvation or damnation: this was a debate that gained significant momentum across Christian Europe in the aftermath of the Protestant Reformation, which, upholding the centrality of Grace in determining one's fate, challenged the capacity of human reason and will to effect meaningful moral change. The other strand concerns the notion that counsel and advice are key to one's journey through life. The theme of counsel, as recently argued by Lupić, is central to early modern English drama, which inherits it from both classical theatre (Seneca in particular) and the many facets of Renaissance political philosophy.[8]

Expanding beyond its original sphere of political matters, counsel functions as an important structuring trope in assessing the very features of performative genres. The peculiar entanglement of morality, free will and counsel is evident, albeit idiosyncratically, in Iago's words, especially in the infamous monologue that follows his exchange with Roderigo at the end of Act 1. After celebrating will as the most powerful weapon for self-determination and reason's ability to control the senses, Iago sharpens his own will in hatred toward Othello, instantiating how a vicious and clever agent can reduce virtue to its raw natural form, a Machiavellian competence focused solely on the goal or activity at hand. What, in the end, allows the villain to prevail is Othello's inability to distinguish real honesty from its mere simulation and, furthermore, malevolent dissimulation, of which Iago is an indisputable master:

---

[7] For an introduction to the psychomachia tradition, stemming from Prudentius's seminal poem, see *The Psychomachia of Prudentius: Text, Commentary, and Glossary*, ed. Aaron Pelttari (U of Oklahoma P, 2019); and more broadly on the reception of *Psychomachia*, see Joanne S. Norman, *Metamorphoses of an Allegory: The Iconography of the Psychomachia in Medieval Art* (Peter Lang, 1988).

[8] Lupić, *Subjects of Advice*.

The Moor is of a free and open nature
That thinks men honest that but seem to be so,
And will as tenderly be led by th' nose
As asses are.
I have 't. It is engender'd. Hell and night
Must bring this monstrous birth to the world's light. (1.3.442–7)

Iago's monologue combines refined knowledge of the mechanisms of human psychology and the lucidity needed to bring his plot to completion. While Othello is incapable of seeing what is hidden behind the mask of simulation, Iago is a skilled dissimulator who embodies the very opposite of what a good adviser should be: instead of using his keen grasp of human psychology to guide his interlocutors toward moral good, Iago uses it to serve his own ego, to further his own evil scheme. By characterising him in this way, Shakespeare offers merciless insight into the risks that come from bad advice and the difficulty of sussing out one's advisers—a topic that, in the wake of Machiavelli's discussion of the interaction between prince and ministers, gained momentum in early modern political theory.[9]

Performing Good Counsel alongside Wit and Wisdom

Iago's subtle analysis of human nature and its implicit meta-theatrical dynamics—that is, his ability to give dramatic shape to his thoughts and scheming—resonates with the tradition of moralities from which, as a Vice figure, Iago himself originates. Focusing on the nexus of counsel and drama, I would like to look briefly at one text from the Shakespearean corpus, *Sir Thomas More*, which will bring us one step closer to the Venetian moralities of Fabio Glissenti.[10] Here, Thomas More embodies on stage, as he did in life, the type of the good adviser.

---

[9] Eugenio Refini, "'*Sufficienti e fedeli*': Aristotelian and Biblical Patterns in *The Prince*, Chapter XXII', in *Machiavelli's 'Prince': Traditions, Text and Translations*, ed. Nicola Gardini and Martin McLaughlin (Viella, 2017), 153–64.

[10] Lupić, *Subjects of Advice*, 30–55. For the text of the play, see *Sir Thomas More*, ed. John Jowett (Arden Shakespeare, 2011). The play's complex issue of authorship (Anthony Munday and Henry Chettle; revised by Henry Chettle, Thomas Dekker, Thomas Heywood and William Shakespeare) is beyond the purview of this chapter.

He does it in a twofold manner, first, meta-theatrically, by present-ing the moral interlude, *The Marriage of Wit and Wisdom*, to his illustrious guests within the fiction of the play, and, second, person-ally, through the power of his own virtue. Not simply a remnant of a dramatic tradition on the verge of disappearing, this moral interlude demonstrates that towards the end of the sixteenth century morali-ties continued to be a living tradition spawning generic hybridisa-tions that dramatised important moral questions of the day.[11] The early modern preoccupation with dissimulation on stage and in life reveals the intimate relation between one's judgement of things and the crucial importance of receiving good counsel. Iago's and More's dramatic speech and action indeed resonate with concurrent discus-sions about other forms of counsel and their role in facilitating or vitiating moral will. Along with other Shakespearean characters such as Paulina, whom Benjamin Parris examines in his chapter in this volume, Thomas More, as the good adviser, performs the proper cor-rective to Iago's vicious manipulation of his interlocutors.

The example of *The Marriage of Wit and Wisdom*—a play that recalls a number of actual moralities still popular in Shakespeare's lifetime—suggests how counsel and drama are intertwined through the performative dimension. In an ironic turn of events, More, in order to enact the role of good adviser, must fill in when the actor playing the part of Good Counsel is running late. In this way, More performs good counsel in both the main action and the play-within-the-play on stage, as in life. Typical of moralities, the plot of the interlude is straightforward: the Vice character, Inclination, invites Wit (personification of the intellect) to marry Lady Wisdom, who,

---

[11] Lupić, *Subjects of Advice*, 47–9; see also David M. Bevington, *From Mankind to Marlowe: Growth of Structure in the Popular Drama of Tudor England* (Harvard UP, 1962); Ineke Murakami, *Moral Play and Counterpublic: Transformations in Moral Drama, 1465–1599* (Routledge, 2011), 171; Pamela M. King, 'Morality Plays', in *The Cambridge Companion to Medieval English Theatre*, ed. Richard Beadle and Alan J. Fletcher (Cambridge UP, 1994), 240–64 (240); Alan C. Dessen, 'The Morall as an Elizabethan Dramatic Kind: An Exploratory Essay', *Compara-tive Drama* 5.2 (Summer 1971): 138–59; and Dessen, 'On-Stage Allegory and its Legacy: *The Three Ladies of London*', in *Locating the Queen's Men, 1583–1603: Material Practices and Conditions of Playing*, ed. Helen Ostovich, Holger Schott Syme and Andrew Griffin (Ashgate, 2009), 147–58 (149).

102] *Eugenio Refini*

by enacting the ability to make a decision based on careful consideration of the circumstances, embodies moral prudence. The plan sounds very appealing to Wit, whose most urgent desire, 'inclination', is to unite with Wisdom. What Wit does not realise is that the woman to whom he is unwittingly introduced is not Lady Wisdom, but Lady Vanity. Crucial to the happy ending, More, intervening as Good Counsel, unveils the true nature of Vanity and thereby guides Wit's understanding and will back to the desired end of the marriage of Wit and Wisdom:

> *More* I tell thee, this naughty lewd Inclination
> Does lead thee amiss in a very strange fashion.
> This is not Wisdom, but Lady Vanity,
> Therefore list to Good Counsel, and be ruled by me.
> [. . .]
> *Wit* Art thou Good Counsel, and wilt tell me so?
> Wouldst thou have Wit from lady Wisdom to go?
> Thou art some deceiver, I tell thee verily,
> In saying that this is Lady Vanity.
> *More* [*as Good Counsel*] Wit, judge not things by the outward show:
> The eye oft mistakes, right well you do know.
> Good Counsel assures you upon his honesty
> That this is not Wisdom, but Lady Vanity. (9.267–70, 275–82)

In his capacity as Good Counsel, Thomas More displays his renowned ability to perform the duties of the wise adviser. Not only does he prevent Wit from falling prey to Vanity, he also articulates an invaluable teaching: never judge things 'by the outward show' for the eyes are often deceived by what they see. Othello was not fortunate enough to have a thoughtful adviser such as Thomas More. The Moor's tragedy banks precisely on his 'free and open nature / That thinks men honest that but seem to be so' (1.3.442–3), a quality that might have landed Wit in ruin were it not for Good Counsel's ability to spot Vanity's dissimulation.

Iago's remarks on man's reason and More's participation in the staging of *The Marriage of Wit and Wisdom* ultimately key into the individual, self-reflective dimension of counsel. The metaphorical psychomachia evoked by Iago and the dramatic psychomachia staged by the Cardinal's players in the moral interlude of *Sir Thomas More* disclose the internal struggle that any individual undergoes

Morality on Stage [103

when making decisions about one's own life and conduct. The staging of such struggle as a dramatic discourse tapping the transformative potential of theatrical performance is the primary focus of the morality play tradition. If Iago turns dramatic psychomachia into an overtly secular reflection on reason, virtue and will, Thomas More revives it properly within the sphere of spiritual practice through a witty merging of play and life. As we shall see in the next section, when the morality play tradition is rekindled within the context of confessional education, the experience of the performance turns into moral and spiritual training toward embodied wisdom, the skilful practice of virtue in everyday life.

Staging Self-Counsel: Performance as Moral and Spiritual Practice in Glissenti's Moralities

The preoccupation with self-counsel, which early modern drama brings on stage either through soliloquy or through allegorical discourse, becomes particularly urgent in contexts in which the themes of counsel and self-counsel align with concerns about disciplining, self-disciplining and relevant confessional matters. Drawing on inter-European intertextuality, a historical case in point locates itself in the same city of Venice where the fictional Iago delivers his powerful, if unsettling, statements. Alongside numerous occasions to attend lively performances of secular theatre—with the *commedia dell'arte* holding a priority position—late Renaissance Venice afforded abundant opportunities to see morality plays not so different in inspiration from *The Marriage of Wit and Wisdom*.[12] Among them, the corpus of moralities ('favole morali', literally, moral fables) authored by the physician-playwright Fabio Glissenti (1542–1615) stand out. Composed for the female orphans based at the local hospitals, these allegorical plays aimed to teach both the performers and their audience about the ways in which one can reach spiritual salvation after

---

[12] On the place of *commedia dell'arte* in Venice, see Richard Andrews, *Scripts and Scenarios: The Performance of Comedy in Renaissance Italy* (Cambridge UP, 1993); Robert Henke, *Performance and Literature in the Commedia dell'Arte* (Cambridge UP, 2002), particularly 50–68; Peter Jordan, *The Venetian Origins of the Commedia dell'Arte* (Routledge, 2014).

death.[13] The moral theory undergirding Glissenti's dramatic works is similar to Iago's recommendation that reason be used to tame the senses and control the challenges that come from them, with the key difference that Iago marshals that wisdom toward vicious rather than virtuous ends. Glissenti's moralities resonated with their author's passion for moral discourse, bringing forth notably a voluminous philosophical dialogue, the *Discorsi morali contra il dispiacer del morire* of 1596 ('Moral discourses against the unpleasantness of dying').[14] The *Discorsi* and the moralities are part of a consistent educational project that gives voice and dramatic shape to popular moral concerns of early modern Europe regarding the conflict between reason and sense, the never-ending battle of virtues and vices, and more strictly confessional issues such as the place of conscience, remorse and penitence in Christian life.[15] Thomas More wrote on similar topics of Christian piety as counsel for his daughters in *The Four Last Things* and *A Dialogue on Conscience*, though other examples worth mentioning include Juan Luis Vives's early sixteenth-century *Education of a Christian Woman*, which, written for the education of Mary I of England, was widely read across Europe.[16]

Glissenti's *Discorsi morali* and his moralities share a profoundly theatrical vision of the world, according to which the world is a stage on which men and women conduct their lives as players.[17] The Greco-Roman trope of the *theatrum mundi*, widespread in the Renaissance and further revamped in the Baroque age, is taken literally by Glissenti, who reads the urban space—specifically, the urban space of Venice—as

---

[13] See Refini, *Staging the Soul*, 1–18, 135–208.

[14] Fabio Glissenti, *Discorsi morali* [. . .] *contra il dispiacer del morire* (Domenico Farri, 1596); on this peculiar work, see George W. McClure, 'The *Artes* and the *Ars moriendi* in Late Renaissance Venice: The Professions in Fabio Glissenti's *Discorsi morali contra il dispiacer del morire, detto Athanatophilia (1596)*', *Renaissance Quarterly* 51.1 (Spring 1998): 92–127; Refini, *Staging the Soul*, 81–134.

[15] Eugenio Refini, ' "*Quasi una tragedia delle attioni humane*": le tragique entre allégorie et édification morale dans l'œuvre de Fabio Glissenti (1542–1615)', *Cahiers d'études italiennes* 19 (2014): 185–98.

[16] *The Essential Works of Thomas More*, ed. Gerard B. Wegemer and Stephen W. Smith (Yale UP, 2020), 504–33; Juan Luis Vives, *The Education of a Christian Woman: A Sixteenth-Century Manual*, trans. and ed. Charles Fantazzi (U of Chicago P, 2000).

[17] Richard Bernheimer, 'Theatrum Mundi', *The Art Bulletin* 38.4 (December 1956): 225–47; Frances A. Yates, *Theatre of the World* (U of Chicago P, 1969); Lynda Gregorian Christian, *Theatrum Mundi: The History of an Idea* (Garland, 1987).

Morality on Stage

[105

a theatrical stage, a veritable mirror of the world. Here, I will explore examples from Glissenti's work that speak to the interplay between free will and good counsel, the focus of this chapter. Iago's statement— man's will *is* responsible for one's successes and failures—is indeed a cornerstone of early modern moral drama. As such, free will was often dramatised in interplay with good counsel, expanding out to questions of self-counsel, which became more pressing in the aftermath of the Catholic Counter-Reformation. While the discourse on free will centred broadly around man's ability to play an active role in his actions, discussions of counsel and self-counsel overlapped effectively with concurrent reflection on the place of conscience and self-examination as tools for the moral assessment of one's own behaviours.

The interconnectedness of these themes comes to the fore in Glissenti's *Discorsi morali*, which, in the genre of *ars moriendi* (art of dying well), aims to convince the readers that true happiness is not found on earth, but after death, as long as one manages to die in God's grace. In line with the author's concern with counsel and self-counsel, the whole dialogue is built as an exchange between two unnamed characters: a Philosopher attempting to persuade a Courtier that death should not be feared but desired. Crucial to the Philosopher's argument is the Christian notion of free will: that what eventually would save or ruin man is the way he exercises his own will, which would rely properly on reason to avoid the traps of the senses. Regardless of the outcome of this spiritual guidance (unsuccessful in this case), the staging of free will through the dialogue of two interlocutors dramatises how the performance of counsel can directly affect a wise exercise of free will.

Glissenti further develops the intermingling of counsel and free will in the morality plays, for theatre allows him to translate the dramatic potential embedded in the philosophical dialogue into dramatic action proper. The transition from dramatic dialogue to theatre, however, is not entirely smooth, for Glissenti shared many of the concerns that fed long-standing biases against the dramatic arts, particularly within the post-Tridentine Christian context.[18] For one thing, moral censors of drama railed against the hypocritical nature

---

[18] Andrews, *Scripts and Scenarios*, 204–26; Bernadette Majorana, 'Commedia dell'Arte and the Church', in *Commedia dell'Arte in Context*, ed. Christopher B. Balme, Piermario Vescovo and Daniele Vianello (Cambridge UP, 2018), 133–48.

of theatre, in which everything is false and nothing is true. Meta-the-atrically speaking, actors were considered to be deceivers par excellence, all of them dissembling like skilful Iagos—a point Glissenti makes himself in the *Discorsi morali* with an articulate reflection on drama and the possibility of reforming it. Through a conversation between the Philosopher and a professional actress, Glissenti makes his position on drama very clear: drama, qua vehicle of deception, should be utilised cautiously, only in the aim of moral education.[19] Predictably, such education is heavily inflected towards spiritual practice and tightly connected with explicitly confessional agendas.[20] More important for the purposes of this discussion is Glissenti's view that the fictional nature of any performance is valid only when it becomes actualised. Performance becomes useful when moral agents have a chance to digest and interiorise moral teachings by performing a given narrative on stage.

Glissenti's own commitment as a playwright gives a fuller picture of what he means by moral drama: a form of educational theatre built around the interplay of will, counsel and, ultimately, self-counsel—key elements of the process of confession, self-examination and repentance that the theatrical performance is meant to activate. Reviving the medieval convention of morality plays, Glissenti turns to allegory to stage this interplay: the dialogic exchange between two interlocutors in the *Discorsi morali* becomes an articulate dramatisation of the fights—both internal and external—that characterise man's spiritual life. By turning to the dramatic code of the morality, Glissenti splits the human being into his material and spiritual parts, from the main dichotomy of Body and Soul to the distinction of the various components that participate in man's experiences and decision-making. On the one hand, human physiology and psychology are, so to speak, dissected, with Sense, Inclination, Reason, Intellect and Memory negotiating their often conflicting needs, a kind of allegorical dramatisation that resonates with

---

[19] Glissenti, *Discorsi morali*, 339r–421v; Eugenio Refini, 'Reforming Drama: Theater as Spiritual Practice in the Works of Fabio Glissenti', in *Innovation in the Italian Counter-Reformation*, ed. Shannon McHugh and Anna Wainwright (U of Delaware P, 2020), 169–89.

[20] Giovanna Zanlonghi, *Teatri di formazione: Actio, parola e immagine nella scena gesuitica del Sei-Settecento a Milano* (Vita e Pensiero, 2002).

Morality on Stage [107

similar dynamics in the earlier morality play tradition of England.[21] On the other hand, the playwright brings on stage the moral tools that Christian doctrine, especially after the Council of Trent, recommended in order for the faithful to cope with their material dimension: Conscience, Remorse, Penitence. By introducing them as personified allegories, Glissenti exposes the workings of the human soul in a double perspective, at once physio-psychological and doctrinaire.[22]

Crucial to such staging of the human soul is the way in which Glissenti introduces the theme of free will. Free Will (now duly capitalised) is not only one of the main recurrent characters in Glissenti's plays, but also the subject-matter at their core as well as the setting of the action. As subject-matter, free will is evoked at the very beginning of Glissenti's first documented dramatic work, *La Ragione sprezzata* (Reason scorned, 1606).[23] An ambitious morality that aims to recount the whole itinerary of human life, the play centres around the notion that Justice and Truth, banned from the world, have found shelter at Death's place. Man, the protagonist of the play, is married to Soul: instead of seeking advice from his wife's maids—Reason, Memory and Will—he follows his own servants, the Senses. The striking resonance here with the psychomachia of Shakespeare's Othello discussed earlier in this chapter is not merely coincidental. As is customary of cautionary tales, the end of the story and the moral that goes with it cannot be but tragic: when Man realises that his conduct has led him towards eternal damnation, it is too late to repent. The importance of Free Will to the unfolding of human life—a kind of life that, within the post-Tridentine moral framework upheld by Glissenti, is meant to be focused on the Christian salvation of the soul after death—is highlighted from the very beginning of the play. Delivered by Man's Custodian Angel, the prologue explains that the most powerful tool that God has assigned to Man is indeed free will: 'in order for Man to be a god to himself, God decided to grant him freedom of counsel

---

[21] Eleanor Johnson, *Staging Contemplation: Participatory Theology in Middle English Prose, Verse, and Drama* (U of Chicago P, 2018); Julie Paulson, *Theater of the Word: Selfhood in the English Morality Play* (U of Notre Dame P, 2019).

[22] On the interconnectedness of physiology, psychology and moral practice, see Langis, *Passion, Prudence, and Virtue*, 1–29.

[23] Fabio Glissenti, *La Ragione sprezzata, favola tragica morale* (Marco Claseri, 1606).

[*libero consiglio*]'.[24] Interestingly enough, Glissenti's phrasing ('libero consiglio') stresses the interconnection of will and counsel, thus introducing one idea that informs the playwright's whole corpus: namely, the notion that free will—while certainly 'free'—is not a given, but the result of a process that must involve forms of self-counsel. As a matter of fact, the idea of free will celebrated by the Custodian Angel in the prologue to *La Ragione sprezzata* does not lead to that unbound freedom of action, which Iago's Machiavellianism promoted with strenuous confidence. Rather, it prioritises Man's freedom to make decisions based on careful consideration of a given situation, hence the centrality of Reason to Man's decision-making.

This point, which is one of the tenets of Glissenti's dramaturgy, is of particular importance to *La Ragione sprezzata*, where the unfolding of the action comes to coincide with the psychological dissection that I have labelled 'anatomy of the soul', a process of dramatisation of Man's inner conflicts offering both performers and public a pathway to virtue and spiritual salvation. The interaction of Man, Reason and the Senses in this play eloquently stages the intellectual processes involved in the handling of will, counsel and self-counsel. It is Man himself who shares concerns about his indecision between Reason's advice and the counterarguments set up by the Senses. In Act 3, Man's growing restlessness is caused by some unidentified inner rancour that gnaws his heart ('l'interno / livor di non so che, che 'l cor mi rode') and triggers self-examination: 'I will consider within myself who I was and who I am'.[25] Reason has instilled in him the awareness that death is unescapable, yet Man's mind is unresolved whether to act according to Reason's counsel ('come Ragion *consiglia*').

If Reason stresses the importance of looking into one's own inner self as a way to check the status of one's conscience, counsel (*consiglio*) is the process by which Man may save himself. Later in the play, the struggle occurring within Man's interiority is rekindled by the advice the protagonist receives from the Senses. They recommend that Man ban Reason from his life, arguing that, in fact, she is not the good adviser that he believes her to be; in a sort of ironic and temporary

---

[24] Glissenti, *La Ragione sprezzata*, 12[r].
[25] Glissenti, *La Ragione sprezzata*, 75[r–v].

reversal of the play's moral, the Senses claim their own priority over Reason by stating that it is sense perception that initiates all sorts of reasoning: 'Reason would not even be able to talk about a bread roll if it weren't for us, the Senses, who give it to her already chewed.'[26] Man does not immediately take to the convenience of living without Reason, as he believes in both the importance of counsel and—trusting his ability to discern—the possibility of rejecting it when deemed harmful: 'when someone else's advice is not useful, one can always reject it; however, to listen to any counsel may bring wise advice and guide the intellect', where the Italian phrasing ('restringe il pensier a miglior *senso*') plays with the ambiguity embedded in the word *senso*, which may signify, as in English, both 'sense' (as in sense perception) and 'meaning'.[27] The Senses explain that Reason is not essential nor beneficial to life: indeed, as demonstrated by the animals, who are devoid of reason, it is possible to live virtuously without it. The fact that only those animals provided with reason—human beings—go to hell is brought up here as evidence of Reason's harmful effect on Man's life.

The somewhat paradoxical argument—the idea that a virtuous life lived according to nature does not need reason—finds a fitting counterpart in Act 4, where Reason performs her advising duties as part of a conversation with Man's wife, Soul, and her maids, Will and Memory. After describing her primary function as that of offering counsel, Reason recommends to Soul a reform of the household, whereby the Senses should not be excluded, for they are, after all, Reason's 'siblings', kept under control.[28] Assisted by Memory, Reason reminds Soul that her bond with Man is meant to affect the afterlife of both: it is not enough for Soul to 'divorce' her husband to be saved, for eternal salvation will only be granted to either both or neither of them, depending on whether or not they—as a couple—have behaved in accordance with virtue. By reshaping the relationship between body and soul as a morality in which each component of human life gets to play its part, Glissenti underscores the centrality of counsel as a two-pronged concept: on the one hand, *consiglio* is

---

[26] Glissenti, *La Ragione sprezzata*, 102ʳ.
[27] Glissenti, *La Ragione sprezzata*, 102ʳ.
[28] Glissenti, *La Ragione sprezzata*, 140ʳ.

indeed the relational process through which one considers what to do, seeking advice either internally or externally; on the other hand, *consiglio*—particularly in the phrasing *libero consiglio*—coincides with free will proper, that is, the ability to decide on one's own destiny. Within the allegorical fiction of the play, free will proves instrumental to Soul's commitment to restrain Man's inclination towards the senses, hence to his moral and spiritual fall.

Even more explicit—and literally proactive—is the role of free will in two plays that build on the 'everyman' trope: *L'Andrio* (1607) and *L'Androtoo* (1616).[29] Both addressing Man's journey through life and the difficulty of handling earthly temptations, these two plays stage the complex relationship between the Christian notions of free will and divine grace, which fuelled some of the fiercest theological conflicts before and into the Protestant Reformation and the Catholic Counter-Reformation. How can one be actually free to act in one way or another if salvation is eventually possible only through God's grace? In Glissenti's plays, the question is repackaged for performers and audiences not necessarily at ease with complex theological disputations. The translation of the question about will and grace into a theatrical form has significant bearings in terms of dramaturgy. Indeed, what might look like an insoluble matter becomes more easily manageable thanks to the allegorical dissection pursued by the playwright, a device that fits the educational scope of the plays particularly well. In *L'Andrio*, Man is tempted to marry Flesh, but Intellect—Man's butler—dissuades him from doing it. The Devil then makes Intellect lose his mind: left without counsel, Man can finally marry Flesh. It is only thanks to the intervention of divine Grace, which makes Intellect come to his senses, that Man is eventually diverted from the inevitable fall that would come through his union with Flesh. In a similar vein, *L'Androtoo* shows how Man may end up hanging in the balance between Vanity and Innocence. Incapable of discerning amongst the conflicting advice received from his servants (Discourse, Will, Sense, Thought, Memory), Man falls prey to Vanity, who deceives him by disguising

---

[29] Fabio Glissenti, *L'Andrio cioè l'huomo virile favola morale* (Giovanni Alberti, 1607) and *L'Androtoo cioè l'huomo innocente, favola morale* (Marco Ginammi, 1616).

herself as Innocence. (The situation staged by Glissenti draws on the same trope that we have seen at work in *The Marriage of Wit and Wisdom*, where Lady Vanity attempts to deceive Wit by disguising herself as Lady Wisdom.) Once again, it is thanks to a special gift received from God—namely, the combined action of Conscience, Remorse and Penitence—that Man is able to see the truth and save himself.

As these brief summaries suggest, by personifying the various components of Man's physical and spiritual life, Glissenti manages to keep together the centrality of free will and the crucial help that—emblematically captured by Grace's intervention—comes to Man from God. The transformation of Man's inner conflicts into a dramatic action in which various allegorical characters pursue their different functions makes those conflicts easier to handle (and interiorise) for both the performers and their audience. By use of allegory, Glissenti's moralities aim to make both performers and audiences see Man's spiritual life from within. The playwright's ambition is that of deconstructing the complex entanglement of conflicting drives that populate the human mind whenever one is asked to take moral decisions. Far from endorsing the idea that, in the end, it all depends on God's grace, Glissenti insists on Man's responsibility when it comes to assessing a given set of circumstances and acting accordingly. In this respect, both *L'Andrio* and *L'Androtoo* are illuminating, for they stage a kind of interaction among the characters in which Free Will's struggle with decision-making relies heavily on his ability (or inability) to seek the right source of counsel.

Even more relevant to the present discussion is the fact that counsel is understood here as self-counsel in the first place, a point that, as we have seen, underpins Glissenti's staging of the interaction between Man, Reason and the Senses in *La Ragione sprezzata*. In this respect, the case of *L'Andrio* is particularly instructive, as it makes the argument more explicit. In the play, Free Will is not only a character, but also the very space within which the action takes place. As announced at the end of the list of characters, the play is set in the 'campo del Libero Arbitrio', where the term 'campo' (literally, field) refers to a typically Venetian urban space, the city square, while also evoking the idea of the battlefield typical of the psychomachia.[30] As

---

[30] Glissenti, *L'Andrio*, A5ᵛ.

is the case with other plays by Glissenti, a real location—the square, a traditional setting in Renaissance drama—merges with a mental projection, in which the various components of the human mind are given the status of characters. As such, they interact on stage in the same way in which regular characters interact, including forms of interaction that border on counsel and—given that all characters are, in fact, projections of Man's inner conflicts—self-counsel.

The convergence of free will and self-counsel dramatised in *L'Andrio* is especially visible in a scene of the play that is worth exploring in detail. As recalled above, the protagonist of the play, Andrio (Man), is unable to decide whether to follow Sense or stick to the stern recommendations received by Intellect. At this key juncture in the storyline, Andrio's indecision takes the shape of a dialogue with his own Echo. Rich in classical resonances—Ovid's *Metamorphoses* come readily to mind—the Echo device is a most common feature of early modern drama, including the burgeoning genre of opera (for instance, in Claudio Monteverdi's *Orfeo*, first performed at the Gonzaga court of Mantua the same year as *L'Andrio*'s publication in Venice). Incapable of taking decisions on his own, Andrio wishes that some good advice ('buono consiglio') could come to him from Free Will. Given that Andrio finds himself literally at Free Will's abode ('this is the campo of Free Will'), the desire to be counselled by him is quite fitting. What he faces is, instead, Echo's replies. As customary when Echo is involved, the replies—which repeat the last few syllables of each sentence—prove both self-reflexive and inconclusive. The dialogue (or should we call it a monologue?) is worth sampling, for it illuminates the dynamics at stake in the play:

Andrio	Da me stesso non so quel che mi voglia,
	Ma questo è 'l campo del Libero Arbitrio;
	Almen egli, che sta su queste strade,
	Mi dasse per pietà buono consiglio.
Eco	Consiglio.
Andrio	Che mi consigli, o tu? Che vuoi che faccia?
Eco	Che faccia.
Andrio	Che faccia che? Dimmi quel che t'aggrada.
Eco	Quel che t'agrada.
[. . .]	
Andrio	Non resta il mio voler al tutto libero.

Morality on Stage

[113

Eco	Al tutto libero.
[. . .]	
Andrio	Al mio dubbio non porgi altro consiglio.
Eco	Altro consiglio.
[. . .]	
Andrio	Né al mio quesito risponderai altro.
Eco	Ai altro.
Andrio	Confuso resto più che non fui prima.[31]

Andrio	*Of my own, I do not know what I want,*
	But this is the campo of Free Will;
	If only he, who resides in these streets,
	Were able to pitifully give me good counsel!
Echo	*Counsel.*
Andrio	*What do you suggest? What do you want me doing?*
Echo	*Doing.*
Andrio	*Doing what? Tell me what pleases you.*
Echo	*What pleases you.*
[. . .]	
Andrio	*My will is not completely free.*
Echo	*Completely free.*
[. . .]	
Andrio	*To my doubts you do not bring further advice.*
Echo	*Further advice.*
[. . .]	
Andrio	*And to my question you will not answer anything else.*
Echo	*Anything else.*
Andrio	*I find myself more confused than before.*

The overarching theme of Free Will becomes at the same time an opportunity for dramatic action and a way to stage a scene of self-counsel. By introducing Echo, the playwright externalises Man's inner conflict while also turning what would normally be a monologue into a dialogue. Not devoid of irony, the scene aims to stress the fact that, ultimately, it is up to the individual to take decisions about themselves, and nobody else can step in. If Glissenti's 'anatomy of the soul' dissects Man's components into personified allegories, with Free Will becoming one of the players involved in Man's management of his

---

[31] Glissenti, *L'Andrio*, 135–6.

own life, the echo device makes it clear that, in the end, the ability to take decisions does rely on Free Will. Man's final statement, 'I find myself more confused than before', is not only the comedic peak of a somewhat nonsensical climax, but also the acknowledgement that the most important form of counsel must come from within.

In a similar vein, the play *L'Androtoo* builds on Glissenti's notion of Free Will as crucial to Man's salvation by exposing the connection between Free Will and Man's ability to assess his own moral status. Consistently with the blossoming of spiritual literature that, in the aftermath of Ignatius of Loyola's *Exercitia spiritualia* (1548), was flooding the devotional book market of Counter-Reformation Europe, Glissenti stages the very interaction between Conscience and Remorse at the core of any itinerary of spiritual cleansing. In a scene that dramatises the examination of conscience—in fact, a form of self-examination—the playwright turns the theatrical performance into spiritual practice. As part of an articulate conversation about Man's behaviours and spiritual weaknesses, the allegorical personifications of Conscience, Remorse and Recollection perform their respective functions: activated by Conscience's call for self-examination, Recollection triggers the work of memory so as to allow for Remorse's own action, which builds on the combined stimuli received by the two other characters. As such, the morality play offers both the performers and their audience a clear example of what the process of spiritual purgation is meant to be.[32]

Conclusion

While it is difficult to say whether the moralities staged in the Venetian hospitals produced any real effect on those who consumed them, their intended scope surfaces in authorial statements that accompanied their written afterlife. For instance, in the preface to Glissenti's *La Ragione sprezzata* one reads that the play, performed by the girls of the hospital of the Derelitti, did trigger a sort of collective catharsis, which led the bystanders to self-examination, confession and repentance more effectively than preaching:

---

[32] For a detailed discussion of this dynamic as it appears in the play *L'Androtoo*, see Refini, *Staging the Soul*, 183–99.

Morality on Stage [115

> Speaking of the usefulness that fits similar fables, that is, purging the souls from vice and spurring them to virtue, it certainly proved most useful: indeed, this play frightened many and led others to consider their own actions; as such, it accomplished what many and well-attended sermons by preachers and strict reprimands by priests were not able to; . . . moved by the example [brought in front of their eyes] more than by words, the audience (who for many years lived without considering or regretting their sins) resolved to confess and acknowledge the guilt caused by their many excesses.[33]

The notion that a staged morality is more effective than sermons and homilies is of particular interest, as it stresses the truly performative potential embedded in the play. In other words, the play has the power to effect moral and spiritual change by providing the audience with a mirror on to which to displace their own interiority, assess their moral condition and act accordingly. In a similar vein, a manuscript copy of the play *La Morte innamorata* (Smitten Death, 1607), which provides plenty of details about the occasion of its performance at the Derelitti, informs us that the 'moral fable was represented . . . with great applause of the entire city, in spite of its sad ending and the fear and terror it brought to many'.[34]

Statements of this kind are probably exaggerated; yet, they give us a sense of the work that morality plays such as those by Glissenti were meant to perform. In fact, it is through statements like these that the convergence of performance and spiritual practice pursued by the playwright is visible: indeed, as auspicated by Glissenti himself in his critique of theatre in the *Discorsi morali*, the value of the dramatic experience comes to full fruition when the performative act (that is, the staging of the morality play) coincides with the moment when both actors and public assimilate the moral and spiritual prescriptions conveyed by the play and put them into practice.

This chapter commenced with Iago, a brilliant spokesman for free will and an infamous embodiment of Vice. Shakespeare's skilful habit of lending lines of wisdom to flawed characters not

---

[33] Glissenti, *La Ragione sprezzata*, A7[r–v].

[34] Fabio Glissenti, *La Morte innamorata* (1607), Biblioteca Nazionale Marciana, Venice, MS. Ital. IX.316, fol. 2[r]; the play was also printed as *La Morte innamorata, favola morale* (Giovanni Alberti, 1608).

only illuminates the perplexing moral realm he portrays but also underscores the moral ignorance that defines these characters. An apposition of Shakespeare's plays with Glissenti's didactic dramas suggests how an old device from the medieval morality toolkit, the anatomy of the soul, may be revisited in today's spiritually impoverished world as a tool for ethical self-counsel and self-examination, offering staging as a means to question and probe the ethics of a particular action. Shakespearean scholars, moreover, might see the benefit of anatomising in Glissentian fashion Brutus's failed attempt at self-counsel in his speech 'It must be by his death' (*Julius Caesar*, 2.1.10–35).[35] While Iago, like so many demagogues, influencers and peddlers of dis- and misinformation in our post-Truth world, may captivate audiences through his subversion of ethical discourse, morality plays, with their explicitly instructive intent, offer a practical antidote to the allure of evil in an ethically confusing world, in the form of a virtuous manual of moral conduct on stage. The expansive, productive space between Iago's deconstruction and Glissenti's construction of virtue is ultimately the '*campo del Libero Arbitrio*', the field in which we struggle to cultivate wisdom.

---

[35] *The New Oxford Shakespeare: The Complete Works, Modern Critical Edition*, ed. Gary Taylor, John Jowett, Terri Bourus and Gabriel Egan (Oxford UP, 2016). Oxford Scholarly Editions Online. doi:10.1093/actrade/9780199591152.book.1

Part II:

Oikeiôsis and Ecology

CHAPTER 5

JAQUES THE PYTHAGOREAN: ECOGNOSIS AND PYTHAGOREAN WISDOM LITERATURE IN *AS YOU LIKE IT*

Todd Andrew Borlik

In Kenneth Branagh's 2007 film adaptation of *As You Like It* set in Meiji Japan, Kevin Kline reincarnates the melancholy Jaques as a Buddhist. We see him assuming the lotus pose to meditate in a Zen rock garden and practising T'ai chi to the dulcet strains of the koto. His lament for the wounded stag endorses Buddhism's compassion for animals and he even embraces the Buddhist monk's vegetarian diet, storming off in disgust at the mention of the deer hunt and smiling appreciatively when the Duke later serves him vegetable potage instead of venison. Branagh's film has been understandably accused of Orientalism (T'ai chi is Chinese, associated more with Daoism than Buddhism) and lambasted for its regrettable failure to cast East Asian actors in any major roles—revealingly, the Japanese actor (Nobuyuki Takano) who plays the sumo wrestler Charles never speaks.[1] Without dismissing these charges, one might critique the film as an exposé of the cultural appropriation it self-consciously commits.[2] Filmed on the Wakehurst estate in rural Sussex, it is, as the haiku prologue cautions, 'a dream of Japan', not a historically accurate documentary. If not a snapshot of authentic Buddhist practices, Kline's performance, nonetheless, captures the Western fascination with Buddhism and Eastern spirituality in general as more ecocentric or attuned to nature.

---

[1] Elizabeth Klett, 'Dreaming of Orientalism in Kenneth Branagh's *As You Like It*', *Borrowers and Lenders: The Journal of Shakespeare and Appropriation* 3.2 (Fall/Winter 2008): 1–6. https://borrowers-ojs-azsu.tdl.org/borrowers/article/view/66/131

[2] Credit for this argument goes to my former student, Holly Prue, who wrote an outstanding essay on Branagh's film as an exposé of Orientalism.

Such fascination is not a uniquely modern phenomenon. While Shakespeare's contemporaries had only the foggiest notions of Buddhism and Hinduism, Renaissance humanists noticed some striking parallels between Western and Eastern belief systems and surmised that, rather than originating independently, they shared a common source in ancient wisdom traditions with wellsprings outside of Europe.[3] Such assumptions should not be dismissed offhand. The establishing of eastern trade routes and administrative links connecting Greece with the Indus Valley in the sixth century BCE under the First Persian Empire of Cyrus the Great, followed by Alexander the Great's incursions and founding of Indo-Greek states, created conditions ripe for intellectual exchanges between Indo-Greeks and Buddhists.[4] As Chapter 1 elucidates, the Renaissance might be reframed to some extent as an Indo-European cultural achievement, a re-germinating of ancient Greek thought partly rooted in religious and philosophical ideas articulated in dialogue with Sanskrit. From this macro-historical viewpoint, Kline's Buddhist Jaques does not seem quite so fanciful.

In the voluminous scholarship on *As You Like It*, Jaques has himself played many parts: the barb-tongued satirist railing against the Bishops' Ban; a poster child of the melancholic temperament; a prototype of the 'man of feeling'; the Italianate or Frenchified English traveller estranged from his homeland; an embodiment of negation that makes possible comic affirmation; and a republican critic of the tyranny of the hunt.[5] He has been compared to, among others, Philip Sidney, John Marston, John Harington, Ben Jonson, Michel

---

[3] See Frances A. Yates's landmark work, *The Occult Philosophy in the Elizabethan Age* (Routledge & Kegan Paul, 1979).

[4] For more on this topic, see M. L. West, *Early Greek Philosophy and the Orient* (Oxford UP, 1971); Richard Seaford, *The Origins of Philosophy in Ancient Greece and Ancient India: A Historical Comparison* (Cambridge UP, 2019); Georgios T. Halkias, 'When the Greeks Converted the Buddha: Asymmetrical Transfers of Knowledge in Indo-Greek Cultures', in *Religions and Trade: Religious Formation, Transformation and Cross-Cultural Exchange between East and West*, ed. Peter Wick and Volker Rabens (Brill, 2014), 65–116.

[5] Tristan Samuk, 'Satire and the Aesthetic in *As You Like It*', *Renaissance Drama* 43.2 (Fall 2015): 117–42 (130); Sabina Laskowska-Hinz, '*Jaques and the Wounded Stag* by William Hodges, Sawrey Gilpin and George Romney: (Re) Painting Shakespeare's Melancholic Figure', *Anglica: An International Journal of English Studies* 25.3 (2016): 37–50; Myrddin Jones, 'Gray, Jaques, and the Man

Jaques the Pythagorean   [121

de Montaigne, the 2nd Earl of Essex and even Laurence Sterne.[6] As is often the case with Shakespeare, these seemingly disparate interpretations provide an index of the character's complexity. Nevertheless, if Shakespeare compounded him from many sundry personas, Jaques does possess a certain intellectual consistency. Namely, this chapter will argue that early modern audiences would have perceived Jaques as a disciple of the Greek sage Pythagoras, a prominent figure in the Renaissance revival of wisdom literature. Although often misunderstood and caricatured, Pythagorean philosophy was a vital conduit between East and West in antiquity and stands as an important precursor of ecological thinking in its advocacy of vegetarianism, the animal soul, mutability and cosmic harmony. Situating *As You Like It* within this global wisdom tradition, this chapter aims to recover Jaques's Pythagorean sympathies and align them with a kind of ecological sapience that Timothy Morton calls 'ecognosis'. By ballasting Jaques's quest for knowledge with Touchstone's insistence on human folly, Shakespeare's pastoral comedy offers an enlightening commentary on the benefits and pitfalls of seeking wisdom abroad in the hopes of achieving greater harmony with nature. More broadly, this play that famously proclaims all the world a stage offers a convenient launch-point for considering whether Global Shakespeare has elevated Shakespeare's own corpus to a kind of secular wisdom literature that might help nurture a global-minded ecocosmopolitanism.

The Pythagorean Wisdom Tradition

The Greek polymath Pythagoras must be ranked among the most foundational thinkers in Western history, one of the architects of

---

of Feeling', *The Review of English Studies* 25.97 (February 1974): 39–48; Cynthia Marshall, 'The Doubled Jaques and Constructions of Negation in *As You Like It*', *Shakespeare Quarterly* 49.4 (Winter 1998): 375–92; Z. S. Fink, 'Jaques and the Malcontent Traveler', *Philological Quarterly* 14 (1935): 237–52; Claus Uhlig, '"The Sobbing Deer": *As You Like It*, II.i.21–66 and the Historical Context', *Renaissance Drama* 3 (1970): 79–109.

[6] *As You Like It*, ed. Richard Knowles, New Variorum Edition of Shakespeare (MLAA, 1977), 537–8; *As You Like It*, ed. Alan Brissenden (Oxford UP, 1993), 28–31; *As You Like It*, ed. Juliet Dusinberre (Thomson Learning, 2006), 104–7. On Jaques as Jonson, see Katherine Duncan-Jones, *Ungentle Shakespeare: Scenes from his Life* (Thomson Learning, 2001), 123–35. Edward Dowden compares him to Sterne in *Shakespeare: A Critical Study of his Mind and Art* (Henry S. King, 1875), 77.

the Axial Age (800–200 BCE) that witnessed the emergence of many of the world's major spiritual and intellectual traditions.[7] Indeed, Pythagoras has a strong claim to be crowned the first philosopher, as he allegedly coined the word from the Greek meaning 'lover of wisdom'. Pythagoras' legacy has suffered from the fact he left no substantial body of writing behind him, preferring, like Socrates, Buddha and Jesus, to relay his teachings orally to a small group of initiates out of a suspicion that writing them down might cause them to be misinterpreted or overly codified as dogma. Early Pythagorean texts tend to be fragmentary and gnomic—enhancing the impression that they contain occult wisdom of oracular force—but thanks to his later disciples and critics, Renaissance humanists were able to piece together at least a fuzzy picture of the man and the main credos of the sect he founded.[8] Born around the year 570 BCE on the isle of Samos, Pythagoras was apparently dissatisfied with the Milesian philosophy he studied as a youth, and set off on extended sojourns in Egypt and Babylon to absorb their religious customs and advanced knowledge in mathematics, music and astronomy. When he returned home to find Samos governed by a tyrant, Pythagoras exiled himself to Crotona in southern Italy, founding a philosophical community that would endure for over two centuries and cast a long shadow across Western thought. At the core of their beliefs was a reverence for mathematics as a sacred science and the theorisation of the universe as a cosmos (or unified whole) governed by mathematical principles. Although the geometrical theorem that bears his name was first worked out by the Babylonians, Pythagoras appears to have imported it to the Greek-speaking world, brandishing it as proof of the world's underlying orderliness. An apocryphal legend tells how hearing the various timbres of blacksmiths' hammers inspired Pythagoras' experiments

---

[7] First proposed by Karl Jaspers in 1949, the Axial Age remains a generative concept in the history of religion. See Robert N. Bellah and Hans Joas, eds., *The Axial Age and its Consequences* (Harvard UP, 2012).

[8] Much biographical lore about the philosopher derives from the early fourth-century account of Iamblichus, *Iamblichus' Life of Pythagoras*, trans. Thomas Taylor (Inner Traditions, 1986). A handy anthology of early writings about the sect can be found in Kenneth Sylvan Guthrie, trans. and comp., and David R. Fideler, ed., *The Pythagorean Sourcebook and Library: An Anthology of Ancient Writings Which Relate to Pythagoras and Pythagorean Philosophy* (Phanes, 1987).

with the monochord (a single-stringed instrument with a moveable bridge), from which he discovered that the musical intervals correspond to mathematical ratios. This eureka moment led him to postulate that the relative distances of the planetary orbits correspond to similar ratios and their motions emit a heavenly music, the famous 'harmony of the spheres'.[9]

Crucially, the Pythagoreans regarded numbers not simply as inert quantities but as infused with qualitative values, so their study of mathematics had a pronounced ethical component. First and foremost, the fundamental Oneness of the universe extends across and binds all living things and hence entails certain moral duties to other creatures. Accordingly, Pythagoras was the first Western thinker to advocate vegetarianism, a belief underpinned by the doctrine of metempsychosis, the transmigration of the soul across the species line. In addition to abstaining from animal flesh and even beans (perhaps because they were deemed a nexus between plants and animals), Pythagorean novitiates obeyed strict laws of hygiene and swore vows of silence. Believing that true friends share all goods in common (*amicorum communia omnia*), the Pythagorean community sought to embody the ideal of achieving oneness out of multiplicity.

Although the sect suffered persecution and gradually petered out around 400 BCE, a neo-Pythagorean revival occurred during the late Roman republic and early centuries of the Common Era, when his teachings were promoted by the likes of Cicero's friend Nigidius Figulus, Apollonius of Tyana (who reportedly travelled to India), and Moderatus of Gades.[10] Amidst this revival, the Roman poet Ovid assigned the Greek sage a prominent role in the final book

---

[9] Consequently, Pythagoreanism exerted a powerful pull upon Renaissance astronomy. Copernicus recognised that the sect had long ago proposed a sun-centred cosmos; he and his English translator Thomas Digges packaged heliocentrism not as a revolutionary new discovery but as a vindication of Pythagorean teachings, which also provided a major impetus behind Kepler's research into planetary orbits.

[10] On neo-Pythagoreanism, see Charles H. Kahn, *Pythagoras and the Pythagoreans: A Brief History* (Hackett, 2001), and Phillip Sidney Horky, 'Italic Pythagoreanism in the Hellenistic Age', in *The Oxford Handbook of Roman Philosophy*, ed. Myrto Garani, David Konstan and Gretchen Reydams-Schils (Oxford UP, 2023), 3–26.

of his *Metamorphoses*, where he delivers a lecture on sacred physics and expounds the doctrine of transmigration, lending the poem's unifying motif of transformation a sheen of scientific credibility. Ovid's magnum opus would help disseminate Pythagorean lore in the Renaissance, enshrining his reputation as the founder of a countercultural philosophy that clashed with the anthropocentric dogma of the Judeo-Christian tradition. Pythagoras' fame in Renaissance Europe also received a boost from the Florentine Marsilio Ficino, who upheld the pre-Socratic philosopher (despite his unorthodox views on the animal soul) as a transmitter of a *prisca theologia*, an ancient wisdom that unified the world's religious traditions.[11]

Although we now think of Pythagoras as a mathematician, most Renaissance humanists regarded him chiefly as a moral philosopher and the font of a tradition of wisdom literature. Pythagoras ranks among the most-quoted sages in Erasmus's *Adagia* and William Baldwin's *Sayings of the Wise . . . A Book of Moral Wisdom Gathered from the Ancient Philosophers*. A forerunner of *Bartlett's Familiar Quotations*, Baldwin's compendium (which went through twenty-three editions between 1547 and 1651) features over two dozen maxims attributed to this pre-Socratic genius, including his celebrated comparison of the world to a public spectacle or competition (like the Olympic games) that the philosopher watches from the sidelines, and recounts how he brought the knowledge of Egypt and Babylon west to Greece and Italy.[12] Thanks to texts like *Sayings of the Wise*, Pythagorean apothegms enjoyed an almost proverbial status in early modern England and echo throughout the era's literature, including (as we shall see) the works of William Shakespeare. Although recent scholarship has disputed whether Pythagoras did and said all that his

---

[11] Ficino produced Latin translations of the Pythagorean symbola and the *Commentaries of Hierocles on the Golden Verses of Pythagoras*, as well as Iamblichus' biography and treatise *On the Pythagorean Life*. On Pythagoras in the Renaissance, see S. K. Heninger Jr, *Touches of Sweet Harmony: Pythagorean Cosmology and Renaissance Poetics* (Huntington Library, 1974), and Christopher S. Celenza, 'Pythagoras in the Renaissance: The Case of Marsilio Ficino', *Renaissance Quarterly* 52.3 (Autumn 1999): 667–711.

[12] William Baldwin, *A treatise of Morall Phylosophie, contayning the sayinges of the wyse* (Edward Whitchurch, 1547), ed. Robert Hood Bowers (Scholars' Facsimiles and Reprints, 1967), B5^{r-v}, A1^{r}.

later disciples claimed, Shakespeare's contemporaries were less sceptical: they understood the Pythagorean brotherhood as a distinct philosophical/religious movement with Eastern origins, which promoted a combination of mathematical study, music theory and ascetic practice to discipline the self to bring it into greater harmony with nature and the universe.[13]

Metempsychosis as Ecognosis

The preceding sentence hints at why Pythagorean wisdom literature deserves renewed attention in the twenty-first century, an argument this chapter will develop by highlighting its compatibility with what Timothy Morton calls 'ecognosis'. Broadly speaking, one might define ecognosis as ecological wisdom, but this would oversimplify a complex term that is deliberately convoluted. Morton qualifies it further as a humble knowing that accepts its own limitations so as to enact 'coexistence' with other species:

> It is like knowing but more like letting be known ... It is like becoming accustomed to something strange, yet it is also becoming accustomed to strangeness that doesn't become less strange through acclimation. Ecognosis is like a knowing that knows itself. Knowing in a loop— a weird knowing.[14]

To put this another way, ecognosis signifies a self-reflexive knowing that refuses to blunt its awareness of its own ignorance or the strangeness of a universe that is not designed merely for human purposes. It is just such a wise receptivity that Ovid's neo-Pythagorean epic seeks to cultivate.[15] It is highly fitting that Golding's Elizabethan translation

---

[13] Walter Burkert contends that many Pythagorean cult practices derived from the Orphic and Eleusinian mysteries in *Lore and Science in Ancient Pythagoreanism*, trans. Edwin L. Minar Jr (Harvard UP, 1972). Leonid Zhmud questions that continuity, arguing that several Pythagorean doctrines did not originate with the founder but were probably accretions, in *Pythagoras and the Early Pythagoreans*, trans. Kevin Windle and Rosh Ireland (Oxford UP, 2012).

[14] Timothy Morton, *Dark Ecology: For a Logic of Future Coexistence* (Columbia UP, 2016), 5.

[15] See the collection *Ovid's 'Metamorphoses' and the Environmental Imagination*, ed. Giulia Sissa and Francesca Martelli (Bloomsbury, 2023).

126]   *Todd Andrew Borlik*

begins with 'Of shapes transformde [*sic*] to bodies *straunge*', for the poem's repeated tales of transformation gradually accustom us to a non-anthropocentric universe, the strangeness of which (relayed with poetic estrangement by Ovid) does not stale with repetition. It is likewise apt that the poem culminates in a defence of Pythagorean natural philosophy, a prime example of 'weird knowing' in its flagrant violation of the Aristotelian law of non-contradiction. Within the spiritual ecology of metempsychosis, humans are beasts and beasts humans; other species must be regarded as our parents, siblings or comrades, 'alyed to us eyther by sum freendshippe or sum kin'.[16] Ovid's exposition of Pythagorean philosophy limns a universe of mind-bending mutability and constant change in which everything is in the process of becoming something else, even its opposite, confounding the possibility of distinction. If the first step towards ecognosis begins with the recognition that, in Morton's words, 'a human is made up of nonhuman components and is directly related to nonhumans', that idea finds its greatest precedent in Western philosophy in Pythagorean metempsychosis.[17]

Designating a nondualistic wisdom flowing from a radical openness to the environment, ecognosis can help us to cross bridges that divide West from East and to theorise the startling affinities between Pythagoreanism and Buddhism. The two traditions share a belief not only in rebirth across the species line but also in a universe of incessant flux, encouraging an understanding of the environment as a dynamic process. In Pythagorean physics, elements mingle and meld into one another, and even the sea and land can swap places, as Ovid's Pythagoras posits the extreme antiquity and geomorphologic malleability of the earth centuries before James Hutton and Charles Lyell:

> For I have seen it sea which was substanciall ground alate,
> Ageine where sea was, I have seene the same become dry lond,
> And shelles and scales of Seafish farre have lyen from any strond,
> And in the toppes of mountaynes hygh old Anchors have beene found.[18]

---

[16] *Ovid's Metamorphoses: The Arthur Golding Translation of 1567*, ed. John Frederick Nims (Paul Dry Books, 2000), 15.513.

[17] Morton, *Dark Ecology*, 18.

[18] *Ovid's Metamorphoses*, 15.288–91.

Such passages illustrate how ancient wisdom traditions can foster ecognosis by enabling us to think in 'temporal and spatial scales that are unfamiliar, even monstrously gigantic'.[19] Although Pythagoreanism fed into and was infused by Platonism, the latter dreamt of a transcendent realm of immutable forms, whereas the former's emphasis on mutability brings to mind the Buddhist doctrine of impermanence (*anitya*). The Pythagoreans also veer closer to Buddhists than Platonists in their adoption of ascetic practices and dietary strictures that recognise the embodied human subject as constituted by its ecological surround. From this standpoint, transmigration is 'not an eschatological escape from Being, but an affirmation of the all'.[20] This affirmation involves certain ethical obligations, namely compassion for other beings, non-violence and vegetarianism.[21]

The vision of Pythagoras as an ethical philosopher who straddles the East/West divide was circulating in the late seventeenth century, when the health writer and vegetarian Thomas Tryon praised 'the Eastern sages [who] . . . declared against these inhumanities and sanguinary customs [i.e. meat-eating], as Pythagoras and his followers'.[22] Recognising that Pythagorean creeds bore a strong resemblance to those of Hinduism and Buddhism, Tryon classifies this Greek sect as Eastern. While it is conceivable that the similarities in their metaphysics may have arisen from similar social and environmental conditions rather than via direct influence, or that theories such as transmigration were posthumously attributed to Pythagoras by later followers after they fell under the spell of Greco-Buddhism, historians as far back as the second century CE have assumed that Pythagoras must have gleaned his teachings on reincarnation and the animal soul by journeying to India or from Indian sages he met in Babylon during

---

[19] Morton, *Dark Ecology*, 25.

[20] James Luchte, *Pythagoras and the Doctrine of Transmigration* (Continuum, 2009), 5.

[21] Just as a *bodhisattva* defers his or her own individual liberation (*moksha*) from the cycle of life and death (*samsara*), Pythagoras believed religious practice entails more than the selfish pursuit of transcendence or personal salvation, devoting himself to the edification of others.

[22] Thomas Tryon, *The way to health, long life, and happiness, or, a discourse of temperance* (Andrew Sowle, 1683), 353.

128]   *Todd Andrew Borlik*

his *Wanderjahre*.[23] In retrospect, Pythagoreanism not only offers a lightning rod for proto-ecological thinking in the Renaissance, as I have argued at length elsewhere, but also complicates facile dichotomies that would construct ecological coexistence as a purely Eastern philosophy in opposition to a Western ethos of dominion.[24]

Jaques the Pythagorean

If one were to search for a historical basis for Shakespeare's awareness of Eastern or Near Eastern wisdom traditions, or for inklings of 'ecognosis' in his plays, one might start by examining his evident fascination with Pythagoras. Shakespeare would undoubtedly have known Pythagoras' magisterial oration in Book 15 of the *Metamorphoses* and his own writings testify that he was particularly intrigued by metempsychosis. In *The Merchant of Venice*, Graziano invokes it to dehumanise Shylock:

> Thou almost mak'st me waver in my faith
> To hold opinion with Pythagoras
> That souls of animals infuse themselves
> Into the trunks of men. (4.1.130–3)[25]

---

[23] Apuleius reports Pythagoras studied with the 'Brahmins, a race of wise men who live in India' in his *Florida*, trans. Harold Edgeworth Butler (Clarendon, 1909), 184. On the origins of metempsychosis in the East, see West, *Early Greek Philosophy and the Orient*, 61–2. Seaford acknowledges the similarities with Buddhism but views them as coincidental in *The Origins of Philosophy in Ancient Greece and India*, 187. In contrast, David H. Sick upholds the Asokan rule as evidence of 'a concrete connection between the Pythagorean and Buddhist orders' in 'When Socrates Met the Buddha: Greek and Indian Dialectic in Hellenistic Bactria and India', *Journal of the Royal Asiatic Society* 17.3 (July 2007): 253–78 (264). Alberto Bernabé and Julia Mendoza, 'Pythagorean Cosmogony and Vedic Cosmogony (RV 10.129). Analogies and Differences', *Phronesis* 58.1 (2013): 32–51. Montaigne, meanwhile, suggests Pythagoras learnt of metempsychosis from the Egyptians, in *The Complete Essays of Montaigne*, trans. Donald M. Frame (Stanford UP, 1958), 316.

[24] Todd A. Borlik, *Ecocriticism and Early Modern English Literature: Green Pastures* (Routledge, 2011), 24–74. For a sobering look at the pitfalls of idealising Buddhism as a religion of eco-harmony, see David Arnold, 'Unsettling the Harmony Stereotype in Buddhist American Poetry', *ANQ: A Quarterly Journal of Short Articles, Notes and Reviews* 33.4 (2020): 293–305.

[25] Unless otherwise stated, all citations from Shakespeare in this chapter are from *The Norton Shakespeare*, 3rd ed., ed. Stephen Greenblatt et al. (Norton, 2016).

Jaques the Pythagorean [129]

The wise fool Feste quizzes the imprisoned Malvolio in *Twelfth Night* on 'the opinion of Pythagoras concerning wildfowl' and judges him insane until he resolves never to kill a bird 'lest [he] dispossess the soul of [his] grandam' (4.2.44–6). The jest underscores Malvolio's transformation from uppity steward into a bird-like gull. But Feste's facetious tone belies the depth and seriousness with which Shakespeare entertains Pythagorean philosophy. When Timon of Athens rebukes the thieves' craving for meat by observing 'The bounteous housewife Nature on each bush / Lays her full mess before you' (4.3.413–14), Shakespeare is paraphrasing Ovid's Pythagoras, who points to the 'great abundance' of fruits and vegetables that 'our mother / The earth dooth yeeld most bounteously' and concludes 'there needs no slaughter nor no blood to get your living by'.[26] Post-Enlightenment readers have sometimes dismissed Pythagoras' oration as a parody, but Ovid's early English translators such as Arthur Golding, George Sandys and John Dryden regarded it as a grand summation of the poem and its philosophical climax. Golding even defends metempsychosis by reinterpreting it as the transcorporeal respiration of the same air between beasts and humans since 'both they and we draw all one breath', and appealing to Aristotle's spiritual taxonomy that endows animals with a sensitive soul.[27] In the tradition of Ovid *moralisé*, Pythagorean teachings could be harmonised with Christian doctrine, and the *Metamorphoses* made one of the most important repositories of ancient ecological wisdom not only accessible but also respectable.

Shakespeare need not have been indebted purely to Ovid for his knowledge of this Greek philosopher. The theatrical impresario Philip Henslowe recorded in his so-called 'Diary' that the Admiral's Men repertory included a play entitled *Pythagoras*, which was staged twelve times at the Rose playhouse between January and July of 1596.[28] The popularity of this lost play helps account for the sudden rash of allusions to Pythagoras in Shakespeare's work from this time and would have enabled Shakespeare's audiences to savour these otherwise obscure, pedantic jests. Given the likelihood

---

[26] *Ovid's Metamorphoses*, 15.88–90, 98–100.
[27] *Ovid's Metamorphoses*, Epistle, line 49.
[28] *Henslowe's Diary*, ed. R. A. Foakes, 2nd ed. (Cambridge UP, 2002), 34–48.

130]   *Todd Andrew Borlik*

this play was revived circa 1598–1600, it should come as no surprise that Shakespeare namechecks Pythagoras in *As You Like It* as well.[29] Cloyed by the repetitive praise of herself in Orlando's verses, Rosalind declares that she was 'never so be-rhymed since Pythagoras' time that I was an Irish rat' (3.3.161–2). The joke requires the audience to suspend disbelief in two seemingly outlandish ideas: in Irish legends that bards could deploy rhyme as a pesticide, and in the Pythagorean doctrine of the soul's transmigration from animals into humans. But the comedy's brush with Pythagorean philosophy is not confined to this single passage; nor is its attitude as glib as this quip implies. As Julia Lupton has shown, *As You Like It* broadcasts recognisably Pythagorean ideals of virtue and intellectual community filtered through Erasmian humanism.[30] Extending and refining this argument, the ensuing paragraphs will demonstrate that these Pythagorean allusions tend to cluster around Duke Senior and Jaques (making it likely that the latter abstains from meat for ethical reasons) and that Shakespeare's comedy anticipates modern ecological thought by looking backwards and eastwards to an ancient wisdom tradition.[31]

The Duke's opening monologue primes the audience to view him and his 'brothers and co-mates in exile' as a kind of Pythagorean brotherhood. In *Sayings of the Wise*, Baldwin reports that the exiled Pythagoras 'with all his disciples, lyued in common to gether, as well in

---

[29] The 'Pethagores' play crops up again in Henslowe's papers in an inventory of playbooks 'bought since the 3[r]d of March 1598' (323–4). Since the Admiral's company probably purchased the play with the intention of restaging it, it seems likely that *Pythagoras* was revived at the Rose, Fortune or at court between 1598 and 1602. During this period the Admiral's Men and the Lord Chamberlain's Men dominated the London theatre scene, and 'each company', as Andrew Gurr has remarked, 'was well aware of its rival's offerings'. *Playgoing in Shakespeare's London*, 2nd ed. (Cambridge UP, 1996), 153.

[30] Julia Reinhard Lupton, '"Good in Every Thing": Erasmus and Communal Virtue in *As You Like It*', *Journal of Medieval and Early Modern Studies* 52.3 (2022): 567–91. Also see Donald Wehrs, 'Touching Words: Embodying Ethics in Erasmus, Shakespearean Comedy, and Contemporary Theory', *Modern Philology* 104.1 (August 2006): 1–33.

[31] Joan Fitzpatrick notes that venison was regarded as unhealthy for melancholics in *Food in Shakespeare: Early Modern Dietaries and the Plays* (Ashgate, 2007), 61–3.

loue, as in other maners. For he taught them, that true fr[i]endship was, to make one harte and mynde of a greate many hartes & bodyes.'[32] Appropriately, the name of the singer Amiens whose music Jaques so enjoys puns on the French *ami*, meaning friend, and his lyrics decry fair-weather friends. The Pythagorean exaltation of friendship—to the point of sacrificing one's goods and life for one's friends—constitutes a prominent theme in *As You Like It*.[33] The Duke's 'loving lords' show this extreme devotion, as does Celia, who likewise relinquishes her possessions and rank to share the misfortunes of her friend Rosalind. When Rosalind attempts to dissuade her, Celia retorts with a Pythagorean aphorism about 'the love / Which teacheth thee that thou and I am one' (1.3.92–3). The seemingly ungrammatical use of the singular 'am' in lieu of the plural 'are' brilliantly conveys (underscored by her use of the intimate, informal 'thou') the Pythagorean equation of friendship as making one from two, unity from multiplicity.

To an Elizabethan audience, Jaques's most iconic lines in the play, the celebrated comparison of the world to a stage, would mark him in particular as a devotee of Pythagoras. While the metaphor was a Renaissance commonplace, the numerous analogues unearthed by Shakespearean source hunters have obscured its well-known attribution to the pre-Socratic sage. A significant precursor of the speech occurs in the Elizabethan comedy *Damon and Pythias* by Richard Edwards. The titular heroes and friends profess their allegiance to the Pythagorean brotherhood, and the former explicitly credits the phrase to the sect's founder.

Pythagoras said that this world was like a stage
Whereon many play their parts. The lookers-on the sage
Philosophers are, says he, whose part is to learn
The manners of all nations, and the good from the bad to discern.[34]

A quarto of *Damon and Pythias* was printed in 1571, a second edition appeared in 1582, and Shakespeare's chief rivals, the Admiral's

---

[32] Baldwin, *Treatise of Morall Phylosophie*, B6ᵛ.

[33] For more on Renaissance friendship, see Laurie Shannon, *Sovereign Amity: Figures of Friendship in Shakespearean Contexts* (U of Chicago P, 2002), 4–5.

[34] *The Works of Richard Edwards: Politics, Poetry, and Performance in Sixteenth-Century England*, ed. Rosalind King (Manchester UP, 2001), 7.71–4.

132]

Todd Andrew Borlik

Men, mounted a remake (now lost) in early 1600, so this Pythagorean comedy was being performed across the street from the Globe around the same time Shakespeare composed *As You Like It*.[35] We know Shakespeare was familiar with the story, for Hamlet addresses Horatio as his 'Damon dear' (3.2.260) in another play written circa 1600. The lost plays about Pythagoras and his followers would almost certainly have given the *theatrum mundi* new currency, making it a safe assumption that Shakespeare and his audiences would have recognised 'All the world's a stage' as a Pythagorean adage. The speech's division of human life into seven ages may also reflect this sect's teachings since Pythagorean numerology regarded seven as the sacred number of growth and maturation: '[the Pythagoreans said] things which are natural appear to have their decisive moments of fulfilment in birth and growth by sevens. Humans, for example, . . . reach adolescence in the second span of seven years and get a beard in the third.'[36] The fact that Jaques utters this speech during a meal further amplifies its Pythagorean timbre, since the Elizabethans were aware of the Greek custom of philosophising during banquets: 'The feasts of Pythagoras, Socrates, Xenocrates, and the Sages of Greece, were the discourses of learned matters & philosophy.'[37] This passage appears in a work by Robert Allot published in 1599 (making it contemporaneous with *As You Like It*) whose title, *Wits theater of the little world*, invokes the same Pythagorean trope of *theatrum mundi*. Clearly, Pythagorean ideas circulated widely in the intellectual climate of Elizabethan London, and Shakespeare's fondness for the metaphor of the world-stage indicates he held Pythagorean teachings in higher esteem than his gags about metempsychosis imply.

A Pythagorean streak can also be discerned in Jaques's character in his touting the intellectual benefits of travel abroad (a practice Renaissance humanists associated with the wandering sage Pythagoras), his espousing the virtues of taciturnity and silent rumination (Pythagorean initiates notoriously had to take vows of silence), and most of all

---

[35] *Works of Richard Edwards*, 91. In early 1600 Philip Henslowe made four payments totalling £6 to Henry Chettle for a 'damon and Pytheas' (131–3).

[36] See Alexander's *Commentary on Aristotle's Metaphysics*, qtd. in Richard D. McKirahan, *Philosophy Before Socrates: An Introduction with Texts and Commentary* (Hackett, 1994), 109.

[37] Robert Allot, *Wits theater of the little world* (Nicholas Ling, 1599), 30.

Jaques the Pythagorean [133]

in his enthusiasm for music.[38] In his first appearance in the play, Jaques sits entranced by Amiens's crooning and vaunts his ability to 'suck melancholy out of a song as a weasel sucks eggs' (2.5.11–12).[39] The simile rests on a Pythagorean belief that music, like food, has medicinal properties and that certain melodies or harmonic modes could enkindle or alleviate 'despondency and lamentation'.[40] Amiens warns Jaques that solemn music will aggravate his melancholy, yet when we next hear of Jaques, the First Lord reports he 'was merry hearing of a song' (2.7.4). By counteracting his melancholy through music, Jaques is following Pythagorean practice. The news startles the Duke: 'If he, compact of jars, grow musical / We shall have shortly discord in the spheres' (2.7.5–6). Here Duke Senior invokes the well-known Pythagorean doctrine of the harmony of the spheres. The Duke assumes that since Jaques is an anti-social contrarian he, like Shylock, must have no ear for the concord of sweet sounds. An interest in Pythagorean philosophy and its promotion of music therapy would help account for this seeming inconsistency in Jaques's character.

The ending of *As You Like It* reveals just how integral Pythagorean ideals of harmony are to Shakespeare's conception of the comedy as a whole, when Hymen's wedding song strikes a distinctively Pythagorean chord:

Then is there mirth in heaven
When earthly things made even
Atone together. (5.4.99–101)

The belief that musical harmony on earth echoes a cosmic harmony pervading the heavens is an *idée fixe* of Pythagorean philosophy and

---

[38] Pythagoras' travels and his stipulation that novitiates observe a quinquennial silence are described in Iamblichus' *Life of Pythagoras* (7–9, 38) and were well known to Elizabethan writers. In a chapter from *Wits theater* on the benefits of 'Perigrination', Allot upholds Pythagoras as an exemplar, claiming he 'visited the Aegiptians, Arabians, and Chaldeans, and went also into Iury [Jewry]' (144ʳ).

[39] A similar expression occurs in a Pythagorean play *Damon and Pythias*: 'Come out you weasel, are you seeking eggs in Damon's chest?' (11.21–2).

[40] Iamblichus, *Life of Pythagoras*, 59. For a Buddhist-inflected reading of Jaques's fondness for sad music, see Lisa Myōbun Freinkel, 'Doing Time: Shakespeare's Weasel, Chao-Chou's Dog, and the Melancholy Lyric', *The Yearbook of Comparative Literature* 57 (2011): 213–29.

was trumpeted by Thomas Morley, the composer of 'It was a lover and his lass' and self-styled 'Pythagorian'.[41] The preponderance of songs in *As You Like It* has prompted James Shapiro to compare it to a musical comedy but it might be more historically accurate to label it a Pythagorean comedy.[42] Figuratively speaking, the plot appears to function like a harmonic equation that, through its working out, balances Pythagorean dyads such as male/female, odd/even, one/many.[43] Hymen's song features a pun with notable Pythagorean resonance, for the accompanying music induces a feeling of social harmony through musical notes *at tone*—or 'attone' as the Folio spells it—with one another, by virtue of which binary oppositions are unified and '*at/one* together'. Shakespeare's comedy culminates in a Pythagorean vision of unity in multiplicity, a oneness that ripples outward from the cast on stage to the audience in its communal experience of lyrical drama.

Unmasking Jaques as a neo-Pythagorean also calls for a reappraisal of his lament for the wounded stag, revealing this *locus classicus* for ecocritical readings of *As You Like It* as a prime example of ecognosis. Although actors sometimes perform it as sentimental or emotionally overwrought, Jaques's harangue draws upon a time-honoured wisdom tradition that recognised cross-species kinship as sacred. For obvious reasons, the Pythagoreans despised the chase. In *The Metamorphoses*, Pythagoras voices this disapproval with impassioned eloquence: 'Away with springdes, snares, and grinnes, away with Risp and net . . . No feared fethers pitche yee up to keep the Red deere in'.[44] Ovid's Pythagoras also asserts that early humans were herbivores and therefore inhabited a 'golden world' without

---

[41] Morley expounds the mathematical basis of harmony and defends the Pythagorean identification of notes with planets as 'not without reason', while acknowledging that in some respects the theory has been justly called '*nugatrix graecia*', in *A plaine and easie introdvction to practicall mvsicke* (Peter Short, 1597), 2, ¶2r–3r.

[42] James Shapiro, *1599: A Year in the Life of William Shakespeare* (HarperCollins, 2005), 224.

[43] Alan Brissenden has suggested the eight people joined by Hymen in the final scene symbolise the eight notes of the octave or Pythagorean diapason. Aristotle describes the Pythagorean theories of opposition in *Metaphysics*, 1.5 986a; see McKirahan, *Philosophy Before Socrates*, 107–8.

[44] *Ovid's Metamorphoses*, 15.527–29.

Jaques the Pythagorean [135

violence or predation.[45] *As You Like It* imagines exile in Arden as a return to such a 'golden world' (1.1.104). Charles the Wrestler here precisely echoes Pythagoras' phrase in a line that clarifies the motives for Jaques's objections to the hunt and lends a pointed significance to Orlando's identifying the food consumed by the Duke and his men as 'fruit' (2.7.99). While Jaques never explicitly alludes to metempsychosis as Rosalind does, the Duke pictures him 'transformed into a beast' (2.7.1), and the wounded stag undergoes a figurative transmigration through similes that consistently erode the distinction between human and non-human nature.[46] The Lord describes the stag as clad in a 'leathern coat' and 'velvet' (2.1.37, 50), punning on the downy fuzz on growing antlers, while Jaques variously compares it to a dying citizen bequeathing his wealth to the rich, a solitude-seeking melancholic and an abandoned bankrupt. Schooled in Pythagorean philosophy, Jaques can easily transfuse a human soul inside a stag, even if he is less successful in entering the stag's non-human *Umwelt*.[47]

Recognising *As You Like It* as a Pythagorean text and reading it through wisdom traditions that accept interspecies fluidity invites a reconsideration of its anthropomorphism. In an incisive critique of the play, Robert N. Watson highlighted the problematic aspects of Jaques's erasure of the species-divide, cautioning that anthropomorphism obscures the alterity of the non-human.[48] While there is much to recommend this view, the play's Pyrrhonic scepticism (another philosophy with roots in Eastern thought) does not invalidate its Pythagorean morality or its concern for other species. We do not need to know what it is like to be a bat or a lobster or a stag, or know how exactly their experience of pain differs from ours,

---

[45] *Ovid's Metamorphoses*, 15.105.

[46] Gabriel Egan, *Green Shakespeare: From Ecopolitics to Ecocriticism* (Routledge, 2006), 100–1.

[47] Jaques's subsequent presiding over the post-kill celebrations seems at odds with his denunciation of the hunt. But the scene effectively mocks the hunter by dressing him in the horns of the cuckold, while also evoking the therianthropic deer gods and species-crossing rituals found throughout the world, from Zuni deer dances to Tibetan stag masks to England's Herne the Hunter.

[48] Robert N. Watson, *Back to Nature: The Green and the Real in the Late Renaissance* (U of Pennsylvania P, 2006), 82.

to perceive that they are capable of suffering.[49] Shakespeare emphasises this capacity when he writes that the stag has 'ta'en a hurt' (2.1.34) and depicts it as groaning and sobbing, behaviour mirrored by Jaques's own 'weeping' (2.1.65). Just as the Buddhist Jātaka tales mobilise anthropomorphism to promote environmental virtues such as *ahimsā* (non-harm), Jaques's personifying of the stag undermines the Duke's reduction of a living creature to mere 'venison' (2.1.21), thereby supporting Pythagoras' equation of carnivorism with cannibalism.[50] Jaques even protests that over-hunting deer will 'kill them up' (2.1.62), that is, extirpate the local population in Arden. If he, like several characters in *As You Like It*, tends to view nature as a mirror or book rather than an 'autonomous entity', Jaques, nonetheless, 'brings a possibility of a more ecocentered awareness to the Duke'.[51]

The possibility that the melancholy Jaques's commentary imparts ecognosis is further bolstered by Morton's defence of melancholy as a symptom of ecological awareness:

> Depression or melancholia is . . . the inner footprint of coexistence, a highly sensitive attunement to other beings, a feeling of being sensitized to a plenitude of things. De-pressed by them . . . Melancholy is irreducible because it's ecological; there is no way out of abjection because of symbiosis and interdependence. To exist is to coexist.[52]

---

[49] William N. West has made a similar point, remarking that a 'strategic anthropomorphism can serve to move us even if it is not exact'. *As If: Essays in 'As You Like It'* (Punctum, 2016), 56. On scepticism's Eastern origins, see Christopher I. Beckwith, *Greek Buddha: Pyrrho's Encounter with Early Buddhism in Central Asia* (Princeton UP, 2015).

[50] *Ovid's Metamorphoses*, 15.533. The Jātaka tales relay Buddhist doctrine via fables describing the Buddha's myriad incarnations in non-human form. See Anand Singh, 'Buddhist Environmentalism: Narratives from the Jātakas', *Journal of the Royal Asiatic Society of Sri Lanka* 60.2 (2015): 59–79.

[51] Jamin C. Rowan, 'Ideas About Nature: An Ecocentric Look at *As You Like It*', *The Upstart Crow* 21 (2001): 15–26 (22). Also see Jeffrey S. Theis, *Writing the Forest in Early Modern England: A Sylvan Pastoral Nation* (Duquesne UP, 2009), and Dipanwita Pal, 'Forest of Arden Revisited: Re-assessing the Role of Jaques in Shakespeare's *As You Like It* from an Ecocritical Perspective', *RAIS Journal for Social Sciences* 4.2 (2020): 5–13. https://journal.rais.education/index.php/raiss/article/view/127/96

[52] Morton, *Dark Ecology*, 129.

Whereas Freud defines melancholy in pathological terms as the diminishing of an ego that narcissistically identified with the lost object, Morton redefines it as an ecological intimation of the human ego's fragility, a receptivity or hyper-sensitivity to our coexistence with other beings, including non-humans. This would explain why the musings of Elizabethan melancholics voice such an acute sense of a shared biological mortality and often verge on ecospheric thinking. Consider, for instance, Hamlet's ruminations on the worm-fish-beggar, or the claim by Chapman's Dowsecer that after death he

> will creep into this stubborn earth
> And mix my flesh with it, and they shall breed
> Grass to fat oxen, asses, and such like.[53]

Telling his father to seek his grandchildren among his cattle, the melancholy Dowsecer shifts transmigration on to a material plane to envisage human kinship with other species in a comedy that provided the key template for Shakespeare's depiction of melancholy in *As You Like It*. The seemingly narcissistic impulse to glimpse oneself in the other can trigger a reciprocal awareness that I, too, am an it and the it is a me. The pathetic fallacy is not entirely fallacious: ecology dovetails with both Pythagorean monadism and Buddhism in perceiving the ego/world dichotomy as the fundamental delusion.[54] If Shakespeare wanted to insinuate that Jaques is simply projecting himself on to the stag he could easily have described him as a bankrupt like Timon; instead, the scene appears more interested in documenting an experience of affective contagion and empathy across the species line. Rather than self-indulgent whinging, Jaques's lament presents an early modern antecedent of the eco-melancholy that suffuses contemporary sentiments such as species loneliness and climate grief.[55]

The overlap between ecognostic melancholy and abjection is underlined by a pun on Jaques's name that, to my knowledge, has

---

[53] George Chapman, *A pleasant comedy entituled: An humerous dayes myrth* (Valentine Syms, 1599), D3ʳ.

[54] For a defence of pathetic fallacy, see Sylvia Bowerbank, *Speaking for Nature: Women and Ecologies of Early Modern England* (Johns Hopkins UP, 2004).

[55] Ashlee Cunsolo and Neville R. Ellis, 'Ecological Grief as a Mental Health Response to Climate Change-Related Loss', *Nature Climate Change* 8 (2018): 275–81.

escaped the attention of Shakespearean commentators. While critics who take a dim view of the character make much of the notion that his name sounds like jakes or privy, Jaques also plays on the Latin *jaces*, to lie recumbent, the very position in which he is first described as he mourns the stag—'he lay along / Under an oak' (2.1.30–1)— and which he may adopt in his first appearance in Act 2, scene 5, when Amiens sings to him as one 'who loves to lie' under the green-wood tree (2.5.2). Elizabethans would have been familiar with this verb from its common inscription on gravestones (*hic jacet*), and this gloss is reinforced by the Folio spelling of his name with a capital 'I' as 'Iaques' (in accordance with Latin usage), making it appear more Latinate than French or English. The quibble implicates the character in the embodied devotions condemned by Elizabethan Puritans but promoted by many religious and wisdom traditions.[56] In his jacent grovelling in the earth, Jaques performs an act of eco-piety, a renunciation of human bipedalism and the supposed prerogatives it confers while mirroring the horizontal posture of the wounded stag with whom he commiserates.[57] Renaissance portraits of melancholics, such as Henry Percy, the Wizard Earl (who had a keen interest in Pythagoras) and Edward Herbert, often depict them stretched out upon the ground, attesting that Elizabethans would have associated a recumbent pose with this humour.[58] But the melancholic's affinity with the element of earth in early modern Galenic medicine (as well as Morton's diagnosis) suggests that Jaques's pose is not merely a symptom of lassitude but rather an act of ego-debasing prostration that enables

---

[56] The continued use of prostration in the Anglican service on Good Friday might even invite comparison between Jaques's mourning for the stag and mourning for Christ's death. On outdoor prayer and prostration, see Alec Ryrie, *Being Protestant in Reformation Britain* (Oxford UP, 2013), 162–99.

[57] On grovelling in early modern drama, see Jean E. Feerick, 'Grovelling with Earth in Kyd and Shakespeare's Historical Tragedies', in *The Indistinct Human in Renaissance Literature*, ed. Jean E. Feerick and Vin Nardizzi (Palgrave Macmillan, 2012), 229–52.

[58] Roy Strong, 'The Elizabethan Malady: Melancholy in Elizabethan and Jacobean Portraiture', *Apollo* 79 (1964): 264–9. George Peele praised Percy for 'following the ancient reverend steps / Of Trismegistus and Pythagoras' in *The honour of the garter Displaied in a poeme gratulatorie* (Iohn Busbie, 1593), A4ʳ. Many Elizabethan and Jacobean tomb effigies portray the subject lying on their side with their cheek on their palm, further attesting to the popularity of this pose in Shakespeare's time.

Jaques the Pythagorean [139

him to feel how profoundly connected human beings are to other life forms and the humusy earth that sustains us. A similar rationale explains the melancholic's fondness for solitude, which provides more scope for communing with the more-than-human world than human conversation alone can afford: we need to be alone in nature to realise how unalone we are. Even if he is partially grieving for his own isolation and mortality, Jaques's melancholy, transcending sadness, flows from and gives voice to an ecological apprehension of oneness that is as consoling as it is daunting and thus should not be confused with depression. As Camus said of Sisyphus, one must imagine Jaques happy.[59] Or to use the more nuanced word the play prefers, 'content'.

Rather than a symptom of a cynical, unsociable personality, Jaques's refusal to join in the dance might also be read in the same ecognostic light. In rejecting 'dancing measures' (5.4.18) for 'other' measures, Jaques maintains a commitment to an ethical life of measure or moderation and reflection consistent with Pythagorean teachings. First, his abstention enacts his Pythagorean belief in the philosopher's vocation as a bystander or objective observer of both humanity and the universe, an idea Pythagoras advances in his famous parable of the world as a stage or spectacle, which Jaques himself paraphrases at length. Secondly, Jaques's retreat to converse with an 'old religious man' (5.4.151) and the converted Duke Frederick bespeaks a yearning to remain in a spiritual community resembling a Pythagorean brotherhood. After all, Ovid's Pythagoras was an old religious man who lived in a cave, opposed tyranny and advocated non-violence toward humans and non-humans alike. Like the exiles in Arden, the Pythagoreans practised communal living and idealised friendship rather than heteronormative marriage. Arden is the right place for Jaques, who must stand apart from the orderliness or oneness of the universe to bear witness to it, for such is the price of wisdom.[60] From the perspective of the couples in newly wedded bliss,

---

[59] This chimes with Morton's argument that eco-awareness suffuses melancholy with pleasure (*Dark Ecology*, 158). Albert Camus, *The Myth of Sisyphus and Other Essays*, trans. Justin O'Brien (Vintage, 1955), 91.

[60] As Robert Bennett remarks, 'his departure is not absurd . . . but is fitting and calls for reluctant acceptance, not censure, from those who like his company and respect his choice'. 'The Reform of a Malcontent: Jaques and the Meaning of *As You Like It*', *Shakespeare Studies* 9 (1976): 183–204 (202).

140] *Todd Andrew Borlik*

Jaques's pursuit of wisdom might look like folly, but the comedy as a whole does not reject Jaques's Pythagorean philosophy outright so much as stress that a well-tempered, measured life must reconcile intellectual wisdom with lived experience and a sense of our own fallibility.

Ecognosis and the Folly of Human Wisdom

At first glance it might seem imprudent to categorise *As You Like It* as a foray into wisdom literature. After all, part of the comedy's charm and beguiling complexity is that its own knowingness is balanced by a wry sense of the folly of wisdom, of wisdom as scepticism towards the self-proclaimed wise. This idea is most succinctly expounded by the fool Touchstone in a rhetorical chiasmus: 'The fool doth think he is wise but the wise man knows himself to be a fool' (5.1.28–9). Such paradoxes can be traced back to Socrates and were echoed by the Apostle Paul: 'if any man among you seem to be wise in this world, let him be a fool, that he may be wise' (1 Corinthians 3:18). In the sixteenth century, Erasmus would popularise the oxymoron of the wise fool in his *Praise of Folly*, a work that had a profound impact on Shakespeare's conception of clowns such as Touchstone, who aim 'to speak wisely what wise men do foolishly' (1.2.76–7). Parsed carefully, these paradoxes reveal that Shakespeare's mockery of the wise does not entail a renunciation of wisdom *tout court*. Inspired in part by Erasmus's joco-serious philosophy, *As You Like It* clowns on an ancient wisdom tradition not to reject it but to reform it: to fashion a comic Pythagoreanism that can laugh at itself.[61]

Naturally, Touchstone sparks much of this philosophical laughter. In his battle of wits with the bumpkin William, he parodies intellectual pretentiousness and excessive reverence for the ancients by invoking an unidentified 'heathen philosopher' (5.1.29) who opened his lips to eat grapes to signify that grapes are for eating and lips for opening. Touchstone's satire appears to be directed at the very concept of the philosopher, which was, incidentally, established by Pythagoras. A few lines later, Touchstone attempts to flaunt his wisdom by using

---

[61] On Erasmus's brand of Pythagoreanism as an influence on the play, see Lupton, '"Good in Every Thing"', 569.

a Latin pronoun: 'writers do consent that ipse is he' (5.1.39). In early modern England, *ipse* was commonly associated with Pythagoras, thanks to the notorious Pythagorean saying *ipse dixit* (he said so), dismissed as a logical fallacy by Cicero, who criticised the Pythagoreans' blind faith in their leader's infallibility.[62] If Touchstone's *ipse* quip were another dig at Pythagoreans, it would afford further proof of the play's scepticism that wisdom is whatever the reputedly wise say. More directly, Rosalind spoofs Pythagorean metempsychosis when she cracks wise about her past life as an Irish rat 'in Pythagoras' time' (3.2.161). Shakespeare also makes it clear that the Pythagorean Jaques is not beyond ridicule. Both Orlando and Rosalind tease him about his foreign affectations and sullen negativity, while the pun on privy in his name appears to encrypt a warning not to take him too seriously as a sapiential figure.

Yet the alternative pun on lying recumbent reveals a different facet of his character and Jaques himself is not too proud to be above self-deprecating humour, even disavowing his own reputation for wisdom. He implicitly includes himself among the 'gross fools' who have 'turn[ed] ass' (2.5.43, 48) by abandoning a life of comfort to squat with the Duke in the forest, and he speaks enviously of the fool Touchstone. When he begs the Duke to make him his fool and invest him in motley, Jaques stipulates one important condition: 'provided that you weed your better judgements / Of all opinion that grows rank in them / That I am wise' (2.7.45–7). Jaques's scepticism towards the self-presuming wise is audible even in his Pythagorean speech regarded as the apex of Shakespearean wisdom. The Seven Ages of Man sounds distinctly dubious about the 'wise saws' (2.7.156) of the pompous justice, while Jaques's description of him with a paunchy 'round belly with good capon lined' (2.7.154) betrays a Pythagorean disdain for meat-eating. From this angle, Rosalind's quip about her past life as a rat is less a send-up of Pythagoras than a comic affirmation of the play's sense of the fluidity of human identity and the instability of our knowledge. Ultimately, the comedy promotes a counterintuitive sense of wisdom as cognisance of one's own folly in

---

[62] Hannah Čulík-Baird, 'Ipse dixit: Citation and Authority', *Sententiae Antiquae*, April 23, 2019. https://sententiaeantiquae.com/2019/04/23/ipse-dixit-citation-and-authority/

Todd Andrew Borlik

ways that chime with the philosophy of Michel de Montaigne, whose slogan *Que sçais-je?* [What do I know?] was in fact an underhanded assertion of his knowingness. Such self-reflexive humble knowingness is also characteristic of Morton's ecognosis. If *As You Like It* is dubious about humanity's purchase on pure nature, as Robert Watson has shown, reframing this doubt in less negative terms as ecognosis might help us embrace a healthy scepticism that does not doom us to environmental alienation. Montaigne offers a precedent for such a balancing act: his doubts about our literal kinship with animals do not prevent him from citing Pythagoras' speech in Ovid to denounce animal cruelty and resign humanity's 'imaginary kingship' over other creatures.[63] In professing a similar epistemological humility, *As You Like It* is likewise compatible with ecognosis, a knowing that seeks to understand others across lines of gender, class, race, creed and even species, while retaining a keen awareness of the limitations of the enterprise.[64]

Global Shakespeare as Contemporary Wisdom Literature: From Ecognosis to Ecocosmopolitanism

Shakespeare's Duke Senior is by no means the first person to hear sermons in stones. In fifth-century China, a monk named Tao Sheng had an epiphany that all things partake of the Buddha nature and, scorned by his fellow monks as a heretic, preached the good news to a field of rocks, who promptly nodded in assent. Thrilled by the miraculous affirmation of his insight (only confirmed after his death by the translation of *The Nirvana Sutra*), Tao Sheng rushed to inform the Zen master Ungan, who coolly replied, 'the rocks had been nodding even before you began to talk'.[65] If some Western scholars find within *As You Like It* evidence of the mind's alienation from pure nature, the Zen parable of Tao Sheng's sermon to the stones offers

---

[63] Montaigne, *Complete Essays*, 316–17.

[64] Shakespeare's negative capability makes his oeuvre a valuable repository of ecognosis—or 'knowing in a loop'—in that it demands and imparts the mental agility to toggle back and forth between the contradictory truths that we are all one but we are not but we are (*ad infinitum*).

[65] Daisetz Teitaro Suzuki, *Zen Buddhism: Selected Writings of D. T. Suzuki*, ed. William Barrett (Doubleday, 1956), 247–8.

a salutary reminder that there is no such thing as 'pure' mind or 'pure' nature. A Pythagorean or Eastern viewpoint would look more charitably on Shakespeare's pastoral rhapsodising as a statement of the fundamental entanglement of humanity and the environment, an anti-dualist metaphysics that resembles ecognosis.

Although the term 'ecognosis' may be new, the wisdom that underpins it is not. This chapter has endeavoured to illustrate that *As You Like It* achieves something like an environmental ethos by tapping into an ancient wisdom tradition that first took root during the Axial Age as a reaction against the nature-culture dualism of agrarian-urban civilisations (what Morton terms 'agrilogistics'). Yet the play also reveals that Pythagoras' radical teachings on the animal soul and holistic cosmology remained a marginal viewpoint in Shakespeare's England. In the West, a Platonic and Aristotelian logos or reason (seen as a distinctly human attribute) prevailed over the pre-Socratic Pythagorean cosmos and its Orphic animism. This raises the question of how ecognosis might be made more central when Shakespeare's plays are studied or adapted by Eastern cultures which stressed harmony and the collective over individualism and Darwinian competition, and where principles such as *advaita* (non-dualism), reincarnation, *ahimsā* (non-harm) and vegetarianism were a vital part of mainstream spiritual traditions. In other words, what are the implications of this chapter for Global Shakespeare?

In the *Damon and Pythias* play, the metaphor of the world as a stage amounts to a Pythagorean imperative to travel abroad to understand other cultures. Pythagorean wisdom literature attained such renown because its founder refused to accept that the Milesian philosophy of his homeland had a monopoly on truth and set out to glean the knowledge of other cultures beyond the borders of Greece. By the same token, Shakespeare's much-vaunted universality stems in part from his willingness to entertain and explore ideas and philosophies from outside England, including Pythagoreanism. Indeed, *As You Like It*'s intellectual generosity and ecumenical outlook stem in part from a 'Pythagorean cosmopolitanism' championed by Renaissance humanists.[66] While Shakespeareans everywhere would do well to be mindful of Shakespeare's limitations as a culture-bound thinker,

---

[66] Lupton, '"Good in Every Thing"', 569.

this volume has shown that readings of his work informed by Eastern philosophy may not be so far-fetched, given his participation in a shared thoughtworld of Indo-European wisdom traditions, and that Shakespeare's plays are marked by a sapiential openness characteristic of these traditions.

There is a lesson here for Shakespearean ecocriticism, which could be more receptive to critical and theatrical interpretations from outside the Anglosphere. For instance, the Buddhist elements in Noh-inflected adaptations of Shakespeare by Akira Kurosawa, Yukio Ninagawa and Kuniyoshi Munakata might offer different ways of conceptualising human-environmental relations that would privilege coexistence over dominion or encourage an acceptance of human transience. Ninagawa's acclaimed *Macbeth* infuses Shakespeare's tragedy with a Buddhist ethos, reimagining the stage as a *butsudan* or Buddhist altar for the dead and blanketing it with falling cherry blossoms, which, as Minami Ryuta notes, the Japanese have long revered as a Buddhist emblem of impermanence.[67] Likening Jaques's melancholy not only to ecognosis but to *mono no aware* (the pathos of transitory things, like cherry blossoms) is an example of how Eastern concepts might open up new, more inclusive perspectives on Shakespearean texts. Falling cherry blossoms also feature prominently in the finale of Branagh's *As You Like It* as signifiers of springtime and of *Japonisme*. Despite the film's flaws and questionable status as an example of Global Shakespeare, its recontextualisation succeeds in presenting Shakespearean lyrics such as 'life was but a flower' (5.3.30) as seamlessly compatible with Buddhist philosophy, capturing that a sense of our shared evanescence with other living things can also be joyful.

If one were obliged to play the moral philosopher and pin a tag on this chapter, it might be this: Global Shakespeare demands a Global Ecocriticism. But rather than treat the Shakespearean text as sacrosanct wisdom literature, Global Shakespeare might harness his cultural prestige to broadcast non-Western wisdom traditions and Indigenous knowledge systems, overcome Nimbyism, and foster collective solutions to environmental problems unfolding on local,

---

[67] Minami Ryuta, '"What, has this thing appear'd again tonight?" Re-playing Shakespeares on the Japanese Stage', in *Re-playing Shakespeare in Asia*, ed. Poonam Trivedi and Minami Ryuta (Routledge, 2010), 76–96.

Jaques the Pythagorean

[145

regional and global levels. Conducted in that spirit, Global Shakespeare might help us all recognise that the wide and universal theatre holds more woeful (and blissful) pageants than the scene wherein we play, counteracting both the Anthropocene and the 'Anglocene' to become a platform for an ecocosmopolitanism.[68]

---

[68] I have borrowed the term 'Anglocene' from Christophe Bonneuil and Jean-Baptiste Fressoz, *The Shock of the Anthropocene: The Earth, History and Us*, trans. David Fernbach (Verso, 2016), 117. On ecocosmopolitanism, see Ursula K. Heise, *Sense of Place and Sense of Planet: The Environmental Imagination of the Global* (Oxford UP, 2008).

CHAPTER 6

SOVEREIGN CARE AND NATURAL GOODNESS: STOIC WISDOM IN *THE WINTER'S TALE*

Benjamin Parris

The phrase 'natural goodness' in this chapter's title is taken from a speech by King Leontes in *The Winter's Tale* that is quite out of step with the idea itself. Though not exactly a negation of the concept, Leontes's screed grossly distorts it by suggesting that his identity as sovereign makes him the bearer of a particular and unique sort of natural goodness that feeds a range of personal virtues. These include capacities of peerless epistemological discernment, as well as an ethical and political singularity that Leontes claims elevates him above the need for the benefit of counsel or communal support—even in decisions that determine the broader lives of court and kingdom that Leontes is meant to care for in the exercise of his monarchical authority. Here is the king's statement in full:

> Why, what need we
> Commune with you of this, but rather follow,
> Our forceful instigation? Our prerogative
> Calls not your counsels, but our natural goodness
> Imparts this, which if you—or stupefied
> Or seeming so in skill—cannot or will not
> Relish a truth like us, inform yourselves
> We need no more of your advice. The matter,
> The loss, the gain, the ord'ring on't, is all
> Properly ours. (2.1.161–70)[1]

Leontes responds in this passage to Antigonus and an unnamed lord as they seek to counsel him against his rash accusations of infidelity

---

[1] All quotations of Shakespeare in this chapter are from *The Complete Works*, ed. Stephen Orgel and A. R. Braunmuller (Penguin, 2002).

Sovereign Care and Natural Goodness [147

against Hermione. His insistent repetitions of 'our' affirm in an absolutist tone his royal identity as the sovereign incorporation of bodies natural and politic. But the possessive pronoun and his yoking of it to the word 'properly' also underscore the ethical mistake that Leontes is making at this moment, a mistake that colours his tyranny throughout the first part of the play. He believes that everyone and everything must bend to the particular authority that belongs solely and properly to him. As Bradin Cormack puts it, Leontes both desires and seeks to claim a sovereignty that is 'uniquely, coherently, and absolutely itself'.[2] The king believes he embodies a natural goodness that constitutes its own brand of sovereign being and sets him completely apart from others. It is a truth like no other, this 'truth like us', as he asserts. Yet the frantic quality of Leontes's repetition of 'ours' also gives the lie to the position he stakes out. No single 'I'—not even this ostensibly sovereign 'I'—is ever truly singular as a bearer of royal authority, since there are always other monarchs ruling other kingdoms, and that fact implies a different truth behind the monarch's use of 'we'. For Cormack, Leontes's assertion of a peerless and indivisible sovereignty is both the cause of his madness and a logical absurdity that gives Shakespeare reason to explore another, more viable model of sovereignty constituted through jurisdictional difference and commonality. *The Winter's Tale* thus posits sovereignty as a general principle to be instantiated and distributed among a number of particulars—a power that is in some ways distinctive but also held in common.

In this chapter, I build on Cormack's insightful account of the limits of sovereign singularity and the play's countering investments in what he calls a 'plurality of excellences', while shifting the focus from political sovereignty to matters of ethical virtue and wisdom. Leontes's speech in Act 2 and his appeal to a 'natural goodness' suggest that the king misconstrues something important about the relationship between nature and the good, which is fundamentally a question of ethics. He seems to grasp vaguely that the authority of the king and his capacities for governance must in some way deal with the question of what is good for king and kingdom alike, even if

---

[2] Bradin Cormack, 'Shakespeare's Other Sovereignty: On Particularity and Violence in *The Winter's Tale* and the Sonnets', *Shakespeare Quarterly* 62.4 (Winter 2011): 485–513 (485).

148] *Benjamin Parris*

he mistakenly asserts that this determination can only be a function of his own singular perspective as it emerges from a natural goodness that belongs solely to him. I want to argue that Shakespeare will go on to reveal that the mistake Leontes makes here is not in thinking that the good can or should be seen as an extension of principles visible in the natural world, but rather in insisting that his identity as sovereign makes him the singular embodiment of this form of ethical value to the exclusion of all others. The play ultimately strengthens the bonds between nature and virtue in a plurality of ways that therapeutically correct the king's lapse in judgement and eventually restore the royal family and kingdom of Sicily, while also suggesting that the craft of virtue bears more than a passing resemblance to the craft of literary *poiesis*.

My argument draws on some core principles of the ancient Athenian wisdom traditions that contributed to Shakespeare's own ethical thought in conceiving a strong affiliation between nature and virtue, or *areté*, in its dual senses as both natural capacity and activity of excellence. For ancient Greek thinkers, the natural world exhibits forms of value or goodness that are meant to be developed and embodied to their fullest extent in the human pursuit of wisdom, or the knowledge of how to live well. Aristotle, for instance, argues in the *Nicomachean Ethics* that we are given the capacities for virtue by nature, but must train those capacities in accordance with their teleological orientation toward the good in order to achieve excellence. Likewise, the ancient Stoics organised their ethical thought around the concept of *oikeiôsis*, which describes the living being's natural orientation toward its bodily constitution and proper objects of care, beginning with itself and expanding outward as circles of inclusion and mutual support. The process of Stoic *oikeiôsis* is grounded in a form of reason given to human life by nature but which must be developed in accordance with the motions of natural reason that also sustain the living cosmos at large. Because human reason is simply one part of the reason permeating the entire living organism that is the cosmic whole, to be wise means to perfect one's capacity to embody what is given by nature to human life. For this reason, the Stoic ethical paradigm of living in accordance with nature—a process captured by the school's concept of *oikeiôsis*—will serve as this chapter's ancient touchstone in its discussion of Shakespeare's attributions of natural goodness and restorative virtues to the pastoral

Sovereign Care and Natural Goodness [149

locale of Bohemia and its denizens. Rosalie Colie aptly describes Shakespeare's pattern of dramatic pastoral as a 'recreative sojourn' that leads to a 'return in moral strength reinforced by the country experience of kind and kindness'.[3] In *The Winter's Tale*, the pastoral kindness of Bohemia stands in sharp contrast to the Sicilian court's threat to the natural bonds of kinship and the collectively suffered psychosomatic afflictions of a king whose reason is overruled by a tyrannical passion of jealousy.

Strikingly, Leontes's reference to 'natural goodness' suggests that Sicily's ruler actually imagines himself to embody virtues broadly associated with the abilities of the sage, who is the paradigmatic embodiment of wisdom in Stoicism and other schools of ancient Greek thought organised around the care of the self. Yet while Leontes appeals to a notion of 'natural goodness' that supposedly guarantees his sovereign sagacity in the passage under consideration, his actual state of confusion and subjection to fantasy show him to be a mockery of such wisdom. Early in the play, Polixenes notes that Leontes 'hath on him such a countenance / As he had lost some province and a region / Loved as he loves himself' (1.2.366–8). The king has indeed lost himself, first in the apparatus of governmental administration and later in the fantasies that emerge from his jealous passion. He has failed to care for himself practically as a human being whose life is intimately connected with the lives of others, which in the case of a sovereign involves special obligations of caring for family and kingdom alike while also remaining open to the care of others. Shakespeare thus uses Leontes's illness and fantasy as foils to the kinds of goodness and care that the play goes on to suggest are genuinely grounded in natural affiliation and senses of belonging, yet must be developed through necessarily interconnected and mutually sustaining relations—from the nurturing of children and the benefits of friendship to the cultivation of floras and the interconnected flourishing of kingdoms.

I argue that two characters in the play come closest to embodying the wisdom of the sage, though for somewhat different reasons. Paulina brings a form of therapeutic speech as wisdom to bear on Leontes's mad condition, and in doing so thwarts a range of established social norms that would otherwise serve as guides for human action among

---

[3] Rosalie Littell Colie, *Shakespeare's Living Art* (Princeton UP, 1974), 245.

the Sicilian elite. In refusing to abide by established courtly norms while crafting new norms for action, Paulina acts as the sage, who in the Stoic tradition is unconcerned with bucking convention when a given situation calls for taking an unconventional path to virtue. I go on to show how Perdita embodies a virtue that resonates with Stoic accounts of goodness and cosmic harmony further developed by the seventeenth-century polymath and philosopher G. W. F. Leibniz. Perdita's virtue is constituted through her ongoing openness to the physical motions and living impulses that shape the natural world and the lives of others who share that world, revealing the extent to which she is part of a unified cosmic whole. Her wisdom—as Florizel suggests through his poetic figurations of Perdita's virtue as forms of crowning and cresting—emerges in its clarity and distinctness from the relatively confused background hum of bodies and causes in the infinitely expansive mixtures of nature, but this background is nonetheless a necessary and sustaining condition of her own virtuous mode of individuation.

For both Paulina and Perdita, virtue is not a state of standing apart from others in radical singularity; it is rather an ongoing activity exercised in accordance with principles given by nature that human beings must work to discern and cultivate properly through constant attention to the interactions between self and world. Through an understanding and attunement of their actions to such principles, Paulina works from the inside to slowly heal the illness that plagues Leontes and his court, while Perdita returns home from the outside to reverse her father's mistaken insistence upon absolute particularity and bring clarity to his distorted and tyrannical notion of 'natural goodness'— not to mention his rejection of the very idea of the common. Grounded in an understanding of mutual co-affection, these women's excellences serve a therapeutic function in the play that resonates deeply with the Stoic paradigm of living in harmony with nature through care for the soul, care for others, and even care for the cares that weigh on human life in its physical and spiritual struggles. Ultimately, Shakespeare blends these principles of ancient Greek ethical thought with elements of Renaissance literary theory to generate his own dramatic 'mixture' in the form of tragi-comic romance. His literary craft in turn provides an early modern assessment of the complicated yet unavoidably close relationship between norms and nature on which wisdom depends.

* * *

Sovereign Care and Natural Goodness [151

Drawing on Eric Santner's linkage of sovereignty and psychosis, Julia Reinhard Lupton argues that 'Leontes disavows his dependencies on his wife, friend, son, and unborn child. As rejected "affection" precipitously coils into inward "infection" . . . his foreclosure of all attachments returns in the real as paranoid delusion. Moreover, because the husband, friend, and father is also a king, his paranoia contracts and deforms the public sphere of the court itself.'[4] Lupton's analysis of the king's illness and its deforming effects on the common terrain of the Sicilian court shows how the sovereign's malady cannot belong solely to him. The king's disavowals of familial care and domestic support are not simply a failure to care for his spouse and progeny, however. They also constitute a failure to cultivate the relational forms of dependence and affection—understood as a bivalent capacity to affect and be affected—that are necessary to his own flourishing as a living being. This relational affectivity serves as the basis of what is held in common among the Sicilians, and thus the domain in which ethical action and virtue take shape.

The same normative principles that Leontes fails to uphold form the basis of the ancient Stoic school's theory of *oikeiôsis*. According to the Stoics, this process begins at birth for all living animals. While there is no perfectly adequate English translation of the term, it includes a range of meanings—attachment, affiliation, being near and dear, appropriation—that describe the living animal's original impulse to feel and care for its own constitution as an embodied being. What begins as an initial awareness of its bodily constitution expands as the animal grows, however, and learns to care for those things that are proper to its flourishing as the sort of creature it is. In the case of human beings, *oikeiôsis* involves growing into sustaining relations of care that begin with the family but eventually include all citizens of the cosmic whole. One cannot care virtuously for the self without also caring for others who are likewise parts of this unified being that is the cosmos, itself understood as a living organism guided by the rational cause or living fire of the *pneuma* that is synonymous with Zeus.

One might expect the Stoic cosmos to reveal an elegantly programmed perfection, working in each instance to achieve the good

---

[4] Julia Reinhard Lupton, *Thinking with Shakespeare: Essays on Politics and Life* (U of Chicago P, 2011), 169.

in easy accordance with the rational agency that permeates all corporeal entities. However, in so far as all causes are bodies guided creatively and responsively by *pneuma*, each body responds actively to situations and to the infinitely subtle corporeal mixtures that can and do behave in an unpredictably volatile manner as they spread across the universe. Human action is guided by the impulse of the soul's ruling principle, or *hêgemonikon*, which is uniquely affected by the physical mixtures of corporeal matter and *pneuma* within a given ecological milieu in which any human being is immersed. In order to act—whether virtuously or viciously—humans must in turn be capable of being acted upon, and this capacity for co-affection necessarily opens the soul to the subtle and unpredictable physics of bodies acting as causes among the infinitely fine mixtures of the cosmos. In ethical terms, human souls are uniquely capable of forming judgements about the ways these mixtures take hold of and affect their surrounding environment as well as themselves, meaning that humans are also uniquely capable of making mistaken judgements that open the door to unnatural and destructive passions that obstruct the embodied soul's path to excellence. In short, while bodies may well be acting in such a way as to ultimately affirm the reason of the cosmos, from the limited perspective of any given human being who in the moment lacks wisdom, the overarching harmony of the cosmos remains imperceptible. The mistaken judgements of a soul agitated by passion lead to mistaken actions, which in turn contribute to a further disruption of natural harmony, and the passion spreads. Embodied human souls are in this way susceptible to the passing currents of a present and turbulent moment when they lack the clear-sighted vision of the sage.

This latter point explains, for the Stoics, why virtue and wisdom are extensions of a fundamentally natural capacity for goodness. Reason is an active cause propelled by the *pneuma*, and it is present in the form of a subtle yet persistent mixture with denser corporeal matter that is found in all the bodily entities that form the parts of the cosmos. From the tiniest of pebbles to flowering plants to cattle and humans, all bodies within the cosmic web are made up of subtly blended mixtures of corporeal matter and *pneuma*. Because *pneuma* acts in different ways among the variety of bodies it causes to cohere, some bodies are given by nature a wider range of capacities than others. For all living animals, however, *pneuma* causes the unfolding process of care

Sovereign Care and Natural Goodness [153

that begins with an attachment to their bodily constitution and guides the arc of their life. For humans, this process includes the ability to discern truths about the natural world, including truths about the human uses of reason that can lead to its flourishing in the forms of virtue and wisdom. Passion is the name given to an unnatural disturbance or distortion of these conditions, which obstructs the embodied soul's path to excellence and its balanced attunement of self and world. Learning to be wise, according to the Stoics, involves living in harmony with nature and with the guiding motions of cosmic reason that flow through all parts of the whole. Like many of their ancient counterparts, the Stoics describe this state of being as *eudaimonia*, a life that, as Katja Vogt explains, 'goes well because divinity [*daimon*] is present in it'.[5]

A relevant Stoic aphorism appears in the fourth book of the *Meditations* of Marcus Aurelius. It is an image that both condenses and transposes into a newly ethical and cosmic register two well-known poetic figurations of martial fortitude as a rock-like hardness causing waves to break and scatter in Book 15 of Homer's *Iliad* and Book 7 of Vergil's *Aeneid*.[6] The turbulent motions of Marcus Aurelius's wave are, like those of Homer and Vergil, meant to figure the force of a passion as it collides with a steady and sufficient defence against its influence. As Aurelius writes, 'Be like the headland, on which the waves break constantly, which still stands firm, while the foaming waters are put to rest around it'.[7] Aurelius's Stoic variant of this classical poetic figure conveys a subtle yet decisive difference in meaning from its predecessors: the waves are themselves transformed through their encounter with the firmness of the promontory, which must be understood as a form of resilience in reason that is simultaneously therapeutic. Christopher Gill's 'put to rest' translates the ancient Greek verb *koímaō*, which can mean lull, put to sleep

---

[5] Katja Maria Vogt, 'The Stoics on Virtue and Happiness', in *The Cambridge Companion to Ancient Ethics*, ed. Christopher Bobonich (Cambridge UP, 2017), 183–99 (194).

[6] See Homer, *The Iliad*, trans. Richmond Lattimore (U of Chicago P, 1951), 15.617–21, pp. 325–6; Vergil, *The Aeneid*, trans. Shadi Bartsch (Modern Library, 2021), 7.586–590, p. 167.

[7] Marcus Aurelius, *Meditations, Books 1–6*, trans. with intro. and comm. by Christopher Gill (Oxford UP, 2013), 4.49.1, pp. 28–9.

or calm. The translation thus adeptly preserves and conveys a sense of the mutual co-affection among all bodies in the cosmos, which the Stoics call *sumpatheia* and recognise as a core principle in their explanation of the subtle mixtures and behaviour of physical bodies. The sage-as-promontory does not stand in radical isolation from the turbulent waves of passion as they crest and break upon them; she is rather causally and affectively open to the waves in a manner that preserves her virtuous disposition while also bringing calm to her surroundings. Aurelius's meditation thus reveals that Stoic wisdom is a virtue not only embodied steadfastly by the wise in a way that protects their own soul from the undue influence of a passion. Virtue is also actively therapeutic toward others, and even toward the broader web of causes and nested material processes that stand in an immediate and reciprocal relation of co-affection with human beings, who are themselves part of these same nested organic processes and the expansive web of physical causation that spreads across the cosmos. Aurelius's cosmic sage thus soothes the surge of passion in human souls and in their ecological surroundings alike. And this Stoic notion of the therapeutic responsiveness of a virtue grounded in co-affection is a key feature of Shakespeare's own visions of the caring wisdom and excellences embodied by both Paulina and Perdita in their particular forms of responsiveness to the ills of the Sicilian court that first take shape as maladies of the human heart.

To live the Stoic way—in harmony with nature—requires us to relate to all the parts of the cosmos affectively, as Vogt explains in her study of ancient Stoic cosmopolitanism.[8] The heart is the physical seat of this capacity, since it houses the soul's common sense organ in ancient thought. According to the Stoics, the heart is the location of the impulse that guides *oikeiôsis* and attunes the soul's ruling principle, or *hêgemonikon*, to the rational motions of the cosmos. This also makes the heart the physical site from which judgements are made about the surrounding world and one's place within it. For Shakespeare, the language of the heart likewise registers Stoic insights concerning mutual affection and co-constitution as the physical basis of the good, beginning with Archidamus's description of Mamilius

---

[8] Katja Maria Vogt, *Law, Reason, and the Cosmic City: Political Philosophy in the Early Stoa* (Oxford UP, 2008).

Sovereign Care and Natural Goodness [155

as a prince who 'physics the subject' and 'makes old hearts fresh' (1.1.36–7). The nurture and developmental growth of the prince—his *oikeiôsis*—is thus woven into the fate and well-being of the political community with whom he has a natural and mutual relation of affectionate care. Both, in turn, are natural objects of the sovereign father's care, who bears a special obligation to cultivate their mutual flourishing. Yet while the heart is the seat of a potential for nurturing co-affection that benefits the soul and encourages living well, the neglect or abuse of this capacity can likewise result in abject isolation. Thus, when Leontes sees Hermione reach for Polixenes's hand while convincing him to remain in Sicily, her husband mistakenly calls the gesture 'too hot' and uses the figure of an arrhythmically tapping heart to capture his malady: 'I have *tremor cordis* on me; my heart dances, / But not for joy, not joy' (1.2.110–11). What Leontes falsely judges as infidelity and a discordant turn in his otherwise harmonious union with Hermione is in fact the result of a distempered and discordant motion of his own soul. This passion originates as a mistaken judgement that shocks heart and mind, causing both to recoil further inward.

Maladies of the heart likewise register the loss of clear perception and sense-making capacities amid the condensed and fuzzy clusters of imprecise language or overdetermined speech in the play. Despite their agreement upon its importance, critics have long been puzzled by the exact sense of Leontes's ruminative statement in 1.2 as he reflects further on the implications of his judgement against Hermione:

> Sweet villain,
> Most dear'st, my collop—can thy dam, may't be
> Affection!—thy intention stabs the centre.
> Thou dost make possible things not so held,
> Communicat'st with dreams—how can this be?
> With what's unreal thou coactive art,
> And fellow'st nothing. (1.2.135–41)

For Stephen Orgel, one crucial implication of these lines is that 'in talking about Hermione, Leontes is talking about himself'.[9] Whether

---

[9] William Shakespeare, *The Winter's Tale*, ed. Stephen Orgel, Oxford Shakespeare (Clarendon, 1996), 102.

the 'affection' is to be understood as a passion of lust overtaking Hermione, whose 'intention' is to wound Leontes's heart, or whether 'thy' refers to Leontes himself and to his mistaken belief that his mind is getting to the heart of the matter between them, it is clear that their relational capacity for co-affection is the necessary principle under-writing Leontes's musings. The murkiness of meaning here, I would suggest, is part of the point: the fuzziness of Leontes's speech, his distorted capacity for judgement, and the dreamlike currents of his sensorial experience of the world all reveal the state of an embodied soul that is immersed and 'coactive' with the agitated and volatile currents of a passion. The 'thou' is both Hermione and Leontes, in so far as his perceptions of the world are compelled by—'coactive' with—the unreality of the mistaken judgements he delivers concerning his wife. The first part of the play thus tracks the multifaceted consequences of Leontes's failures as husband, father, king and self in ways that illustrate that the boundaries dividing these roles are quite permeable. Likewise, the volatile mixture of bodies and the capacity for co-affection open the sovereign to mistaken judgements, whose subtle physical beginnings circulate inconspicuously throughout the natural world before taking hold in the form of a passion. Leontes's lack of practical care for his own soul plays a central role in this pro-cess, which further confirms that the circles of the king's care overlap and complicate one another, even while revealing the dire need for a properly balanced attunement of self and world that involves an open and compassionate heart.

While Hermione's imprisonment and apparent death rob the sover-eign of the chance to be cured of his ills through her own virtuous care, her ally Paulina—with more than a touch of astringency—brings a necessary form of therapeutic sagacity to the ailing king. Laurie Shan-non argues that Paulina's designation of Leontes as a tyrant is in fact 'appropriate' and that she 'serves well when she lies', drawing atten-tion to Paulina's audacity in confronting the king and her recalibra-tion of gender norms in the face of the patriarchal court's ongoing misogyny and gynaephobia.[10] What Shannon describes in Paulina as a form of daring liberty enabled by the codes of early modern friendship

---

[10] Laurie Shannon, *Sovereign Amity: Figures of Friendship in Shakespearean Con-texts* (U of Chicago P, 2002), 212–13.

can also be described as a virtuous and creative mode of action that displays wisdom. Paulina acts as the sage, who is renowned in Stoic thought for being unconcerned or even eager to refute conventional norms in favour of crafting action that is truly *kalon*—action that embodies the unified perfection of goodness and beauty in the philosophical sense because its uniqueness is precisely appropriate for the situation.[11] Paulina says it best herself: she comes to Leontes to calm, soothe and 'bring him sleep' (2.3.32), just as Marcus Aurelius suggests the Stoic sage calms the agitated waters of the wave that crashes over and breaks upon her. Sleep, as I have argued elsewhere, occupies a distinctive place in the history of Stoic thought as both a foundational natural virtue and a restorative therapy tied to the school's ethical theory of *oikeiôsis*.[12] Paulina's action thus takes the form of a benefit to the king that is at once biological and ethical but that also corrects the physically life-draining and harmful effects of the court that his male counsellors only augment:

> 'Tis such as you
> That creep like shadows by him and do sigh
> At each his needless heavings, such as you
> Nourish the cause of his awaking. I
> Do come with words as medicinal, as true—
> Honest as either—to purge him of that humour
> That presses him from sleep. (2.3.33–9)

In calling out his counsellors for contributing to the king's unnatural state of agitated 'awaking', Paulina reminds Shakespeare's audience of the early back-and-forth between Leontes and Polixenes, when the latter jests that he has 'stayed / To tire your royalty' and Leontes assures him 'We are tougher, brother, / Than you can put us to't' (1.1.14–16). Through his commitment to a form of wakefulness that seeks to outdo his masculine peer, Leontes reveals his sovereign care has been captured and directed toward ends that ultimately prove

---

[11] Richard Bett, 'Beauty and its Relation to Goodness in Stoicism', in *Ancient Models of Mind: Studies in Human and Divine Rationality*, ed. Andrea Nightingale and David Sedley (Cambridge UP, 2010), 130–52.

[12] Benjamin Parris, *Vital Strife: Sleep, Insomnia, and the Early Modern Ethics of Care* (Cornell UP, 2022).

harmful to himself and his kingdom. Their exchange suggests the inscrutably subtle beginnings of a psychosomatic agitation that will eventually grow into a full-blown passion of jealousy, which as Paulina rightly recognises entails a corrosive form of sovereign vigilance. Her virtuous intervention in the life of the king thus takes aim at the core of his embodied soul, beginning with a form of therapeutic and truthful speech that undoes the patriarchal strictures of the court and restores Leontes's ill 'humour'. Like Shannon, Orgel suggests that 'Paulina's behavior is vindicated' in this regard, though he ultimately finds the play ambivalent concerning the ethical value of Paulina's action, in so far as 'even her admirers impugn her shrewish tongue and her harsh manner'.[13] Rather than the shrew, I suggest Paulina's closest kin in this scene is the ancient sage, in so far as her unique blending of therapeutic and acerbic qualities in truthful speech ultimately disperses confusion and heals the sovereign in body and soul. Such effects are likewise attributed to the speech of sages described in Stoic thought, as well as Platonic and Cynic figures such as Socrates and Diogenes who are known to sting, shock or disarm their interlocutors with forcefully unexpected and often painful words of wisdom. What Orgel describes as the play's ambivalence is better seen as the ambivalence of certain misguided and unappreciative male courtiers whose own patriarchal perceptions are muddied by the turmoil of their king and the spread of his impassioned soul's malady into their common domain.

Sixteen years are needed to treat this illness, as Paulina continues caring for Leontes and (secretly) for her queen. This prolonged concealment suggests that the therapy Paulina brings to Leontes is both part of a natural cycle of generational renewal and a process that requires steady, uninterrupted work in order to secure the transformation of a king and court in tumult. Yet while the initial setting and events taking place in Sicily tend to emphasise chaotic or disordered attempts by humanity to regulate and control the natural world, the move to Bohemia instead shows humans to be functionally part of nature.[14] The play's pastoral scenes underscore the extent to which

---

[13] *The Winter's Tale*, ed. Orgel, 28.

[14] Jennifer Munroe, 'It's all about the gillyvors: Engendering Art and Nature in *The Winter's Tale*', in *Ecocritical Shakespeare*, ed. Lynne Bruckner and Dan Brayton (Routledge, 2016), 139–54.

Sovereign Care and Natural Goodness   [159

human beings can never succeed in subjecting nature to their own designs: as the Stoics teach, they can flourish only by working and living in accordance with nature, a condition exemplified for Shakespeare by Perdita. As she grows up in Bohemia under the care of her surrogate parents in their pastoral abode, we might think of Perdita's steady maturation as an arc of increasing intensity whose *telos* is the embodiment of wisdom, or virtue, flourishing in harmonious relation to her natural surrounds. The sheep-shearing festival of Act 4 serves as the coming-out party for her character in this regard, taking place in a pastoral domain that is a space of regeneration and, for both Cormack and Colie, one that actively cultivates excellence. According to Cormack, the 'shepherd's place' affirms a plurality of distinctive excellences that supersedes the singularly absolute sovereignty endorsed by Leontes. Colie, meanwhile, suggests that for Shakespeare and other Renaissance poets, pastoral is the mode through which the grounding principles of aesthetic and ethical norms alike are reconfigured and made anew.[15] In need of a salutary transformation, both the conventions of literary craft and courtly decorum come to the shepherd's surrounds for guidance. In other words, matters of virtue and poetry alike involve forms of practical wisdom whose starting impulses come from nature but must be shaped through skilful exercises of human care.

The horticultural exchange between Perdita and Polixenes in 4.4 is typically read as the play's decisive statement on the interplay between the processes of nature and the actions of human beings. I would like instead to emphasise Florizel's figuration of a garlanded Perdita as the goddess Flora at the opening of the scene, along with his estimation of her singularity as a unique 'function' cresting in the form of a wave. Building on Jenny Mann's insightful discussion of figures of Orphic eloquence in early modern poetry, I suggest that crowning and cresting serve in *The Winter's Tale* as two of Shakespeare's key poetic figures for the activity of virtue and for the human capacity to recognise and respond to its presence through poetic creation—even as the playwright simultaneously draws our attention to the paradoxical nature of human encounters with wisdom by emphasising our propensity to lose hold of the insights it

---

[15] Colie, *Shakespeare's Living Art*, 3–9.

brings.[16] For Mann, the poetic figure is a condensation of perceptible form and energetic capacity in language, and it is the means by which poets both theorise and bring about the affective and physical transformations associated since classical antiquity with the sublime. Along such lines, Florizel uses 'crowning' and 'cresting' as poetic figures to articulate Perdita's virtue as the unified perfection of natural goodness and beauty, or what ancient thinkers designated as the *kalon*. These poetic figures in turn disclose Shakespeare's investments in a close affiliation between nature and virtue: the play reveals that our capacities for wisdom and virtuous action do not separate us from the natural world but rather affirm our belonging to it—even as virtue stands out clearly in visible relief from the backdrop of material processes and embodied causes that engender it.

Act 4, scene 4 begins with Florizel's description of his beloved's body as a site of nested processes that give rise to a mythological and poetic recognition:

> These your unusual weeds to each part of you
> Does give a life; no shepherdess, but Flora
> Peering in April's front. This your sheep-shearing
> Is as a meeting of the petty gods,
> And you the queen on't. (4.4.1–5)

Florizel begins his conceit by imagining a relation of benefit—the giving of 'a life'—that extends from the 'unusual weeds' of Perdita's garland to each part of his beloved. In line with Seneca's Stoic description of the good as a form of benefit that is corporeal, active and enriching for the whole, Florizel also suggests that Perdita's embodied life consists of many parts that are both sustained by the multiple floras she wears yet cohere in such a way as to reveal the singular Flora who 'peer[s]' outward to be recognised and honoured as queen of the festival.[17] Perdita's *daimon* thus appears in a manner that affirms its embeddedness within the physical mixtures and nested processes of a natural world that nonetheless make possible

---

[16] Jenny C. Mann, *The Trials of Orpheus: Poetry, Science, and the Early Modern Sublime* (Princeton UP, 2021).

[17] Seneca, *Letters on Ethics*, trans. with intro. and comm. by Margaret Graver and A. A. Long (U of Chicago P, 2015), 117.2, p. 464.

Sovereign Care and Natural Goodness   [161

the emergence of a clear and distinct recognition—a crowning—that stands out from this backdrop precisely at the moment that Flora emerges from floras and Perdita becomes 'queen' of the festival. In so far as 'Art seems part of the regenerating power of the play', as Northrop Frye argues, Florizel's poetry reveals a key means by which this form of pastoral regeneration takes place.[18] The human crafts of poetry and virtue converge in a moment of mythological recognition that identifies Perdita with the goddess of spring and the spirit of renewal whose fated transformation from Chloris into Flora appears in Book 5 of Ovid's *Fasti*.

To better grasp the dynamic interaction between floras and Flora in Shakespeare's figures of crowning and cresting, a brief turn to the work of G. W. F. Leibniz is in order. Leibniz's system draws resources from ancient Greek thought, including the Stoic school, and Leibniz himself uses the cresting wave as a poetic figure to explain his theory of clear perception as an event involving a multiplicity of subtle and confused perceptions. As Leibniz contends, 'Nothing takes place suddenly . . . *nature never makes leaps*',[19] and this principle of continuity holds true for all acts of perception. Put simply, 'noticeable perceptions arise by degrees from ones which are too minute to be noticed', showing that perception 'always and everywhere involves an actual infinity'.[20] Leibniz in turn uses 'the example of the roaring noise of the sea' to illustrate his point: 'To hear this noise as we do, we must hear the parts which make up this whole . . . although each of these little noises makes itself known only when combined confusedly with the others . . . We must be affected slightly by the motion of this wave, and have some perception of each of these noises, however faint they may be.'[21] The phenomenon Leibniz describes—the genesis of a noticeable and sufficiently clear sound—correlates with the

---

[18] Northrop Frye, *Fables of Identity: Studies in Poetic Mythology* (Harcourt, Brace, 1963), 112.

[19] Gottfried Wilhelm Leibniz, *New Essays on Human Understanding*, trans. and ed. Peter Remnant and Jonathan Bennett (Cambridge UP, 1996), 57.

[20] Leibniz, 54.

[21] Leibniz, 54. Leibniz bases this argument on an ancient argument about the sound of a bushel of millet grain made by the pre-Socratic Zeno of Elea. See *Zeno of Elea: A Text, with Translation and Notes*, trans. and ed. H. D. P. Lee (Cambridge UP, 1936), 108.

experience he aims to bring about in his readers: the emergence of a 'clearer idea' of the process of perception. The figure of the cresting wave thus becomes the poetic means of bringing about a clear and distinct idea in the minds of his readers. Leibniz goes on to suggest some broader implications to his theory of perception and its situating of the soul in relation to the natural world and, indeed, to the entire cosmos:

> These minute perceptions . . . constitute that *je ne sais quoi*, those flavours, those images of sensible qualities, vivid in the aggregate but confused as to the parts; those impressions which are made on us by the bodies around us and which involve the infinite; that connection that each being has with all the rest of the universe . . . by virtue of these minute perceptions the present is big with the future and burdened with the past . . . all things harmonize—*sympnoia panta*, as Hippocrates put it . . .[22]

Without the buzz and hum of background sensations, confused perceptions and bodies acting as causes, there would be no genesis of noticeable qualities or clear apperception of anything. Every perception and every bodily cause is part of an aggregate mass or infinite chain that spreads across the entire cosmos, and for Leibniz such infinite extension reveals the central principle of harmony that guides God's creation and connects past, present and future while maximising the degree of beauty that the cosmos expresses.[23]

In Florizel's description of Perdita's beauty, Shakespeare, like Leibniz, imagines that which is beautiful, or *kalon*, to emerge from a relatively confused aggregate of natural bodies and sensations. The floras that make up her garland provide the necessary condition for the deity Flora to appear, by giving life to Perdita along a continuum that transforms her many parts into a singular manifestation of the cyclical beauty and harmony of spring. The Stoic theory of *sumpatheia* provided Leibniz and Shakespeare alike with

---

[22] Leibniz, *New Essays on Human Understanding*, 55.

[23] On the centrality of beauty and harmony as aesthetic values underpinning Leibniz's view of the cosmos, see the discussion of philosophy as an aesthetic object in Richard Halpern, *Leibnizing: A Philosopher in Motion* (Columbia UP, 2023), 167–77.

Sovereign Care and Natural Goodness [163]

a systematic model from the ancient world for conceptualising an infinitely expansive interconnectedness of all bodies and souls in the cosmos, and the extent to which any perception or action is in some way the result of an infinite chain looking backward into the past while at the same time having infinite repercussions for the future. In so far as the Stoic sage embodies wisdom by achieving the state of a soul ruled by reason, they embody within themselves the principle of harmony that is also at work in the larger cosmos, thereby connecting them to its guiding motions and making their embodied soul function as a fully realised part of the cosmic whole—much as Shakespeare imagines the transformation of Perdita into Flora as a manifestation of the natural goodness and cosmic beauty of her pastoral surrounds that in turn peers out as a god.

For Shakespeare, however, such beauty also bears a special relation to the craft of poetry, as Harold Wilson explains: 'The idea of cosmic nature as guiding and controlling the development of poetic art occurs in Petrarch . . . and this normative conception of "nature" is further applied to all literary art and to human arts in general by a succession of Renaissance writers in Italy, France, and England.'[24] Frye similarly argues that the controlling power behind the emblematic sheep-shearing scene and the play's dramatic action more broadly is 'something identified with both the will of the gods, especially Apollo, and with the power of nature'.[25] These critics show that Shakespeare's conception of poetic art is tied to principles of natural goodness and beauty that simultaneously invoke divinity. Yet while Frye argues that the providential grace indicated by Hermione's return is ultimately secularised by Shakespeare's alignment of such return with the cycles of nature, I suggest that Shakespeare's notions of cyclical return, natural harmony and goodness in the crafts of virtue and poetry alike involve a view of nature that is closer to the ancient Stoic vision of a providential cosmos that nonetheless involves moments of disruptive and passionate upheaval emerging from the volatility of physical mixtures when seen from the limited

---

[24] Harold S. Wilson, '"Nature and Art" in *Winter's Tale* IV, iv, 86 ff', *The Shakespeare Association Bulletin* 18.3 (July 1943): 114–20 (115).
[25] Frye, *Fables of Identity*, 111.

164]   *Benjamin Parris*

perspective of the present moment.[26] Moreover, Shakespeare's conception of the alignment between virtuous action and poetry shares the Stoic insight that the *kalon* is both ethically and aesthetically beautiful because, in its uniquely singular appropriateness for the given state of affairs, it manifests a form of unique perfection.

Along such lines, figures of cresting and crowning enliven Florizel's poetic description of Perdita's virtue as a unique capacity for action that improves that which it acts upon. 'What you do', he tells her,

> Still betters what is done. When you speak, sweet,
> I'd have you do it ever; when you sing,
> I'd have you buy and sell so, so give alms,
> Pray so, and for the ord'ring your affairs,
> To sing them too. When you do dance, I wish you
> A wave o'th' sea, that you might ever do
> Nothing but that; move still, still so,
> And own no other function. Each your doing,
> So singular in each particular,
> Crowns what you are doing in the present deeds,
> That all your acts are queens. (4.4.135–45)

On the one hand, Florizel offers us a kind of cascading list of 'do's'—from Perdita's speech to her singing to acts of economic and spiritual

---

[26] Notably, the oracle's pronouncement on Perdita has a salutary influence on Hermione: 'Knowing by Paulina that the oracle / Gave hope thou wast in being, have preserved / Myself to see the issue' (5.3.126–8). Her faith in prophecy is relevant to the Stoic notion of a providential cosmos working ultimately to actualise the good. A number of Stoic philosophers remark on the virtues of prophecy and divination, including Marcus Aurelius, who claims that in the 'natural order' of things providence will help in a 'variety of ways, by dreams, by prophecy'. Similarly, Seneca notes that a diviner is a useful person because they are a 'servant of fate', and just as our health is a matter of fate being realised through the expert care of a doctor, the work of prophecy aims to bring forth the good that we are fated to realise in our lives. See *The Meditations of the Emperor Marcus Antoninus, Volume 1: Text and Translation*, trans. A. S. L. Farquharson (Oxford UP, 1944), 9.27, p. 211, and Seneca, *Natural Questions*, trans. Harry M. Hine (U of Chicago P, 2010), 2.38.4, p. 182. On Epictetus and divination within a wider historical context of the long-standing affinity between Stoicism and prophetic divination, see Erlend D. MacGillivray, 'Reassessing Epictetus' Opinion of Divination', *Apeiron: A Journal for Ancient Philosophy and Science* 53.2 (2020): 147–60.

Sovereign Care and Natural Goodness [165

exchange to dance—that seem to constitute a mounting force that culminates in the figure of the cresting wave whose constant 'function' he both envisions and desires as a pinnacle of her many glorious ways of doing. Yet on the other hand, each of these successive actions also in its own particular mode constitutes a form of 'singular' excellence by which it stands out, crowning each action like a queen in Shakespeare's phenomenology of virtue.

While capable of discerning something true about the nature and appearance of Perdita's virtue, Florizel seems ignorant in other important respects as to its nature and deeper implications. Seeing and wishing for Perdita's virtue to manifest as a dancing wave that endlessly repeats one function to the exclusion of all others misses an important fact about the nature of waves. Namely, they emerge and fall away as part of the rhythmic cycles of a more expansive ocean whose waters act as the cause of its cresting. The perfection, beauty and singularity embodied by the cresting of any particular wave must therefore also draw our attention to its fleeting nature and return to the relatively obscure or confused depths from which it emerged. Misconceiving the truth that her many singular actions emerge continuously from the motions of the cosmic whole, Florizel risks seeing and attributing to Perdita the very sort of isolated singularity and imagined perfection of 'natural goodness' that Leontes attributes to himself. To be wise is to be attentive and apperceptive to the natural ebb and flow of the cosmos and its will, as things come into being and pass away, including that which is *kalon*. Appropriately, Perdita tells Florizel his 'praises are too large', and even jokingly introduces the notion that her own sagacity warns her against his excessiveness: 'With wisdom I might fear, my Doricles, / You wooed me the false way' (4.4.150–1). And of course Polixenes makes the same mistake as his son as he watches the two dance, remarking that everything Perdita does 'smacks of something greater than herself, / Too noble for this place' (4.4.158–9). Like Florizel, Polixenes wants to sever Perdita's beautiful and virtuous actions from the very 'place' on which they fundamentally depend. Both members of the Bohemian court reveal the limitations of their understanding of the pastoral domain and the fact that its plurality of excellences, including Perdita's modes of crowning and cresting, affirm their harmonious belonging to a continuum with the natural world.

166] *Benjamin Parris*

Perdita's fateful return to Sicily manifests the cyclical and sympathetic motions captured in Leibniz's figure of the wave. She brings to the court a cosmic mixture of rejuvenating energy and sadness in which present joys remain burdened by past memories of her lost sibling and parent, while simultaneously pointing to a future ripe with virtuous potential. Paulina again offers sagacious words for Leontes at the opening of the final act, appropriately pitched to both the realities of his loss and the wisdom of seeing and relating to the world in a new and better way that takes to heart the lessons of Stoicism while also anticipating elements of the Leibnizian cosmos: 'If one by one you wedded all the world, / Or from the all that are took something good / To make a perfect woman, she you killed / Would be unparalleled' (5.1.12–15). Like her daughter, whose excellence emerges from a cosmic plurality, Hermione is said to have embodied a virtue that was both distinctively its own yet of a kind with each of these other instances of the 'good' among the 'all'. Yet Paulina reminds Leontes that Hermione is irreplaceable because, in the end, no accumulated sum of goods could ever reproduce the singularity of her own goodness. Soon thereafter, a servant describes Perdita upon her entry to the Sicilian palace as 'the most peerless piece of earth . . . that e'er the sun shone bright on' (5.1.94). Like Florizel's earlier estimation of Perdita's virtue, the servant's praise of Perdita's singular goodness gets something right and something wrong. His comparison of her virtue to a 'piece' of sun-soaked earth implies a grounded yet isolated fixity that the play has already called into question, by presenting more apt figures for virtue modelled on the natural rhythms of cresting waves and crowning blossoms that connect the manifestation of natural goodness to cyclical processes of the cosmos—and therefore to the inevitability of decay, death and rebirth. Paulina thus reminds the servant that he once praised Hermione's peerlessness in the same terms he now praises Perdita's, so that while then his 'verse flowed with her [Hermione's] beauty', his praise now 'ebbs' like the tide that draws waves in and out of their cresting cycles (5.1.95–103).

In her wisdom—and hidden knowledge that Hermione lives—Paulina knows that the peerless virtue of Perdita is in fact not absolutely singular, and that such forms of praise miss their mark by imagining excellence as a quality divorced from the surroundings that engender it. While her exchange with the servant thus recalls the ethical failures caused by Leontes's passion and his denial of

Sovereign Care and Natural Goodness [167

the living grounds of co-affection, we soon learn that Sicily's sovereign has taken Paulina's wisdom and advice to heart. As the third unnamed gentleman who serves as Paulina's steward reveals, the reunion of the two sovereigns becomes a mounting crescendo of joy in common that mirrors Florizel's figuration of Perdita's virtuous crowning of action: 'There might you have beheld one joy crown another so and in such manner that it seemed sorrow wept to take leave of them, for their joy waded in tears' (5.2.43–6). These crowning joys emerge from the midst of watery reminders of impermanence and loss, as the buoyant energies gathered by the cresting wave of Perdita's return must also release, disperse and give way to memory of her mother's absence: 'Our King, being ready to leap out of himself for joy of his found daughter, as if that joy were now become a loss, cries, "O, thy mother, thy mother!"' (5.2.49–51). Shakespeare thus subtly captures a sense of the necessary ebb and flow that characterises life and *eudaimonia* amid the circulating affections and cyclical realities of the cosmos. 'O grave and good Paulina' (5.3.1), Leontes remarks, cementing his grasp on the ethical truth that eluded him in earlier years, the truth of the joy conferred by the cresting and crowning recognition of the *kalon* as it comes into being, passes away, yet eventually returns through the cosmic cycles of life, death and natural goodness.

Part III:

A Kinaesthetic Ethics of the Heart-Mind

CHAPTER 7

PRAJÑĀPĀRAMITĀ AND THE BUDDHIST PATH OF WISDOM IN *KING LEAR*

Marguerite A. Tassi

I loved her most, and thought to set my rest
On her kind nursery.

King Lear, 1.1.121–2[1]

Maternity of the daughter toward the father.
Profound subject!

Victor Hugo[2]

King Lear is Shakespeare's greatest wisdom play and artistic realisation of the transformative powers of suffering, compassion and
selflessness. Yet Shakespeare depicts the brutal realities of the human
condition with such anguishing intensity that some critics and audiences have found the tragedy unbearably pessimistic, nihilistic and
absurd.[3] The preference for Nahum Tate's comedic revision of *King
Lear*, which replaced Shakespeare's play in English theatres for 150
years, is a case in point. The play challenges us to penetrate its rough,
unpalatable surface to find gems of wisdom at its core. While scholars

---

[1] I would like to express my deepest appreciation to Unhae Park Langis, Julia Reinhard Lupton and Elizabeth Mattis Namgyel, fellow wisdom-seekers and exuberant
intellectual spirits. All quotations from *King Lear* in this chapter are taken from *The
Norton Shakespeare*, 3rd ed., ed. Stephen Greenblatt et al. (Norton, 2016). Unless
indicated with a Q for the 1608 Quarto, quotations are from the First Folio.

[2] Victor Hugo, *William Shakespeare*, trans. Melville B. Anderson (McClurg,
1899), 244.

[3] See especially criticism of the 1960s, with pessimistic readings of *King Lear* from
Barbara Everett, William Elton, J. Stampfer and Jan Kott. The latter, for example,
argues that in *King Lear*, 'there is nothing, except the cruel earth, where man goes
on his journey from the cradle to the grave'. Jan Kott, *Shakespeare Our Contemporary* (1964), trans. Boleslaw Taborski (Norton, 1974), 146–7.

have looked productively to Hellenic, Hebraic and Christian traditions to meet this challenge, I would like to consider a fresh perspective by turning to an Asian wisdom tradition, specifically Buddhism, to see what capacity this ancient religion has to illuminate spiritual truths in *King Lear*. In Mahāyāna Buddhism, which includes Chan/Zen, Pure Land and Vajrayāna lineages, we find a treasury of wisdom revealed in a body of sacred literature known as the *Prajñāpāramitā sūtras* (Sanskrit, 'Perfection of Wisdom scriptures').[4] Expressing a refined understanding of the nature of reality (dependent origination, or *pratītyasamutpāda*), these wisdom texts have transformed civilisations, teaching the path to enlightenment through accurate discernment (*prajñā*), emptiness (*śūnyatā*), skilful means (*upāya*) and active compassion (*karuṇā*). In Buddhism, *path* is a 'synonym for "mind"' and 'the mental process of developing our basic human potential to its fullest'.[5] This process engages the heart, as well, which is revealed in the translation of the word *citta* (Pāli/Sanskrit) as both 'mind' and 'heart'; thus the great Buddhist sages regard *bodhicitta* as simultaneously 'the mind of enlightenment' and 'the awakened heart'. Resonating with Mahāyāna Buddhism, *King Lear* reveals the path of wisdom as the path of *bodhicitta*, dramatised poignantly as a *via negativa*, which strips away worldly illusions and egoic attachments,[6] preparing the heart-mind for spiritual awakening. This path is arduous, but it leads to release from suffering and refuge in love's 'kind nursery'.

---

[4] Buddhism reaches back 2,500 years to the teachings of the historical Siddhārtha Gautama, who became the Buddha ('Awakened One'). The Mahāyāna ('Greater Vehicle') Buddhist tradition developed in northern India as early as the first century BCE and emerged at the same time as Christianity.

[5] Karl Brunnhölzl, *The Heart Attack Sūtra: A New Commentary on the 'Heart Sūtra'* (Shambhala, 2012), 24–5.

[6] The path of negation (also known as *via negativa* and apophatic theology) is followed in other spiritual traditions, including Advaita Vedanta and mystical Christianity. Melinda E. Nielsen has applied the Christian traditions of *via negativa* and asceticism to Lear's experience. She argues: 'In order to understand the subsequent miracles—which, like Creation, proceed ex nihilo—Lear must first descend into the void of nothingness that he had evoked so lightly and experience for himself the negation of all he had assumed.' '"Nothing almost sees miracles / But misery": Lucretian Philosophy and Ascetic Experience in *King Lear*', *Logos: A Journal of Catholic Thought and Culture* 19.4 (Fall 2016): 101–16 (102–3).

Prajñāpāramitā and the Buddhist Path of Wisdom   [173

To understand *King Lear* in light of Buddhist wisdom is to acknowledge how responsive Shakespeare's dramaturgy is to non-Western spiritual traditions. Shakespeare's openness to myriad languages, theatrical styles and cultural habitations renders a great tragedy of the human condition such as *King Lear* powerfully resonant with Eastern wisdom. The Renaissance motifs of mirror and *theatrum mundi*, intrinsic to Shakespeare's conception of theatre, reveal how his dramas participate in an ongoing transcultural and transhistorical endeavour to awaken wisdom and ethical consciousness in audiences everywhere. From a Buddhist perspective, *King Lear* functions as an introspective mirror in which audiences 'see feelingly' how humans on a spiritual path grapple with suffering, seek love and compassion, and aspire to wisdom. In his greatest tragedy, Shakespeare has imagined a world of seemingly unbearable suffering, yet many of his characters bear pain with grit and grace, and do not avert their gaze from the suffering of others. Compassionate witnessing complements and arises from wisdom, an intrinsically spiritual 'organ of vision' for Mahāyānists and an all-seeing bringer of light to dispel 'the blinding darkness' of delusion.[7] In Mahāyāna Buddhism, this light of wisdom is associated in profound ways with the figure of the Mother.

In many ancient world religions and cultures, wisdom manifests as the divine mother and sacred feminine. These manifestations include Sarasvatī (Hinduism), Gaia, Athena, Mêtis (Paganism), Sophia (Hellenism, Platonism, Gnosticism, Christianity), Amaterasu, Benzaiten (Shinto, Buddhism), Isis, Seshat (Egyptian religion), Shekhinah (Kabbalah) and Wisdom/Chokmâh (Judaism). Indian and Tibetan Mahāyāna lineages exalt *Prajñāpāramitā*, the personified deity of transcendental wisdom, who is known by her distinctive epithets 'Mother of Perfect Wisdom' and 'Luminous Mother of All Buddhas'. *Prajñāpāramitā* is the primordial wisdom figure who became the 'ancestress and prototype' of a pantheon of Buddhist female deities, such as Tārā (Tibet) and Guānyīn (China).[8] *Prajñā* is a Sanskrit word that translates as 'the sharpening of intellect' and 'the mind's process

---

[7] *The Perfection of Wisdom in Eight Thousand Lines and its Verse Summary*, trans. Edward Conze (Sri Satguru Publications, 1973), 135.

[8] Miranda Shaw, *Buddhist Goddesses of India* (Princeton UP, 2006), 185.

174] *Marguerite A. Tassi*

of attaining clear seeing/knowing'. To add *pāramitā* ('perfection') to *prajñā* renders *Prajñāpāramitā* the supreme vehicle and antidote to suffering.[9] She is the great mother who carries her children across the ocean of suffering to *nirvāṇa*, the ultimate state of liberation from the cyclic world. The journey from suffering on 'the near shore' to liberation on 'the other shore' involves the awakening of the heart-mind (*bodhicitta*) and realisation, or the dawning of wisdom in the mind. The feminine noun *prajñā* (*pāramitā* is also feminine) expresses wisdom's gender and, more precisely, as Miranda Shaw observes, 'deep metaphorical resonances between motherhood and the matrix of wisdom and reality she represents'.[10] *Prajñāpāramitā*'s epithets reveal her liberating fecundity: she is womb of all buddhas and *bodhisattvas*, birth-giver of enlightenment, nurse and instructress who illuminates and brings to fruition the essence of the Buddhist path. The radicalness of this philosophy, as Shaw argues, lies in its 'premise that the birth-giver is greater than the one who is born'.[11]

Wisdom's maternal manifestation is elusive and subtle in the world of *King Lear*. There are no biological mothers in the play, yet Lear's daughters function behaviourally and symbolically as mothers in their relationship to Lear—the eldest two in an aggressive display of power and status and the youngest in a transcendent, salvific role.[12] The Fool

---

[9] My understanding of the etymology and meaning of *prajñāpāramitā* has been informed by Greg Seton's linguistic explanation in conversation with Elizabeth Mattis Namgyel, 'Unlocking the Meaning of Prajnaparamita', Open Question Conversations, The Middle Way Initiative, June 18, 2022. The Sanskrit can be translated as follows: *pra*, 'supreme, best'; *jñā*, 'awareness, understanding, knowledge'; *pārama*, 'supreme, perfect'; *pāram*, 'the other shore'; *i*, 'to go'; *tā*, 'state of'. Seton clarifies that the Sanskrit verb 'to go' also means 'to know', thus *prajñāpāramitā* conveys a sense of the mind's movement in coming to know the nature of reality.

[10] Shaw, *Buddhist Goddesses*, 167.

[11] Shaw, *Buddhist Goddesses*, 187.

[12] Feminist interpretations of *King Lear* have included psychoanalytic readings of the absent mother/wife and Lear's fear of 'the mother'. See, particularly, the interpretations of Coppélia Kahn and Janet Adelman, who focus on Lear's pathological fantasy of maternal contamination, his destructive vision of Goneril and Regan as monstrous mother-daughters and Cordelia as sacrificial mother-daughter. Coppélia Kahn, 'The Absent Mother in *King Lear*', in *Rewriting the Renaissance: The Discourses of Sexual Difference in Early Modern Europe*, ed. Margaret W. Ferguson, Maureen Quilligan and Nancy J. Vickers (U of Chicago

Prajñāpāramitā and the Buddhist Path of Wisdom   [175

chastises Lear for his folly in creating punitive mothers out of his eldest daughters: 'thou madest thy daughters thy mothers . . . [and] gavest them the rod and puttest down thine own breeches' (1.4.138–40). Lear acts like a 'child of spleen' (1.4.244), full of rage and curses, which rightly prompts his mother-daughters to chide him 'for want of wisdom' (1.4.306). Yet when they drop their masks of filial piety, they act without wisdom themselves, becoming vindictive and triggering cruelty and shame in Lear. Lear curses Goneril with sterility or a tormenting child, which karmically calls forth her '[s]harp-toothed unkindness'. He feels her unkindness like 'a vulture' 'tied' to his heart, constricting blood flow and suffocating him (2.2.299, 298). As terror of 'the mother' threatens his mental and physical health, Lear can barely control his hysteria, crying out,

> O, how this mother swells up toward my heart!
> *Histerica passio* down, thou climbing sorrow;
> Thy element's below.—Where is this daughter? (2.2.225–7)

Lear's startling association of the maternal with a bodily disease known in Shakespeare's time as *hysterica passio* (Greek; *hystera* means 'womb') reveals his primal fear of the non-nurturing female, manifesting literally in Goneril and Regan, and psychosomatically within himself as a rising, 'suffocating maternal womb'.[13] His delusional fantasy transposes the natural or 'kind' place for gestation in a woman's body to his own body as a 'disease' in his 'flesh' (2.2.387).

Despite the terrifying misogynistic vision of the mother as bodily disease, Lear possesses an alternative vision of the mother as a beloved figure, deeply rooted in lovingkindness, nurturance and sanctity. He reveals this hidden, intuitive feeling for the mother when he invokes 'her kind nursery' (1.1.122) and 'shrine' (2.2.295). The latter image comes spontaneously to Lear's mind when he seeks a glad

---

P, 1986), 33–49; Janet Adelman, *Suffocating Mothers: Fantasies of Maternal Origin in Shakespeare's Plays, 'Hamlet' to 'The Tempest'* (Routledge, 1992). More in line with this chapter's argument is Steven Shankman's Buddhist reading of the positive connotations of 'the mother'. '(m)Other Power: Shin Buddhism, Levinas, *King Lear*', in *From Ritual to Romance and Beyond: Comparative Literature and Comparative Religious Studies*, ed. Manfred Schmeling and Hans-Joachim Backe (Königshausen & Neumann, 2011), 229–37.

[13] Adelman, *Suffocating Mothers*, 114.

welcome from Regan. He exclaims passionately that he would think her mother an adulteress if the daughter lacked gladness (*muditā*, for Buddhists, or rejoicing in the well-being of others) and would 'divorce' himself from her 'mother's shrine' (2.2.295). Regan's gladness dries up quickly and with her displeasure comes Lear's promised 'divorce' from the mother's sacred 'shrine' and his final estrangement from all three mother-daughters. Unkind Goneril and Regan stand in solidarity against their child-like father, ordering Gloucester to shut his doors, denying him essential human needs—dignity, shelter and compassion. Yet Lear has done much the same in banishing Cordelia, and it is she, his youngest mother-daughter, who possesses the curative maternal womb. Now more elusive than ever, Cordelia's kind nursery is the sublime alternative to the tormenting, suffocating womb of Lear's diseased, ignorant mind and imbalanced body. What Lear intuits in Cordelia is the maternal womb of protective, life-giving warmth, 'dear shelter' of the gods (1.1.179).

Looking at the function of Cordelia from the perspective of a non-Western wisdom tradition reveals the transcendent value of 'the mother' not as a biological/familial/social figure mired in a patriarchal system, but rather as a compassionate, salvific presence who addresses the spiritual health of the heart-mind. In the revelatory light of Mahāyāna, Cordelia appears as an emanation of Mother *Prajñāpāramitā*, a Buddhist Sophia, who is the 'shelter, defence and protection' of the wisdom-seeker, to echo the words of *The Perfection of Wisdom in Eight Thousand Lines*.[14] In meditation, Buddhist practitioners devote themselves to *Prajñāpāramitā* as the feminine principle of wisdom teachings, but there is also, especially in Tibetan Buddhism, the practice of regarding all living beings, male and female, human and non-human, as 'mother sentient beings', as if they may have been one's mother in a previous life. This morally efficacious mindset is possible given the Buddhist belief in rebirth, which broadens the horizon of life well beyond the bounds of a single lifetime. As Lauren Shufran observes, perceiving 'motherness' in all beings activates our natural 'impulse . . . to repay that kindness', to 'become deeply invested' in the 'welfare' of all sentient beings.[15] The kindness

---

[14] *Perfection of Wisdom*, 147.

[15] Lauren Shufran, *The Buddha and the Bard: Where Shakespeare's Stage Meets Buddhist Scriptures* (Mandala, 2022), 157.

Prajñāpāramitā and the Buddhist Path of Wisdom [177

harboured in Cordelia is essential to her 'motherness', as is her desire for the welfare of others, particularly Lear. Yet the perfection of motherness begins and ends with *prajñā*, the mind's capacity to cut through illusion. Cordelia/Wisdom's stance in the face of Lear's ignorance is to 'Love and be silent' (1.1.60). When forced to speak, she utters the provocative word 'Nothing', which sets the wheel of *dharma*, the wisdom teachings of the Buddha, turning antidotally against the wheel of *saṃsāra*, the world of illusory appearances perpetuated by greed, anger and ignorance.[16]

Similar to Western traditions of apophatic theology, which strive to understand God by what He is not, Cordelia's 'Nothing' teaches wisdom through negation and disruption of ordinary conceptual mind. The verbal exchanges involving ignorance and wisdom initiated by Cordelia in the play's first scene are taken up later by her proxy, the Fool, who uses his mirror-like wit to show Lear his mind's stubborn resistance to seeing its destructive proclivities. 'Nothing' is a provocation reminiscent of medieval Chan/Zen enlightenment narratives and paradoxes known as *kōans*.[17] As Lex Hixon observes, the 'inner affinity between the *Prajnaparamita Sutra* and the later approaches of Mahamudra and Zen is particularly striking'.[18] Eastern apophatic approaches to wisdom cut through the veil of appearances—worldly comforts and 'accommodations', illusions and mental projections of ego—until there is nothing left to cling to. The ritual rejection and physical removal of Cordelia, an embodiment of the wise heart, from Lear's presence initiates Lear's journey into wisdom, which will be marked by self-indulgent venting and a persistent rejection of experience, eventually wearing down into a painful, complete kenosis, or self-emptying. Lear's anguished image of himself 'bound / Upon a

---

[16] In his translation of *The Perfection of Wisdom in Eight Thousand Lines*, Lex Hixon, *Mother of the Buddhas: Meditation on the Prajnaparamita Sutra* (Quest Books, 1993), 96, writes: 'It is Mother Prajnaparamita alone who turns the wheel of true teaching.'

[17] The Japanese word *kōan* literally means 'public case'. Unhae Park Langis analyses Cordelia's 'Nothing' in relation to a famous Chan *kōan*, the dialogue between Emperor Wu and the legendary Buddhist monk Bodhidharma. 'Humankindness: *King Lear* and the Suffering, Wisdom, and Compassion within Buddhist Interbeing', in *Literature and Religious Experience: Beyond Belief and Unbelief*, ed. Matthew J. Smith and Caleb D. Spencer (Bloomsbury, 2022), 209–26 (216).

[18] Hixon, *Mother of the Buddhas*, 7.

178]   *Marguerite A. Tassi*

wheel of fire' (4.6.39–40) reveals not only a sense of Purgatorial or Ixion-like punishment, but also an experience of the burning process of surrender to transcendent wisdom, as one illusion after another is ruthlessly burnt away. Once his rage is fully extinguished on this 'path of burning and destroying', as Anam Thubten calls the Buddha's path,[19] he comes unbound in madness and then finally surrenders to sleep. When he awakens literally and spiritually, Lear finds Cordelia has returned as the healing presence of feminine wisdom and love, the matrix of grace welcoming him to her 'kind nursery'.

Mother Prajñāpāramitā, *the* Heart Sūtra *and the Mahāyāna* Bodhisattva *Ideal*

While Buddhism is based on the four noble truths,[20] which initiated the first turning of the wheel of *dharma*, the Mahāyāna movement gave rise to a second turning with the *Prajñāpāramitā sūtras*.[21] The earliest text was most likely *The Perfection of Wisdom in Eight Thousand Lines*, but a later highly condensed version known as the *Heart Sūtra* superseded this and other longer texts in popularity and renown. Revered as the *hṛdaya*, or 'heart essence', of Mahāyāna, the *Heart Sūtra* teaches the spiritual path as a *via negativa*, a self-emptying through a *kōan*-like

---

[19] Anam Thubten, *No Self, No Problem: Awakening to our True Nature* (Snow Lion, 2009), 112.

[20] After his enlightenment, the Buddha gave his first teaching on what has become known as the 'four noble truths': the truth of suffering; the truth of its causes in worldly cravings and self-attachment; the truth of its cessation; and the truth of the path leading out of suffering (the path of wisdom, virtue and mental discipline). The realisation and application of these truths renders one 'noble'.

[21] The *Prajñāpāramitā* literature of Buddhism is vast, as is the commentarial literature, which has elucidated its meanings over the centuries. The original thirty-eight sacred scriptures, known as *sūtras* (Sanskrit, 'rules', 'threads', 'strings', from the root *siv*, meaning 'to sew'), contain hundreds of thousands of verses dating between c. 100 BCE and c. 550 CE. Prior to written scripture, *sūtra* was a descriptive word for how the oral teachings were strung together with common themes; later, the word described how the books' palm leaves were sewn together. These ancient Indian wisdom texts are as significant to world religion as the Hebrew Bible, the Gospels and the Qur'an. Their distinctive contribution lies in the profound view of *śūnyatā* and the moral exemplar of the *bodhisattva*.

Prajñāpāramitā and the Buddhist Path of Wisdom   [179

series of nos.[22] The effect of daily chanting of this poetic devotional text, like the repeated singing of the Psalter in Shakespeare's time, is incantatory, leading to intuitive insight into the illusoriness of worldly appearances. The process of awakening through negation can be felt in this extract:

> [I]n emptiness, there is no form, no feeling, no perception, no formation, no consciousness; no eye, no ear, no nose, no tongue, no body, no mind; no appearance, no sound, no smell, no taste, no touch, no phenomena, no quality of sight and so on, until no quality of thought and no quality of mind-consciousness . . .[23]

Two verses in the *Heart Sūtra* serve as memorable distillations of Mahāyāna wisdom, illuminating the emptiness view and framing the cascade of nos. First, there is the famous formulation: 'Form is emptiness. Emptiness is form. Emptiness is no other than form; form is no other than emptiness.'[24] Form refers to the relative dimension of dependently arisen appearances, and emptiness refers to the ultimate reality of phenomena. The concept of emptiness (Sanskrit, *śūnyatā*; *śūnya* means 'empty', 'nothing', 'zero') can be misunderstood to mean a nihilistic void, but *śūnyatā* is far from nihilism; rather, the term refers to the open-dimensional nature of all phenomena, free of singular, static and permanent existence. In perceiving the union of emptiness and appearance, it becomes apparent that forms appear vividly to the senses, yet are not solid, frozen entities existing independently in time and space; change, movement, interrelatedness and ephemerality define the nature of all forms and of reality itself. The emptiness view counteracts conceptual fabrications the mind projects onto the world of forms. Second, there is the *Sūtra*'s culmination in a mantra expressing the emptiness teaching as a devotional invocation to the Great Mother *Prajñāpāramitā*: '*Gaté Gaté Paragaté Parasamgaté Bodhi Svaha*' ('Gone, gone, gone beyond, gone far beyond to the

---

[22] Karl Brunnhölzl makes this revealing connection between *kōans* and the *Sūtra*'s enigmatic negations in *Heart Attack Sūtra*, 9.

[23] Anam Thubten, *The Fragrance of Emptiness: A Commentary on the Heart Sutra* (Dharmata, 2018), xvi.

[24] Thubten, *Fragrance of Emptiness*, xvi.

180] *Marguerite A. Tassi*

other shore, to awakened wisdom, so may it be').[25] The mantra implicitly distils the five paths of awakening within the greater Mahāyāna spiritual path: accumulation, engagement, seeing, meditation and no-more-learning.[26] *Paragaté*, the path of seeing, is the transformative stage of insight where the eye of *prajñā* opens, 'gone beyond' dualism and delusion to perceive reality directly, or non-conceptually.

The progressive nos of the *Heart Sūtra*, like the repeated 'nothings' of *King Lear*, are aimed at opening the eye of wisdom to emptiness, which is the view that sees there is nothing to be grasped anywhere in the ever-changing phenomena of mind and world. Significantly, in the Mahāyāna, emptiness is the 'symbolic mother' and 'feminine principle', which pervades the nature of reality.[27] Because everything is empty or dependently arisen, there is rich potential for dynamic, vital forms to be born out of the feminine principle. Thus, emptiness is meaningfully captured in the symbols of the womb and the figure zero. Karl Brunnhölzl explains,

> in India the circle of *śūnya*, or zero, means 'fullness', 'completeness', or 'wholeness'. In the same way, 'emptiness' does not mean 'nothingness', but rather 'fullness' in the sense of full potential—anything can happen in emptiness and because of emptiness.[28]

Bringing this understanding to Shakespeare's Globe theatre, we can see the Wooden O as a space of pure potentiality in which 'forms are momentary manifestations in time and space'.[29] In light of Zen, in which '"nothing" is the key word', expressive of emptiness rather than nothingness, the Globe is a 'Theatre of Nothing', like the Japanese Noh theatre, consisting only of weather, a bare stage and 'Shakespeare's words, words, words'.[30]

---

[25] My translation. I have followed Seton's linguistic analysis in Namgyel and Seton, 'Unlocking the Meaning', and Brunnhölzl, *Heart Attack Sūtra*, 158–62.

[26] Thubten, *Fragrance of Emptiness*, 208, 210–11.

[27] Judith Simmer-Brown, *Dakini's Warm Breath: The Feminine Principle in Tibetan Buddhism* (Shambhala, 2001), 81–9.

[28] Brunnhölzl, *Heart Attack Sūtra*, 13.

[29] Mu Soeng, *The Heart of the Universe: Exploring the Heart Sutra* (Wisdom, 2010), 42.

[30] Yoshio Arai, 'Shakespeare in Japan's Zen Philosophy: The Plays of Nothing at the Theatre of Nothing', *Ilha do Desterro: A Journal of English Language, Literatures in English and Cultural Studies* 49 (July–December 2005): 143–57 (143–4).

Prajñāpāramitā and the Buddhist Path of Wisdom   [181

Such a transcendent vision of emptiness/wisdom/nothing, however, requires grounding in the relative world where skilful means and tender compassion are needed to minister to those who suffer. Departing from the earlier Buddhist model of a predominately male *arhat*, who strove for *nirvāṇa* only for himself, Mahāyānists made a spiritual advance in imagining the *bodhisattva* (Sanskrit, 'enlightened or awakening being') as one who is 'male or female, monastic or lay',[31] dedicated to liberating all suffering beings from *saṃsāra* before entering into *nirvāṇa* themselves. The Perfection of Wisdom *sūtras* were 'champions of the new paradigm of the bodhisattva',[32] celebrating the heroic compassion of such beings who 'abide by means of transcendent wisdom'.[33] Female *bodhisattvas* (*Prajñāpāramitā* as *bodhisattvadevi*) reflect wisdom's maternal capacity for boundless compassion.

In the *Heart Sūtra*, it is not the Buddha who teaches, but rather the *bodhisattva* Avalokiteśvara, a figure who appears in both male and female forms in Asian religious iconography. The *Sūtra* depicts the Buddha sitting in deep meditative silence with a gathering of monks, nuns and *bodhisattvas* at Vulture Peak in India. The Buddha's silence powerfully demonstrates his numinous wisdom while Avalokiteśvara's words convey the truth of ultimate reality. The *bodhisattva*'s attitude of *bodhicitta* moves him to call out to his student, the monk Śāriputra, 'just like a mother calling out to her only child', to answer his spiritual needs and to awaken *prajñā*.[34] Avalokiteśvara's name in Sanskrit identifies him as the 'lord who gazes down', seeing the world with eyes of compassion. Iconographical representations of Avalokiteśvara and other *bodhisattvas* often depict them as 'thousand armed' with an eye on the palm of every hand. 'Boundless suffering is met with boundless seeing, boundless response,' writes Ejo McMullen. 'This is the bodhisattva's activity.'[35] *Bodhisattvas* see the relative world as resplendent with spiritual opportunity and practise six 'perfections' (*pāramitās*):

---

[31] Soeng, *Heart of the Universe*, 77.

[32] Soeng, 77.

[33] Thubten, *Fragrance of Emptiness*, xvi.

[34] Dosung Yoo, *Thunderous Silence: A Formula for Ending Suffering* (Wisdom, 2013), 69.

[35] Ejo McMullen, 'Your Whole Body Is Hands and Eyes', *Lion's Roar*, May 16, 2022. https://www.lionsroar.com/your-whole-body-is-hands-and-eyes/

generosity, moral discipline, patience, diligent effort, concentration and wisdom. Wisdom, the greatest of the perfections, infuses these core virtues with her generative energy.

Lear's 'imperfections of long-engrafted condition' (1.1.291–2) are notable in relation to the Mahāyāna perfections. According to Buddhist karmic ethics, causes and conditions contribute to the 'engrafting' of mental and emotional habits; without self-knowledge and moral intentionality, individuals are driven from one life to the next by the vagaries of their own ungoverned minds. When Goneril and Regan confer about their father's 'condition', they diagnose him accurately:

> 'Tis the infirmity of his age; yet, he hath ever but slenderly known himself . . . [T]hen must we look from his age to receive not alone the imperfections of long-engrafted condition, but therewithal the unruly waywardness that infirm and choleric years bring with them.
> (1.1.288–9, 291–4)

Because Lear's deeply rooted habits of mind have formed without the foundation of wisdom, he is subject to ungovernable eruptions of pride, wrath and shame. In 'the infirmity of his age', his mental condition worsens and in his ignorance he becomes the cause of great suffering to himself and others. Suffering, as the play poignantly demonstrates, gives rise to the profound need for *bodhisattvic* characters—Kent, Edgar, the Fool and, most urgently, Cordelia.[36]

Cordelia's Nothing Kōan

The Buddha's first teaching after his enlightenment focused on suffering and the path out of suffering. 'Suffering' is the most common translation of *dukkha*, the original Pāli word used by the Buddha, but other translations bring out nuances in the concept: 'dissatisfaction',

---

[36] In the parallel story of Gloucester and his sons, Edgar appears as a *bodhisattva*, 'pregnant to good pity' (4.5.216). Elsewhere, I examine Edgar's *bodhisattvic* journey, which begins with ritual self-emptying, 'Edgar I nothing am' (2.2.178), and leads to adoption of a salvific role with his despairing father. Marguerite A. Tassi, 'The Way of the *Bodhisattva*: A Buddhist Understanding of *King Lear*', *Critical Survey* 35.2 (2023): 80–91.

Prajñāpāramitā and the Buddhist Path of Wisdom   [183

'disease', 'sorrow', 'flawed', 'awry', 'lack of peace' and 'existential anguish'. All of these meanings resonate strongly with Shakespeare's depiction of Lear. As Karen Armstrong observes, 'The Buddha had always seen old age as a symbol of the *dukkha* which afflicted all mortal beings'; in his later teachings, he focused more specifically on 'the vulnerability of the old' who are preyed upon even by their own children in a ruthless, violent 'world where all sense of sacredness is lost'.[37] The play's opening scene expresses the old king's sense of *dukkha* as he attempts to empty himself of worldly cares so he can '[u]nburdened crawl toward death' (1.1.39). 'Crawl' captures a poignant sense of ageing with the shadow figure of the baby anticipating care in the maternal nursery. Lear's figurative language reveals a truth he cannot see yet, that he is the aged child/spiritual aspirant seeking its wise, loving, symbolic mother, and that the unburdening process will involve far more than dispensing with earthly property, powers and wealth. It will take shocks to his physical well-being and injuries to his ego to get the spiritual process going, to make him aware of further unburdenings, which require the failure of every strategy he might try to accommodate his worldly self. Steven Shankman points out that Lear's name, derived from the Middle English *lere* and Old English *gelaer*, means 'empty' or (as the *OED* confirms) 'having no burden or load'.[38] Of significance, as well, are the Old and Middle English verbal forms *laeran* and *leren*, which are related to instruction and guidance. Lear's very name possesses the wisdom of a pun, pointing the way to a dramatic arc and spiritual path in which self-emptying is the necessary condition for learning.

Instruction in wisdom comes unexpectedly from Lear's youngest daughter, Cordelia, who emerges out of the shadows of courtly drama with an uncompromising fierceness and a diamond-like precision in thought and speech. Her karmic relationship with Lear becomes evident as she displays a magnanimity he lacks; she reveals herself in a Buddhist disposition as the knowing presence of *Prajñāpāramitā*. Her first words are delivered as an aside in response to her sister

---

[37] Karen Armstrong, *Buddha* (Viking Penguin, 2001), 164.

[38] Shankman, '(m)Other Power', 230. Following the etymology of Lear's name, Shankman observes, 'Lear tries to empty himself of his kingship, but the emptying keeps getting filled up by the attachments of an ego driven more by self-power (what Shin Buddhists refer to as jiriki) than by Other Power (tariki)' (230).

184] *Marguerite A. Tassi*

Goneril's grandiloquent profession of love for their father-king: 'What shall Cordelia speak? Love and be silent' (1.1.60). Invoking her own name calls attention to an allegorical dimension of her presence and purpose. Deriving from Latin *cor/cordia* and French *coeur*, meaning 'heart', and Greek *dēlos*, meaning 'clear', 'plainly evident due to inner perception', 'manifest',[39] Cordelia's name can be translated as 'manifest heart'. She names herself again in another aside in response to her second sister's profession of love, this time confident in love's unspeakable profundity: 'Then poor Cordelia— / And yet not so, since I am sure my love's / More ponderous than my tongue' (1.1.74–6). Resonating with the *Heart Sūtra*, Cordelia's silence, like the Buddha's, is a powerful manifestation of *prajñā*'s sureness. Yet the worldly conditions of her father-king's court press upon her the need to express wisdom through speech, much as Avalokiteśvara does in the *Sūtra*.

With Lear's command, 'Speak', Cordelia breaks her silence and says, 'Nothing', which opens up a provocative exchange:

Lear	what can you say to draw
	A third more opulent than your sisters? Speak.
Cordelia	Nothing, my lord.
Lear	Nothing?
Cordelia	Nothing.
Lear	Nothing will come of nothing. Speak again.
Cordelia	Unhappy that I am, I cannot heave
	My heart into my mouth. I love your majesty
	According to my bond, no more nor less. (1.1.83–91)

Responding directly to Lear's 'what can you say', Cordelia's 'Nothing' reveals magnanimity in her refusal to make love transactional; at the same time, she uses language paradoxically to expose truth. This word, like all that Cordelia says, functions powerfully to teach, like the words of the compassionate Avalokiteśvara, in order to awaken wisdom. Like a swift figurative slice of *prajñā*'s sword, Cordelia's

---

[39] 'δῆλος', in Joseph Henry Thayer, *Thayer's Greek Lexicon* (American Book Company, 1889), Internet Archive. https://archive.org/details/greekenglishlexi00grimuoft/mode/2up

Prajñāpāramitā and the Buddhist Path of Wisdom [185

'Nothing' cuts through Lear's delusion, exposing the interior hollowness of her sisters' rhetoric. As Karl Brunnhölzl indicates, *prajñā* is often depicted iconographically as a double-bladed, flaming sword. *Prajñā* is 'threatening to our ego and to our cherished belief systems since it undermines our very notion of reality and the reference points upon which we build our world'.[40] Importantly, *prajñā* 'also includes the quality of compassion',

> but it is a somewhat merciless kind of compassion in that it cuts through wherever it is needed ... [I]t cuts through what needs to be exposed or what we need to let go of. In brief, prajñā questions everything that we are, everything that we think, everything that we perceive, and everything that we value.[41]

Prajñā shines the spotlight on the main actor, the ego, but the ego is, paradoxically, 'the blind spot in the show'.[42]

Accordingly, Goneril and Regan indulge Lear's blindness, playing out their karmic relationship with him. They rhetorically mimic wisdom's silence in saying they 'love ... more than words can wield the matter' (1.1.53). Yet it is clear that they 'wield the matter' in the worldly way of self-interested courtiers. By contrast, Cordelia's image of heaving her heart into her mouth suggests a terrible labour involved in speaking truth, the panting of breath in the chest and the forcing upward of a vital organ. This compact physical image of the distressed breathing and unnatural dislodging of the heart throws into relief the terrible ease with which her sisters speak insincere words. Pressed to speak, Cordelia chooses words with a discerning rhetoric of balance and bond, which recognises the natural duties of love between parent and child. The underlying subtle point belongs to absolute *prajñā*, however, which conveys the impossibility of calculating love, hinted at with cutting irony when Cordelia says she gives 'no more nor less' (1.1.91). She then expands upon this idea, speaking more and less than Lear wants to hear, with notions of 'right fit' and 'half' (1.1.95, 100). The mirror of this subtle teaching reflects how immeasurable qualities like lovingkindness cannot be expressed truthfully through

---

[40] Brunnhölzl, *Heart Attack Sūtra*, 25.
[41] Brunnhölzl, 26.
[42] Brunnhölzl, 27.

186] *Marguerite A. Tassi*

a flattering rhetoric of 'all'. Paradoxically, the rich silence implicit in 'nothing' expresses the true nature of a loving bond.

Cordelia is frank, precise and true, yet her wisdom seems enigmatic because her student's mind is clouded by ignorance and passion. 'But goes thy heart with this?' Lear asks uncomprehendingly. 'Ay, my good lord,' Cordelia responds. 'So young and so untender?' he persists. 'So young, my lord, and true,' she asserts (1.1.102–5). Lear perceives Cordelia as untender only because she strips away pretence and teaches unaccustomed truth to egoic power. While some Western scholars may criticise Cordelia's bluntness as harsh, preferring a tactic of gentle persuasion, a Buddhist audience can see *Prajñāpāramitā*'s attempt to clear away Lear's mental obscurations. She means to slice through Lear's sense of absolute self and sovereignty.

Lear's response reveals a stubborn refusal to comprehend Cordelia's wisdom, which leads to a wrathful declaration of estrangement. She who was known to be Lear's 'best object, / The argument of [his] praise, balm of [his] age, / The best, the dear'st', as France attests (1.1.211–13), is now rendered 'a stranger' to Lear's heart and self (1.1.113). Even so, Lear cannot help but declare his love for this bold daughter—'I loved her most'—and betray his hidden intention to 'set [his] rest / On her kind nursery' (1.1.121–2). By Lear's own confession, he loves Wisdom and desires the abode of her kind care. The past tense 'loved' indicates the sharp hurt his ego has just suffered and the distance he has suddenly created from the very 'rest' he desires. *Nursery*, *rest* and *kind* are multivalent words whose meanings resonate poignantly throughout the play. *Nursery* refers not only to a house's designated place for nurturance and care of children, but also, according to the *OED*, to places in nature and other environments where desirable qualities, attributes, skills and growth are fostered.[43] Lear intuits his need for such a place in his vulnerable old age, yet he has tried to control his entrance therein. What is obscured from his view is how Cordelia will serve as his 'ultimate teacher—the beacon, torch, and instructor' of 'liberating insight' and wisdom.[44]

Lear's phrase 'to set my rest' not only reveals his desire to take up residence for the remainder of his days in Cordelia's 'nursery', but also implicitly expresses the stakes involved in such a manoeuvre.

---

[43] 'nursery, n. and adj.', *OED* online.
[44] Shaw, *Buddhist Goddesses*, 169.

Prajñāpāramitā and the Buddhist Path of Wisdom   [187

The phrase is taken from a popular Renaissance card game called 'primero' in which 'to set one's rest' meant to bet all of one's reserves on a big win.[45] In his division of the kingdom, Lear stakes his all, gambling his entire well-being, his heart and mind, his earthly and spiritual care, on 'our joy', Cordelia (1.1.80), the most desired win. As the *OED* clarifies, the stakes in primero were 'kept in reserve by a player' and 'were agreed on at the beginning of the game, and on the loss of which the player was out'.[46] Lear is Primero, poised to control his world—daughters, dowries, kingdom, sovereignty and old age—as if all of it were a game to win with conditions he can impose. The set-up of the game, however, reveals that Lear has suppressed an awareness of the possibility of loss by reserving the authority and power to answer his own question—'Which of you shall we say doth love us most' (1.1.49)—and to distribute property and goods as he sees fit. He declares that he will 'retain / The name and all th'addition to a king' (1.1.133–4). In his ignorance, Lear poises himself to lose the game he has orchestrated, as his bond with Cordelia is not a thing to be lost or won.

Lear's desire to win what can only be given freely reflects a profound lack of moral clarity and discernment regarding love and, furthermore, the question of how to bow out of his worldly affairs with grace and magnanimity. In his anger (the most destructive passion in Buddhist teachings), he renounces a sacred bond of nature with Cordelia, disavowing 'paternal care, / Propinquity, and property of blood' (1.1.111–12). With a revealing locution, he swears, 'So be my grave my peace as here I give / Her father's heart from her' (1.1.123–4). *Give* is a deeply ironic word to use for what is a theft and deprivation of the heart's natural generosity. Lear fails to see how he has set up the causes and conditions for tremendous suffering. Lacking the eye of *prajñā*, he sees the proceedings with his daughters through the egoic lens of pride, ignorance and gamesmanship, denying the challenge Cordelia offers to shine a light on his mind's proclivities. Thus, he proclaims, 'we / Have no such daughter, nor shall ever see / That face of hers again' (1.1.260–2). His wilful estrangement from Cordelia underscores his estrangement from wisdom, the feminine face of enlightenment. Once

---

[45] 'primero, n.' and 'rest, n.3', *OED* online.
[46] 'rest, n.3', *OED* online.

188]   *Marguerite A. Tassi*

the terrible allegory of the banished heart is set to run its course, Lear will find that losing the face of Cordelia drives him further into existential anguish (*dukkha*), where the world appears as a frightening mirror of his own disturbed mind rather than a mirror of wisdom.

Failing on an ontological level to recognise the deeper truth of Cordelia's Nothing, Lear's 'Nothing will come of nothing' asserts a pagan view at odds with Christian theology (*creatio ex nihilo*) and Buddhist wisdom alike.[47] Cordelia's teaching on nothing will come back to haunt him with the tough spirit of a *kōan*. In the *kōan* tradition of Chan/Zen Buddhism, emphasis is placed on the teacher's unorthodox means of provoking the student's awakening to the nature of reality: shouts and blows, question-answer sessions, and the use of paradoxical statements, dialogues and vignettes. Such means are used to disrupt rational thought and turn the mind towards enlightenment. As Zenkei Shibayama observes, 'Etymologically the term *koan* means "the place where the truth is". In actual training its role is to smash up our dualistic consciousness and open our inner spiritual eye to a new vista.'[48] Cordelia's Nothing *kōan* acts upon Lear in just such a manner and is reminiscent particularly of the Zen student's first *kōan* known as 'Jōshū's Dog', or 'Mu'.[49] In the thirteenth-century classic Japanese collection of forty-eight cases called the *Gateless Gate* (*Mumonkan*), 'Mu' is presented this way: a monk came to the great master Jōshū and asked him, 'Does a dog have buddha nature or not?' Jōshū said, 'Mu.' As Shaku Soen indicates, '*Mu* is written with the character which means "No, not have"'; the word

---

[47] The pagan philosophical doctrine of *ex nihilo nihil fit* was first articulated by Parmenides, then discussed by Aristotle and Lucretius. See *Parmenidean Fragments*, 1–19, trans. John Burnet, in *Early Greek Philosophy*, 2nd ed. (Adam and Charles Black, 1908), 196–203, Lexundria: A Digital Library of Classical Antiquity, https://www.lexundria.com/parm_frag/1-19/b; Aristotle, *Physics* I.8.191a 30–1; *De Rerum Natura* 1.148–56. I am grateful to Unhae Langis for these references.

[48] Zenkei Shibayama, 'Joshu's Mu', trans. Sumiko Kudo, in *The Book of Mu: Essential Writings on Zen's Most Important Koan*, ed. James Ishmael Ford and Melissa Myozen Blacker (Wisdom, 2011), 83–93 (85).

[49] For a reading of Shakespeare's *Timon of Athens* in light of Jōshū's Dog, see Lisa Myōbun Freinkel, 'Empson's Dog: Emptiness and Divinity in *Timon of Athens*', in *Shakespeare and Religion: Early Modern and Postmodern Perspectives*, ed. Ken Jackson and Arthur F. Marotti (U of Notre Dame P, 2011), 188–204.

Prajñāpāramitā and the Buddhist Path of Wisdom   [189

is also translated to mean 'nothing', 'non-' and simply 'no'.[50] 'Mu' startles its auditor with its emphatic negation, in part because the expected answer to the monk's question would be 'yes, he does'. The Buddha taught that all sentient beings (dogs included) are endowed with buddha nature, the primordial intelligence that poises the mind for enlightenment. Like Lear's question to his daughters, the monk's question begs other questions and the 'answer', which seems like a mystifying 'wrong answer', throws him off balance. 'Mu'/Nothing is a difficult 'turning word', perplexing and easy to misunderstand, uttered to direct the auditor's mind away from ego-centred thinking.

The 'Mu' *kōan* is itself known as the 'gateless gate', the paradoxical barrier which obstructs the mind until one can drop the ego and conceptual thought, 'pass through' and see with the eye of wisdom. Cordelia's 'Mu' *kōan* defies reason and convention, shining a light on the closed 'gate' of Lear's mind. But Wisdom's light cannot penetrate; there is no sudden enlightenment for Lear, only blinding wrath when he realises that his 'game of thrones' has been exposed by Cordelia. From one perspective, the game resembles the high-stakes gambling of primero, but from another, the exchange with Cordelia unfolds more subtly like a game of words, akin to literary games in the Chinese tradition from which *kōan* study derives.[51] Like a Chan/Zen student, Lear will find his mind goaded and puzzled by the singularly haunting word at the centre of this literary game—*nothing*. That word and its profound resonance will alter Lear's consciousness and confront him with his folly again and again. Similar to the Zen gate, Shakespeare uses the figure of the gate to refer to the head and, more specifically, the obstructed mind. Distressed over Goneril's ingratitude and his own ignorance, Lear cries out, 'O Lear, Lear, Lear! / Beat at this gate that let thy folly in / And thy dear judgement out' (1.4.232–4). 'Beating at the gate' is precisely the Zen master's spiritual function, both literally with swift kicks and beatings and figuratively in directing a student's mind towards enlightenment. Lear's arduous inner work

---

[50] Shaku Soen, 'Teisho on Joshu's Dog', trans. Victor Hori, in *Book of Mu*, 35–43 (35), and James Ishmael Ford and Melissa Myozen Blacker, Introduction to *Book of Mu*, 1–15 (1).

[51] This argument comes from the foremost scholar of *kōan* introspection, Rinzai Zen priest Victor Hori. See Ford and Blacker, Introduction to *Book of Mu*, 2–3.

with Cordelia's *kōan* begins early in the drama, yielding painful yet instructive moments of insight.

In Cordelia's absence, the Fool delivers his own renditions of the Nothing *kōan*, which beat at the gateless gate of Lear's mind, teaching proverbial wisdom through aphorisms, riddles and songs. 'I'll teach thee a speech,' he says to Lear and Kent. 'Have more than thou showst, / Speak less than thou knowest . . . Learn more than thou trowest, / Set less than thou throwest' (1.4.101, 104–5, 108–9). His instruction reflects the wise virtues of restraint, thrift and discerning knowledge. Lear's folly in gambling all ('setting his rest'), then showing his hand in the kingdom's uneven division, reveals his lack of such virtues. When Kent insists, 'This is nothing, fool' (1.4.114), the Fool turns to Lear with a needling challenge: 'Can you make no use of nothing, nuncle?' (1.4.116–17). Lear answers, as if by rote, with the classical formula from his disastrous exchange with Cordelia: 'Why no, boy. Nothing can be made out of nothing' (1.4.118). Exhibiting skilful means (*upāya*), the Fool uses sly humour to expose Lear's folly and school him in karmic consequences: 'Thou wast a pretty fellow when thou hadst no need to care for her frowning. Now thou art an O without a figure. I am better than thou art, now. I am a fool; thou art nothing' (1.4.157–9). This teaching is driven home swiftly when Goneril and Regan 'disquantity' (1.4.210) Lear's retinue to zero. While the older sisters pursue a heartless self-interest in stripping down their father, Cordelia and the Fool aim at illuminating the wisdom of the 'pregnant zero', as Joanna Macy calls *Prajñāpāramitā*.[52] Zero is 'pregnant' because it is full of potential and empty of all attachment. Lear must learn the painful wisdom of being an O without a 'figure', a social nothing in his own kingdom, as all the 'figures' that once amplified his royal condition fall away or are forcibly stripped from him.

Lear now has new, urgent questions about the very self he took to be solid, sovereign and knowable:

---

[52] Joanna Macy, *World as Lover, World as Self: Courage for Global Justice and Ecological Renewal*, 30th Anniversary Edition, ed. Stephanie Kaza (Parallax, 2021), 115–18.

Prajñāpāramitā and the Buddhist Path of Wisdom [191

Does any here know me? This is not Lear.
Does Lear walk thus, speak thus? Where are his eyes?
Either his notion weakens, his discernings
Are lethargied—ha, waking? 'Tis not so.
Who is it that can tell me who I am? (1.4.191–5)

Unhae Park Langis observes that Lear's 'questioning remarkably resembles the Buddhist chanting of the Heart Sutra, intended to instill no-self'.[53] In doubting the solidity of 'me', and detaching from his Lear-self with its distinctive body and afflictive thoughts, Lear is spiritually preparing for the Fool's answer to his questions: 'Lear's shadow' (1.4.196). Yet the knowledge of no intrinsic self is hard to bear, as Lear's bewildered, angry repetitions of 'nothing', 'not' and 'no' attest. To awaken his dormant wisdom, however, bearing suffering in the relative world is precisely what he needs. Moments of insight arise when the Fool, like a Zen master, relates instances to shake his student's mind out of the stickiness of ego. In one key exchange, seemingly absurd, he puts the question to Lear: why is the nose in the middle of the face? The answer suggests the keen sensory perception called up in wisdom's service: to keep the eyes on either side so that 'what a man cannot smell out, [he] may spy into' (1.5.20–1). With these words, Lear's mind is struck with a sudden realisation of his transgression against Cordelia, which flashes brightly like lightning streaking the night sky: 'I did her wrong' (1.5.22).

Lightning, thunder and 'wrathful skies' (3.2.42) in the natural world provoke protest and anguished rants from Lear, but more importantly insight and a softening of the heart. As the storm pummels his body, his heart-mind begins to change, and he spontaneously vows to practise the *pāramitā* of patience: 'No, I will be the pattern of all patience. / I will say nothing' (3.2.36–7). Cordelia's Nothing *kōan* has begun to touch him. In Act 3, before the hovel, Lear's compassion awakens with a dawning awareness of other beings' suffering. Lear speaks with newfound care for his fool: 'How dost, my boy? Art cold? / I am cold myself'; 'Poor fool and knave, I have one part in my heart / That's sorry yet for thee' (3.2.67–8, 71–2). 'In boy; go first,' he insists (3.4.26), in a radical dispensing of privilege

---

[53] Langis, 'Humankindness', 217.

192]   *Marguerite A. Tassi*

and hierarchy.[54] *Bodhicitta*'s quiet transformative power begins to uncover Lear's buddha nature. The 'one part' of his heart that feels for the suffering of one human being quickly grows more expansive to encompass '[p]oor naked wretches, wheresoe'er you are, / That bide the pelting of this pitiless storm' (3.4.28–9). He realises that the same 'contentious storm' which '[i]nvades' him 'to the skin' (3.4.6–7) drenches living beings both close and far—his fool, Kent and all houseless poor.

At the threshold of shelter, Lear crosses another threshold, from 'I am suffering' to 'There is suffering', realising the Buddha's first noble truth as a direct experience.[55] But there comes more—a heart-piercing insight: 'O, I have ta'en / Too little care of this' (3.4.32–3). 'Take physic, pomp,' he counsels himself. 'Expose thyself to feel what wretches feel' (3.3.33–4). He is becoming aware of his disease—indifference and ignorance—and discovers in the same moment a desire to cure it. The physic lies in his capacity to 'feel' for other living beings, which unites him with all 'wretches'. With this realisation comes a recognition of his capacity for generosity, magnanimity and justice: 'thou mayst shake the superflux to them / And show the heavens more just' (3.4.35–6). From the perspective of 'nothing', Lear experiences a genuine sense of moral agency and an aspiration to serve the well-being of others in the relative world of causes and conditions. At this moment, he enters through the gateless gate into the heart of Cordelia's *kōan*.

Eventually Lear's sanity, the final buffer between ego and nothing, is stripped away. Literally homeless, he finds an inner refuge which affords him a penetrating vision of reality. With the breakdown of ordinary cognition, Lear paradoxically sees better. His encounter with the blind Gloucester poignantly demonstrates the tough vulnerability of two old men who, when reduced to zero in worldly terms, are propelled to feel their way into a late-dawning wisdom. Lear, who formerly commanded love and speech, mocked forgiveness and called for vengeance, speaks in a language of realisations, of *kōans*

---

[54] Melvin Sterne regards the Fool in light of the Buddhist master as clown figure and 'agent of redemption'. The Fool 'turns Lear from madness to sanity' when he becomes the agent who gives rise to Lear's compassion. 'Shakespeare, Buddha, and King Lear', *Journal of Buddhist Ethics* 14 (2007): 129–52 (142).

Prajñāpāramitā and the Buddhist Path of Wisdom [193

and *sūtras* that affirm nothing: 'To say "ay" and "no" to everything that I said "ay" and "no" to was no good divinity,' he now understands (4.5.97–8), and 'They told me I was everything; 'tis a lie, I am not ague-proof' (4.5.102). What he and Gloucester both come to understand through brutal, raw experience is the unreliability of *saṃsāra*. They learn to embrace self-emptying as the path to wisdom. Lear's heart has become tender and open; he is now ready for Cordelia's 'kind nursery'.

Cordelia's Kind Nursery

From a Buddhist perspective, Cordelia's return to the kingdom can be understood as the return of *Prajñāpāramitā*, the *bodhisattvadevi*, to the *saṃsāric* world. Her boundless compassion sends her back to Lear to nurse his 'heart-struck injuries' (3.1.8). As Lex Hixon observes, '[B]odhisattvas live in tender solicitude for all beloved sentient beings ... Bodhisattvas themselves become Goddess Prajnaparamita's fully conscious expression.'[56] Cordelia's 'better way' is the *bodhisattva*'s way of wisdom, compassion and patience. When she hears of the inhumane treatment Lear received at the hands of Goneril and Regan, she weeps tears, which a gentleman describes to Kent '[a]s pearls from diamonds dropped' (Q: 17.20, 23). Her 'heavenly eyes' spill forth tears like 'holy water' (Q: 17.31). The sacred image of Cordelia's tears resembles the Buddhist symbol of the wish-fulfilling jewel (Sanskrit, *cintāmaṇi*), often depicted iconographically as a pearl held by Avalokiteśvara and other *bodhisattvas*. Symbol of the enlightened mind of compassion and wisdom, the pearl was thought to remove poverty, suffering and afflictions of the eyes.[57] In that vein, Cordelia's diamond eyes can be seen as metaphors for transcendent healing, like the miraculous diamonds of *Prajñāpāramitā*

---

[55] Similarly, Sterne interprets Lear's recognition of the relationship between his own suffering and others' suffering in light of the four noble truths, 143–4.

[56] Hixon, *Mother of the Buddhas*, 40.

[57] For the pearl's symbolic meanings in Buddhist iconography, see R. A. Donkin, *Beyond Price: Pearls and Pearl-Fishing: Origins to the Age of Discoveries* (American Philosophical Society, 1998), esp. 173–81, 228–35. See also the entry on 'cintāmaṇi' in www.tibetanbuddhistencyclopedia.com/en/index.php?title=Cintamani

194] *Marguerite A. Tassi*

that 'can clear away . . . any limit or obscuration that may exist in awareness'.[58]

Lear's mental and moral obscurations now yield to 'burning shame', which as Kent observes, stems from the knowledge of 'his own unkindness' (Q: 47, 43) to Cordelia. Kent, too, has received unkindness from Lear, yet has chosen in Cordelia's absence to serve the fallen king with a *bodhisattva*'s care. Cordelia recognises Kent's virtue when she says, 'O thou good Kent, how shall I live and work / To match thy goodness? My life will be too short, / And every measure fail me' (4.6.1–3). She has been a moral exemplar for Kent; he feels confident she will 'give / Losses their remedies' (2.2.154–5). In the stocks, Kent reflected (with Cordelia's letter in hand) from the depths of his 'nothing' how 'Nothing almost sees miracles / But misery' (2.2.150–1). Cordelia's goodness is the 'miracle' he 'sees' with wisdom's eye, which views reality from the vantage point of 'nothing'. Rather than pursue the ego's business, she has vowed, 'No blown ambition doth our arms incite, / But love, dear love, and our aged father's right' (4.3.27–8). Cordelia is literally a warrior-queen, head of France's army in the First Folio, yet her words reveal an allegorical and a karmic significance in her return. She is a spiritual warrior-*bodhisattva* whose cause is love and whose abode, whether a makeshift military tent or a prison, is a spiritual refuge from worldly fields of vulnerability and violence. Shakespeare writes no battles scenes in *King Lear* for good reason; his drama enacts the arduous nature of the spiritual journey to such an abode.

The association between sight and wisdom, profoundly woven into the play's language, continues to deepen as Cordelia anticipates nursing Lear in the French camp. '[B]ring him to our eye,' she commands a soldier (4.3.8), then turns to an attendant to ask, 'What can man's wisdom / In restoring his bereavèd sense, / He that helps him take all my outward worth' (4.3.8–10). She reflects the *bodhisattva*'s heroic effort to alleviate suffering whether, as *The Perfection of Wisdom in Eight Thousand Lines* proclaims, it 'cost them their entire wealth or even their lives'.[59] The attendant offers Lear medicinal herbs to aid sleep, the 'foster-nurse of nature', and 'close the eye

---

[58] Hixon, *Mother of the Buddhas*, 88.
[59] Hixon, 145.

Prajñāpāramitā and the Buddhist Path of Wisdom   [195

of anguish' (4.3.12, 15). In the Quarto, a doctor ministers to Lear, but in the Folio, it is Cordelia who is doctor, nurse and 'cordial', yet another meaning contained within her name: she is the medicinal restorative that invigorates Lear's heart and eases his anguished eye.

Cordelia invokes the 'kind gods' to '[c]ure this great breach' in Lear's 'abusèd nature' (4.6.12–13), yet she herself possesses and embodies a vision of lovingkindness that promises to cure breaches. Seeing the degraded condition of her 'child-changèd father' (4.6.15), she exclaims,

> Mine enemy's dog, though he had bit me, should have stood
> That night against my fire. And wast thou fain, poor father,
> To hovel thee with swine and rogues forlorn
> In short and musty straw? (4.6.30–3)

Cordelia's kindness resonates with the Mu *kōan* and echoes Kent's appeal to Regan when he is stocked: 'Why, madam, if I were your father's dog / You should not use me so' (2.2.126–7). While Regan treats Kent as her enemy, worse than a dog, Cordelia perceives that even her enemy's dog has buddha nature. Getting to the very bottom of Mu, to the place of truth, she finds all creatures deserving of care and hospitality. Carolyn Sale notes the radical nature of Cordelia's kindness which, in offering warmth to all sentient creatures without discrimination, represents a cure for 'a human culture of division'.[60] The 'sheltering warmth of [Cordelia's] fire' goes beyond Lear's more abstract speech about the 'superflux' by literally imagining a 'better place' (1.1.271) where Cordelia 'is willing to risk further hurt to herself rather than exclude any creature'.[61] Cordelia's hearth offers 'the sign of an all-embracing kindness', Sale argues, 'one of an inclusion so radical it makes nonsensical the impulses in which other characters in the play indulge as they seek to reduce others to something less than human'.[62] Cordelia desires to repair such destructive impulses, even with her own body. Her speech takes on the quality

---

[60] Carolyn Sale, 'Cordelia's Fire', in *Shakespeare's Virtuous Theatre: Power, Capacity and the Good*, ed. Kent Lehnhof, Julia Reinhard Lupton and Carolyn Sale (Edinburgh UP, 2023), 25–48 (35).

[61] Sale, 35.

[62] Sale, 35.

196]   *Marguerite A. Tassi*

of a sacred vow as she looks with tenderness upon her sleeping father in his reduced state:

> O my dear father, restoration hang
> Thy medicine on my lips, and let this kiss
> Repair those violent harms that my two sisters
> Have in thy reverence made! (4.6.23–6)

Lear 'hath slept long' (4.6.16) and now awakens from his terrible dream of suffering in a scene that can be understood as an allegory of awakening to wisdom. When his eyes open, Lear looks directly into the 'heavenly eyes' (Q: 17.31) of Wisdom. Cordelia's kiss and tears, like the wish-fulfilling pearls that remove afflictions, become benedictional 'medicine', given in the spirit of 'perfect' or transcendent generosity.

Lear's vision of Cordelia as 'a soul in bliss' and 'spirit' (4.6.39, 42) reveals his perception of her as a transcendent being, one who has 'gone beyond to the other shore', in the words of the *Heart Sūtra*. He questions his sense of reality, knowing he is not in his 'perfect mind' (4.6.56); he confesses he 'should ev'n die with pity / To see another thus' and 'know[s] not what to say' (4.6.46–8), which echoes his earlier words of humility and empathy for suffering 'wretches' in the storm. He has come to understand the wisdom of Cordelia's stance: 'Love and be silent' (1.1.60). When Cordelia kneels before him, saying 'O look upon me, sir, / And hold your hands in benediction o'er me' (4.6.50–1), he responds by kneeling before her, which creates a poignant stage image of reciprocal blessing. Recognising himself as 'a very foolish, fond old man' (4.6.53) and Cordelia simply as 'my child' (4.6.63), Lear cannot fathom that she still loves him. He offers to drink poison, to die as recompense for his terrible ignorance and ill treatment of her. She has 'some cause', he believes, for withholding love and retaliating. Cordelia responds with perhaps the most moving line of the play: 'No cause, no cause' (4.6.68). With *prajñā*'s eye, she regards Lear with profound lovingkindness, beyond the conventional logic of revenge, beyond personal accountability, karmic debt and the causes and conditions of *saṃsāra*. She sees from 'the other shore' (*pāramitā*) of enlightenment where all wrongs have been forgiven.

The numinous quality of Lear and Cordelia's reunion is unmistakable. Lear has at last found the warm hearth of Cordelia's 'kind

Prajñāpāramitā and the Buddhist Path of Wisdom   [197

nursery'. This is the figurative birthplace of wisdom and compassion described in *The Perfection of Wisdom in Eight Thousand Lines* as 'a true shrine for beings,—worthy of being worshipped and adored, . . . a shelter for beings who come to it, a refuge, a place of rest and final relief'.[63] Lear has had to 'abjure all roofs' in his kingdom (2.2.373) in order to find Wisdom's abode of kindness. In truth, Lear has carried Cordelia's tough and tender nursery within his mind as a vision of human potentiality; only after intense suffering and spiritual maturation does he find himself in the presence once again of the very being who inspired that vision.

In Cordelia, Shakespeare displays the extraordinary sacrificial offering of one being for the enlightenment of others. Her final speech expresses compassion for all sentient beings who have 'incurred the worst' despite their devotion to 'best meaning' (*prajñā*) (5.3.4). She embodies the *bodhisattva*'s fierce commitment to free the oppressed who suffer in the *saṃsāric* world where all are cast high and low on the wheel of 'false fortune':

> We are not the first
> Who with best meaning have incurred the worst.
> For thee, oppressèd King, I am cast down,
> Myself could else outfrown false fortune's frown.
> Shall we not see these daughters and these sisters? (5.3.3–7)

Her last words are a question meant to rouse courage and insight in the face of Lear's and her sisters' karmic transgressions. Lear's response sounds like a denial, yet his words can be understood as yet another instance of letting go: 'No, no, no: Come, let's away to prison' (5.3.8). He aspires to 'go beyond' fortune, karmic afflictions and familial conflict to a place of perpetual benediction, where he and Cordelia can 'take upon [themselves] the mystery of things' (5.3.16). Cordelia's Nothing *kōan* has led Lear to another great *kōan*, that of unconditional love. As the *Prajñāpāramitā sūtras* reveal, 'the consecrated heart of love is identical with the clear mind of transcendent insight'.[64]

---

[63] *Perfection of Wisdom*, 105.
[64] Hixon, *Mother of the Buddhas*, 47.

Yet transcendent wisdom includes the 'realization of losing every-thing'—every illusion, every 'thing' or person one might cling to.[65] In the end, Lear must lose even Cordelia. The final moments in the play, when Cordelia lies dead in her father's arms, press upon Lear, as surely as they press upon us all, a deeply felt anguish in the face of impermanence and sudden death of one's child. Lear laments how other sentient beings have life, yet his beloved Cordelia is dead:

> And my poor fool is hanged. No, no, no life?
> Why should a dog, a horse, a rat have life,
> And thou no breath at all? (5.3.280–2)

The figure of 'my poor fool' poignantly captures Lear's recognition that his wisdom teachers, now gone, have been his own child and fool. The keening of a grieving father is almost unbearable to wit-ness, as Lear's on-stage and off-stage audiences must feel. If it seems that a Buddhist understanding of Lear's journey breaks down here, at ground zero, we might consider how Buddha's teachings never sug-gest that humans should not feel grief at death. Mourning the loss of Cordelia, youngest daughter of Lear, newly married queen, mother sentient being and earthly emanation of the sacred feminine, is a natural response in the human realm of conditioned existence. Yet in Lear's cry '[t]hou'lt come no more. / Never, never, never, never, never' (5.3.282–3), the radical nature of Shakespeare's ethical-aesthetic vision comes to the fore. Such a vision resonates with a Buddhist view of a blessed end to Cordelia's rebirths in *saṃsāra*. Cordelia's death is the inexorable, logical end to *Prajñāpāramitā*'s role as wis-dom teacher; she has reached 'the other shore' of enlightenment. Lear's final test as her student lies in fully letting go into the empti-ness of reality. Lear's last words, spoken as he gazes upon Cordelia's face, suggest that he does just that as he looks beyond personal grief and despair. He says to Kent, the character who admonished him in the first scene to '[s]ee better' (1.1.156), 'Do you see this? Look on her. Look, her lips. / Look there, look there' (5.3.285–6). Lear's final words are mysterious, indeterminate markers like a Zen pointing out instruction, which cannot be conceptualised or pinned down.

---

[65] Thubten, *No Self, No Problem*, 114.

Prajñāpāramitā and the Buddhist Path of Wisdom   [199

When seen in the light of *Prajñāpāramitā*, *King Lear* can be understood as a drama that contributes to and draws upon global wisdom literature. The achievement of Shakespeare's tragedy lies not only in its unflinching portrayal of suffering as a 'noble truth', but also in its illumination of the human potential to transform suffering into wisdom. The transformation of consciousness that comes with the apophatic quality of nothing shows how wisdom is innate in human beings and can arise even, or perhaps especially, within catastrophic conditions. In Cordelia lies the dramatic embodiment of wisdom and compassion, the 'feminine principle' which demonstrates humanity's capacity to meet *saṃsāra*'s challenges. Lear may have had only glimpses of his own buddha nature and enlightenment, but theatregoers and readers of *King Lear* gain a greater perspective in their encounter with Shakespeare's vision of human potentiality. In a tragedy notorious for withholding consolation, the audience may yet find spiritual sustenance in the wise, resplendent figure of Cordelia, the 'manifest heart' 'burning with love in a world [she] can't fix':[66] her example of 'all-inclusive befriending, a fearless kindness rooted in mindfulness and insight', encourages us to 'widen the circle of our concern and care, understanding we can be intentional participants in the healing and awakening of our world'.[67]

---

[66] I borrow this description of the *bodhisattva*'s fierce tenderness from Elizabeth Mattis Namgyel, *The Logic of Faith: A Buddhist Approach to Finding Certainty beyond Belief and Doubt* (Shambhala, 2018), 105.

[67] Christina Feldman, *Boundless Heart: The Buddha's Path of Kindness, Compassion, Joy, and Equanimity* (Shambhala, 2017), EPUB.

CHAPTER 8

LOVING 'NOT WISELY BUT TOO WELL': RACE, RELIGION AND SUFI THEOEROTICISM IN *OTHELLO*

Unhae Park Langis

Against the grain of secular treatments of love in Shakespeare, I propose that 'a love-song, or a song of good life' (*Twelfth Night*, 2.3.31), is not necessarily a binary choice. This chapter explores the idea that *Othello* dramatises a spiritual quest described as theo-eroticism: a finely wrought commingling of divine and sensual striving, channelled in both metaphorical and physical ways within the greater Mediterranean thoughtworld that comprehends Greek, Sufi and Abrahamic traditions. Sixteenth-century Venice and Cyprus were archetypal city-states where Beauty and Love interacted toward ends of transcendence and pleasure. Cosmopolitan Venice, aspiring to domestic harmony and justice for its citizens, was overseen and protected by a conflation of Venus and Virgin even as it was known for the unparalleled beauty of its courtesans and the unruly licentiousness to which Iago sardonically refers as 'our country disposition' (3.3.197).[1] Cyprus, Venice's Ottoman-adjacent outpost, was the home of Venus's votaries since the goddess, according to Hesiod's *Theogony*, was known to have risen from the billowy sea off Cyprus from the severed genitals of Uranus (Aphrodite means 'risen from

---

[1] Margaret F. Rosenthal, *The Honest Courtesan: Veronica Franco, Citizen and Writer in Sixteenth-Century Venice* (U of Chicago P, 2012), 3. All citations from Shakespeare in this chapter are from *The New Oxford Shakespeare: The Complete Works, Modern Critical Edition*, ed. Gary Taylor, John Jowett, Terri Bourus and Gabriel Egan (Oxford UP, 2016). Oxford Scholarly Editions Online. doi:10.1093/actrade/9780199591152.book.1

Many thanks to Joan Pong Linton for helping me toward a more coherent expression of my multifaceted argument.

foam' in Greek).[2] As such, Cyprus channelled both the divine Venus, inspiring her beholder with love as desire for the Good (as equivalent with Beauty; Greek *kalon*), and the 'mortal Venus' (*Troilus and Cressida*, 3.1.29–30), whose lustful energy posed a threat of male castration or cuckoldry.[3] The play's embodiment of Venus is accordingly the great-souled Desdemona, who binds herself—'soul and fortunes' (1.3.348)—to Othello, noble Moor of Venice, in their joint aspiring to the 'perfect soul' (1.2.30). Together, they represent at once mythical and terrestrial travellers, who, awakened to unitive being, embark on a Sufi-Christian path toward God/Good. The difficulty of such a spiritual enterprise in the sublunary worlds of Venice and Cyprus, the play's settings, lies in what Black feminist Audre Lorde would diagnose as 'an incomplete attention to our erotic knowledge', resulting from a false 'dichotomy between the spiritual and the political'. A true understanding of the 'erotic as power', Lorde claims, would recognise that 'the bridge which connects them is formed by the erotic—the sensual—those physical, emotional, and psychic expressions of what is deepest and strongest and richest within each of us, being shared: the passions of love, in its deepest meanings'.[4]

Lorde's 1978 essay 'Uses of the Erotic: The Erotic as Power' attests to the ever-perpetuating structures of sexual power that cannot hold eros and divinity, sex and sacredness, as a whole. Reminding us that '[t]he very word erotic comes from the Greek word eros, the personification of love in all its aspects—born of Chaos, and personifying creative power and harmony', Lorde defines the erotic specifically 'as an assertion of the lifeforce of women; of that creative energy empowered, the knowledge and use of which' women

---

[2] Hesiod, *Theogony*, in *Homeric Hymns, Epic Cycle, Homerica*, trans. H. G. Evelyn-White, vol. 57 of Loeb Classical Library (William Heinemann, 1914), fragment 176, accessed October 6, 2023. https://www.theoi.com/Text/HesiodTheogony.html

[3] Plato, *Symposium*, in *Plato: Complete Works*, ed. John M. Cooper and D. S. Hutchinson (Hackett, 1997), 180d–185c, 206d. The integration of noble and sensual love, as discussed in *Marsilio Ficino's Commentary on Plato's Symposium*, trans. and ed. Sears Reynolds Jayne (U of Missouri P, 1944), ch. 7, is revitalised variously in the Italian Renaissance through the works of Petrarch, Dante and Ficino, which in turn inspired Neoplatonically infused paintings such as Botticelli's *The Birth of Venus* and Titian's *Sacred and Profane Love*.

[4] Audre Lorde, 'Uses of the Erotic: The Erotic as Power', in *Sister Outsider: Essays and Speeches* (Crossing, 2012), 53–9 (56).

must reclaim now more than ever before 'in our language, our history, our dancing, our loving, our work, our lives'.[5] As precisely the bridge between the spiritual and the political, and between the spiritual and the sexual—domains which Western society has placed in false dichotomies—the erotic, she underscores, is 'an internal sense of satisfaction to which, once we have experienced it, we know we can aspire': 'the fullness of this depth of feeling and recognizing its power' makes us 'demand the most from ourselves, from our lives, from our work'.[6] It is precisely through this Lordean lens of eros's energetic power at the node of the spiritual, the sexual and the political that we must view Othello and Desdemona's courtship and coupling. Their conjoined aspirations to 'perfect soul' (1.2.30) can be seen as the theoerotic pursuit of a Lordean triplicate 'excellence', resonating furthermore with Diotima's account of *erōs* as 'giving birth in beauty' (*kalon*, the beautiful, good, noble) in Plato's *Symposium*.[7] And if the erotic is, as Lorde intimates, 'a measure between the beginnings of our sense of self and the chaos of our strongest feelings', we can surely feel 'oh . . . the pity' (4.1.180) of this divine comedy descending into tragedy as race and gender muddy their political interchange with the theoerotic realm.

According to Lorde, 'the male world . . . values' erotic power, 'this depth of feeling enough to keep women around in order to exercise it in the service of men', but simultaneously 'fears this same depth too much to examine the possibilities of it within themselves'.[8] A similar sexual politics, intertwined with historical English xenophobia, plays out in Shakespeare's play as Othello's interaction with Iago directly fuels and is fuelled by the Moor's psychomachia. Just when Othello, inwardly, is about to transcend the sexual divide to pledge allegiance to something greater than individual self, Ego, allegorised as Iago, turns Othello from the trinity of God, Love and Desdemona to a hell of defensive manhood, engendered by imagined injury compounded by racial and religious hatred. In other words, Iago manipulates 'identity politics' to reduce eros—incarnated in Desdemona—to lust, stripping it of its synthetic, ecstatic powers. Having

---

[5] Lorde, 55.
[6] Lorde, 53–4.
[7] Lorde, 54–5; Plato, *Symposium*, 206b–c.
[8] Lorde, 'Uses of the Erotic', 54.

Loving 'Not Wisely But Too Well' [203

successfully braved the tumultuous seas physically, Othello flounders psychomachically between the 'Perdition' of loving Desdemona and the 'Chaos' (3.3.89–91) of not loving her. Just as he is about to moor himself in Desdemona and the cosmic Self, Othello descends to his egoic self of defensive manhood through the noxious influence of Iago, who destroys the brief union of the political, the spiritual and the sexual that materialised in Desdemona's noetic-erotic presence. Less important than Othello's circumstantial downfall at the nexus of sex, race, religion and interrelational politics is the often overlooked ecstatic and devotional power of eros, which this chapter brings to light through a hermeneutic of Sufi theoeroticism.

Being on the Sufi Path of Love (as the Absolute) is a journey of 'unselfing', being 'a host to God' rather than 'a hostage to your ego'.[9] The lover's single aim is to keep from deviating from the Path of Love. The cause of Othello's divergence from the Path (Arabic *ṭarīqah*) is embedded in us all: the centrifugal force of ego that continually lures us away from unconditional love and goodness. Through the unitive reality sublating the worldly concerns of sex, race and politics, Othello's story involves the inherent condition of self-division in human beings—with regard to self, others and the divine Other. Within this perspective, Othello's self-division ineluctably involves a diversion from the Divine that embraces all: to wit, his fatal misperception that Desdemona has committed adultery blinds him from his own greater 'adultery in nature'.[10] *Othello* presents jealousy in the sensible world as a gross parody of divine love: autogenic jealousy is a form of sexual love within egoic being, which represents the key target of one's spiritual journey within the Abrahamic religions. Grounded in an expansive, transpersonal love of all sentient beings and all creation, the Abrahamic as well as other global wisdom traditions teach that the all-loving heart grows inversely to self-emptying kenosis: apophatically, the knot of spiritual self-cultivation—as both problem and salvific union—lies in the naught, as Marguerite Tassi also argues in this volume in her Buddhist reading of *King Lear*'s 'nothing'.

---

[9] Iris Murdoch, *The Sovereignty of Good* (Routledge, 2013), 82; Wayne W. Dyer, *Change Your Thoughts—Change Your Life: Living the Wisdom of the Tao* (Hay House, 2009), 124.

[10] Cynthia Bourgeault, 'The Way of the Heart', *Parabola*, January 31, 2017. https://parabola.org/2017/01/31/the-way-of-the-heart-cynthia-bourgeault/

Othello's uxoricide caps his tragically botched navigation between the political and the spiritual, this world and the Absolute. Loving unwisely to this extremity is an abrupt deviation from his accustomed piety, judgement and equanimity, according to the intertwined Peripatetic-Platonic and mystical Islamic understandings of wisdom that constitute Sufism. In the influential scholarship on the English contact with Islamic culture in early modern theatre, Othello is often presented as turning into a barbaric 'Turk' (code for Muslim), with Desdemona 'as the victim of Islamic erotic tyranny', a theme echoed in a host of early modern English plays.[11] A Lordean perspective of eros at the integrative node of the political, the spiritual and the sexual reveals how Daniel Vitkus and others in these discussions have 'politically weaponized [eros] to destroy the ethical' in the tragic mode, and in so doing, engage in the very dualism Lorde rejects.[12] For Shakespeare does not merely replicate but exposes false dichotomies in *Othello*: in the Venetian-Cypriot world of racial, religious and sexual tension, Iago scripts the trope of 'turning Turk' into a plan of action that successfully thwarts Othello and Desdemona's beneficent union. Othello's spiritual devolution occurring by circumstance points up the true substance of the play: the far-reaching possibilities of eros's devotional and aspirational power in connections and collaborations within and beyond the traditional romantic relationship.

As the tragedy of Othello and Desdemona suggests, the long-standing separations between the political and the ethical, and between the spiritual and the sexual, have had real transhistorical consequences. We witness these consequences today in overt hate crimes as well as racial injustices built into our systems of education, health, housing, justice, commerce and disaster relief. By braiding together race and wisdom hermeneutics, this chapter taps into the play's sapiential possibilities resonating on the Shakespearean stage, but better yet materialising in the care-centred activisms of today. These rhizomatic

---

[11] For a list of plays of this narrative, see Daniel J. Vitkus, *Turning Turk: English Theater and the Multicultural Mediterranean, 1570–1630* (Palgrave Macmillan, 2003, 2016), 90, 99, 212; Samuel C. Chew, *The Crescent and the Rose: Islam and England during the Renaissance* (Oxford UP, 1937; Octagon Books, 1965), 478–90.

[12] Joan Pong Linton, reader's report on *Shakespeare and Wisdom*.

Loving 'Not Wisely But Too Well' [205

possibilities confirm what sages and activists as diverse as Lao Tzu, Aristotle, Gandhi, Martin Luther King, Thich Nhat Hanh and Grace Lee Boggs have reaffirmed: that politics and ethics, structural transformation and self-transformation, must go hand in hand, furthering humanist values of 'hope, cooperation, stewardship, and respect'.[13] Radical social change, Boggs claims, must be viewed 'as a two-sided transformational process, of ourselves and of our institutions, a process requiring protracted struggle'.[14] 'What comes forth' from such a heart-centred practice 'feels [less] political' and more 'like spirit leading me to truth', reveals activist adrienne maree brown: a calling 'to lead from spirit toward liberation'.[15] In this vein of spiritual politics, this chapter re-envisions *Othello*'s proto-colonialist trope of 'turning Turk' through Sufi theoeroticism in the hope that non-Western hermeneutics can offer Black, Muslim and other members of marginalised groups a transformative ethics that transcends binary stances of submission and assimilation to reworld our present ego-logy into a truly life-giving ecology.

Here, I reimagine Othello as a spiritual traveller in the Sufi tradition of his native North Africa, following a Path of Love informed by the thirteenth-century Persianate School of Love, the most influential and widespread of the Sufi love traditions.[16] Joseph Lumbard conceptualises this path in four stages:

> (1) the wayfarer loves what is other than the [B]eloved; (2) the wayfarer becomes attached to what pertains to the [B]eloved; (3) the wayfarer loves only the [B]eloved; and (4) the wayfarer transcends the duality of lover and beloved and is immersed in the ocean of Love.[17]

---

[13] Marc Andrus, *Brothers in the Beloved Community: The Friendship of Thich Nhat Hanh and Martin Luther King Jr.* (Parallax, 2021), PDF, 15; Grace Lee Boggs and Scott Kurashige, *The Next American Revolution: Sustainable Activism for the Twenty-First Century* (U of California P, 2012), 15, 17.

[14] Boggs and Kurashige, 39.

[15] adrienne maree brown, *Emergent Strategy: Shaping Change, Changing Worlds* (AK, 2017), PDF, 14.

[16] For a reading through the lens of universalist Sufi ethics, see Mochammad Dwi Teguh Prasetya and Muhammad Arif Rokhman, 'A Journey to Ethical Life: A Moral Reading of Shakespeare's *Othello* through the Nasirean Ethics of Naṣīr Al-Dīn Al-Ṭūsī', *Lexicon* 6.2 (October 2019): 139–55.

[17] Joseph E. B. Lumbard, 'Love and Beauty in Sufism', in *Routledge Handbook on Sufism*, ed. Lloyd Ridgeon (Routledge, 2020), 172–86 (179).

What animates this path is *'ishq*, a passionate, exclusive love for the Divine, which is 'a reality beyond the duality of lover and beloved that characterizes *maḥabba*', the broader Arabic term for love.[18] Desdemona proceeds steadfastly through the first two stages as her love for Othello as Stranger (on which more later) harmonises divine and profane love. Upon losing the Moor's love, she passes critically to the latter two divinisation stages in the 'Willow Song' scene, followed by her death when she aligns with her heavenly rather than her earthly lord (5.2.125). A full account of Desdemona's path as the Sufi-Sophianic Feminine is offered in a diptych essay elsewhere, which details her path of divinisation through her exclusive love for the Divine.[19] In Othello's case, however, Iago interrupts Othello's 'attach[ment] to what pertains to the [B]eloved' just as he is entering a divinisation stage after his 2.1 theophanic experience linking Desdemona to the Divine. Othello's spiritual journey runs aground in the shoals of race, religion and gender as his ethnic vulnerability in a male-defensive erotic economy proves no match against Iago's machinations of ego. Through Iago's corruptive influence upon his *nafs* (egoic self), Othello becomes derailed from the Sufi Path of Love. Resulting from his temporary 'derangement', his uxoricide, in cutting Desdemona off from all others, becomes a tragic, hubristic parody of *'ishq*. When the Moor comes to, his suicide, performing Sufi annihilation into the Divine, marks his proper return to the Path, thereby recuperating 'turning Turk', or turning Muslim, from an act of barbarism to one of speechless remorse and divine atonement.

Othello the Stranger: Imagining a Sufi Traveller in Christian Lands

Sufism was a strong influence in the early modern Islamic world, and more particularly in North Africa, Othello's place of origin, a 'once thriving world of devotion and pious foundations'.[20] Islam is

---

[18] Lumbard, 174.

[19] Unhae Park Langis, 'Sufi Theoeroticism, the Sophianic Feminine, and Desdemona's Tragic Heroism', in *Shakespeare's Virtuous Theatre: Power, Capacity and the Good*, ed. Kent Lehnhof, Julia Reinhard Lupton and Carolyn Sale (Edinburgh UP, 2023), 205–27.

[20] Nabil Matar, *Europe through Arab Eyes, 1578–1727* (Columbia UP, 2008), 79.

Loving 'Not Wisely But Too Well' [207

centred on the idea that God is the only Reality (*tawḥīd*), by 'which all aspects of creation and spiritual aspiration are presented as an unfolding of Divine Love'.[21] Sufism is understood as an internalisation of this idea, as reinforced by its etymology. One lexical root of the word 'Sufism' is *ṣūf* (Arabic, wool), referring to woollen clothing historically associated in the Mediterranean littoral with ascetics and mystics. The other lexical root is *ṣafā* (Arabic, purity). Combining these two meanings, ninth-century Sufi mystic al-Rudhabari aptly defined the Sufi as 'one who wears wool on top of purity'.[22] According to present-day Sufi teacher Jamal Rahman, Sufis try to practise pure living on a daily basis, without getting too 'enmeshed in rituals or theology'—a universalist outlook for which Sufism is known.[23] Whether a native Moor or a 'Christianised' *morisco* displaced from Andalusia to North Africa a century after the Spanish Reconquista in 1492, Othello hails from this cross-cultural heritage, and from what Nabil Matar calls a 'saint-oriented' society, where 'holy men, Sufis, and sheikhs played a decisive role in their communities' religious and political decisions'.[24]

Resonating with the Greco-Christian aestheticisation of Aphrodite in Venice and Cyprus, the interplay of Beauty and Love is a salient element also in Sufism through both pre-Islamic Arabic literature and Islam from its inception. In *udhrī* (chaste love) ghazal poetry, in particular, 'the beloved becomes the personification of the ideal and the lover is condemned to die in love', as in the Layla-Majnūn story.[25] The Sufi tradition, Joseph Lumbard explains, 'transformed these stories into a discussion of spiritual annihilation (*fanā'*) in the Divine Beloved or in Love Itself',[26] aligning with the topoi of beauty and love fundamental to Islam. In one saying from a compendium of sayings

---

[21] Annemarie Schimmel, *Mystical Dimensions of Islam* (U of North Carolina P, 1975), 17; Lumbard, 'Love and Beauty', 173.

[22] G. F. Haddad, 'Sufism in Islam', Living Islam: Islamic Tradition, accessed October 6, 2023. https://www.livingislam.org/k/si_e.html

[23] Schimmel, *Mystical*, 17; Jamal Rahman, 'Sufi Stories of Laughter', interview with Farah Nazarali, Banyen Books, YouTube, January 22, 2020. https://www.youtube.com/watch?v=BuY1ajuvXY8

[24] Matar, *Europe*, 57.

[25] Lumbard, 'Love and Beauty', 172.

[26] Lumbard, 172.

ascribed to the Prophet Muhammad (*hadith qudsi*), God is reported to have said, 'I was a hidden treasure. I wanted to be known and I created the creation in order to be known.'[27] The younger brother of the famous Persian theologian Abu Ḥamid al-Ghāzāli, Aḥmad al-Ghāzāli (d. c. 1126 CE), who dedicated himself to the Sufi aim of purifying the heart through spiritual realisation, was the first to place love at the centre of Sufi metaphysics, and God's statement in the *hadith qudsi* lies at its core. Lumbard offers al-Ghāzāli's explanation of our metaphysical relationship with God: love is 'the essence of God and the substance from which all else is woven. From this perspective, every existent thing is a self-disclosure of the Divine; everything is what he refers to in [his treatise] the *Sawāniḥ* as "a glance from loveliness".'[28] In early Sufism, 'a human love for God which is absolute' gradually evolved into 'a love which is the Absolute Itself'.[29] All lower forms of love were regarded as reflections of this highest form, and secular love as one way station toward the Divine Beloved—a path resonating with the Neoplatonic journey of descent and return to the One. Attested by the 132 uses of the word 'heart' in the Qur'an,[30] Sufism is indeed the religion of the heart, a more passionate expression, if you will, of its noetic Neoplatonic counterpart. Augustine and his followers embraced a similar passionate devotion to God, evolving into a 'kyndely' medieval wayfaring and aesthetics of love and 'sweetness' regarding Christ.[31] In the spiritual interweaving between pagan, Christian and Judaic-Muslim mysticism, the aesthetics of love and beauty operates beyond doctrinal differences as a common feature of the Christian-Muslim spiritual path in a similar way that Islam and Neoplatonism share expression in the mysticism of the One.

This yearning for Reality in Sufi theoeroticism—Love equated with the Absolute—sets one on an inner path whereby the lover's

---

[27] Annemarie Schimmel, *I Am Wind, You Are Fire: The Life and Work of Rumi* (Shambhala, 1992), 74.

[28] Joseph E. B. Lumbard, 'From *Ḥubb* to *'Ishq*: The Development of Love in Early Sufism', *Journal of Islamic Studies* 18.3 (September 2007): 345–85 (350).

[29] Lumbard, 'From *Ḥubb*', 348.

[30] Rahman, 'Sufi Stories'.

[31] Mary Carruthers, '"Sweet Jesus"', in *Mindful Spirit in Late Medieval Literature: Essays in Honor of Elizabeth D. Kirk*, ed. Bonnie Wheeler (Palgrave Macmillan, 2006), 9–19.

Loving 'Not Wisely But Too Well' [209

single aim is to keep from falling out of the Path of Love. The tropic braiding of love and pilgrimage in the Shakespearean canon, I suggest, is most poignantly dramatised in *Othello*, where the concept of 'pilgrimage', as the Moor calls his life's traverse, belongs to both Islam and Christianity through their common Neoplatonic heritage. The Lover seeking Beauty embodies the spiritual path, and he thus purified by the Beloved is a Sufi.[32] Sufi theoeroticism represents the internal side of the one and same spiritual journey, which can manifest itself also as a physical pilgrimage—both in Othello's vast experience as a worldly traveller and in his relative inexperience of the erotic landscape. *Othello* dramatises such a journey integrating the noetic and the erotic in Desdemona's ardent desire to join 'soul and fortunes' (1.3.248) with Othello in that quintessentially Neoplatonic endeavour to integrate the sensible and intelligible worlds. This unusual wooing results in a mythic-theoerotic joining of Mars and Venus, of male and female energies (also witnessed in *Antony and Cleopatra*), to facilitate their journey of soul to the ultimate Beloved. Together, they optimally represent the androgynous *insan al-kamil*, or the archetypal 'perfect human': in Maria Dakake's words, 'not the masculine Adam as opposed to the feminine Eve, but the as-yet-undifferentiated Adam, the "single soul" from which both men and women were created', consisting of both masculine and feminine qualities.[33] This mythical union of male and female qualities is reinforced by more earthly models of conjugal piety offered in both Qur'anic and Christian teachings of conjugal love as inspired by and aspiring toward Divine Love.[34]

Resembling Christian pilgrimage to the Holy Places and to monasteries in Egypt, Greece and Russia in the centuries after Christ, travel functioned similarly within the Islamic paradigm of the Path and the *rihla*, the theo-literary genre it produced alongside a rich oral tradition.[35] An Islamic teaching (*hadith*) underscores a core idea

---

[32] 'Ali ibn Uthman al-Hujwiri, *The 'Kashf al-Mahjub'*, qtd. in Schimmel, *Mystical*, 16.

[33] Maria Massi Dakake, '"Walking upon the Path of God like Men"? Women and the Feminine in the Islamic Mystical Tradition', in *Sufism: Love and Wisdom*, ed. Jean-Louis Michon and Roger Gaetani (World Wisdom, 2006), 131–51 (139).

[34] Ephesians 5:22–8; Hermann von Wied, *The Glasse of Godly Love*, trans. Haunce Dekin (J. Charlewood, 1588).

[35] Luke Dysinger, 'Wisdom in the Christian Tradition', in *The World's Great Wisdom: Timeless Teachings from Religions and Philosophies*, ed. Roger Walsh (SUNY, 2014), 29–54 (45).

210] *Unhae Park Langis*

about the spiritual journey within the mystical traditions of Alexandria centuries before and after Christ: 'Be in this world as if you were a stranger or a traveller', akin to the Christian idea of being in the world but not of it, or in Shakespeare's words 'becom[ing] / As new into the world, strange' (*Troilus and Cressida*, 3.3.12).[36] Since the ninth century, travel had become 'a path to discovery' for the Muslim seeker—'discovery not of something considered foreign and exotic but of the character and meaning of *Islām* itself' as the process of engaged surrender to God. In a ghazal 'Aṭṭar (c. 1145–c. 1220 CE) advises, 'Leave this ocean like rain and travel, / for without travel you will never become a pearl', an idea also resonant in Rūmī (1207–1273 CE).[37] As Natalie Zemon Davis explains, travel was a test, 'hardships being welcomed as an ascetic challenge: the mountain and the desert were places where encounters with the sacred might be expected'.[38] An influential pilgrimage by Andalusian Ibn Jubayr (1145–1217 CE), who died in Alexandria, 'took him from Granada to Egypt, Syria, and Iraq, with a return across the Latin kingdom of Jerusalem and the Norman kingdom of Sicily'.[39]

Such a circuit through mountain and desert from Andalusia to the Middle East to Italy echoes Othello's own 'pilgrimage' (1.3.152), which Shakespeare probably cobbled together from classical travel accounts from Pliny and Herodotus. The forms of social otherness (by differences of religion, race and gender) which Othello encounters as travails in Christian lands might be regarded from a spiritual perspective as exercises of estrangement to keep him on the Path, aligned with the Stranger. Indeed, the spiritual role

---

[36] *Sahih al-Bukhari* 6416, 'To Make the Heart Tender', accessed October 6, 2023. https://sunnah.com/bukhari:6416; John 2:15, 15:1–19.

[37] 'Aṭṭar, *Dīwān*:689; qtd. in Annemarie Schimmel, *A Two-Colored Brocade: The Imagery of Persian Poetry* (U of North Carolina P, 1992, 2014), 439. See Apostle Thomas, *Hymn of the Pearl* (first–second century CE), influential to Sufism. 'Hymn of the Pearl', trans. G. R. S. Mead, in *Echoes from the Gnosis*, vol. 10 (Theosophical Publishing Society, 1908), accessed October 6, 2023. http://gnosis.org/library/hymnpearl.htm

[38] Natalie Zemon Davis, *Trickster Travels: A Sixteenth-Century Muslim between Worlds* (Hill & Wang, 2006), 98; Houari Touati, *Islam et Voyage au Moyen Âge: Histoire et anthropologie d'une pratique lettrée* (Éditions du Seuil, 2000), chs. 1, 2, 5 and 7.

[39] Davis, 98.

Loving 'Not Wisely But Too Well' [211

of travel for Muslims and their hospitality contrasted sharply with the suspicion and hostility they actually encountered in Christian lands, as opposed to Christians travelling to North Africa. Reflecting historical and travel accounts, Othello is commonly known as a stage Moor, an early modern mythic amalgam of 'lust, cruelty, and aggression', to quote Vitkus, bringing together a slew of ethnicities—Moor, Turk, Ottomite, Saracen, Mahometan, Egyptian, Judean, Indian—'all constructed and positioned in opposition to Christian faith and virtue'.[40] Although 'Turk' and 'Moor' could refer specifically to the people of Turkey or historical Mauretania—the North African Barbary states including Morocco—given Europe's fear of Ottoman expansion, the terms were more frequently used by the late sixteenth century to signify a Muslim indiscriminately.[41] The word 'Moor' also took on a colonialist, melanotic meaning in the medieval period since the English viewed Moors stereotypically as black or dark-skinned, a connection reinforced by the sixteenth-century Iberian transatlantic slave trade of sub-Saharan Africans, along with (mostly) dark-skinned *moriscos*, or Andalusian Moors.[42]

English xenophobia against Moors and other foreigners manifested itself doubly. The state attempted to maintain social order through homogeneity, for instance, when Elizabeth sanctioned the expulsion of 'blackamoors' in 1601. The English people also exhibited anti-alien sentiments, whether it be merchants displaying anti-Muslim attitudes or London rioters 'scapegoating foreigners, prostitutes, and gentlemen's servingmen' in protest against economic ills.[43] Shakespeare's *Othello*, within the intersectionality of race, religion and sex, brings to the fore English displacement onto foreign elements its own inability to control the vicious and transgressive energies from within—with particular

---

[40] Vitkus, *Turning Turk*, 90.

[41] Vitkus, 91.

[42] Aurelia Martín Casares, *La esclavitud en la Granada del siglo XVI: Género, raza y religión* (Editorial Universidad de Granada, 2000), 94–7; cited in Emily Weissbourd, '"I Have Done the State Some Service": Reading Slavery in *Othello* through *Juan Latino*', *Comparative Drama* 47.4 (Winter 2013): 529–51 (532).

[43] Paul L. Hughes and James F. Larkin, eds., *Tudor Royal Proclamations*, 3 vols. (Yale UP, 1964), 3:221–2; cited in Jerry Brotton, *This Orient Isle: Elizabethan England and the Islamic World* (Penguin, 2016), PDF, 288.

focus here on the schizophrenic concept of manhood contingent on male superiority but dependent on female chastity, the conceptually and practically unknowable *secreta mihi*.[44] Elizabeth and London's Barbary and Levant merchants inhospitably refused to transport Abdul Wahid al-Annuri's embassy back to Morocco in 1600. Othello, installed as a military commander, is later unexpectedly recalled by the Venetian senators. As Jerry Brotton observes, these two men, 'one real, the other fictional, move into a Christian world that first embraces but eventually rejects and expels them'.[45] From such a perspective, Othello's pious 'traveler's history' is regarded as suspiciously 'exorbitant', even as 'the North African coastline' had in fact become 'the free range of marauding pirates from Christendom', making travel for Moorish envoys and travellers a terrifying ordeal, 'whether from highway brigands, angry mobs, or whimsical rulers'.[46]

In this anti-Muslim and racist context, Othello's account of his pilgrimage was often received by both the early modern audience and modern Eurocentric scholars as a 'conversion narrative of a man who starting in darkness has come to the light'.[47] Given, however, the harsh Islamic punishment against apostasy, it is more likely that Othello exercised *taqiyya*, that is, 'precautionary dissimulation of one's faith and religious practices under circumstances of coercion'.[48] Recent early modern Arab historiography prompts an account of a Muslim/Sufi Othello whose travels are ultimately configured as part of that spiritual journey and longing for home. Leo Africanus's *Geographical historie of Africa* (trans. Pory, 1600) has long been considered one of the sources for the play. Scholars have apposed Othello with the Andalusian Moor Leo Africanus (c. 1495–c. 1554) for a number of striking resonances, including their cultural hybridity. Like Othello, Leo Africanus recounts that 'in the flower of his youth, he had traveled in great hunger and danger and had investigated things

---

[44] Mark Breitenberg, 'Anxious Masculinity: Sexual Jealousy in Early Modern England', *Feminist Studies* 19.2 (Summer 1993): 377–98 (390).

[45] Brotton, *This Orient Isle*, 22.

[46] Matar, *Europe*, 79, 232.

[47] Ana Manzanas Calvo, 'Conversion Narratives: Othello and Other Black Characters in Shakespeare's and Lope de Vega's Plays', *SEDERI* 7 (1996): 231–6 (234).

[48] Davis, *Trickster Travels*, 179.

Loving 'Not Wisely But Too Well' [213

in the name of God'.[49] Later captured and enslaved by Italian pirates, Africanus, as a skilled diplomat and jurist, did not end up in the galleys but instead was delivered to Pope Leo X (Giovanni di Medici), who took the Moor under his wing. Leo Africanus, or Yūḥannā al-Asad (Arabic, John Leo, after his patron), remained in Italy for eight years. Like the fictional Othello, al-Asad was an alien living in hostile Christendom, who, after his forced baptism, was commissioned to write a book on (mainly North) Africa for a European readership. In an unusual third-person reflection, al-Asad 'admits to not a little shame and confusion in . . . disclosing the vices and disgraceful qualities of Africa, having been nourished and raised there, and known as a man of purity. But it is necessary for anyone who wants to write to tell things as they are.'[50] In this revelation, al-Asad makes a subtle allusion to the challenge of navigating between two cultural worlds without tainting his soul, between *taqiyya*, prudent religious dissimulation, and *adab*, the outer manifestation of inner alignment with the Divine. *Adab*, in Sufi courtesy, was regarded as a 'code of honorable conduct that follows the example of the prophets, saints, sages, and the intimate friends and lovers of Allah'.[51] Resembling his *morisco* predecessor in Sufi courtesy, the fictional Othello pursues the 'perfect soul' (1.2.30) as much as al-Asad strove to be 'a man of purity' throughout his long sojourn among Christians, whose Eurocentric perspective must have been taxing on his nerves on many an occasion.

Adab, this 'inner purity' of soul aligning 'inner attitude [with] outer act', was the mark of 'superior character and behavior', the

---

[49] Davis, 153; Brotton, *This Orient Isle*, 304. His full Arabic name is al-Hasan ibn Muhammad ibn Ahmad al-Wazzān. See also the striking similarities with Othello in Leo Africanus's self-description in Amin Maalouf's novel *Léon, l'Africain* (Lattès, 1986), 9, which relies considerably on Alexis Épaulard's translation, *Description de l'Afrique* (Adrien-Maisonneuve, 1956, 1981), reputed to be the most accurate translation as a line-by-line comparison between the Ramusio text and al-Asad's Italian version.

[50] Al-Asad, qtd. in Davis, *Trickster Travels*, 106.

[51] Abul-Husayn îbn Sam'un, *The Way of the Sufi Warrior*, ed. Tosun Bayrak al-Jerrahi, 6; qtd. in Llewellyn Vaughan-Lee, 'Adab—Sufi Etiquette in the Outer and Inner Worlds', *SUFI: Journal of Mystical Philosophy and Practice* 86 (December 2013), republished by The Golden Sufi Centre, accessed October 6, 2023. https://goldensufi.org/adab-sufi-etiquette-in-the-outer-and-inner-worlds/

way of the *fata*, 'the ideal, noble, and perfect man whose hospitality and generosity would extend until he had nothing left for himself', resembling kenosis, Jesus's self-emptying love to suffer, serve and save humankind.[52] Imtiaz Habib entertains the historical possibility that Shakespeare may have known some of the Moors living near the Globe theatre.[53] Wafting on this perfume, a Sufi imaginary suggests that something of these 'saint-oriented' traditions has rubbed off onto al-Asad and the fictional Othello and manifests its effects as they resided far from North Africa: specifically, both appear to be attuned to the inner nobility of the Path in their aspiration to be 'a man of purity' or 'the perfect soul'. In Davis's telling words, 'Yuhanna al-Asad displayed little mystical sensibility in his writings that have come down to us, but he held dear the tradition of al-Ghazali with its mystic strains'.[54] I see a similar pious demeanour in Othello. Though cynics might regard the religious dissimulation of *taqiyya* as a form of Iago's 'I am not what I am' (1.1.63), noetic grounding in Good distinguishes Othello as much as *All's Well*'s Helena, whose virtuous actions externally resemble those of true villains in appearances of stealth and calculation. In joining inner with outer, Sufi courtesy suggests how in Aristotelian terms practical wisdom is subsumed in noetic wisdom. In further Arabic-Aristotelian confluence, 'certain circumspect dissimulation', in the words of al-Asad's contemporary Baldassare Castiglione (1478–1529), is required to 'move strategically between different cultural positions' as the Moor, in this reimagining, aspires to a life of purity amidst emotionally, economically and politically taxing situations that foreigners often faced in Christian lands.[55] Davis frames the dilemma more in terms of fulfilling responsibility and using *hila*, or ruse, to evade sticky situations, emblematised by the trickster amphibian bird who flies between land and sea to avoid taxation. Othello's 'circumspect

---

[52] Vaughan-Lee, n.p. See also Philippians 2:6; Cynthia Bourgeault, *The Heart of Centering Prayer: Nondual Christianity in Theory and Practice* (Shambhala, 2016), 33–6, 68.

[53] Imtiaz Habib, 'The Black Alien in *Othello*: Beyond the European Immigrant', in *Shakespeare and Immigration*, ed. Ruben Espinosa and David Ruiter (Ashgate, 2014), EPUB.

[54] Davis, *Trickster Travels*, 216.

[55] Castiglione, 2.40: '*una certa avvertita dissimulazione*'; qtd. in Davis, 107.

Loving 'Not Wisely But Too Well' [215

dissimulation', however, is grounded in the striving for spiritual purity. As such, *taqiyya* should be viewed less in terms of confessional differences than in terms of the shared goal of the Christian-Islamic path—a heart of unconditional love.[56] Such would be the universalist, heart-centred Sufi corrective to the dualistic Eurocentric conversion narrative and the anti-Muslim trope of 'turning Turk'.

Divine Courtship

Beneath a rousing narrative of 'hair-breadth scapes', Othello's storytelling at Brabantio's home depicts an understated 'pilgrimage' for the 'perfect soul' (1.3.135, 152; 1.2.30). In this latter account, Desdemona and Othello's theoerotic courtship offers two devotees the opportunity to conjoin their practice as Desdemona plays 'half the wooer', actively responding to Othello's tales—a gender reversal of Scheherazade's *Arabian Tales* resonant with this Sufi reading. Their courtship literalises what Romeo and Juliet say and do in their secular wooing, invoking the 'saint[ly]' language of palmers to join 'palm to palm' in physical intimacy (*Romeo and Juliet*, 1.5.97). This sacred courtship instantiates the ideas of the sublime in Islamic philosophy. In his influential *Alchemy of Happiness*, Abu Ḥamid al-Ghazālī (1058–1111 CE) reflects on beauty and love and their relationship to virtue. In Domenico Ingenito's words, al-Ghazālī 'hints at the intimate bonds that place lyric poetry within the scope of the experience of sexuality and desire', hearkening back theophanically to the Platonic notion of *erōs* as a ceaseless striving for beauty.[57] Othello's powerful narration has Desdemona mesmerised, figuratively clambering over the precipitous crags of his hazardous journey. This sublime experience acts like a thunderbolt upon Desdemona, sparking a 'storm' of emotions between them and, a hundred lines later, 'downright violence and storm of [fused] fortunes' (1.3.243) for the theoerotic couple. Al-Ghazālī figures 'the heart as an iron which, if struck by a stone, delivers a mysterious spark signifying a spiritual com-

---

[56] Davis, 109. In Aesop's Fables circulating during al-Asad's time, the 1520s, the bird's counterpart is a bat.

[57] Domenico Ingenito, *Beholding Beauty: Saʿdi of Shiraz and the Aesthetics of Desire in Medieval Persian Poetry* (Brill, 2020), 165; Plato, *Symposium*, 203c.

motion before the visual or aural contemplation of beauty'.[58] When Desdemona 'Devour[s] up [his] discourse' 'with a greedy ear' and makes 'a prayer of earnest heart / That [he] would all [his] pilgrimage dilate' (1.3.148–52), these actions can be read as not merely stirrings of profane love but also 'a powerfully charged arousal' upon seeing in Othello a Lover who has undergone tests of virtue along the Path.[59] The ecstatic sublime achieved by Othello's moving travel account operates as the sympathetic reflection of divine presence in the world, especially in figures of human beauty and virtue—founded on the 'correspondence between the proportions of the visible world and the balanced architecture of the supernal realm'.[60] In such a theoerotic experience, Desdemona weds compassion with desire, fusing the Passion of Christian theology—the appropriation of human sin and suffering—with sensual passion in her exchange of 'kisses' for Othello's 'pains', which she finds 'wondrous pitiful' (1.3.158).[61] '[S]w[earing], in faith', in joyful bewilderment, ''twas strange, 'twas passing strange' (1.3.159), Desdemona lifts, vertically, into a numinous experience that converts Othello from the strange Moor into a visible emblem of God as Stranger. Horizontally, on a social plane beyond private courtship, Desdemona, as the Sophianic Feminine, enacts a radical spirituality antidotal to English xenophobia against Moors: to this end, she goes beyond Brabantio's pursuit of entertainment to model the human-heartedness of hospitality, which 'as both an act and an attitude to life, demands a transformation of the self towards goodness and grace—to how God wants us to be with one another'.[62] May we not forget such hospitality in view of the rising hostility toward present-day African Muslim refugees, who cross the treacherous Mediterranean seeking new lives in Europe. Desdemona's radical spirituality, embracing friend and foe, operates 'as a

---

[58] Abu Ḥamid al-Ghazālī, qtd. in Ingenito, 474.

[59] Stephen Halliwell, *Between Ecstasy and Truth: Interpretations of Greek Poetics from Homer to Longinus* (Oxford UP, 2012), 340.

[60] Ingenito, *Beholding Beauty*, 473.

[61] A possible analogue might be the sacred union of Jesus and Mary Magdalene. See Cynthia Bourgeault, *The Meaning of Mary Magdalene: Discovering the Woman at the Heart of Christianity* (Shambhala, 2010).

[62] Mona Siddiqui, *Hospitality and Islam: Welcoming in God's Name* (Yale UP, 2015), 14.

Loving 'Not Wisely But Too Well' [217

Christomorphic trace in the universe' and accords with Sufi customs of heart-centred hospitality.[63] In welcoming him unconditionally, she meets him eye to eye in Sufi-Sophian fashion within an Islamic-Christian blending of the courtly romance and the spiritual journey.[64]

Desdemona as a Divine Ocean

The counterpart to Desdemona's theophanic experience in courtship occurs when, in reuniting with Desdemona at Cyprus after a dangerous sea voyage, a wonder-struck Othello states that he could die 'content' in that eternal moment, merely gazing upon Desdemona as a lustrous image of the divine (*ayat*):[65]

> If it were now to die,
> 'Twere now to be most happy; for, I fear,
> My soul hath her content so absolute
> That not another comfort like to this
> Succeeds in unknown fate. (2.1.180–4)

Othello's speech, like the devotional poetry of contemplatives East and West, attests to the highs and lows of the spiritual endeavour through the common trope of the sea voyage. Here, Othello savours the consummate happiness he is feeling in this present moment beyond time, as reflected in the beatific image of Desdemona, who, before Iago's sinister ministry, embodies *eudaimonia*, his 'soul's joy', the north 'star to [his] wandering bark' (Sonnet 116.7). In Qur'anic terms, she is 'the divine gift sent to comfort him in his loneliness'.[66] Desdemona is the manifestation not of the stormy sea he had traversed but 'of that divine ocean which [Adam] had left' according

---

[63] Siddiqui, 122.

[64] For possible Arabic influence on European courtly love tradition, see Abdulla Al-Dabbagh, 'The Oriental Sources of Courtly Love', *International Journal of Arabic-English Studies* 3.1 (2002): 21–32; Alasdair Watson, 'From Qays to Majnun: The Evolution of a Legend from 'Udhri Roots to Sufi Allegory', *La Trobe Journal* 91 (June 2013): 35–45 (39).

[65] See Martin Lings, *Shakespeare's Window into the Soul: The Mystical Wisdom in Shakespeare's Characters* (Inner Traditions, 2006), 62; Schimmel, *Brocade*, 83.

[66] Qur'an, Sura 7:189.

218]   *Unhae Park Langis*

to the Andalusian Sufi Ibn 'Arabi's (1165–1240 CE) theory of the Sophianic Feminine. As Annemarie Schimmel explains, the woman in Ibn 'Arabi's conceptual world becomes 'the highest, sublime *object* of masculine yearning; she becomes the personification of the Divine, which encompasses within Itself active and passive, masculine and feminine traits'.[67] In Biron's words, 'women's eyes' are 'the books, the arts, the academes, / That show, contain, and nourish all the world' (*Love's Labour's Lost*, 4.3.323, 326–7). This Shakespearean example of courtly love might be seen as a tame Western counterpart to the nondual practices of Buddhist and Kashmiri Tantrism, Shaivism or Vajrayana (Sanskrit, Thunderbolt or Diamond Vehicle), not to mention Audre Lorde's Black feminist affirmation of the erotic—in all of which the Sophianic Feminine represents a primal theoerotic vehicle to attaining wisdom.[68]

Othello's ecstatic moment approximates the kind of theophanic experience elaborated in the Sufi tradition with which Shakespeare would be acquainted via Christian Neoplatonism. Muslim and Christian sages and poets on both sides of the Mediterranean have regarded beautiful youths—male and female—as vehicles unto the Divine. The heart-mind is the homing device receiving this beautiful image to tap into unitive being: as Cynthia Bourgeault explains, 'if the heart is awake and clear', released from 'the small, reactive ego-self', it can 'directly receive, radiate, and reflect [the usually] unmanifest divine Reality'.[69] Yet Othello's peak experience implies descent back to earth. In this regard, Plotinus's query, 'How on earth is it in the nature of soul to associate with body?', might well be Othello's at this liminal moment.[70] Souls, in the Plotinian account of the cycle

---

[67] Annemarie Schimmel, *My Soul Is a Woman: The Feminine in Islam*, trans. Susan H. Ray (Continuum, 1997), 107; emphasis in original.

[68] Schimmel, *My Soul*, 106. For further references for Buddhist Tantrism and Shaivism, see Alan Watts, *The Way of Zen* (Vintage, 1999), PDF, 77, 93; Watts, *Nature, Man and Woman* (Thames & Hudson, 1958), 170, 176.

[69] Cynthia Bourgeault, *The Wisdom Way of Knowing: Reclaiming an Ancient Tradition to Awaken the Heart* (Wiley, 2003), 35, 87.

[70] Plotinus, *Enneads*, IV.8.2, 4, 56, in *Ennead IV.8: On the Descent of the Soul into Bodies*, trans. with intro. and comm. by Barrie Fleet (Parmenides, 2012). On scholarship regarding the 'consummation' question, see Katharine Cleland, *Irregular Unions: Clandestine Marriage in Early Modern English Literature* (Cornell UP, 2021), 118–32 (166).

Loving 'Not Wisely But Too Well' [219

of descent and return to the One, 'come to have two lives': 'forced to live one life "there" and one "here", [they] turn and turn about [between the intelligible and the sensible worlds]. Those more able to consort with Intellect live more of their life "there", while those in the opposite state, either by nature or chance, live more of their life "here".'[71] Othello, an Islamic-Christian seeker of the 'perfect soul' (1.2.30), is joined to another soul in a marriage yet to be consummated. Consciously or not, he may wonder how he will fare in the perennial attempt to harmonise mind and body, spirit and flesh (with further difficulties posed by his Stranger/stranger status in Venetian society).

This challenge has been met with variations of *discordia concors* offered in Islamic and Christian forms of holy matrimony, crafted not solely as a ritual but as a way of life in which the conjugal partners mutually love and support each other in their daily devotion to God/Good. Desdemona's life-embracing reply, 'The heavens forbid / But that our loves and comforts should increase / Even as our days do grow' (2.1.190–2), envisions such a harmonious integration of the intellective and sensible worlds, of divine and profane love. She looks upon the journey of soul as one that can be shared and aided through the well-tempered communion of marriage, which according to a famous Islamic *hadith* (teaching) is half the faith.[72] With her benevolent influence, Othello would have had a fair chance at harmonising the divine and the worldly, following Christian, Muslim and Sufi precedents of conjugal piety—whether modelled after Pauline and Muhammadan love between spouses or the theoeroticism of Valentinus (100–160 CE).[73] The 'only early Christian on record

---

[71] Plotinus, *Enneads*, IV.8.4, 32–5, 61; Franklin Merrell-Wolff, *The Philosophy of Consciousness without an Object: Reflections on the Nature of Transcendental Consciousness* (Julian, 1973), 38–55; qtd. in Amit Goswami, *Quantum Creativity: Think Quantum, Be Creative* (Hay House, 2014), 215.

[72] Camille Adams Helminski, *Women of Sufism: A Hidden Treasure—Writings and Stories of Mystic Poets, Scholars and Saints* (Shambhala, 2003), 39; al-Mu'jam al-Awsaṭ 992, Daily Hadith Online, accessed October 6, 2023. https://www.abuaminaelias.com/dailyhadithonline/2013/04/16/nikah-half-deen/

[73] Sara Munson Deats, '"Truly, an obedient lady": Desdemona, Emilia, and the Doctrine of Obedience in *Othello*', in *Othello: New Critical Essays*, ed. Philip C. Kolin (Routledge, 2002), 233–54; Gilles Quispel, *Gnostica, Judaica, Catholica: Collected Essays of Gilles Quispel*, ed. Johannes van Oort (Brill, 2008), 167.

who spoke lovingly about sexual intercourse and womanhood', Valentinus, who imbibed the syncretic mystical traditions arising from Alexandria and died fittingly in Cyprus, the birthplace of Venus, recommended intercourse only between *pneumatics*, that is, 'men and women who were able to experience it as a mystery and a sacrament', such as Othello and Desdemona of Shakespeare's Venetian-Cypriot tale.[74]

Coitus interruptus

Given, however, the gender tensions underlying patriarchal societies, Christian and Muslim, Othello's intimation of death during a peak experience may suggest the dangers he feels subliminally as a black Muslim entering a miscegenous marriage in Venetian society. Othello's vague misgivings become a self-fulfilling prophecy when Iago politicks race, sex and anti-Muslim hatred to topple Othello. A common early modern metaphor for sex in discussing sexuality is the sea and its attendant perils. Alexander Niccholes links female sexuality to death and loss at sea: as Parolles puts it, 'A young man married is a man that's marred', marooned in the gynocentric 'dark house' (*All's Well*, 2.3.273, 267). As Mark Breitenberg states, 'Niccholes's linkage of marriage and "shipwrecke" depends upon an *a priori* fear of disempowerment and loss of identity that derives from two forms of dependence—erotic and matrimonial—on women'.[75] Defined by eleventh-century Sufi writer Al-Hujwiri (1009–1077 CE) as 'the heart's being pure from the pollution of discord', Sufism directly bears on Othello's attempt to love wisely and well. As Al-Hujwiri explains further, 'Love is concord, and the lover has but one duty in the world, namely to keep the commandment of the beloved, and if the object of desire is one, how can discord arise?'[76] The commandment is so simple—'Love, full stop'—and yet how easy it is to swerve from it—swerve so grossly as the otherwise wise Othello does. Niccholes's contemporary, Joseph Swetnam, speaks of male

---

[74] Quispel, 167.

[75] Joseph Swetnam, *The arraignment of lewde, idle, froward and unconstant women* (1615), qtd. in Breitenberg, 'Anxious Masculinity', 393.

[76] Al-Hujwiri, qtd. in Schimmel, *Mystical*, 15–16.

Loving 'Not Wisely But Too Well' [221

desire as 'being carried headlong into the deep and dangerous Sea of raging affection . . . into the bottomless gulf of endless perdition'.[77] Such an admonition alerts us to the autogenic aspect of jealousy that mires Othello between 'perdition' and 'chaos' (3.3.89–91) until he sinks apoplectically into uxoricide.

According to the Qur'an, a husband and wife should be an astral 'garment' of comfort for each other spiritually and emotionally, and coitus serves as the consummation of this conjugal *koinonia*.[78] Whether actually consumed or not, wine is the celebrated symbol of divine love, accompanied by sexual love or not: Persian poet Rūmī equates bewilderment, 'the indescribable intoxication caused by ecstasy', with 'the intoxication caused by wine'.[79] Desdemona has accompanied Othello to Cyprus for the chance that the newlyweds may fulfil 'the rites for why I love him [still] bereft me' (1.3.251). A sacred union of the pneumatic sort would consecrate profane love of the sensible world as lovers would open themselves to divine ecstasy. Emblematic of religious ritual in its etymological sense of religature to the One, this 'Sufasm' would 'fast' Othello's divine orientation with 'seals and symbols', marking that he has assumed his 'royal siege' (1.2.10, 21; 2.3.306) in the Beloved, rather than being divided by egoic passions.[80] By these lights, consummation becomes pivotal in his difficult endeavour to integrate not only the sensible and divine but also the Christian and Muslim worlds. Othello's testiness at having his nuptial slumbers interrupted reveals itself in his stern speech reprimanding his men for having 'turned Turks, and [doing] to ourselves . . . that / Which heaven hath forbid the Ottomites'

---

[77] Swetnam, qtd. in Breitenberg, 'Anxious Masculinity', 393. All early modern texts are cited in modernised spelling.

[78] *Surah al-Baqarah* 2:187; qtd. in Helminski, *Women of Sufism*, 39. According to Plotinus, *Enneads*, IV.8.4.12, 62, the soul 'encounters and serves the need of another in its progress'.

[79] Jalāl al-Dīn Rūmī, *Spiritual Verses: The First Book of the Masnavi-ye Ma'navi*, trans. Alan Williams (Penguin, 2006), I, 311–15; Annemarie Schimmel, 'Rumi and the Symbols Used by Him', *Ilm* 7.3 (December 1981–February 1982): 29–31. https://www.iis.ac.uk/media/nlhdbdrn/rumi-symbols-3-470185473.pdf

[80] Cleland, *Irregular Unions*, 118–32. 'Sufasm' is my adaptation of Robert Thurman's word 'buddhasm', meaning a theoerotic Buddhist-inspired mindful awareness, in *Wisdom Is Bliss: Four Friendly Fun Facts That Can Change Your Life* (Hay House, 2021), PDF, 17.

(2.3.148–50). Othello's speaking in the royal 'we' becomes all the more ironic when he, beside himself, 'turn[s] Turk', precisely within the Sufi tradition of steadfastly according himself with God/Good. Othello and Desdemona's nuptial union, which should be capped by divine intoxication, is instead derailed by vicious drinking and fighting connived by Iago: the signal consummation of their marriage becomes vitiated through Iago's scheme of 'fasten[ing] but one cup upon' Cassio (2.3.38). If *coitus interruptus* is the sign and source of Iago's machinations within the elision of public and private spheres, then Cassio, who acts as both Othello's lieutenant and liaison in the Moor's recent courtship, is framed as the drunken brawler perfidiously responsible for the newlyweds' *coitus interruptus*. Othello's 'mamm'ring' (3.3.69) hesitation to reinstate his lieutenant—so exasperating to Desdemona—can well be understood in the context of this sinuously manipulated *ménage à trois*. Divine ecstasy backstage, interrupted and upstaged by vicious intoxication, opens the trapdoor to Othello's further debasement into jealousy, with all its inexorable consequences.

Haraam *to Harem, Zealous to Jealous*

We have yet to understand, internally, viscerally, how and why loving and judicious Othello, who both adores his wife and exhibits laudable self-discipline (1.3.266), could become 'perplexed' (5.2.344) to the point of uxoricide. A phenomenological account of this 'turning Turk' must be situated within the broader context of Othello's vulnerability as a Muslim living in Christendom. Spurred by Iago, who mongers evil for evil's sake, Othello downshifts from divine to egoic orientation, from zealous to jealous love, turning himself into a complete perversion, yea, adulterer, of his native Sufism. This is the ethical and interspiritual rather than Eurocentric, racist interpretation of 'turning Turk' at the heart of Sufi Othello. As Nabil Matar's studies of early modern Arab travel writing suggest, Othello, caught between divine and profane love, between Sufi piety and Venetian worldliness, confronts conflicting social conventions regarding women. In the Islamic tradition, aristocratic women, veiled as emblems of the sacred as well as for protection, resided in their own quarters, or *haram*. Keeping in mind its clear potential for and vast history of abuse in patriarchal societies East and West into the present, hinted at by

Loving 'Not Wisely But Too Well' [223

the English word *harem*, the concept of *haraam*, as Matar explains, began 'as a description of a sacred space that then [became] applied to woman/women who should be treated with the appropriate sacredness and forbiddenness as a holy place',[81] as associated with passionate love for God. Within the context of early Arab travel writing, an absence of *haraam* in more secularised Christian lands—through culturally crude translations—came to be positively valorised as 'an absence of jealousy', thereby distorting and usurping 'zealousy' as sacred love.[82] The reference to jealous Moors (along with all other mentions of jealousy in North Africans) in John Pory's translation of the numerously published and widely translated Yuhanna al-Asad/ Leo Africanus's *Description of Africa* (in Ramusio's *Delle Navigationi et Viaggi*, 1550) clearly reveals cultural and ethnic distortion: 'No nation in the world is so subject unto jealousy; for they will rather lose their lives, then put up any disgrace in the behalf of their women.'[83] Al-Asad wrote another version in simple, lively Italian, *Cosmographia and Geographia de Africa*, an elaboration of a probable, no longer extant Arabic draft. Despite its lingering status as 'a multi-handed work [*un'opera a più mani*]',[84] al-Asad in this version describes jealousy ('*gelus[ia]*') in a notably different manner from the extremely negative way that Pory does in the context of profane love. These Moors of Barbaria (North Africa), al-Asad avers, are 'men of

---

[81] Matar, *Europe*, 107.

[82] Matar, 108.

[83] Leo Africanus, *A geographical historie of Africa, written in Arabicke and Italian by Iohn Leo a More, borne in Granada, and brought vp in Barbarie* [. . .], trans. John Pory (Georg. Bishop, 1600), 40; Davis, *Trickster Travels*, 395; Federico Cresti, '*Il Manoscritto della Cosmographia de l'Affrica di Giovanni Leone Africano. Note in Margine all'Edizione Critica del Testo*', *Mediterranea: Ricerche Storiche* 31 (August 2014): 383–96 (388). According to Tom Verde, a Venetian official, Giovanni Batttista Ramusio, published the *Cosmographia* in 1550 under its better known title and pseudonym, Leo Africanus's *Description of Africa*, as part of *Delle Navigationi et Viaggi*, a five-volume collection of geographical texts and travel narratives. This popular but translatively inaccurate version was the source of its various translations into French, Latin, English and Dutch. Verde, 'A Man of Two Worlds', *AramcoWorld* 59.1 (January/ February 2008), accessed October 6, 2023. https://archive.aramcoworld.com/ issue/200801/a.man.of.two.worlds.htm

[84] Cresti, '*Il Manoscritto*', 386.

great souls in acquiring things and honour [*homini de grande animo in acquistare robbe e honore*]'.[85] In the context of the saint-oriented North Africa from which both the historical al-Asad and the fictional Othello hail, the language of 'great soul' and 'honour' resonates with the Sufi aspiration to be a man of purity, a 'perfect soul' (1.2.130), as echoed in *Othello*, through a shared language of interspirituality. In these misappropriations of culture and language occurring in Christian-Islamic encounters between the sacred and secular spheres, the Qur'anic concept of *haraam*, I submit, was misprised as excessive possessiveness, without due understanding of the respect toward sacred place and toward women that underlies the divine prohibition. If so, then this cultural and linguistic mistranslation by Europeans is as much 'turning Turk'—turning vicious—as Othello's own eventual slippage from divine to profane, from zealous to jealous love, in navigating his Muslim-Christian duality.

In negotiating his religious-racial hybridity, Othello appears indeed to be affected by this and other theo-cultural misunderstandings. Unlike their Islamic counterparts, European ladies at court were 'socially interactive', often producing disturbing effects on Moorish envoys visiting and living in Christian lands, who in *Dar al-Islam* 'hardly ever got to see a well-guarded woman outside [their] own immediate famil[ies]'.[86] While more cosmopolitan than these Moorish envoys, Othello is evidently inexperienced in the intricacies of navigating the Venetian-Cypriot aristocratic scene. According to *The Book of the Courtier*, Baldassare Castiglione's Neoplatonic treatise and manual on virtuous conduct, the court lady was subject to contradictory demands of courtesy: she 'must

---

[85] Leo Africanus (al-Asad), *Libro de la cosmogrophia et Geographia de Affrica*, 1526, National Central Library of Rome, 40v, accessed October 6, 2023. http://digitale.bnc.roma.sbn.it/tecadigitale/manoscrittoantico/BNCR_V_E_953/BNCR_V_E_953/92

Elsewhere, for instance on page 20v–21r, the overall effect of al-Asad's original version is that the Numideans of the Libyan deserts are far more civilised, liberal ('*liberali*'), than their portrayal in Pory's translation, notably without the references to the jealousy or the 'savage and brutish manner' that Pory describes, not to mention an aesthetics against 'grosse, corpulent, and . . . swart complexion' (21), absent in al-Asad's more neutral descriptions. I thank Kelly Lehtonen for translation assistance.

[86] Matar, *Europe*, 107; Schimmel, *My Soul*, 100.

Loving 'Not Wisely But Too Well' [225

observe a certain difficult mean' of being 'no less chaste, prudent and benign than she is pleasing, witty and discreet'.[87] Female courtesy thus proves to be as challenging for Desdemona as agent as it is perplexing for Othello as observer. Venetian courtiers, however, appear to have no trouble discerning Desdemona's virtue. In his so-called Annunciation speech, the otherwise foolish Rodrigo calls Desdemona 'blessed', rightly reading as 'courtesy' social gestures Iago tries to stain as 'lechery' (2.1.232–8). Lodovico, likewise knowing her for a virtuous, 'obedient lady' (4.1.230), later protests Othello's most unseemly act of slapping her face.

Unlike the Venetian courtiers, Othello has trouble reading the social and ethical conduct of a lady who mingles freely in Cypriot high society as well as in a military setting. Theo-social differences contribute to Othello's failure to sustain a sacred-zealous view of Desdemona. Claiming to be 'Rude . . . in . . . speech, / And little blessed with the soft phrase of peace' (1.3.81–2), Othello may be unaccustomed to the Italian courtly version of Sufi courtesy, which resembles the cosmopolitan refinement customised by the Persian Safavid dynasty (1500–1736)—courtly decorum, originally conceived as the external manifestation of *adab*, the inner striving for purity. Othello is apparently far less practised than Rodrigo and Lodovico in distinguishing truly virtuous character within the milieu of cultivated learning and polished manners of Cypriot high society. As an initiate to Divine Love, the formerly judicious Moor becomes the perfect dupe for Iago's machinations. '[W]ith a learned spirit / Of human dealings' (3.3.253–4), Iago perceives Othello's subaltern vulnerabilities within two overlapping patriarchal economies of desire that fuel anxious masculinity from Christian and Muslim contexts. Gleefully turning concord into discord, he simply sets Othello's ethnic and gender troubles against each other, targeting and weaponising the Moor's capacious love and martial decisiveness to serve his egoic evil. Recognising how Othello's uxoriousness fuels 'his weak function' (2.3.310), this perverter of Good turns Desdemona's virtue into pitch and retools his commander into an ensign of causeless hate.

---

[87] Baldassare Castiglione, *The Book of the Courtier*, trans. and ed. George Bull (Penguin, 1976), PDF, 291–2.

226]   *Unhae Park Langis*

Trying to maintain his hybrid identity, Othello initially shuns the stereotype of the jealous Moor, an overcompensation that will fuel a subsequent swing to its exact opposite. He affirms: "'Tis not to make me jealous / To say my wife is fair, feeds well, loves company, / Is free of speech, sings, plays, and dances' (3.3.179–81). To use an inter-spiritual seafaring metaphor for the ethical pursuit, Othello, fronting a liberal attitude toward Desdemona's courtesy, tries to maintain a Sufi-Stoic constancy against waves of external forces that perturb his contentment.[88] Against such disturbances, Tibetan Buddhist teacher Chögyam Trungpa explains that true gentleness 'comes from experiencing the absence of doubt', which stems from 'trusting in the heart, trusting yourself'; the consequences otherwise are 'the tremors and the shaking and the shortsightedness of anxiety, which make your behavior totally inaccurate', as Othello and Leontes come to know.[89] At the nexus of Greek, Buddhist and Sufi wisdom traditions, Trungpa's teachings point to the autogenic quality of jealousy, as Emilia does in the play (3.4.48–51): the root of the problem lies within the jealous person as his unreliable physical eyes become decoupled from the noetic Third Eye. 'Trusting in the heart' dissolves when Othello cannot trust himself as Iago points up all his erotic liabilities—age as well as religion and race, implicit in the Moor's difference from courtiers 'Of [Desdemona's] own clime, complexion, and degree' (3.3.225). Othello makes a brave if brief show of a 'free and open nature' (1.3.370) as his confidence begins to crumble, signalling Othello's 'turning Turk', his slippage from zealous to jealous love.

Limed in Iago's trap of misogynist, racist and anti-Muslim ideologies, Othello can no longer exercise reason and virtue. The externals and 'accidents' of his skin colour and his Muslim affiliation unmoor the Moor from the Beloved and, by extension, from Desdemona's 'solid virtue' (4.1.248), and his own in their now asundered 'marriage of true minds' (Sonnet 116.1).[90] Being in the world and not of it is a special challenge to a member of a racial and religious minority

---

[88] Sadiq, 'A Sufi Parable of Sea', *Technology of the Heart*, January 24, 2012. https://www.techofheart.com/2012/01/parable-of-sea-niffari-travel.html

[89] Chögyam Trungpa, *Shambhala: The Sacred Path of the Warrior*, ed. Carolyn Rose Gimian (Shambhala, 2009), 49–50.

[90] 'Accidents' are distinguished from 'substance' in Castiglione, *Book of the Courtier*, 300.

group such as Othello, whose yearnings for freedom, justice and dignity are acute, given his oppressed status. His socio-political and spiritual inclinations seemingly work at cross purposes: whereas surrender is the signal motion for liberation spiritually, his socio-political and sexual instincts are to resist and avoid personal degradation.[91] Actions guided by 'cultural conditioning and the hidden agendas of the lower self, with its compulsive wanting and needing', in Othello's case, are exacerbated by his subaltern status into his derangement by imagined cuckoldry, the ultimate sexual affront to egoic love.[92]

A kernel of doubt—Iago's artful insinuation ('Indeed') that Cassio was a '[dis]honest', adulterous mediator in the couple's courtship (3.3.99–101)—is all it takes to foam up in a frightful image of Aphroditic castration all of Othello's insecurities and uncertainties regarding his standing and livelihood in Venetian society and his conduct toward women. Despite the Venetian counsel's quick deployment of the Moorish commander against Turkish threat, Othello, as his sudden recall in Act 4 shows, remains an outsider with uncertain prospects. Exploiting Othello's status as an ethnic stranger, Iago, in a counterfeit alliance of injured manhood, invokes cuckoldry to rile him up in self-defence. The Moor becomes unable to cope with another source of insecurity in his life added to racism and Islamophobia. Othello, in Coppélia Kahn's words, 'flees from unbearable doubts about women to identify with men as the passive, fated victims of women, an identification coded into marriage through cuckoldry'.[93] Kahn's salient point that cuckoldry, 'like rape, is thus an affair between men' is borne out in evolutionary biology, which reveals that cuckoldry, prevalent across cultures through time, is at heart about male-male competition over mates and resources, about male insecurity vis-à-vis each other.[94]

---

[91] For post-colonial and ecological critiques of the narratives of freedom, see Dipesh Chakrabarty, 'The Climate of History: Four Theses', *Critical Inquiry* 35.2 (Winter 2009): 197–222; Pierre Charbonnier, *Affluence and Freedom: An Environmental History of Political Ideas*, trans. Andrew Brown (Polity, 2021).

[92] Bourgeault, *Wisdom Way*, 76–7.

[93] Coppélia Kahn, *Man's Estate: Masculine Identity in Shakespeare* (U of California P, 1981), 144.

[94] Kahn, 150; David C. Geary, 'Coevolution of Paternal Investment and Cuckoldry in Humans', in *Female Infidelity and Paternal Uncertainty: Evolutionary Perspectives on Male Anti-Cuckoldry Tactics*, ed. Steven M. Platek and Todd K. Shackelford (Cambridge UP, 2006), 14–34 (14).

Unable to heed what Rūmī might have advised, 'Be generous / to what nurtures the spirit and God's luminous reason-light', namely, Desdemona, Othello proceeds to 'honor what causes / dysentery and knotted-up tumors', or apoplexy, in his case.[95] Before Iago's viral influence regarding *vir* (Latin, manliness), Othello was properly installed in his 'royal siege' (2.3.306), attuned to the Beloved and his portion of Divine Being, or *Anima Mundi*, the animal essence that joins the noetic and seminal powers. Now, his heart-mind, that 'fountain from the which my current runs' (4.2.53), solely registers lust and evolutionary self-protection, and the sacred fusion of his and Desdemona's psychic and seminal spirit becomes 'a cistern for foul toads / To knot and gender in!' (4.2.57–8).[96] Othello tragically rejects Desdemona as the Lordean incarnation of eros, feminine creative and aspirational power that bridges the spiritual, the political and the sexual.[97] Mix in biology, and Othello might well be revolting against becoming an evolutionary dead end, investing emotional and seminal energy to father other men's offspring.[98] In yogic terms, Othello is assailed at all the chakra points, notably the midbrain (third eye), heart, stomach and genitalia, respectively inducing confusion not clarity, jealousy not love, unworthiness not pride, lust not sacred sexuality.[99] Erotic love, in Amit Goswami's words, is 'an agreement between the immune systems . . . of the two lovers', whereby the immune systems do not 'distinguish between "me" and "not me"', but rather 'the feeling would be "you are mine and I am yours"'.[100] But when the heart and other chakras go awry as in Othello's case, his immune system immediately erects a barrier between self and other. In an imagined fight-or-flight situation against a viral enemy, Othello's noetic link to the Beloved and to Desdemona as its votary becomes severed, as the cuckold's horn pierces to the core of his zoetic being. Othello's 'weak function' (2.3.310), induced by erotic, racial and

---

[95] Rūmī, 'A Basket of Fresh Bread', in *The Essential Rumi*, trans. Coleman Barks (Castle, 1997), 256.

[96] Compare Proverbs 5:15 (KJV): 'Drink waters out of thine own cistern, and running waters out of thine own well.'

[97] Lorde, 'Uses of the Erotic', 53–6.

[98] Geary, 'Coevolution', 22.

[99] Goswami, *Quantum Creativity*, 74.

[100] Goswami, 75.

Loving 'Not Wisely But Too Well' [229

religious vulnerabilities unable to resist Iago's evil contriving, results in the euphemistic folly of '[t]hrow[ing] out a pearl / Richer than all his [masculine] tribe' (5.2.345–6).

The dissipation in a mere 150 lines of Othello's strivings for 'perfect soul' (1.2.130) is astonishing, to say the least. This 'unnatural' degradation occurs when Othello naturalises an ethnic anthropology that white cleaves to white, Christian to Christian. Iago's weaponising of eros shatters his aspiration to 'being in the world without being of it' at the node of identity politics and unitive being. Othello's sacred alignment with the Stranger is subverted by his sense of social inferiority as a stranger in white Venetian Christendom. Such are the mitigating factors surrounding the marginalised subject as moral agent, which fuel Othello's 'adultery in nature', his tragic swerving from his natural inclination toward God/Good.[101] Without his ethnic and cultural vulnerabilities, the Moor may well have withstood Iago's attempts to malign Desdemona as the Venetian courtiers Rodrigo and Lodovico successfully do, correctly reading Desdemona's behaviour as licit rather than illicit conduct for the court lady. As it stands, however, Othello's misreading of Desdemona's courtesy can be more deeply understood as a deviation from Sufi courtesy, *adab*, a way of sacred being, bringing 'innermost respect into daily life, into his way of being with others, with himself, and with God'.[102]

Loving 'Not Wisely But Too Well': A Miscarriage of Experiential Wisdom

More broadly speaking, Othello's diversion from Good can be viewed as a miscarriage of experiential wisdom in conditions adverse to the flourishing of marginalised people. Islamic wisdom, *hikma*, is associated with moral judgement, restraint, strength, knowledge based on clear evidence, and revelation put into practice. The Neoplatonic harmonising of the sensible and divine worlds also resonates in Islamic thought thanks to the uptake of Greek thought in Arab philosophy. As U. Isra Yazicioglu explains,

---

[101] Bourgeault, 'Way of the Heart'.
[102] Vaughan-Lee, 'Adab'.

230]   *Unhae Park Langis*

hikma, wisdom, is traced to the root *h-k-m* and related to *hukm*, which means to judge. Its meaning is also sometimes related to *ihkam*, which means 'to prevent, curb; be strong'. Therefore, wisdom is also defined as preventing harm and guiding to good. When ascribed to a human being, it also communicates that the person is balanced and just.[103]

Accordingly, wisdom to early Islamic exegetes such as Muhammad Ibn Jarir al-Tabari (839–923 CE) was the capacity to discern truth from falsehood, for which reason *hikma* (wisdom) comes from the same root as *hukm* (judgement).[104] For Muslims, such wisdom involved understanding the Qur'an as the revelation of God.

Influenced by the Aristotelian-Avicennan emphasis on virtue as activity, another exegete, al-Harizmi al-Zamakhshari (1075–1144 CE), defines wisdom as 'putting revelation into practice'—altogether important 'because the complexities of lived reality require discernment in applying principles of truth and ethics'.[105] Our ability to apply the principles of truth and ethics is, moreover, subject to moral luck, the circumstances in which agents are blamed or praised for an action or its consequences that they executed voluntarily and without coercion but over which they did not have full control.[106] In general, the propensity to wisdom is dependent on our circumstantial surroundings and the *complexio* of constitutive factors such as the cultural, religious, economic and even melanotic conditions into which we are born, as well as the health, personality and abilities we start with in the *daimonia*, or lottery of life.[107] Despite his inauspicious moral luck, Othello exhibited commendable judgement, restraint and knowledge throughout his single life, but his uxoricide 'Throws

---

[103] İlhan Kutluer, 'Hikmet', in *Türkiye Diyanet Vakfı İslâm Ansiklopedisi*, vol. 17 (Türkiye Diyanet Vakfı, İslâm Ansiklopedisi Genel Müdürlüğü, 1998), 503–11 (503); U. Isra Yazicioglu, 'Wisdom in the Qur'an and the Islamic Tradition', in *The Oxford Handbook of Wisdom and the Bible*, ed. Will Kynes (Oxford UP, 2021), 221–40 (222).

[104] Yazicioglu, 226.

[105] Kutluer, 'Hikmet', 504; glossed in Yazicioglu, 226.

[106] Bernard Williams, *Moral Luck: Philosophical Papers 1973–1980* (Cambridge UP, 1981).

[107] Thomas Nagel, 'Moral Luck', in *Mortal Questions* (Cambridge UP, 1979), 24–38 (31–2).

out [his] pearl [of pure living] / Richer than all his' life (5.2.345–6). Philosopher Veli Mitova argues that the spiritual, emotional and epistemic centrality of Desdemona to his life places upon him a 'duty of inquiry', a duty of wisdom.[108] But to what avail is such a rational analysis when, in his embodied experience as a subaltern in Venice, Othello has already flown from Love's berth in visceral fear? In his flight, he fixes solely on finding and accepting with swift military dispatch the 'ocular proof' (3.3.354) that he thinks will crack him free from 'a serpent's . . . shell' (*Julius Caesar*, 2.1.32–4) of uncertainty. In Othello's egoic hell of doubt, we too might easily grasp at Iago's motley combination of indirect and unreliable evidence offering in sum a spectre of 'ocular proof'.[109] A more empathic understanding of Othello's heart-wrenching experience recognises that his sapiential lapse *in toto* stems from the circumstantial and constitutive elements that 'perplex [him] to the extreme' (5.2.344).

Othello, succumbing to the subtle ways of ego peddled by Iago, takes the 'particular masculine vices of pride and a hunger for domination and conquest' to their logical end.[110] Othello states overtly that the 'cause' for his ritualised 'sacrifice' of Desdemona is to keep her from hurting other men, but covertly it is to stop the source of his maddening, the sheer deranging of her ranging: the apoplectic gall of her 'knot[ting] and gender[ing]' further while he is reduced to living death (4.2.58). Apoplexy is Othello's psychosomatic reaction to lust's imperative, but his imagined loss of her body is nothing compared to the loss of her love and what she represents: divine *'ishq*, the 'cohesive force' and essence, the 'light and love and life and all qualities' of our existence.[111] Thickening the bodily spirits coursing through Othello's veins, the cognitive-emotional disorder provoked

---

[108] Veli Mitova, 'The Duty of Inquiry, or Why Othello Was a Fool', in *The Routledge Companion to Shakespeare and Philosophy*, ed. Craig Bourne and Emily Caddick Bourne (Routledge, 2018), EPUB, 461–78.

[109] Unhae Park Langis, *Passion, Prudence, and Virtue in Shakespearen Drama* (Continuum, 2011), 62.

[110] Dakake, '"Walking"', 142–3, 145.

[111] Murshid Samuel L. Lewis, 'The Perfection of the Heart: An Original Sangatha', PDF, 2, Sufi Ruhaniat International, Murshid Samuel Lewis Archives, accessed October 6, 2023. https://www.ruhaniat.org/index.php/major-papers/sufi-practices-ryazat/2247-the-perfection-of-the-heart--an-original-sangatha

232]   *Unhae Park Langis*

by loveless Iago causes a blood clot in his heart-stream, an obstruc-
tion to 'love-unity'.[112] Rūmī's account of the misguided soul (*nafs*)
aptly describes Othello's 'weak function' (2.3.310):

> Anger and lust make a man squint;
> they cloud the spirit so it strays from truth.
> When self-interest appears, virtue hides: a hundred veils rise
> between the heart and the eye.[113]

Seeing through these veils of 'puddled' (3.4.133) imagination (in
Aristotelian-Avicennan faculty psychology), Othello tragically mis-
interprets the 'sublime' in Desdemona as 'shameful', as something
he must veil, silence and cipher. Vitkus argues that Othello attempts
to 'make the murder a sacrament', a 'pagan "sacrifice" of a pure
virgin'.[114] I contend further that Othello's 'mistaken presumption of
ministry is damnable blasphemy' not only in Christian but, more
acutely, in Islamic-Sufi terms. His silencing her into a 'world / Of one
entire and perfect chrysolite' (5.2.142–3) is ironic undoing of the polished crystal or pearl's symbolic capacity for divine mirroring.[115] As
such, it is the acme of the egoic state of 'separation, distinction, crys-
tallization, atomic activity', 'individuat[ing] . . . or differentiat[ing
oneself] in essence from the Universe of God'.[116]

In the mystical wisdom traditions, 'every person weaves out of one's
thoughts, words, and deeds a garment for one's soul'.[117] As much as
race, religion and gender have contributed intersectionally to weave a
horrific garment for his soul, the veil of the egoic *nafs* lifts lightning-
quickly for Othello, returning him to 'the lap of [His] grace' to reclaim
his astral robe.[118] In Hindu iconography, *vajrā* multivalently signifies
the thunderbolt of Indra, diamond wisdom and diamonds as precious

---

[112] Lewis, 2.

[113] Rūmī, *Mathnawi* (also *Masnavi*), I.333–6, in Kabir Helminski, *The Knowing Heart: A Sufi Path of Transformation* (Shambhala, 2000), 84.

[114] Vitkus, *Turning Turk*, 98.

[115] Schimmel, *Brocade*, 26, 235. See also Tassi, Chapter 7 of this volume, on Diamond Sutra.

[116] Lewis, 'Perfection', 18.

[117] Schimmel, *My Soul*, 122.

[118] Rūmī, qtd. in Schimmel, *My Soul*, 109, 121. Sufi mystic Hallaj's name means 'cotton-carder'.

Loving 'Not Wisely But Too Well'   [233

stones.[119] I suspect that thunderbolt and diamond, along with garment, veil and pearl, were part of a large trove of motifs accessible to poets and sages in the Afro-Eurasian thoughtworld.[120] In *Nāṭya-śāstra* (c. 500 BCE–c. 500 CE), a Sanskrit treatise on the performing arts, these meanings can converge to powerful effect. While, literally, Indra's thunderbolt is the destroyer of *daityas* (demons) in dramatic performance, *vajrā*, figuratively, refers to 'an adamant' and 'harsh words uttered on one's face . . . called thunderbolt', directing us to Othello's sudden illumination when Emilia applies the *vajrā* in the play's denouement.[121] In a Sufi analogy, a man must board a ship in order to seek a pearl (*haqiqah*, ultimate truth) in the sea (*tariqāh*, path).[122] In Act 2, Othello does just that and briefly reunites with his pearl-bride, Desdemona, in Cyprus at his spiritual peak. In Act 5, Othello, through uxoricide, loses this Aphroditic pearl of Venetian society as much as his own pearl of Sufi striving.

But through his self-immolation, Sufi Othello retrieves an eternal pearl, his love of Desdemona, sealing his soul's return to God/ Good. Upon discovering Iago's treachery, Othello kills in himself 'the circumcised dog', the most common Arab metaphor for the *nafs*,[123] thereby restoring Desdemona as a seeker of the higher rather than the lower soul and affirming his own culpability far beyond Iago's 'turn[ing] her virtue to pitch' (2.3.322). But this paradoxical 'turning Turk' does not mean, as Vitkus and others have argued, that Othello

---

[119] *Vajrā*, Wisdom Library, accessed October 6, 2023. https://www.wisdomlib.org/definition/vajra

[120] Several of these motifs converge in 'Hymn of the Pearl', trans. G. R. S. Mead, originally written in Syriac. For similar ontologies of the veil, see Reza Shah-Kazemi, *Common Ground between Islam and Buddhism: Spiritual and Ethical Affinities* (Fons Vitae, 2010), 53–70. According to Thurman, *Wisdom Is Bliss*, 77, the teachings of the 'Second Buddha', Nāgārjuna (100 BCE–500 CE), spread 'as far east as China and as far west as Iran, possibly even Mesopotamia, Egypt, and Greece'.

[121] *Vajrā*, Wisdom Library.

[122] Muhammad Khairi Mahyuddin, Dato' Zakaria Stapa and Faudzinaim Badaruddin, 'The Relationship between the Shari'ah, Tariqah, Haqiqah and Ma'rifah by Wan Sulaiman b Wan Siddik, a 19th Malay Sufi Scholar in the Malay World', *Journal of Islamic Studies and Culture* 1.1 (2013): 1–11 (3).

[123] Lings, *Shakespeare's Window*, 63. See Rūmī, *Spiritual Verses: The First Book of the Masnavi-ye Ma'navi*, trans. Alan Williams (Penguin, 2006), 69.

fulfils a self-prophecy of 'the Europeans' phobic fantasy': the Moor as a 'black devil'.[124] Othello's self-annihilation, in Islamic terms, can be seen not simply as self-damnation but as a Sufi's return to God, submitting to annihilation as part of the soul's path of purification. This *tariqāh* involves 'polish[ing] the interior dimension by removing the evil qualities and acquitting oneself with worthy qualities'[125]—even at the price of life. His last theoerotic words explain the inexorable logic of atonement in the aim of at-Oneness: 'I kissed thee ere I killed thee—no way but this, / Killing myself to die upon a kiss' (5.2.357–8). Othello thus becomes truly moored at the haven of awakening death. This kiss links back to his 2.1 'If it were now to die' speech and forward to his imminent death—literal and metaphorical—as the 'inevitable consequence of ecstatic love', which 'takes us out of ourselves to live in the thing we love'.[126] As this chapter has aimed to show, there is much value in reading Othello through a framework of Islamic wisdom: it is only through universalist, heart-centred Sufism that Othello finally transcends the subaltern denigration rooted in racism and anti-Islamism that he could not escape in human realms.

Transporting Othello into the present, our era of racial and social injustice intersecting with climate crisis reveals an increase in hate crimes, censorship and anti-woke policies against a backdrop of decades-long anti-Muslim Guantánamo Bay injustices and deep reckonings with colonial atrocities against Indigenous peoples.[127] At

---

[124] Vitkus, *Turning Turk*, 106; Calvo, 'Conversion Narratives', 235.

[125] Mahyuddin, Stapa and Badaruddin, 'Relationship', 3.

[126] Eleanor Johnson, *Staging Contemplation: Participatory Theology in Middle English Prose, Verse, and Drama* (U of Chicago P, 2018), 24.

[127] For a selective list, see William Barber, 'Racist Shootings "Don't Happen in a Vacuum": Bishop Barber on DeSantis, Trump & Those Who Spread Hate', interviewed by Amy Goodman, *Democracy Now!*, September 5, 2023, https://www.democracynow.org/2023/9/5/rev_william_barber_jacksonville_florida_shooting; Roxanne Dunbar-Ortiz, *An Indigenous Peoples' History of the United States* (Beacon, 2014); Ned Blackhawk, *The Rediscovery of America: Native Peoples and the Unmaking of U.S. History* (Yale UP, 2023); Geoffrey Skelley and Mary Radcliffe, 'Florida Started a Race to Reshape Conservatism. Now It Has Some Catching Up to Do', *FiveThirtyEight*, May 19, 2023, https://fivethirtyeight.com/features/desantis-florida-conservatism-2024/; Olga Kajtár-Pinjung, 'Finding a Tribe in a Hopeless Place: Mansoor Adayfi and Guantánamo Bay', in *Off Campus: Seggau School of Thought*, vol. 8 of *Stability, Security, and Happiness*, ed. Maureen Daly Goggin and Ursa Marinsek (Leykam, 2022), 57–70.

the time of this revising, November 2023, Israel's genocidal war on Palestinians in Gaza, a disproportionate response to the October 7 Hamas attack, can be seen as a contemporary macrocosmic example of 'turning Turk', premised on never-ending violence (instead of love and kinship) and a 'segregationist apartheid' of 'white' Jews against 'brown' Palestinians that intensifies the intersectionality of race, religion and colonialism operant in *Othello*.[128]

The resurgence of fascism in various forms is all the more reason to heed Patty Krawec's call for kinship through 'unforgetting' and adrienne maree brown's call to 'imagine new worlds that transition ideologies and norms, so that no one sees Black people as murderers, or Brown people as terrorists and aliens, but all of us as potential cultural and economic innovators' in what Madeline Sayet would call an ethics of welcome.[129] These reimaginings are critical in the Ecocene as BIPOC communities fight at the frontline of our CO_2lonialism-induced climate crisis as disparate victims of precarious living and forced migrations.[130] Shakespeare affirms: 'One touch of nature makes the whole world kin' (*Troilus and Cressida*, 3.3.172). But in our present world of bad relations, 'the way of the fat-taker' billionaires (*owasicu owe* in Lakota), having essentially colonised the

---

[128] Ta-Nehisi Coates, 'Ta-Nehisi Coates Speaks Out against Israel's "Segregationist Apartheid Regime" after West Bank Visit', interviewed by Amy Goodman and Nermeen Shaikh, *Democracy Now!*, November 2, 2023. https://www.democracynow.org/2023/11/2/ta_nehisi_coates

[129] Patty Krawec, *Becoming Kin: An Indigenous Call to Unforgetting the Past and Reimagining our Future* (Broadleaf Books, 2022); brown, *Emergent Strategy*, 20.

[130] Krawec, 180; '15 Black Environmental Leaders to Follow', *Yale Sustainability*, February 13, 2023, https://sustainability.yale.edu/blog/15-black-environmental-leaders-follow; Tom Goldtooth and Eriel Deranger. 'Indigenous Activists Tom Goldtooth & Eriel Deranger on the Link between Colonialism & Climate Crisis', interviewed by Amy Goodman, *Democracy Now!*, November 17, 2022, https://www.democracynow.org/2022/11/17/eriel_deranger_tom_goldtooth_at_cop27 For intersections between Sufi-Muslim and Indigenous wisdom cultures and the climate crisis, see Diaa Hadid, 'In Pakistan, residents are returning to ancient practices to deal with melting glaciers', *Weekend Edition Sunday*, NPR, September 3, 2023, https://www.npr.org/2023/09/03/1197461145/in-pakistan-residents-are-returning-to-ancient-practices-to-deal-with-melting-gl; Ananya Jahanara Kabir, 'Deep Topographies in the Fiction of Uzma Aslam Khan', *Journal of Postcolonial Writing* 47.2 (May 2011): 173–85 (183).

entire earth, is making it uninhabitable for all persons and living systems.[131] Even at this level of planetary catastrophe causing grief from layered histories of colonialist suffering, Krawec yet reminds us that 'grief is the persistence of love', that we, as kin, must continue to love and protect the beauty and the web of Life.[132] For Othello, too, who suffered personal tragedy as a victim of proto-colonialist ideology, grief ultimately became the persistence of love. May Othello's trial of wisdom encourage reflection on our own journeys of spiritual growth toward ecological rather than ego-logical action in the world—a world we must nurture and reworld together.[133]

---

[131] Nick Estes, Foreword to Krawec, *Becoming Kin*, xiii.

[132] Krawec, 119.

[133] Jane Hwang Degenhardt, 'Globality: The Virtue of Worlding', in *Shakespeare and Virtue: A Handbook*, ed. Julia Reinhard Lupton and Donovan Sherman (Cambridge UP, 2023), 334–46.

CHAPTER 9

NO MAGISTRATE, NO ENGINE, NO OIL: *CALVIN'S CASE* (1608) AND THE KINAESTHETIC WISDOM OF *THE TEMPEST*

Carolyn Sale

In his final lines in *The Tempest*, Caliban, one of only two characters who exhibit any kind of wisdom across the dramatic action, declares that he will 'be wise hereafter / And seek for grace' (5.1.295–6).[1] Whatever we may think this wisdom would entail, it is not a wisdom that we experience in the time and space of playgoing.[2] This chapter looks for the wisdom of the play in forms that are immanent to the play in performance. While one aspect of the argument here depends on what the actors have to say, the greater part depends on the play's corporeographic dimensions or what we experience as a result of the actors' embodied art. There is a law of nature in this play, one that we experience as spectators of the play's action, with our experience at its most powerful when the actors say nothing at all. The discussion sets this law in relation to the putative wisdom asserted in the jurisprudence of the most consequential law case of the first decade of the seventeenth century, *Calvin's Case* (1608). The jurisprudence established the possibility of English encounters with the Indigenous people of 'Virginia', the Algonquians, that would be anything but peaceful. The play in performance marshals the various arts at its disposal to cultivate the capacity for encounters with the Algonquians that might instead be one of non-violence. Representing something that stands in for the wisdom associated with the Algonquians and other Indigenous peoples

---

[1] William Shakespeare, *The Tempest*, ed. Virginia Mason Vaughan and Alden T. Vaughan (Arden Shakespeare, 1999, 2017). All further references to the text of the play in this chapter will be to this edition.

[2] For the most extended consideration of Caliban's declaration, see Julia Reinhard Lupton, '*The Tempest* and Black Natural Law', *Religions* 10.2 (February 2019): 1–15 (12–13). doi:10.3390/rel10020091

238]   *Carolyn Sale*

of the 'Americas' in the time and space of playgoing, the play makes immanent in performance a form of wisdom that audience members experience kinaesthetically, as they respond to the actors' display of their animate capacity, and from which they might shape another kind of law than that to be found in *Calvin's Case*.

Subditus *and* Transmarinis: *The 'Law of Nature' in* Calvin's Case

In 1608, when the justices of England's central courts convened to hear *Calvin's Case*, they took up a relatively simple question: whether Scots born after James VI of Scotland's accession to the English throne could hold property and prosecute property rights in England. From this question, to use Edward Coke's metaphor in his report, they mined gold. In early modern England, the common law was understood to be a form of common wisdom, spun, as the pretty simile of the legal writer John Davies suggested in 1615, out of the people like silkworms.[3] But the wisdom of the case was, Coke contended, an ancient wisdom to be found in the justices' hearts, where it was written, he claims, by God's finger.[4] High priests presiding over esoteric secrets that they communicated in the casuistry of their mystifying jurisprudence,[5] the justices traded in a charismatic authority in which King, God and Nature were legal fictions in whose names immense violence might be unleashed in the 'new world'.[6]

A central proposition of the jurisprudence was that every Englishman and Englishwoman was 'subditus natus', or a 'subject born',

---

[3] John Davies, *Le primer report des cases & matters en ley resolues & adiudges en les courts del Roy en Ireland* (John Franckton, 1615), *2ᵛ.

[4] Edward Coke, 77 *English Reports* (7. CO. REP. 1.a), 377–411 (381). Originally published in law French in *La sept part des reports Sr. Ed. Coke Chiualer* (Societie of Stationers, 1608).

[5] Peter Goodrich, 'The New Casuistry', *Critical Inquiry* 33.4 (Summer 2007): 673–709 (682).

[6] For other accounts of *Calvin's Case*, see Bradin Cormack, *A Power to Do Justice: Jurisdiction, English Literature, and the Rise of Common Law, 1509–1625* (U of Chicago P, 2007), 242–53; Margaret Franz, 'Legal Rhetoric and the Ambiguous Shape of the King's Two Bodies in *Calvin's Case* (1608)', *Advances in the History of Rhetoric* 20.3 (September 2017): 262–84; and Daniel J. Hulsebosch, 'The Ancient Constitution and the Expanding Empire: Sir Edward Coke's British Jurisprudence', *Law and History Review* 21.3 (Fall 2003): 439–82.

whose 'ligeance' was due to the king as their 'liege lord'.[7] This proposition was a retrograde construction, inasmuch as its logic was feudal, but also a dangerous innovation within English common law culture that lashed the capacity to 'do justice and judgment' to a single person's soul.[8] It was in both respects entirely consistent with the views that James had published in his 1598 *True Law of Free Monarchies*, in which the authority of a king was asserted as 'absolute', with power flowing always from himself.[9]

The subjection required was not, as it was in medieval political theology, to the *corpus mysticum*, or the members of the realm as corporate body, but to the majesty passed from one natural person to another on the death of a king.[10] In other words, the jurisprudence insists that 'ligeance' is due to the king not as the possessor of a second 'mystical body' in which all members of the realm are incorporate, but, rather, to his person, 'the invisible and immortal capacity' not having, of itself, either body or soul. The jurisprudence conspicuously omits any reference to the truisms of English legal and political theory up to this date, most notably the proposition that the king was 'sub deo' or beneath God.[11] In its 'imaginative rules', subjects are bound not to one another or to God, but to the sovereign as 'liege lord' via the figurative 'ligatures' of their subjection.[12]

At its most emphatic, the central proposition of the jurisprudence, that 'ligeance' was due to the king according to the 'law of nature', is expressed in a tortured syllogism that cites Aristotle to conclude that 'magistracy and government are of nature'.[13] The putatively 'natural' magistracy infused into the heart of 'creatures' at the time of their creation is inescapable. The idea of an inalterable subjection as 'not due

---

[7] *Calvin's Case*, 383.

[8] *Calvin's Case*, 390. See Hulsebosch, 'Ancient Constitution', 455.

[9] *The True Law of Free Monarchies* (1598), in *The Political Works of James I*, rpt. from the 1616 edition, ed. Charles Howard McIlwain (Harvard UP, 1918), 82.

[10] For the most extended discussion of the *corpus mysticum*, see Ernst Kantorowicz, *The King's Two Bodies: A Study in Medieval Political Theology* (Princeton UP, 1957), 194–206, 438–43.

[11] This is the proposition famously articulated in the thirteenth-century legal text *Bracton*.

[12] *Calvin's Case*, 400, 382.

[13] *Calvin's Case*, 392.

by the law or constitution of man' but 'by the law of nature' would help to drive forward James's imperial project in the 'new world', starting with the founding of Jamestown in Virginia, as much as the merchant capital that would fund the westward-bound ships of the Virginia Company. Intertwined, the fictions of the king's magistracy and his subjects' inescapable subjection to him would travel under another of the case's 'imaginative rules': that both the king's dominion and his subjects' 'ligeance' were *transmarinis* or still in force wherever subjects went 'beyond the seas'.[14] Subjection, Coke writes, was 'a quality of the mind . . . not confined within any place'.[15]

Historically, as Coke notes, this fiction was necessary to justify the king's ability to command men to go to war outside of England. Natural-born subjects had to be understood as always prospectively natural-born killers fighting the king's wars for him 'beyond the seas'. The historical rationale now had implications for the king's imperial ventures in the so-called 'new world'. This is clearest when Coke addresses the question of the status of the king's law in different places. While, as the jurisprudence had already established, no Englishman could escape his own subjection, he could have the authority to quash elsewhere, in the king's name, any form of law that would not prevail in England. The imagined authority of colonial adventurers to 'abrogate' the laws of peoples they encountered elsewhere flows from the fiction that with conquest 'the laws of the infidel are abrogated, for that they be not only against Christianity, but against the law of God and of nature, contained in the decalogue'.[16] '[I]n that case', Coke continues:

> until certain laws be established amongst them, the King by himself, and such Judges as he shall appoint, shall judge them and their causes according to natural equity, in such sort as Kings in ancient time did with their kingdoms, before any certain municipal laws were given . . .[17]

The transformation of legal order imagined here is not just the imposition of a state of exception on the terms that Giorgio Agamben

---

[14] *Calvin's Case*, 387.

[15] *Calvin's Case*, 388. Hulsebosch, 'Ancient Constitution', sees Coke as 'on the verge of recognising' 'a new kind of imperial subjectship' (466).

[16] *Calvin's Case*, 398.

[17] *Calvin's Case*, 398. See Hulsebosch, 'Ancient Constitution', 461–2.

No Magistrate, No Engine, No Oil　　　　　　[241

has imagined, that is, exception as the temporary suspension of the rule of law.[18] This is exception as obliteration or as the means of permanently razing laws; what English colonisers would find themselves razing in the 'new world' was any 'law of nature' that contradicted the English construction of the 'law of nature' as that which required subjects to express their subjection to their 'liege lord' even 'until the letting out of the last drop of [their] dearest heart's blood'.[19] At the very historical moment, then, in which the English were starting to have sustained encounters with the Algonquians of Virginia—encounters that would lead not just to war with them but to genocide—English jurisprudence was articulating precisely the fiction whereby English venturers stepping on to Virginia's shores were to understand themselves not only as still the king's subjects, but also as the petty sovereigns licensed to 'abrogate' any laws found there deemed inconsistent with the law of nature in *Calvin's Case*—a 'law of nature' that at least some of the Indigenous peoples of the Americas rejected.

Satisfying Nature

Coke could claim that 'the very law of nature itself never was nor could be altered or changed' but in the first decade of the seventeenth century there was a very strong sense (however accurate or inaccurate it may have been) that there were cultures elsewhere living according to a 'law of nature' that had entirely different premises from the law of nature in *Calvin's Case*. It is this very proposition that Shakespeare, by using the passage from Florio's Montaigne for Gonzalo's description of his ideal commonwealth, helped to keep alive, especially in the lines in which Gonzalo declares that his ideal commonwealth will be one in which nature 'bring[s] forth, / Of its own kind, all foison, all abundance, / To feed [his] innocent people' (2.3.163–5). From Vespucci in 1500 onwards, the claim was that there were peoples at various scattered locations in the Americas who had achieved what European cultures purportedly held out as an ideal, the holding of things in common, and who could do so

---

[18] Giorgio Agamben, *State of Exception*, trans. Kevin Attell (U of Chicago P, 2005), esp. 24–5.

[19] *Calvin's Case*, 385.

because they had found ways to live in relation to non-human nature in ways that made use of it without destroying its 'abundance'.[20] Shakespeare would have had more than one possible source for the idea, including Richard Eden's 1555 English edition of Peter Martyr d'Anghiera's 'Decades', which claimed amongst other things that the people of Guadalupe were content to live in ways that 'satisfie[d] nature'. Eden's translation also claims that these people had no understanding amongst them of '"Myne and Thine" (the seeds of all mischief)'.[21] They needed no such regime because they had 'no experience whatsoever of things'.[22]

Introduced into England with the Roman conquest, the regime of 'Myne and Thine' ('meum et tuum') existed in tension with the various forms of property-holding in England which were designated as those of 'communitie' rather than 'propertie'. As the legal historian David Seipp has argued, deep into the fifteenth century the idea that one might hold 'propertie' or own things continued to be considered a 'sin' in England; even as late as the turn of the sixteenth century it remained unclear whether the English common law would develop as a law of property.[23] Across the sixteenth century, however, 'propertie' so decisively supplanted 'communitie' that by 1600 the legal writer William Fulbecke could marshal even God against the proposition that the English were to hold things in common: 'And God woulde not haue sayd, Thou shalt not steale, if he would haue had all things common: for to steale, is to take away goods wherein others haue a propertie.'[24] As a result, by the time that the English men and women aboard the *Sea Venture* set sail for Virginia only to be shipwrecked off the coast of Bermuda in the episode long taken to

---

[20] For a quite different emphasis, see Stephen Orgel, 'Shakespeare and the Cannibals', in *Cannibals, Witches, and Divorce: Estranging the Renaissance*, ed. Marjorie Garber (Johns Hopkins UP, 1987), 40–66 (41).

[21] Richard Eden, *The decades of the newe worlde or West India* (Guilhelmi Powell, 1555), fo. 17ᵛ, sig. Eiᵛ.

[22] Francisco Guicciardini, *Storia d'Italia* (1537–40), as quoted in Alberto Toscano, '"By contraries execute all things": Figures of the Savage in European Philosophy', *Radical Philosophy* 2.04 (Spring 2019): 9–22 (12).

[23] David J. Seipp, 'The Concept of Property in the Early Common Law', *Law and History Review* 12.1 (Spring 1994): 29–91 (29, 91).

[24] William Fulbecke, *A Direction, or Preparative to the Study of the Lawe* (Thomas Wight, 1600), 57ᵛ.

No Magistrate, No Engine, No Oil [243

be an inspiration for Shakespeare's play, people who were on their home ground experiencing a radical diminution or suppression of forms of the 'common' were about to find themselves confronting, in their colonising enterprises, something that resembled the opposite: cultures organised around the holding in common of nature's 'abundance' or 'foison'. These were cultures against which English colonisers were asked to bear their swords in the name of a sovereignty for which *Calvin's Case* had spun their prospective violence's enabling fictions. In his 1625 edition of William Strachey's 'True Reportory' of what happened to those aboard the *Sea Venture*, Samuel Purchas would claim that all of this was to the good; the English, having been civilised by Roman swords, could now bear their civilising swords against others.[25]

As Alberto Toscano has noted, the view of Indigenous peoples of the Americas as the seventeenth century unfolded was of 'an immanent and constitutive alterity' that needed to be suppressed if a legal regime of 'mine and thine' was to be successfully transplanted to the 'new world'.[26] Those aboard the *Sea Venture* who attempted to join the Algonquians in ways of living that 'satisfied nature' were denounced in part 4 of the 1610 book *A true declaration of the estate of the colonie in Virginia* as 'mutinous loiterers'.[27] That book declares 'A Colony is therefore denominated', 'because they should be *Coloni*, the Tillers of the Earth',[28] but the 'mutinous' preferred to join the Algonquians in simply living off Nature's bounty. One of the allegations, directly pertinent to Caliban's resistance to gathering wood for Prospero, was that they would prefer to 'eat their fish raw, rather then they would go a stones cast to fetch woode and dress it'.[29] As Meredith Skura has

---

[25] Samuel Purchas, *Purchas his Pilgrimes, In Five Bookes* (Henrie Fetherstone, 1625), fo. 1755, sig. Gggggggg3ʳ.

[26] Toscano, 'Figures of the Savage', 10.

[27] *A true declaration of the estate of the colonie in Virginia* (William Barret, 1610), fo. 36, sig. E4ᵛ. In a discussion of the relationship of William Strachey's 'True Reportory' as printed by Purchas to the 1610 *True declaration*, Alden T. Vaughan contends that the most likely author of this book was Edwin Sandys. See 'William Strachey's "True Reportory" and Shakespeare: A Closer Look at the Evidence', *Shakespeare Quarterly* 59.3 (Fall 2008): 245–73 (247–9, 255).

[28] *True declaration*, fo. 36, sig. E4ᵛ.

[29] *True declaration*, fo. 36, sig. E4ᵛ.

244]   *Carolyn Sale*

noted, the accounts of the colony written between 1606 and 1610 provide considerable evidence that some of the 'venturers' wished to participate in the 'utopic' possibilities of 'Virginia'.[30] The 'mutinous' were, it seems, refusing to be marshalled as the labourers necessary to the snatching of 'commodities' to be transported back to England in the historical developments which would result in the rise of a view of Nature as inanimate, exploitable stuff to have its goodness wrested from it at as little cost as possible as part of the emergence of the 'capitalocene'.[31] In an account that Purchas cobbled together from various writers' notes there is also evidence of some rejection of the profiteering attitudes amongst them:

> [T]he worst mischiefe was, our gilded Refiners with their golden promises, made all men their slaues in hope of recompence; there was no talke, no hope, no worke, but digge Gold, wash Gold, refine Gold, load Gold, such a brute of Gold, as one mad fellow desired to bee buried in the Sands, least they should by their Art make Gold of his bones.[32]

It is this kind of critique in which we see Shakespeare's play participating.

As Carolyn Merchant has argued, the 'disemboweling' of Nature taking place on both sides of the Atlantic went hand in hand with the destruction of the long-standing idea of a 'world soul' that bound all life together as one organism in a pneumatic cosmology.[33] This transformation in ideology would make possible the destruction of peoples whose cultures involved a continuing reverence for nature. One of the men at the centre of Merchant's account of the ideological transformations, Francis Bacon, helped fashion the arguments in

---

[30] Meredith Anne Skura, 'Discourse and the Individual: The Case of Colonialism in *The Tempest*', *Shakespeare Quarterly* 40.1 (Spring 1989): 42–69 (55–6).

[31] Jason W. Moore, 'The Capitalocene, Part I: On the Nature and Origins of our Ecological Crisis', *The Journal of Peasant Studies* 44.3 (April 2017): 594–630.

[32] Purchas, *Purchas his Pilgrimes*, fo. 1711, sig. Ccccccc5ʳ.

[33] Carolyn Merchant, *The Death of Nature: Women, Ecology, and the Scientific Revolution* (Harper & Row, 1980), 104. Merchant quotes the Roman playwright Seneca on this cosmology as expressing itself in the breath that Earth 'exhales from every part of it day and night' (24). See also Lupton, Chapter 2 of this volume.

Calvin's Case.[34] The Baconian project, as Amitav Ghosh notes, was to make even humans the 'mute resources that enabled the metaphysical leap whereby the Earth and everything in it could also be reduced to inertness'.[35] Encouraged to see Virginia as the site of 'commodities' waiting to be seized, the English were positioned not to concern themselves with the possibility that the Algonquians might offer them one or another form of wisdom worth emulating, including forms of wisdom Europeans had once held. They were encouraged, rather, to see themselves as the 'ligatures' of the racist imperium that might be asserted in the king's name, beyond the seas, as the agents of a 'scheme of differential separations' that cast the Algonquians as less than human and capable of being 'cut . . . off from the face of the earth'.[36] This is what would happen, in 1637, at Mystic in what is now Connecticut, when the English killed members of the Algonquian tribe living there, the Pequots, by setting ablaze their dwellings. The surviving accounts of this massacre by the two men who led it depict God laughing to see hundreds of 'souls' perishing in the 'fiery oven' the English had created.[37] *The Tempest* responds to the exterminist ideology that would license such genocide, in favour of another 'law of nature' imagined to be thriving on the other side of the Atlantic.

No Oil

A great deal has been made of the material that Shakespeare cribs from John Florio's English translation of Montaigne's discussion in his *Essais* of the Tupinamba people of Brazil ('Antartike France'). For the English at the turn of the seventeenth century Montaigne's account of the Tupinamba was the most specific account of Indigenous peoples

---

[34] Gavin Loughton, 'Calvin's Case and the Origins of the Rule Governing "Conquest" in English Law', *Australian Journal of Legal History* 8.2 (January 2004): 143–80 (161–3).

[35] Amitav Ghosh, *The Nutmeg's Curse: Parables for a Planet in Crisis* (U of Chicago P, 2021), 37.

[36] Catherine Keller, *Political Theology of the Earth: Our Planetary Emergency and the Struggle for a New Public* (Columbia UP, 2018), 47–9, and Bacon as quoted in Ghosh, *Nutmeg's Curse*, 26.

[37] Ghosh, 24–5. The lieutenants' names were John Mason and John Underhill.

of the Americas living in ways that 'satisfied nature'. 'The lawes of nature', Florio's translation reads, 'doe yet command them.'[38] Montaigne notes that the Tupinamba were willing to shed blood to protect their own lands from invasion by others and had a cannibalistic rite for dealing with the enemy once he had been defeated, but also that they had no acquisitive impulses whatsoever. Their culture was premised on contentment with the 'abundance' that they had, in the place in which they were nestled—'Whatever is beyond it is to them superfluous'.[39] They spent their days in dancing. To Montaigne's account, which attributes to the Tupinamba 'no use of wine, corn or metal',[40] Shakespeare makes a significant revision when he adds the words 'or oil' (2.1.154). Let us imagine that the words 'or oil' are there to do more than fill out a line of blank verse.

Oil features centrally in the art by which Prospero exercises his dominion in the play, alchemy. Konrad Gesner's alchemical text *The newe iewell of health wherein is contayned the most excellent secretes of phisicke and philosophie* (1576) includes over 1,200 references to the processes by which oil can be derived from flowers, seeds, fruits, spices, gums, dry lees of wine, wood (especially juniper), eggs, amber, honey, wax, paper, linen, metals and salts, as well as 'beastes', 'deade mens bones' and 'excrements of chyldren'.[41] Thomas Tymme's *A dialogue philosophicall. Wherein natures secret closet is opened* (1612) declares that 'out of the . . . three beginnings of minerals, vegetables, and animals, divers oyles, liquors, and Salts, apt for mans vse . . . may by Chymicall Art be extracted', with 'oyle' having a special importance because it is 'by a certaine native hete . . . of a property agreeing to fire'.[42] The alchemical activity is imagined to be beneficent—that is, a means of producing oils that will serve to sustain human health. Dead men's bones may, for example, serve as

---

[38] *Essays vvritten in French by Michael Lord of Montaigne*, trans. John Florio (Edward Blount and William Barret, 1613), fol. 104, sig. K4^v.

[39] *Essays*, trans. Florio, fol. 104, sig. K4^v.

[40] *Essays*, trans. Florio, fol. 102, sig. K3^v.

[41] Konrad Gesner, *The newe iewell of health wherein is contayned the most excellent secretes of phisicke and philosophie* (Henrie Denham, 1576), fo. 170^v, sig. Aaiii^v.

[42] Thomas Tymme, *A dialogue philosophicall. Wherein natures secret closet is opened* (Clement Knight, 1612), fo. 51, sig. H2^r.

No Magistrate, No Engine, No Oil [247

a balm for healing the 'cut' sinews of the living.[43] Prospero, on the other hand, calls for his 'spirits' to 'grind' the 'joints' of his enemies or 'shorten' their 'sinews' (4.1.258–9). Oil may be proscribed, then, because it is associated with the manipulations of nature whereby men like Prospero assert their dominion over others by weakening, possibly destroying, their bodily integrity. But given that Gonzalo also refuses to allow any 'engine' in his commonwealth there may be something more at stake.

European cultures had had hydraulics since the Romans, but the various 'engines' in which oil as viscous spirit might be put to work either to help things burn or to move matter would shape modernity.[44] We see some sense of this in Prospero's characterisation of Ariel's groaning when he discovers him trapped in the 'cloven pine': 'thou didst vent thy groans', Prospero declares, 'as fast as millwheels strike' (1.2.280–1). As Moore notes, the 'new technics—a repertoire of science, power, and machinery'—included the Dutch hydraulics that were being used to move non-human nature in unprecedented ways,[45] and we can see from Agricola's mid-sixteenth-century *De Re Metallica* that oil was lighting the lamps that miners would take with them as they descended into the earth in search of metals or coal.[46] As Amitav Ghosh has noted, at least as early as the eleventh century CE the Chinese celebrated their capacity to turn bitumen into coal, with 'late pre-modern China' exploiting the 'technical vigor and virtuosity' of oil running through bamboo tubing in 'domestic gas cookers, domestic gas lighting, and a primitive form of mobile illuminating using bottled oil'.[47] And as Paula De Vos notes, in sixteenth-century Europe bricks made of clay and bitumen were used to heat the furnaces for the making of 'philosophers' oil'.[48] Oil was

---

[43] See, for example, Gesner, *The newe iewell*, fo. 46ᵛ, sig. Uiiᵛ.

[44] Moore, 'Capitalocene', 616.

[45] Moore, 'Capitalocene', 610, 613.

[46] Georgius Agricola, *De Re Metallica*, trans. from the first Latin edition of 1556 by Herbert Clark Hoover and Lou Henry Hoover (Dover, 1950), 99. Project Gutenberg. https://www.gutenberg.org/files/38015/38015-h/38015-h.htm

[47] Amitav Ghosh, *The Great Derangement: Climate Change and the Unthinkable* (U of Chicago P, 2016), 997–8.

[48] Paula De Vos, 'Rosewater and Philosophers' Oil: Thermo-Chemical Processing in Medieval and Early Modern Spanish Pharmacy', *Centaurus* 60.3 (August 2018): 159–72 (165).

248]   *Carolyn Sale*

already at work, then, in the sixteenth century, firing the 'new technics'. Shakespeare's proscription of oil may derive from a simple and reasonable extrapolation from oil's existing uses in his lifetime to forms of use, and a scale of use, to come, or foresight for which Sycorax as a 'blue-eyed hag' (1.2.269) is one oblique figure. As Kristina Richardson has argued, the 'blue-eyed hag' is almost certainly a reference to the legendary Arabic woman Zarqā' al-Yamāma, who 'possessed vision so acute that she could spot a white hair in milk and thus was able to see into distances that would take three days to reach'.[49] Shakespeare's foresight involves a glance forward across both geography and time, in the imagining of oil, with its 'property agreeing to fire', prospectively animating engines to come that would meet the desire to move beyond dependence upon a 'somatic regime' of either human or 'animal muscle'.[50] But the proscription may have a third dimension: it may spring from a sense of what oil signifies as the end-product of any human art for wresting it from either living or non-living matter.

In a woodcut for the 1618 book *Atalanta fugiens* (see Figure 9.1), Theodor de Bry depicts a magus wearing spectacles like goggles tracking Nature through the night with the assistance of a staff and a lamp in an image that is ominous: 'Nature' may be bent to the magus's will, in places beyond the view of others, so that he may extract from her the oils that serve his purposes, with the arts by which he does so breaking linkages between human and non-human natures at any location to which he may travel. Once the oil is extracted from its source (whether that source is a metal, something long dead or something killed to create it), it too may travel, perhaps across great distances, to have another existence apart from the organic relations from which it first sprang. This can, of course, be a good

---

[49] Kristina Richardson, 'Blue and Green Eyes in the Islamicate Middle Ages', *Annales islamologiques* 48.1 (2014): 13–29, par. 4. https://doi.org/10.4000/anisl.3051 As Richardson notes, Shakespeare had already drawn upon the legends associated with Zarqā' al-Yamāma in *Macbeth*, in the idea of the forest that moves towards Dunsinane.

[50] Nancy Fraser, *Cannnibal Capitalism: How our System Is Devouring Democracy, Care, and the Planet—and What We Can Do about It* (Verso, 2022), 94; Merchant, *Death of Nature*, 217. See also Moore, 'Capitalocene', 607. Fraser notes that the 'principal way to augment available energy' for a somatic regime was 'through conquest' (95).

Figure 9.1 *Magus goggled and tracking Nature through the night with staff and lamp* (by Theodor de Bry, in Michael Maier, *Atalanta fugiens, hoc est, Emblemata nova de secretis naturae chymica*, 1618).

thing. 'Extraction', as Imre Szeman and Jennifer Wenzel note, is not in and of itself a problem. Processes of extraction may, however, lend themselves to *extractivism*, the 'ruthless looting of the environment for the benefit of a distant few—in short, colonialism'.[51] Extractivists have no interest in the reciprocal relations amongst organic forms that are essential to meeting the 'goal' of any 'natural system', the 'proliferation of life'.[52] Extractivism treats nature, instead, as the

---

[51] Imre Szeman and Jennifer Wenzel, 'What Do We Talk About When We Talk About Extractivism?', *Textual Practice* 35.3 (2021): 505–23 (507).
[52] Robin Wall Kimmerer, *Braiding Sweetgrass: Indigenous Wisdom, Scientific Knowledge, and the Teachings of Plants* (Milkweed, 2013, 2015), 334.

'stuff' from which profit may be made without beginning to meet the responsibilities of 'satisfying nature'.

In living systems, as Tyson Yunkaporta notes, 'nothing can be held, accumulated, stored'.[53] Every vial of oil, on the other hand, is an instance of 'Nature . . . decomposed into discrete units' and abstracted from the conditions that made it possible.[54] In the most destructive scenarios, these processes of extraction let power accrue to those who have the capacity not only to manage the extraction but to animate the extra-human nature that may result when oil fuels one or another 'engine'. But given that oils may be found, too, in human flesh, and not just when a person is dead, to ban oil is to ban any process that allows for the use of one person's flesh or animate capacity by another. As Laurie Shannon has noted, we see 'repeated blurrings of personhood and oily substance' in the Shakespearean drama as part of a 'persistent recognition that human matter is fat, oily, grease-laden, meltable, combustible, and consumable'.[55] A category of substance that includes forms of energy that may be captured at one location and released at another, oil lends itself to the necropolitics on display in the play, which allow Prospero to marshal nature's animacy against others.

The Filthy Mantled Pool

The play imagines sites of extraction as places where men like Prospero produce and leave their 'filth'. As Toscano notes, the leftovers of alchemical experiments were called *caput mortuum* or the dead heads,[56] and the first meaning of 'filth', in Old English, was 'decayed

---

[53] Tyson Yunkaporta, *Sand Talk: How Indigenous Thinking Can Save the World* (HarperCollins, 2019), 39.

[54] Moore, 'Capitalocene', 606.

[55] Laurie Shannon et al., 'Editor's Column: Literature in the Ages of Wood, Tallow, Coal, Whale Oil, Gasoline, Atomic Power, and Other Energy Sources', *PMLA* 126.2 (2011): 305–26 (311–12). See Katherine Walker, 'Shakespeare and the Magic of Mummy: *Julius Caesar*'s Consumed/Consuming Bodies', *Preternature: Critical and Historical Studies on the Preternatural* 7.2 (2018): 215–38, for a discussion of the practices of eating mummified flesh.

[56] Toscano, 'Figures of the Savage', 11.

tissue'.[57] When Prospero refers to Caliban as the 'filth' upon whom his 'nurture' will stick, he designates another man as the subject of a failed experiment. That experiment is one in which he would let Caliban have only a limited relationship to his own animate capacity. Prospero would assert himself as the regulatory authority who can determine when this capacity may be exercised and when it may be constrained or frustrated, with Caliban ideally serving as nothing more than the 'animal muscle' that provides Prospero with the fuel that he urgently requires to fire his alchemical furnace. To secure this somatic regime Prospero must sever Caliban's relationship with non-human nature and any other person that might join him in undermining his dominion.

We hear evidence of the first dimension of Prospero's project both in 1.2, when Caliban claims that Prospero keeps him stied in 'hard rock' (344), and in 2.2, when Caliban reports that the spirits that Prospero marshals through his art 'fright him with urchin-shows', 'pitch [him] i'th'mire' and 'like hedgehogs' 'tumbl[e] in [his] barefoot way and mount / Their pricks at [his] footfall' (2.2.5–12). Presumably Prospero does this when Caliban seeks to range from the rock across the 'rest o'th' island' (1.2.245). The hedgehog-spirits direct the wisdom of non-human creatures against Caliban. (One of the perceived signs of a hedgehog's wisdom was its ability to 'enclose' itself in its 'hull' in order to protect itself from any hurt.[58]) They also sever Caliban's relation with non-human nature by keeping him from walking upon the earth. Later Ariel, by making a sound of 'lowing', leads Caliban, Stephano and Trinculo 'calf-like' 'through / Toothed briers, sharp furzes, [and] pricking gorse and thorns / Which entered their frail shins' (4.1.179–81), suggesting that even when Caliban does manage to range beyond his 'rock' he can be subject to a flesh-tearing punishment. The landscape of hedges laced with hawthorn links Caliban's predicament to that of English commoners who lost their access to land through enclosure. The implication is that as English 'venturers' went to the 'new world' to seize its commodities,

---

[57] 'filth, n., 1.a', *OED* online.

[58] Pierre Viret, *The schoole of beastes; intituled, the good housholder, or the oeconomickes. Made dialogue-wise, by M. Peter Viret, translated out of French into English, by I. R.* (Printed by Robert Vvalde-graue, 1585), fo. 53, sig. D3ʳ.

they would bring with them the regime of 'mine and thine' and carve up the landscape of the Americas so that it was no longer a place of 'open gardens'.[59] The English would, in short, transform the landscape of 'Virginia', to make it 'toothed'. But the analytic imagination of the play extends its dark vision of what the men who would prosper off the 'new world' might do when Shakespeare's allegory has Ariel leave the three men 'dancing up to th'chins' in the 'filthy mantled pool' just beyond Prospero's 'cell' (4.1.182–3). In a site of nature degraded by Prospero's experiments, the animate capacity of those who would undermine Prospero's dominion is rendered futile. The conspirators are stuck in a filth that saps them of their own dynamic potential and leaves them using what kinaesthetic power they can muster to one end, survival.

The spectre that lurks here is much grimmer than what we see with the Neapolitan and Milanese courtiers and their entourage who are subjected, along with the mariners, to a storm in which they seem to be drowned but from which they are saved so that Prospero can manage their animate capacity by putting them to sleep or making them 'stand charmed' (s.d. after 5.1.57). In this variation on the play's theme of the drowned/'undrowned', the grim spectre is of living men deposited in an alchemist's 'bath' and, by extension, to borrow a metaphor from Catherine Keller, the possibility of a 'monstrous inequity of lives liquefied as commodities'.[60]

As Stanton Garner has argued, the human body is 'a kinesthetic entity, alive with circulatory, respiratory, tactile, and affective energies', with our experience of this kinaesthetic capacity central to our sense of our autonomy.[61] Trapped in a site of nature degraded by Prospero's experiments, Caliban, Stephano and Trinculo are figures for one person's power to capture the kinaesthetic power of others for his own uses. Immersion of the human in non-human nature is not in itself a negative proposition. As Emanuele Coccia argues, life is properly understood as 'a state of immersion of each thing in

---

[59] Eden, *Decades*, fo. 17ᵛ, sig. Eiᵛ. See the discussion in Margaret T. Hodgen, 'Montaigne and Shakespeare Again', *Huntington Library Quarterly* 16.1 (November 1952): 23–42 (32–3).

[60] Keller, *Political Theology of the Earth*, 32.

[61] Stanford B. Garner Jr, *Kinesthetic Spectatorship in the Theatre: Phenomenology, Cognition, Movement* (Palgrave Macmillan, 2018), 38.

No Magistrate, No Engine, No Oil   [253

all other things'.[62] But as Tyson Yunkaporta notes, any truly self-sustaining system of life must be 'heterarchical': every part of it must be treated as an equal part of the system's 'intelligence' and free to exercise its animate capacity according to its own will.[63] Shakespeare's imagery is of the kinaesthetic power of human persons contained and frustrated by a dominating entity that first renders non-human nature as 'filth' and then uses that 'filth' to deprive others of their agency.

The victims of such processes have a difficult time reclaiming that agency precisely because the 'filth', nature degraded, is also the site of nature 'mantled' or occluded. English commoners usually experienced 'nature' in the late medieval and early modern period in the form of the 'feudal landed property' that they worked, which was 'already by its very nature huckstered land—*the earth . . . estranged from man*'.[64] Even before the onset of significant enclosing in the early sixteenth century, the English were conditioned to think of nature, especially in the form of 'soil', as that which could belong to a few and be only worked by the rest; they were conditioned, in short, to think of land as properly generative only for the lord and of themselves as animate 'stuff' bound to the feudal lord's uses. Prospero's 'filthy mantled pool' extends this estrangement to 'nature' more broadly which he manipulates to gain his mastery over others whose creative capacity, like that of English commoners working the land that belonged to the lord, was mantled to them. Even as new horizons might open to some Englishmen and Englishwomen as they went 'beyond the seas', there was the danger, as Shakespeare's ensuing allegory of the 'glistering apparel' suggests, that they would prefer to relate to the 'new world' as the site of commodities to be plundered rather than the place where they might experience an entirely different way of living, one in which they might not just 'satisfy nature' but have the opportunity to express their animate capacity outside the control of any 'liege lord' and his debilitating fictions. In 4.1, only Caliban has the wisdom to

---

[62] As quoted in Peter Goodrich, 'The Pure Theory of Law Is a Hole in the Ozone Layer', *University of Colorado Law Review* 92.4 (Fall 2021): 985–1,012 (1,009).

[63] Yunkaporta, *Sand Talk*, 82–3.

[64] Marx as quoted in Kohei Saito, *Karl Marx's Ecosocialism: Capital, Nature, and the Unfinished Critique of Political Economy* (Monthly Review, 2017), 36, Saito's emphasis.

254] *Carolyn Sale*

understand that the 'glistering apparel' is 'trash' designed to distract the conspirators from their political goal, with the prospect of their being dehumanised as a result: 'I will have none on't. We shall lose our time, / And all be turned to barnacles, or to apes / With foreheads villainous low' (4.1.246–8). One way or another, Prospero will make them, Caliban declares, 'strange stuff' (4.1.235). The play's appeal to audience members is to extricate themselves from conditions of 'filth' without letting themselves be subject to the culture of the 'glistering', so that they might not only keep themselves from serving as the monstrous 'ligatures' on which the English king's racist imperial dreams might be made, but might liberate themselves in relation to another law of 'nature'.

Sea-Change

The play holds out the promise that the radical transformation of a culture is possible. We find one expression of this in Ariel's most famous song:

> Full fathom five thy father lies;
> Of his bones are coral made;
> Those are pearls that were his eyes:
> Nothing of him that doth fade
> But doth suffer a sea-change
> Into something rich and strange.
> Sea-nymphs hourly ring his knell. (1.2.397–403)

The song asks us to imagine a fantastical process that we cannot observe of human matter subjected to a radical 'sea-change', one in which a human person is transformed into non-human material both biotic and abiotic, human bones into coral and human eyes into pearl. Shakespeare here harnesses Thomas Tymme's idea of the alchemical power of the 'Salt of the Sea', which 'containeth in it the radicall Balsam of Nature': 'it is the cause of the generation, first of most pretious pearles in the shels of fishes, and of Corall, springing out of the bowels of hard stones and rockes, spreading forth branches like a Tree'.[65] The text appeals to this idea of 'sea-change'

---

[65] Tymme, *Dialogue philosophicall*, fo. 56, sig. H4ᵛ.

elsewhere when Ariel claims that he has plunged the Naples-bound travellers into 'foaming brine' (1.2.211) and Prospero claims that brains may be 'boiled' (5.1.60). The question is: what kind of change might the play effect through its art?

The person whose death is being imaginatively knelled is a king (indeed, the play's only on-stage king). This king certainly does not have a power that is 'transmarinis'. The sea, rather, goes to work on him, in a relation that presumes a law of nature quite different from that of *Calvin's Case*. Ariel's song imagines Nature as 'a constantly mutating being ... through which the human passes and which passes through the human'.[66] This flux, like the sounds of the island that Caliban claims are not to be 'feard' (3.2.135), has the potential to create non-exploitative relations between human and non-human nature. The implication is that the play has the power to transform us in a process that is entirely gentle.

In Ariel's song, the idea of the ceremony and its blanched dead king are purely linguistic constructs. But the knelling of the bells that accompanies it marks the theatrical space as the site of a possible transformation into which playgoers are drawn as a matter of sensual experience. Unlike *Hamlet*, which trades in the idea of playgoers participating in a shared experience of breath,[67] *The Tempest* trades in the idea that what passes through playgoers in the time and space of playgoing is sound. As Mayra Cortes has argued, the play stages a great deal of its resistance to Prospero's projection of dominion through elements that are 'acousmatic'.[68] But in addition to this, the experience may alter playgoers not simply because of what they hear but also because of what they are asked to observe, in the form of life in motion, or a representation of exactly what Prospero would thwart in Caliban, his kinaesthetic potential. As Garner notes, 'theatre embraces kinesis, kinesthetic experience, animation, and movement perception as its *sine qua non*'.[69] *The Tempest*'s embracing of the kinaesthetic makes a form of wisdom immanent in the performance.

---

[66] Goodrich, 'Pure Theory of Law', 1,009.

[67] See Carolyn Sale, 'Eating Air, Feeling Smells: *Hamlet*'s Theory of Performance', *Renaissance Drama* 35 (2006): 145–68.

[68] Mayra Cortes, 'Acousmatic Noise: Racialization and Resistance in *The Tempest*'s "New World" Soundscape', *Early Theatre* 25.1 (2022): 79–106.

[69] Garner, *Kinesthetic Spectatorship*, 55.

256]   *Carolyn Sale*

A More Gentle-Kind Generation

Consider what we are asked to observe in 3.3, after we hear some 'Solemn and strange music'. The stage directions indicate that we are to see 'Prospero at the top (invisible)' and then 'several strange shapes', who enter 'bringing in a banquet'. These 'shapes' are to 'dance about [the banquet] with gentle actions of salutations' and then, after inviting the shipwrecked courtiers to eat, are to depart. The music continues, with Alonso asking 'What harmony is this?' and Gonzalo referring to the 'marvellous sweet music' (3.3.18–19). But Gonzalo also draws our attention to the non-linguistic dimension of what we are asked to experience when he declares that what the courtiers have just witnessed are 'manners . . . more gentle, kind, than of / Our human generation you shall find / Many—nay, almost any' (3.3.32–4). We are to find this gentleness in them despite the fact, as Gonzalo notes, the figures are of a 'monstrous' shape.

We cannot know what it is about the actors embodying the 'shapes' that may have made them appear 'monstrous', but Gonzalo's adjective connects them to the play's putative 'monster', Caliban. Their gentleness presumably bears some relation to the gentleness in evidence in Caliban's speech about the isle's sweet noises and the dream they inspire, that of a natural abundance that descends upon him from above as the heavens open their clouds to drop their riches upon him. This is an abundance from which Caliban has been severed.[70] If we understand the 'shapes' to be 'monstrous' because they are, like Caliban, not white, there is a great deal more at stake in their 'manners'.

I can find no earlier critical discussion of the play that considers that the 'shapes' are 'monstrous' because they, like Caliban, may be something other than white, even if they are not of the same 'hue'.[71]

---

[70] See Julia Reinhard Lupton, 'Creature Caliban', *Shakespeare Quarterly* 51.1 (Spring 2000): 1–23 (12–13).

[71] 'Hue' is the language of other plays, especially *Titus Andronicus*. See my discussion in 'Black Aeneas: Race, English Literary History, and the "Barbarous" Poetics of *Titus Andronicus*', *Shakespeare Quarterly* 62.1 (Spring 2011): 25–52. In a brief 1914 article for *The Journal of English and Germanic Philology*, Rachel M. Kelsey noted that 'Indian music and dances are among the features of Indian life most enthusiastically described in [contemporary] accounts and may easily have caught Shakespeare's attention'. 'Indian Dances in "The Tempest"', *The Journal of English and Germanic Philology* 13.1 (January 1914): 98–103 (100).

No Magistrate, No Engine, No Oil   [257

Perhaps this has been assumed, but not deemed notable. Even scholarship on *The Tempest* expressly dedicated to non-verbal eloquence
in the play has nothing to say about what it is we are asked to see in
these figures despite the fact that their actions make them, as Gonzalo
would have it, a 'more gentle-kind' generation than exists elsewhere.[72]
Characterisation of the shapes as 'spirits' with no attention to how
they are represented or what they represent is typical.[73] But what if
we find the shapes to be, like Caliban, figures of 'darkness'? As Ian
Smith has demonstrated, the theatrical company had several ways of
achieving such a representation, including using a mixture of charred
cork and oil,[74] and an early account of the Algonquians claims that
male dancers appeared to Captain John Smith with their skin painted
black, red and white.[75] If we imagine that the actors representing
the shapes are painted figures, we might have in them an idealised
representation of Indigenous persons of the Americas through which
the actors make immanent in the theatrical space a generalised sense
of the wisdom of those persons, whose being is expressed not, as
George Percy would have it, as that of 'Wolues or Deuils', 'shouting, howling, and stamping against the ground, with many Anticke
tricks and faces',[76] but as the epitome of gentle-kindness. Painted,
Shakespeare's 'shapes' would also bear some relation to the figures

---

[72] See, for example, David M. Bevington, *Action Is Eloquence: Shakespeare's
Language of Gesture* (Harvard UP, 1984), and Anthony B. Dawson, *Watching
Shakespeare: A Playgoers' Guide* (St. Martin's, 1988), 231–41. In abbreviating 'the gentle, kind' to the 'gentle-kind', I follow the online edition at http://
shakespeare.mit.edu/tempest/full.html

[73] See, for example, Barbara Fuchs, 'Conquering Islands: Contextualizing *The Tempest*', *Shakespeare Quarterly* 48.1 (Spring 1997): 45–62, for whom only Ariel
and Caliban are 'islanders', and Patricia Akhimie, 'Performance in the Periphery:
Colonial Encounters and Entertainments', in *Acoustemologies in Contact: Sounding Subjects and Modes of Listening in Early Modernity*, ed. Emily Wilbourne and
Suzanne G. Cusick (Open Book, 2021), 65–82.

[74] Ian Smith, 'Othello's Black Handkerchief', *Shakespeare Quarterly* 64.1 (Spring
2013): 1–25 (9–10).

[75] Purchas, *Purchas his Pilgrimes*, fo. 1708, sig. Cccccc3ᵛ.

[76] George Percy, in an account published by Purchas, describing Algonquian dancers
at 'Cape Comfort' (now Point Comfort) in 1606, fo. 1687, sig. Aaaaaaa4ᵛ. For
Percy's genocidal conduct, see Alden T. Vaughan, '"Expulsion of the Salvages":
English Policy and the Virginia Massacre of 1622', *The William and Mary Quarterly* 35.1 (January 1978): 57–84 (67).

that had appeared before an audience at Whitehall a few years earlier when twelve court ladies including the queen represented the goddess Aethiopia and black nymphs who were to be 'laved' in the sea dew called 'ros-marine' and then blanched by the presence of the sun (James I) in Ben Jonson's *Masque of Blackness*.[77] The imagined colour(s) of Shakespeare's shapes would not, however, be something to be blanched or 'laved' away.

As Julia Lupton has argued, through Caliban the play participates in a tradition of 'black natural law' that 'unfixes the *imago dei* from its presumptive whiteness'.[78] As we have seen, in the course of the play's action an imaginary king is reduced to a figure of hyper-whiteness in his death—blanched, as a sign of some whiteness that must die?—even as animated painted figures are presented as the epitome of a gentle-kindness to be admired and emulated. This accords with early accounts of Virginia evidencing, as Skura notes, attempts amongst the English to resist racial prejudice.[79] Catherine Keller's *Political Theology of the Earth* (2018) may also help us recover the kind of thinking that informs *The Tempest*. Keller argues that against the 'bright white supremacy' that would dominate the planet even to the destruction of all life on it, we should set an 'ecogod' of 'brilliant darkness' that nurtures an endlessly creative animate capacity in all through an 'amorous agonism' of 'sensuous intersectionalities'.[80] For Keller the figures for a recovery of the pneumatic cosmology or 'cosmic animacy' that a racist early modern sovereignty repressed appear as hope 'draped in black'.[81]

That the shapes do not speak but simply act is crucial to drawing the audience into an experience of a sensuous intersectionality that resists racist presumptions. As the legal theorist Peter Goodrich has recently argued, new law that would support all sentient beings on

---

[77] Ben Jonson, *The Masque of Blackness* (1605), in *The Works of Ben Jonson*, ed. William Gifford (Phillips, Sampson, 1853), 660–3, Luminarium Editions Online, accessed December 20, 2023. https://www.luminarium.org/editions/maskblack. htm For another linkage of play and masque, see Orgel, 'Shakespeare and the Cannibals', 49.

[78] Lupton, '*The Tempest* and Black Natural Law', 5. John Weemes's *The pourtraiture of the image of God in man* (Iohn Bellamie, 1627), fo. 51, sig. Ff2^r, using the metaphor of sugar found in figs, avers that souls are 'white', but may be found in all bodies.

[79] Skura, 'Discourse and the Individual', 56.

[80] Keller, *Political Theology of the Earth*, 48, 138 and 57 respectively.

[81] Keller, 57.

No Magistrate, No Engine, No Oil

[259

the planet in the full flourishing of their animate capacity must find its genesis in our self-conscious experience of ourselves as embodied beings existing in relation to and bearing moral responsibility for all forms of life in their interconnectedness. 'It is the body', he writes, 'that generates thought, that sees and theorises',[82] with all theorising that might shape new law needing 'communal spaces of intellection' in which 'winged ideas' can 'inhere and expand' as 'an instance and rite of thinking'.[83] It is the theatre that specialises in such theorising. With this play the theatrical company presented audiences in 1611 with a 'corporeography'[84] of 'gentle-kind' life in motion rejecting the reduction of any form of life to the status or stasis of 'thing', with this rejection extending to all persons regardless of any 'monstrosity' imputed to them. The idea that is immanent in the performance—indeed, cannot exist without it—is that of kinaesthetic potential given over only to gentleness and only to kindness. Bones, sinews and energy are marshalled in a corporeographic display of animacy that serves as a retort to any person who would presume to treat others as the 'stuff' on which their 'dreams' might be 'made' (4.1.156–7), and it may have come in the form of painted figures refusing the reduction to 'filth' of all those for whom they stand in. There is a complex mimesis here. Pretending to be persons from some indeterminate elsewhere, persons who might be painted, the actors present the audience with the idea of a racially inflected sensuous intersection that finds its gentle-kindness in a conflation of persons. Embodying their idea of persons elsewhere, the actors hold up a mirror to the audience of what they might be if they embodied the kind of being or 'generation' presented to them. The political potential of this would be enhanced to the degree that members choose to see gentleness rather than monstrosity, and sameness rather than difference, in the represented persons before them.

A Graceful Dance

The audience is asked to experience something similar in Act 4, scene 1, when the actors who play the shapes appear in other non-speaking roles

---

[82] Goodrich, 'Pure Theory of Law', 990.
[83] Goodrich, 'Pure Theory of Law', 994, 999.
[84] Goodrich, 'Pure Theory of Law', 1,010.

260]   *Carolyn Sale*

in the betrothal masque's dance. The 'shapes' split, as it were, into two groups, with some of them remaining like those of 'more gentle-kind' 'generation' in the earlier scene—these play the 'nymphs' summoned by Iris from 'windring brooks' and 'crisp channels'—and the others now appearing as the 'sunburned sicklemen / Of August weary', summoned from their 'furrow' to join the nymphs in making holiday on 'green land' (4.1.128–30). It is fitting that Iris, the goddess of the rainbow and a symbolic bridger, presides over this union, for the performance of their 'graceful dance' is the expression (like that the audience has already experienced in 3.3) of harmony across difference. Both the shapes as the gentle-kind 'islanders' and this dance beg to be set in relation to what the English thought they knew, in addition to George Percy's highly negative account cited above, of the dances of the Algonquians.

The English had a representation of the dances of the Algonquians in the grandest of the de Bry woodcuts in the 1590 edition of Thomas Hariot's *A briefe and true report of the new found land of Virginia* (Figure 9.2), which reports that in their dancing the Algonquians would 'vse the strangest gestures that they can possibly devise'.[85] The woodcut depicts the dancers standing in a clearly demarcated circle. Three dance together in this circle's centre, hands linked, making a circle of their own. Also standing in the outer circle are poles with faces ('like Nunnes, with their vayls', the description in the Hariot notes).[86] In their hands, the dancers hold either gourd rattles or branches that are probably tobacco stalks.[87] De Bry's woodcut heightens an aspect of White's drawing by making the leaves and branches that adorn one of the figures in the foreground more ostentatious while also decking out another of the dancers, top right, in arboreal attire. De Bry also subtly alters the three 'virgins' at the centre so that they appear like the three graces in Botticelli's *Primavera*.[88] While the dance as represented was part of an epistemology that we cannot fully know, it might very well have appeared to English eyes, especially as revised by de Bry, as that of a 'gentle-kind' generation.

---

[85] Thomas Hariot, *A briefe and true report of the new found land of Virginia* (1590), XVIII.

[86] Hariot, *Briefe and true report*, XVIII.

[87] Kim Sloan, *A New World: England's First View of America* (U of North Carolina P, 2007), 116.

[88] See also Orgel, 'Shakespeare and the Cannibals', 44.

Figure 9.2 *Their danses vvhich they vse at their highe feastes* (by Theodor de Bry, in Thomas Hariot, *A briefe and true report of the new found land of Virginia*, 1590), right half.

We know enough to understand the dance as a celebration of nature's abundance and of the Algonquians as part of that abundance. This is heightened by the arboreal attire. But we might also understand the dance as the performance of relations in which everyone is a 'point of connection', a node, in the illimitable patterns and patterning of nature, with each person/part 'carry[ing] the inherent intelligence of the entire system'.[89] As the Potawatomi writer Robin Kimmerer suggests when she writes of her desire to dance 'with a hundred others so that the waters hum with our happiness', the dancing of Indigenous peoples of the Americas may also have been a means of effecting a kinaesthetic transfer of feeling.[90] Dancing on earth—exactly what Prospero would keep Caliban from doing—may not be just the means of expressing a love of nature, but a means of communicating it. One expresses one's love through one's feet as one participates in a system of intelligence in which each constituent part is as important as any other in an activity that is the opposite of any system claiming to epitomise a law of nature in which all but one part are subordinate to a single entity accorded an importance that is its alone. This gives us another way of understanding why the 'gentle-kind' do not (as Gonzalo's speech of his commonwealth suggests) tolerate the existence amongst them of any 'magistrate'.

Whatever the English thought they understood about the dancing of the Algonquians, what they experienced in a performance of *The Tempest* in 1611 was something like what the Algonquians experienced while dancing, which was the experience of their own kinaesthetic potential. Current cognitive science tells us that the act of watching kinaesthetic action activates mirror neurons in us that increase our 'motor potential' to imitate what we see.[91] This response has been called kinaesthetic resonance.[92] The theory of kinaesthetic resonance posits that our attunement to the dynamic movements that we observe in others spawns an internal response, in which the brain experiences movement even as our bodies remain still. This resonance is believed to be at its most powerful where the movements we observe have a repetitive element. This theory, in which we experience an 'inner imitation' of what we observe without ourselves moving at all, makes the theatre a catalytic organ, with our

---

[89] Yunkaporta, *Sand Talk*, 83.

[90] Kimmerer, *Braiding Sweetgrass*, 251.

[91] Florence Hazrat, '"The Wisdom of Your Feet": Dance and Rhetoric on the Shakespearean Stage', in *The Oxford Handbook of Shakespeare and Dance*, ed. Lynsey McCulloch and Brandon Shaw (Oxford UP, 2019), 217–36 (229).

[92] Garner, *Kinesthetic Spectatorship*, 153–8.

No Magistrate, No Engine, No Oil [263

mere observation of the movements of others stirring a kinaesthetic response in us.[93] The *Tempest*'s dance of the nymphs and sunburned reapers may appeal to us, in short, as the possessors of an energy that may be spurred by the energetic displays of others.

For the audience the experience of the movements of the actors in the non-speaking roles is the experience of our own bodies as instruments of attention—instruments through which we might have the immanent experience of the capacity to 'be wise' in relation to the nature of which we are a part, nature that takes more than one form in the actors before us. The play's kinaesthetic aspects appeal to us as the possessors of sinews that will not be cramped and bones that will not be ground down—as living beings, that is, who must not be reduced, by any 'alchemy', to any form of 'oil'. There is, in other words, a law of nature in a dance's kinaesthesis, which not only performs capacity—the capacity of human bodies as energetic instruments—but also defies the abstraction that would make such capacity available to exploitation. The experience, in short, is of a mimesis of a quite different kind than that to which Hamlet so famously speaks when he talks of the theatre's power to 'make mad the guilty and appall the free' (2.2.499),[94] or the kind of mimesis that would prepare early modern audiences for roles in a participatory judicial culture.[95] As the theatrical mirror presents us with gestures and actions ripe with the potential to produce kinaesthetic resonance in us, it makes the theatre its own kind of engine, for what it elicits, by way of its kinaesthesis, is our capacity—our capacity for our animation in non-violent, non-exploitative relations that would make us the source and expression of nature's abundance. Neither an English dance nor an Algonquian dance, the dance of the nymphs and sunburned sicklemen holds out to audiences the possibility that we too may become a 'more gentle-kind' 'generation' by orienting ourselves to what the dance expresses (union and harmony with other persons and non-human nature), especially as a celebration of

---

[93] Garner, 147.

[94] William Shakespeare, *Hamlet*, ed. Ann Thompson and Neil Taylor (Arden Shakespeare, 2006).

[95] On this vastly important aspect of the early modern English drama see Lorna Hutson, *The Invention of Suspicion: Law and Mimesis in Shakespeare and Renaissance Drama* (Oxford UP, 2008), esp. 67–70, 241–53.

Nature's 'foison'. In the case of both the shapes as the gentle-kind islanders and the dance of the nymphs and sunburned sicklemen, we may become something like what we observe in our open responsiveness to what the play offers us in terms of sensuous conjunction with difference, with the theory of kinaesthetic resonance suggesting that the very experience of the actors' movements alters us by making us feel our kinaesthetic potential.

We may feel all of this most strongly when the dance is brought up short—that is, when our pleasure in it is disrupted by Prospero, who 'starts suddenly and speaks' when he recollects the conspiracy against him. It may be too much to contend, as Francis Barker and Peter Hulme have done, that this is the only moment in the play that is truly dramatic, but it is certainly the most powerful instance, as they suggest, of 'Shakespeare's play' interrupting Prospero's.[96] The interruption is acoustically underscored by 'a strange hollow and confused noise' in relation to which the dancers 'heavily vanish' (4.1.139). Sound is once again joined to movement, this time to make us feel a dispossession or deprivation. We feel what we lack as a result of the protagonist's 'beating mind' obsessed with his projects of dominion and revenge, which affects the 'quality of mind' in which we have been participating as we watch the dance. The experience of the interruption of our pleasure in the dance is enhanced by the heaviness of the actors' vanishing, which must mean that the exit of the actors is sluggish or slow.

The theory of kinaesthetic resonance suggests that with this slow vanishing playgoers experience something like the heaviness that we observe, a drag that is a consequence not just of what the actors perform, but of the activities of the play's domineering alchemist. This drag—our sense of our diminished kinaesthetic potential—may be the by-product of what we are to understand as the nymphs and reapers' resistance to Prospero's command. They 'heavily vanish' because they would not go. As Jairus Victor Grove notes, 'drag' can work to impede the progress of what may seem inevitable as part of a larger project of constraining the vicious.[97] Performing their

---

[96] Francis Barker and Peter Hulme, 'Nymphs and Reapers Heavily Vanish: The Discursive Con-texts of *The Tempest*', in *Alternative Shakespeares*, ed. John Drakakis (Methuen, 1985), 194–208.

[97] Jairus Victor Grove, *Savage Ecology: War and Geopolitics at the End of the World* (Duke UP, 2019), 232, 225.

No Magistrate, No Engine, No Oil   [265

resistance to Prospero's command, the actors make it possible for us to feel a diminishment of our kinaesthetic capacity even as their actions give the central dramatic irony of the play its most important expression: the actors (whatever role they are playing) pretend to be subject to Prospero's authority in order to inspire in the audience an energetic rejection of his project through which playgoers join the actors in celebrating the abundance of a kinaesthetic capacity that might be shared in projects that liberate that capacity from any one person's control. All that remains is for the play to provide the rite through which the celebration of that capacity may be formalised as the characters are released from Prospero's spell, and the audience, from the fiction.

The Unmantling

When Prospero speaks of the senses of the shipwrecked courtiers as 'rising' after he releases them from his spell ('The charm dissolves apace, / And . . . their rising senses / Begin to chase the ignorant fumes that mantle / Their clearer reason' (5.1.64–8)), what the audience hears is the need for their own senses to be released from any force that might diminish them. Casting the state in which the characters have been immersed not only as the opposite of any experience of wisdom (they have been kept from one or another kind of knowledge by 'ignorant fumes'), Shakespeare's phrasing underscores what we already know, that the characters have been the subjects of alchemical experiments. So too have we. The difference is that the characters' subjection to 'ignorant fumes' has been for us knowledge-producing. We have seen exactly how the 'mantled' would work, and what they would seek to gain, and understand that it is our own energetic capacity that is at stake in projects of dominion outside the theatre's walls. The play holds up to audiences a mirror not of what they are, but of what they might be, if they could extricate themselves from the 'filth' of a manipulated and degraded Nature and fictions that would require their subjection to a 'liege lord' as a matter of a so-called 'law of nature'.

In 1611, the need for the release of these fictions was urgent. It is possible, as Catherine Keller notes, for such a release to come too late. ('Be not too late' (4.1.133), says Iris to the nymphs and sunburned sicklemen in a proleptic echo.) The invitation of Shakespeare's play in 1611 was for the audience to find in the figures of the shapes and the nymphs and sunburned sicklemen performances of animated difference with which they might identify—performances with which they might resonate—as part of a playgoing experience in which they might experience the possibility of release from a certain 'quality of mind'. The play thus closes with an appeal to playgoers to engage in an act by which they do more than release a character from his 'bands'.

'Good' theatre, Jacques Rancière has argued, 'is a place where an action is taken to its conclusion by bodies in motion in front of bodies that are to be mobilised'. It is the nature of the theatrical contract that for the purposes of the performance the audience agrees to 'relinquish its power'; it will listen, see, attend. 'But its power is revived, reactivated in the performance [of the bodies in motion], in the intelligence which constructs that performance, in the energy it generates.'[98] *The Tempest*'s final rite is one that asks audience members to confirm that they have been moved. In the gesture of our clapping, we confirm that a transfer of energy has occurred as the play as kinaesthetic engine stimulates our kinaesthetic potential in relation to the idea of a more 'gentle-kind' generation. We harness the energy that the play has generated in us, and express it, and what we celebrate when we clap is the possibility of our achieving the reciprocal and heterarchical relations that would permit us to 'satisfy nature' by participating in nature's wisdom as equal parts of its shared intelligence. In 1611, this necessarily involved, as a matter of great urgency, English willingness to find in the difference of peoples on the other side of the Atlantic a wisdom that might animate them as the living rejoinders to any exterminist dream.

---

[98] Jacques Rancière, *The Emancipated Spectator*, trans. Gregory Elliott (Verso, 2009), 3.

Part IV:

Grace-Notes of Creative Wisdom

CHAPTER 10

HOLDING A SPACE FOR POSSIBILITY: A CONVERSATION WITH MADELINE SAYET

Madeline Sayet is a Mohegan theatre maker, who serves as an assistant professor at Arizona State University with the Arizona Center for Medieval and Renaissance Studies (ACMRS). A national tour of her play 'Where We Belong', produced by Woolly Mammoth Theatre Company in association with the Folger Shakespeare Library, included notable venues such as The Public Theater, The Goodman Theater, Seattle Rep, Oregon Shakespeare Festival, Hudson Valley Shakespeare and Portland Center Stage, after its initial performance at Shakespeare's Globe in London. 'Where We Belong' is published by Bloomsbury.

Robin Alfriend Kello is a PhD candidate in English at the University of California, Los Angeles, with interests in Shakespeare and migration. He first came to know 'Where We Belong' and to speak with Madeline Sayet when writing a review of the play for 'Theatre Journal', and went on to assign the play to undergraduate students at UCLA, when the playwright generously joined his class discussion via Zoom. He was delighted to continue for this volume a conversation on the cultural afterlife and vexed inheritance of Shakespeare, the radical possibilities of theatrical performance, and the politics and the ethics of care in the modern world.

Robin Kello: Hi, Madeline. Thanks for making time to talk with me about your play, *Where We Belong*. We have been discussing that it can be tricky to have Shakespeareans like me latch on to the references to Shakespeare in your work. Then you, as the artist, have to say, 'Well, no, that's not the core of what this work is doing'. So, I'd like to start by getting your sense of audience response. The play is on tour now. How have people been engaging with the performances?

A Conversation with Madeline Sayet

Madeline Sayet: It varies a lot. Different cities have a different relationship to colonialism, and different theatrical venues have different expectations from subscribers. And often it's advertised in a way that makes people think it will be a kind of love letter to Shakespeare—which it's not. The version of *Where We Belong* that was performed at Shakespeare's Globe had the least references to Shakespeare in it. It was understood that the context was me pursuing a PhD in Shakespeare, but Shakespeare didn't need to be in the play directly, nor did anyone ask for more of it. He was entirely peripheral, other than a few lines in which academics ask me to talk about specific things [about *The Tempest* and my study of Shakespeare], there wasn't any Shakespeare in the play.

Over the evolution of the play, some audiences wanted more clarity around my specific relationship to Shakespeare, which is problematic because centring Shakespeare is the opposite of what the play is trying to do. But as the politics and the tensions of what was happening in the discourse around theatre and white supremacy shifted, the journey of the play began to more directly address my being forced into an assimilationist context because [Shakespeare] was the only place I could find my voice, and ultimately realising, by the end of the play, that [Shakespeare] is being valued at the expense of something else. That journey was one of the last things that got added to the play. People kept saying, 'Oh, we want to understand why you even like Shakespeare or what your relationship to Shakespeare was', and so I wrote that in.

The arc is structured as a coming-of-age narrative, and as I move through it as a performer now, it's not until I'm giving a lecture on the relationship between Indigenous peoples and Shakespeare at least three-quarters into the play that my voice drops into the place where I naturally speak. I don't become my present self until that point in the play. Up until then, I am a past version of myself very in love with the idea that Shakespeare could have my back or I'm trying to find myself in [his work], and then I realise that I'm only ever going to be boxed in within that. People are only going to expect one thing of me. People aren't going to see me and all my multiplicity inside of Shakespeare.

Robin Kello: Yes, there's that great line in the play when you say you don't want to be the 'Native in front of the word Shakespeare'. Yet

Holding a Space for Possibility [271

the academics in the play keep saying: 'Talk about *The Tempest*, talk about *The Tempest*'. That's a very telling portrait of academia as a space. Now that you're working at a university that is doing such valuable critical work on Shakespeare and race, how do you feel about academia as a space where certain kinds of liberatory possibilities may exist beyond reinforcing the superiority of Shakespeare? Or does it still come back to Shakespeare-centric ways of looking at things?

Madeline Sayet: It's really revelatory being in a space that actually wants to deeply question the work and how we engage with it. We recently recorded a series of conversations with groups of scholars at ASU on each of Shakespeare's plays. I remember looking at the assignments for each play and thinking, 'Wow. I'm not on *The Tempest*.' It was this strange surprise to me because I'm always assigned that play. For the first time, there were enough BIPOC scholars that the Native person wasn't put there as a default.

I have some scholar-peers who really dislike *The Tempest*. I don't dislike the play. The issue for me is that for a long time it has been the only thing that I am asked to talk about. I am constantly asked to talk about *The Tempest*; I am asked to exist inside of *The Tempest*; I am contacted repeatedly because theatre companies decide that they now want to have a Native character playing Caliban. At this point, if you're having one Native person in your cast and you're having them play Caliban, you're just retraumatising them. You're just reproducing colonial dynamics, not actually investigating the thing. How do you do more than that?

I've been co-writing a piece with a theatre company in London about the time Matoaka (Pocahontas) was in London, leading up to her murder. There's a scene between her and Ben Jonson, and [my collaborator] had written a scene in which [Jonson and Pocahontas] were going to bond over *The Tempest*. I immediately wrote in a rebuttal for the character illustrating, 'that play is not about us. It's about you.' It's a gift working at ACMRS, because I was also able to bring other scholars into conversations about what Jonson might say in a scene like that, nuanced by their academic work as early modernists.

Ultimately, the representation of *The Tempest* that made the most sense to me was in the opening ceremonies for the Olympics

272]   *A Conversation with Madeline Sayet*

in London when they had Kenneth Branagh play Isambard Brunel as part of the Industrial Revolution. That made sense. It's England. What does Shakespeare know better than his own island?

Robin Kello: Since we are on *The Tempest* now, you said you don't dislike the play—do you see something there besides the colonial framing that is valuable, that might hold something useful or, to come back to the theme of this collection of essays, even wise?

Madeline Sayet: I don't think you can do the play and not address settler colonialism in some way, but I think that there are other additional things in the play that are interesting. Ariel appearing as multiple genders for one. Nobody's identity in that play is locked. The characters arrive in a new place and suddenly everyone could be anything for a moment. Nobody has to be what they were told they had to be before. A lot of the play deals with the possibility of an alternative world, and a moment of great possibility and great imagining. I think that in production you have to also deal with the toxic elements within the text. Not just Caliban—also the servants, the hierarchies, what a monarchy does to people, the sexism, and so on. It's not like the characters get to the island and they forget everything, but they get to the island, and more is possible than was possible before. I once went through and tracked who is referred to as spirit, monster or man in the text, and was surprised to discover everyone's identity changes depending on who is the one speaking about them. It's all a matter of perception.

Robin Kello: I'm drawn to that idea of possibility, and how to deal with these plays that have such beautiful moments of reconciliation and repair, but often it is the royal characters who are allowed to share in those moments of communal beauty. Coming back to *Where We Belong*, where do you see your own ideas about wisdom coming through in your work? Your play ends on this powerful moment of welcome and, for me, I see a core of wisdom in that, but that's just my reading.

Madeline Sayet: In the draft currently being performed, the moment of welcome is more significant because it deals with multiple repatriations and the welcoming home of the ancestors. It's even more

Holding a Space for Possibility

[273

heightened. My mom convinced me to finally say 'welcome home' in English. I was like, 'Why do I need to say it in English? The end is in Mohegan.' She said, 'Yes, and what is it serving, Madeline, that nobody knows what you're actually saying?' I was like, 'I see your point'. I was being very, 'I say it in Mohegan because it's not for the audience in that moment', and she said, 'But the audience is still there, so you could let them in on what's going on'.

My director, Mei Ann Teo, said to me one time that the tenets of good theatre are to entertain the drunk, reveal the way the world works, and show us how to live. Shakespeare plays are good at entertaining the drunk and revealing the way the world works, but they don't show us how to live, except for maybe a little bit in *As You Like It*.

I don't go to Shakespeare to see Shakespeare; I go to Shakespeare to see what people are thinking about now. How we make meaning out of the text today—how it changes—shows us how humanity has changed. But also in the extratextual choices creative teams make to create relevant complexity given what they've been handed. I think that if he were writing now, Shakespeare would probably want to do some rewrites and adjustments himself, but since he's not here, each production has to confront what they want something to mean, stare at a word and all its possibilities. Knowing nothing is neutral.

Our ability to take the text and make it mean different things is not limitless. Sometimes you have to change a word or a pronoun in order to make it work. That doesn't mean the stories don't have meaning—it means that for them to continue to make meaning, to continue to be relevant, they have to be told in conjunction with the moment in time that is happening and not as if they were released down to earth as some sort of deity that's intrinsically going to heal us all. Because the idea that Shakespeare is going to improve us is deeply steeped in white supremacy and missionary beliefs. I think teaching him in schools, without teaching other playwrights and poets, probably keeps a lot of people out of the field of poetry and theatre.

Robin Kello: Do you feel that the theatre space can do that work of showing us how to live? What kinds of things would theatre makers, audiences or critics need to be attentive to in order to make that possible?

274] *A Conversation with Madeline Sayet*

Madeline Sayet: For me, theatre is a space of transformation of one's concept of what is possible. That's not to say what theatre is for all people, but when I make something, I want to bring people into a space in which they question things, and then leave questioning things in their own lives and around them. The experience has shifted their perspective in some way, even if it's imperceptible. I don't want people to leave with answers. I'm not interested in telling them how to do anything, but I want them, by going on a journey with these characters, to see the world a little differently and have a different understanding of what is possible.

Having a variety of different perspectives on stage is really important, so it's not just one character the audience is hearing from for the entire play. *Where We Belong* is tricky because it's 'a solo show', but I never really wanted it to be that, nor did I ever feel that's what it was. I often think about it as: 'How am I figuring out the world through the journeys of my ancestors?' Together, the ancestors, audience and myself are making sense of the journey as we move through it.

Robin Kello: Yes, it's certainly the most communal and least ego-driven solo show I've ever seen. Not only do you inhabit many voices, but the play itself is about community and belonging.

Madeline Sayet: It's very difficult to do a tour of it because in my culture, we don't have a concept of the self. You are always doing everything with a consciousness of the community. Who shows up to see it is so important. If who shows up is just a wall of 150 old white folks who don't want to question anything and thought they would be seeing something different—I still have to go through that journey in front of them, and it's painful. But when people out there feel liberated by it, when there's one Native person out there in the audience, I can tell, because it's a journey *with* them. You can feel the palpable shift in the space when somebody out there is resonating with the experiences of the play instead of watching you like you're an object.

It was great to perform at Hudson Valley Shakespeare because it was the first time since the Wanamaker I had been back on a thrust stage. Suddenly everybody in the theatre could see each other again and it changed drastically the way the audience behaved. If they

Holding a Space for Possibility [275

know they can be seen and can see each other—they're starting from a place of togetherness. Being outdoors was also profound because we had the duality of being at a Shakespeare festival on Native land that is very close to my homelands. It made the storytelling more easeful. Normally, I'm there in the black box like, 'Come with me. I have to get you to fully imagine what I'm imagining.' There [at Hudson Valley] it was so much easier because the audience reaction was, 'I get it. Shakespeare versus tree. Here we are.'

Robin Kello: Have you had the opportunity to perform the show in front of a predominantly Native audience?

Madeline Sayet: There was an all Indigenous audience performance at The Public Theater. It was by far the highlight of the entire tour for me. It was the first time I could let my guard down and trust the audience would be able to hear what I said, that I didn't need to fear them. Early in the tour there were some white audiences who got mad or yelled, and it put me on guard from that moment on. Suddenly with an all Indigenous audience—it felt like I could be honest and not be afraid of telling the truth—that they understood—that it would be heard. The more Native people are there—the deeper the story is, because I can feel it resonating in the space. There have been performances where a small group of Mohegans come to the show, and they fully get it, and it's so much more electric. Because of their presence there. This tour wasn't structured by the producers to go out to Native audiences; it was structured to go to regional theatres and their subscriber bases, which has its own value, but when I'm not alone, it really matters.

If one person out there who needs to [hear it] hears it, that's enough, but also sometimes, if it's a really hard group, it's hard for me to tune in as much because the play is not me acting as someone else—it's me having to go through my own experiences again. The main thing I stole from Shakespeare in *Where We Belong*, if you want to know what I stole in terms of wisdom, was something I realised at some point in the pandemic. I had this obsession with questions and the ways in which a question gathers people together on a path. I realised that all of Shakespeare's greatest monologues are questions that the character grapples with in front of the audience. They don't answer anything. They say, 'To be or not to be, let me,

276] *A Conversation with Madeline Sayet*

blah, blah, blah, blah, blah, blah, blah. I'm trying to figure it out. I'm trying to figure it out. I'm trying to figure it out.' They don't say, 'Here's the answer'.

Where We Belong has always been very question-centred. I'm not supposed to, as a character, ever figure things out. It's structured so the character, as in Shakespeare, has to think on the line. It's thinking out loud your way through an entire journey to try to figure out where you're going as opposed to knowing what's going to happen next. I think that's a useful device for theatre. To be in a space with somebody when they're genuinely trying to figure something out and maybe never do is more compelling than being with somebody who has all the answers.

Robin Kello: Yes, and in your introduction to the printed text, you give the reader some of those core questions the play explores. I'd like to throw a few back at you now and see what happens. You write: 'How are borders created? Is it possible to be both a bird and a wolf? As an Indigenous person in a globalised society, is there a place where I get to belong?' How has your relationship to those questions, not necessarily in terms of finding clear answers, changed over the course of performing, thinking about, talking to people about, and living with this play for the past few years?

Madeline Sayet: I think people want me to have answers. I think they want *Where We Belong* to be an answer; they don't want it to be a question. My favourite review of the play acknowledged that I didn't answer the question fully, and I think that is the ideal. It's about understanding that things are constructs. 'How do borders get created?' is as much about asking the question of how they got here as forcing people to grapple with the reality that they are all made up. Making them really slow down and think about the fact that they weren't always here. So? How were lines drawn between people? Why do I have to be a bird or a wolf? Why can't I be both? I still don't know if as an Indigenous person in a globalised world there's a place where I get to belong. When having to perform this every day, I'm never able to create any distance for myself from the difficult questions in the play: 'Are my people going to fade into the darkness and will we cease to exist? And is there ever going to be a place I can go home to? What does it mean to fight for a culture

Holding a Space for Possibility [277

that the world isn't fighting for?' Normally, in my day-to-day life, I can create some distance from those kinds of thoughts. Instead, I'm grappling with it [in performance] every single day, so it spills out into my life as well.

Robin Kello: And all while receiving these annoying emails from scholars who want to talk about Shakespeare, too.

Madeline Sayet: I have enough work in theatre that I could choose not to work on Shakespeare. The problem is that I do actually like Shakespeare. For most of my life, it was the thing that brought me profound comfort. Yes, a lot of that is because it was the space in which I had something in common with people when my culture is not something I will ever have in common with society. So, it was the thing that I had that was shared, the shared experience, and I had a profound relationship to it.

My culture is never going to be that because of the state of colonialism in America. I would like to dream it would someday be easy to be Mohegan, but I don't know that it ever will be. Now, my relationship to Shakespeare's plays is complicated. Sometimes I get mad at them and want to throw them at the wall, but for a long time, that was where I went for comfort. I don't think I can go there for comfort any more because I get so frustrated with the fact that people aren't dealing with what's in the plays. They just put them up on stage as if it's fine to be murdered for losing your virginity, targeted by racism, and that toxic colonial behaviour should be the norm. That we're supposed to laugh and cheer at those things with no extratextual interventions. As if putting those things on stage and treating them like they're normal doesn't create harm. But then there are theatres and communities where you can see the work of really grappling with what these texts mean now, in exciting and inspiring ways, questioning the events, characters and language in a way that leads to really exciting dramatic choices. It's just about remembering that no words are neutral and no play is intrinsically pure.

Robin Kello: I am interested in how you denaturalise the idea of a border as a legitimate form of social and political organisation. You also bring into that inquiry communities formed by shared land as well as communities by shared language. In your rider, you ask theatres to

278] *A Conversation with Madeline Sayet*

donate and to become involved with various kinds of cultural reclamation projects, including language reclamation projects.

Madeline Sayet: The hardest thing in the rider for an organisation to do successfully is the language reclamation component because they don't realise how busy those people are and how hard that work is. They think 'Oh, we'll just get someone to come in and talk about language revitalisation', and I tell them over and over again, 'You don't understand, these people who are keeping the language, who are fighting for the language, there's a lot on them. You can't ask them last minute. There's not an infinite number of them.'

The line in the play 'You'd think they can't keep Native peoples out but try telling that to the Indigenous peoples whose territories sit on both sides of the border to Mexico'—I changed it to say just Mexico, because even though it's also true for First Nations folks in Canada, for the average audience, making it clear that the border to Mexico is made up and that there are Indigenous nations whose territories span that border is much more important because they've probably never thought about that, in any of the political conversations around that border.

Robin Kello: You keep coming back to borders in the play; you start at a border, and there is the line in the setting description about the earth 'carved with lines by foolish people'. This critique of the idea of borders is another question without an answer. You don't propose an alternative geographical and political organisation, but you do trouble the idea of the border continually throughout the play.

Madeline Sayet: The first scene of this play takes place the day after Brexit. That's the framework of time from which I was writing. England hadn't fully Brexited yet; it was still in process. Trump was President. In that moment, the metaphor and actual violence of the border was very strong. Trump was trying to build a wall. Countries like the UK and the US were making it actively more difficult to enter. I found it so bizarro for these imperialist [states] specifically to be [militarising their borders] and to feel so self-important about it. I thought things would change. I thought this would become a period piece or something, but it hasn't gone in that direction. Time hasn't gone in the direction I hoped.

Holding a Space for Possibility [279

Robin Kello: And the new Prime Minister, who just stepped in, has a crazy nostalgia for imperialism.[1]

Madeline Sayet: Here we go. I'd been flying from country to country to country so much and one of the strangest things in the borders themselves, they all look the same. The actual customs system looks the same. I always feel like this is a space we're going to get in trouble. I didn't put any of the later border interactions I had in the play, but when I went to the UK to perform the play at Shakespeare's Globe, I got detained at the border because when I withdrew from my PhD, that visa got rescinded, and it drew a flag in the system. I was sitting in this little box of detainees, and I was just like, 'Is this how it's all going to go down? Quitting Shakespeare genuinely makes me unaccepted here.'

Even weirder, I was coming through the Canadian border recently, the border guard asked me what I was doing there, and about the play, and what the play was about. I was trying to say it without saying it, and he said, 'Oh, maybe I'll come see it. Oh, I'm going to be in Seattle then.' I responded, 'Yeah, you should definitely come see it', but of course I'm thinking, 'This is going to be a bad representation of border guards'. He then said, 'I have kids with me. Is it okay for kids?' I said, 'Well, there's swearing in it'. He's like, 'Nah, that's fine'. I was like, 'Well, sometimes I feel nervous about swearing'. He said, 'Listen, as long as you're speaking your truth, as far as I'm concerned, they can go fuck themselves'. And I thought: 'What *is* this border guard interaction?' Even in these spaces that all look the same, depending on the characters and circumstances, there is so much possible variation. The lines that are being made up, are made up by people in power, not by the people who have to monitor the lines.

Robin Kello: Ha, the border guard who says, 'Speak your truth'. That idea of truth takes us back to the theme of wisdom. We've talked some about where you see wisdom in Shakespeare's late plays. Where do you see a gap that needs to be filled by new art and new

---

[1] This interview took place days after Liz Truss was appointed Prime Minister. Her tenure in that position lasted less than two months.

280]   *A Conversation with Madeline Sayet*

theatre artists like yourself who are presenting different forms of being and acting in wisdom that are less steeped in colonial ideas?

Madeline Sayet: I'm looking up the definition of wisdom because I'm curious about what it actually is supposed to mean now.

Robin Kello: You can define it however you like for you.

Madeline Sayet: Right, but I mean that word, because I don't think I'd attribute anything to wisdom. That's why I want to look it up. The first two definitions that come up have the phrase 'good judgement' in them and I don't know what that is. For me, wisdom would be a quality of being able to hold space for difference, hold space for many meanings, and hold space for questions. I think if that is the definition of wisdom, then Shakespeare certainly does have an ability to hold space for many voices. Whenever wisdom becomes 'this thing is good' or 'this way of doing things is good', it's never true. It's always based on one culture or one culture's ethical system.

In Mohegan culture, I'm always thinking about how things affect my community, how things are going to affect my descendants for the generations to come. I don't make a play or tell a story and think about how it is going to make me successful. There are cultures where that kind of ambition is a good quality. Not in my culture. Shakespeare was a commercial playwright. He was trying to tell the version of the story that would reach the most people in the moment he was telling it—so that it would make a lot of money. That is a specific structure, which is why we always joke that if he was writing today, he'd probably be writing for Marvel and Netflix because he was not concerned fundamentally with wisdom, despite his entire art form in that time being a poetic form.

Robin Kello: The way you are pushing back on any idea of universal wisdom, but also thinking about generations that will come later, makes me curious about human relations to the earth. I wonder if those relationships might yield some idea of the good that is not restricted to a single culture.

Madeline Sayet: I would love to say that's true, but most of society's concept of what is good and what correct judgements are involve

Holding a Space for Possibility [281

destroying the planet. Within [Mohegan] culture, it's not like there's us and then beneath us there's these other beings—no, they are literally our relations, our relatives. They told us their names in Mohegan and that is how we spoke together. We are constantly in relation and treating every being around us as a relative. Most white culture would say that is bullshit. I think there's a section in the Bible that says something like it was all given to you to do whatever you want with.

Robin Kello: Yeah, 'have dominion over'.

Madeline Sayet: Have dominion over. You would think that not destroying the planet on which we all reside and depend upon in order to sustain life would be intrinsically wise, and yet we are doing it, so maybe there's no wisdom in humanity. I guess the question is, who gets to decide what wisdom is? A lot of Indigenous peoples recognise and understand that it's not the most important thing for humanity to survive. If the planet decides to be rid of us after we've harmed it, that's probably better for the planet.

Robin Kello: You have a line in the play that the earth will be all right one way or another.

Madeline Sayet: Yes. And the old version of the epilogue said: 'This planet is so small, when will we learn that we're all responsible for each other?' I think that's true, that we are all responsible for each other, but do we choose to actually take on that responsibility? Just like we are all in relation, but are we going to treat our relatives well or badly?

Robin Kello: I very much appreciate that your take on the wisdom question is 'What *is* wisdom anyway?' because this afternoon we're having a particular conversation, but the ideas and language that we use to approach the idea of wisdom will always shift over time. What patterns do you see that have come out of this conversation on wisdom? Where can we find that sense of possibility and space for asking questions?

Madeline Sayet: I think that there's a faulty assumption that academia holds wisdom. What I found most difficult in academia was

282] *A Conversation with Madeline Sayet*

that you're always set up to critique. I find that an odd, negative structure. It's not a particularly collaborative method of behaviour. I think about that as both an academic and a scholar, and as someone who comes from a line of medicine people who would probably question their own wisdom, a lot more than a lot of academics do.

The idea that X, Y and Z must hold wisdom, and that it's something we're trying to attain in a specific format, is really complicated. There are some cultures where wisdom is attained by sitting with oneself and meditating. Are you going to attain wisdom by reading a book? Are you going to attain wisdom by absorbing Shakespeare? Or are you going to attain wisdom by being in relationship with all the people and beings around you? I think what is sustainable is also a question I have around that. What is wisdom's relationship to sustainability? Yeah, wisdom is a weird word. I think anyone who says that they are wise is probably not. Makes me think of the fake medicine people who run around offering paid services to heal people, versus the real medicine people who aren't proud or showy about their work.

Robin Kello: Right. On medicine, the question of the capacity to heal and be healed seems central to any discussion of what it means to be wise.

Madeline Sayet: I think knowing that healing and/or harming are happening is key to wisdom. That what you're doing has an effect. That things are in relation. That if you do something, something else will happen in response to that, and so: what are you actually trying to do? I think about that a lot with academia. Are you trying to critique an argument? For what? Are you teaching that Shakespeare play? Why? What is the hope for humanity that is stemming from these actions? From a pedagogical perspective, that's why I always return to questions, and the thing most useful that Shakespeare does that not all playwrights do is really sit in those questions. It creates a space for more possibility.

We learn the most when we're able to tap into what our brains are able to think of beyond what we're just being handed. If we're just being handed something, and being handed something, we're not going to be trained to be critical of it. When we have space for questions and can think about how each person arrives on the path in a different way, and how we can sit inside of all of the information at the same time without exploding, or fighting, or having the cognitive dissonance that we all have around climate change—how to sit inside all of that information *together* and not lose our minds would, I imagine, be the form of wisdom that humanity is not having a good time attaining.

Robin Kello: I love the emphasis on *together* there. I recently heard a poet say something like 'Conversation is my favourite way of thinking'. You don't get that in a one-to-one relationship between reader and text. That's why I am stuck on that moment of welcome at the end of the play—the theatre itself becomes this communal space. The play offers us a way of thinking about how we're actually all here being welcomed into this space, and then we become more aware. We're sharing, and that's powerful.

Madeline Sayet: Thanks, Robin.

Robin Kello: You deal with Shakespeare as playwright, but also as emblem of the English language, the English language being the colonial tongue and a tool used in these language erasure and re-education projects.

Madeline Sayet: I am conscious of the power he still holds in the education system and that his plays are required learning while Native plays are not. I think that's why I carry a lot of fear around this play becoming a partner text to *The Tempest*, in classes. Everything is always set up to support and hold up Shakespeare at the centre. When in reality, my play wasn't written in response to *The Tempest*—it just happens to be the part that audiences can understand because that's the part they were taught before. Indigenous texts full of joy and humour should be required on their own merit. Only teaching texts that reinforce centring a conversation on Shakespeare, even while complicating it, are problematic.

Robin Kello: *Where We Belong* is nuanced but also direct at the moments where you need to deal with the real violence of colonial erasure. There are also spots of humour and beauty that are deeply human and theatrical that allow us to again share that space of possibility.

284]   *A Conversation with Madeline Sayet*

Madeline Sayet: That's why I say *As You Like It* is the winner in my mind—it's the only one of Shakespeare's plays in which the characters go somewhere outside of the city and it is better. They are able to be in relationship with each other and with everything around them, and then they come back with more wisdom. There's all this ambition and colonial values in the plays, but in *As You Like It*, it's questioned, which is why this is the one that I always come back to as having the most potential when it comes to our culture, even though when I directed *As You Like It*, I didn't direct it with an Indigenous viewpoint specifically. There is a sense that by leaving this place of toxicity, we go somewhere else and then we find something else. But that very framework is very problematic too, so it's like people who are like, 'I'm going to go volunteer on the rez'. There's no winning.

Robin Kello: It's really hard. I also love how Jacques, at the end of *As You Like It*, gives us a perspective of refusal: 'No thanks, I don't really want to go back to court. Court is terrible. I'm just going to stay in the monastery or whatever and live my own truth out here.'

Madeline Sayet: It's not a great place, the court. It's not the thing. But the plays mostly take place in the court.

Robin Kello: True. Thank you, Madeline, for taking the time to speak with me today about the possibilities of theatre and the trouble with wisdom.

Madeline Sayet: I'm going to keep thinking about this word 'wisdom'. I'm going to try to understand the word more because I think that there's something about the word that maybe we need to examine. Are we all meant to have a collective understanding of wisdom? Who holds it and why? Or is it fluid and just reflective of any being that holds knowledge? Do humans have the right to claim it for themselves?

CHAPTER 11

WISDOM AND WELCOME IN MADELINE SAYET'S *WHERE WE BELONG*

Robin Alfriend Kello

'What happens when the poet takes over the cartographer's tools?' asks Tonawanda Band of Seneca scholar Mishuana Goeman.[1] The question she poses in relation to the work of Muscogee Creek poet Joy Harjo illuminates a core pattern in Mohegan theatre maker Madeline Sayet's *Where We Belong*, which reimagines land and language as dual pillars of her artistic project. In the play, Sayet employs Shakespearean references and *The Tempest* as a specific intertext to address catastrophic colonial legacies that reach violently into the present, articulating a form of wisdom rooted in welcome, recovery and repair. While Shakespeare's play has long served as a metaphor for the European imperial project, Sayet diverges from modes of adaptation that maintain the dramatic architecture of Shakespearean precedent or reproduce the drama as a colonial allegory. She instead deploys Shakespearean references strategically while charting a vexed relation to Shakespearean inheritance in which the early modern dramatist becomes an emblem of settler colonialism, as his English tongue sought to supplant Indigenous languages in North America and his English compatriots sought to possess Native territory. Against a colonial project premised on exclusion and erasure, the play poses the question of how communities might form a place, anticolonial and deeply welcoming, where we all belong.

Where We Belong responds to the dual dispossessions of land and language that subtend colonial practices and imaginings by dramatising anticolonial conceptions of places and the names by which they are called. Addressing how colonised Mohegan and other Indigenous

---

[1] Mishuana Goeman, *Mark My Words: Native Women Mapping Our Nations* (U of Minnesota P, 2013), 119.

peoples were forced to 'speak Shakespeare' as political subjects of the US, the play rejects both the inheritance of statist political structures and the presumed dominance of the English language, denaturalising the exclusionary border as a legitimate form of political organisation and staging language reclamation in opposition to a linguistic inheritance grounded in colonial and white supremacist projects.[2] This focus on the violence of borders and attention to language erasure fuels the energies of the play, but the work refuses to be contained within a mode of responsive critique, and ultimately enacts an alternative ethic in which theatre itself becomes a vehicle for collective healing. While Sayet does not explicitly frame the play in terms of wisdom, and is indeed sceptical of such claims, her work expands the inquiry of the essays in this volume into relations between dramatic art and ethical ways of being and forming community.[3] This chapter follows the broader inquiry into knowledge traditions in this volume by considering *Where We Belong*—including its conversation with the inheritance of Shakespeare—as a mode of performance that refuses the prevailing logic of twenty-first-century global capitalism, instead centring language and land reclamation in an expansive theatre of care. The play rejects systems of thought based on exclusion and replaces them with communal belonging, going beyond critique to depict and enact an experiential wisdom of welcome.

Where We Belong, first read as a full play on the set of Larissa Fasthorse's *Thanksgiving Play* at Playwrights Horizons in 2018, later staged at the Sam Wanamaker Playhouse in 2019, and recorded at the Woolly Mammoth Theatre Company in Washington, DC, in association with the Folger Shakespeare Library in 2021, is an autobiographical, one-person show in which Sayet dramatises how she 'became a bird'.[4] That avian metamorphosis occurs as she leaves the Mohegan lands and travels to London to pursue a PhD in Shakespeare studies at the Shakespeare Institute. The core of the plot centres the tension between Sayet's deep and abiding connection to Mohegan community

---

[2] Madeline Sayet, *Where We Belong* (Methuen, 2022), 38.

[3] See Sayet's interview in this volume for her thoughts on the concept of wisdom and theatre as a place of possibility.

[4] Sayet, *Where We Belong*, 6. This chapter responds to the filmed version and the published text, but the work continues in performance, and was playing at Seattle Rep and The Public Theater in New York in autumn 2022.

Wisdom and Welcome in *Where We Belong* [287

and her ostensibly conflicting desire to take flight, boarding planes and seeking forms of belonging away from her Mohegan home. The play expresses that tension in part by way of Shakespeare, as Sayet's interest in the study and performance of those dramas is juxtaposed against an attention to the attempted cultural erasure of settler colonialism. Inhabiting a multitude of voices and tones, Sayet moves the audience through a narrative arc that depicts non-exploitative and attentive relations to land and language which culminate in the communal experience of belonging.

Where We Belong begins at a border, a stark demarcation of unbelonging and emblem of exclusion.[5] Sayet recounts travelling from the UK to Sweden and back shortly after the Brexit referendum. The first characters besides Sayet to speak are enforcers of the increasingly militarised divisions between nations, introducing themes of geopolitical exclusion and gesturing toward Indigenous dispossession by reference to statist conceptions of territory. As she returns to London, she tells the border guard that she is studying Shakespeare, but not that her study involves the relationship of Shakespeare to settler colonialism, since 'Most people don't like talking about colonialism as much as they like talking about Shakespeare'.[6] Placing Shakespeare alongside colonialism, the play asks the audience to ask themselves why 'people'—here, predominantly white, anglophone publics—prefer to discuss one over the other.

That preference for celebrating Shakespeare while ignoring the imperial arc that extends from his time into the present is rooted in what settler scholar Kevin Bruyneel calls 'settler memory', which 'serves to reaffirm the settler claim of belonging to, appropriation of, and authority over lands on the one hand, and the disavowal of the genocide, dispossession and alienation of Indigenous peoples, on the other hand'.[7] *Where We Belong* not only foregrounds that

---

[5] Each performance starts with a prologue that is specific to the location and time it is taking place, which further reinforces the value of place to the theatrical project of the work. What I here refer to as the beginning is 'Borders', the first section of the play following that prologue.

[6] Sayet, *Where We Belong*, 5.

[7] Kevin Bruyneel, *Settler Memory: The Disavowal of Indigeneity and the Politics of Race in the United States* (U of North Carolina P, 2021), 14. Like Bruyneel, I am also a descendant of settlers.

disavowal, upon which the acceptance of the United States as a legitimately recognised political entity depends, but highlights what anglophone societies choose to remember in lieu of colonial violence—the inheritance of the most esteemed writer of their language. The name 'Shakespeare' too often enables settler memory by reinforcing the assumed cultural excellence of a white, European author at the expense of other traditions, which fuels the pervasive bardolatry that Sayet has elsewhere called the 'Shakespeare missionary complex'.[8] The unquestioned presumption of Shakespeare's universality not only obscures Native and other non-anglophone cultures and knowledge traditions but disavows the role of Shakespeare's language and work in settler colonial projects and the attempted erasure of Indigenous languages, lands and ways of knowing.

When the border guard responds by quoting *Macbeth* and gesturing as if cradling Yorick's skull, his comic conflation underscores the ubiquitous, if often spectral, presence of Shakespeare in anglophone culture and education, while also introducing imagistic patterns of blood, conquest and death.[9] The enthusiasm of the guard and other travellers in response to Sayet, travelling on an American passport and studying Shakespeare in the UK, articulates a legacy of Shakespearean uses in projects of language erasure through education. Leah S. Marcus writes that in the English colonial imagination, the capacity of Shakespeare to 'reach into the hearts and minds of conquered nations across the globe' depends upon an ironic claim to Shakespearean 'innocence': 'The more Shakespeare's texts became immersed in the project of civilizing conquered peoples, the less he was imagined as even incipiently complicit in the colonial project.'[10] Marcus's reference to civilising, which can only exist conceptually by way of an acceptance of

---

[8] Madeline Sayet, 'Interrogating the Shakespeare System', *HowlRound*, August 31, 2020. https://howlround.com/interrogating-shakespeare-system

[9] Sayet, *Where We Belong*, 5.

[10] Leah S. Marcus, *How Shakespeare Became Colonial: Editorial Tradition and the British Empire* (Routledge, 2017), 3–4. While I generally follow the scholars who have inspired this chapter by citing them in relation to their settler or Native identity, I am doing so in relation to the self-identification of the author. In this case, I could find no self-identification.

Wisdom and Welcome in *Where We Belong* [289

the civilised/barbaric binary, centres Shakespeare in colonial work, including the purported bestowal of imagined values as well as the systemic erasure of Indigenous languages. The border guard defends Shakespearean and colonial innocence while mounting a more stolid defence of the 'lines drawn in the sand by petulant children with guns', as Sayet puts it, that divide nations and naturalise political entities that emerge from historically specific acts of violence.[11] *Where We Belong* not only highlights the irony of a twenty-first-century moment in which imperialist states such as the US and UK are shoring up their borders—that 2016 double-whammy of Brexit and Trump—but calls attention to the ephemeral and contingent nature of borders themselves. Lines in sand drawn by human actors inevitably shift over time, and nationhood based primarily on territorial holdings can only be maintained through the continual presence of implicit and explicit violence. The Shakespeare-quoting border guard does not see a dagger before him, but his presence alone is an emblem of the razor-edged violence of the twenty-first-century nation-state.

The play's extended engagement with the Shakespearean legacy as a tool of settler colonialism and language erasure is most direct in the sections that recount Sayet's fraught relationship to *The Tempest* and the colonial dynamic between Prospero and Caliban. Dismayed by the dehumanised figure of Caliban as Prospero's enslaved 'savage'—that pernicious binary again—Sayet is spurred to direct a production of *The Tempest* centred on the restoration of both his language and his land, a vision of the play in which Caliban is allowed to belong. She narrates her earlier attempt to reconcile her interest in Shakespearean drama and her Indigenous identity:

> I stare madly at another portrayal of Caliban who babbles like a fool onstage. As if he never spoke at all. As if his language wasn't more complex than his colonizers . . . What would happen if Caliban could get his language back? If as he moved toward freedom his language came back too, replacing that of the oppressor. If Ariel, the airy spirit, too was of here, was blackbirds like me, a flock of blackbirds . . . if their language was my language. And this was a story of something

---

[11] Sayet, *Where We Belong*, 6.

that happened here long ago. After all, in the play, the settlers leave in the end. Maybe I can prove Shakespeare wanted the colonists to leave too.[12]

With a Caliban who speaks Mohegan and colonists who return to Europe, Sayet navigates the complexity of using Shakespeare's significance to address legacies of colonial violence, shifting from the 'as if' that refers to settler assumptions about Native languages and cultures to the theatrical possibility in the 'if', and finally to the textual fact that the colonists leave the island. The focus on Prospero teaching Caliban a European tongue—not *language*, but *Prospero's language*—would not carry the same force it does in modern performance if not for its echo of historical projects of language erasure and Anglocentric educational campaigns, foundational for projects of Native family separation as well as institutions of US higher education that continue to thrive in the present.[13]

While Sayet's production of *The Tempest* aligns with other Indigenous Shakespeare performances of the early 2000s, *Where We Belong* questions the utility of indigenising Shakespeare at all. Those productions, she tells the audience, 'come out of reclamation movements. You don't have a language reclamation movement until after a language removal process . . . So you learn to speak English to survive . . . That's part of the legacy of how we came to speak Shakespeare.'[14] The term 'removal' echoes the Indian Removal Act, gesturing toward interrelated colonial projects of territorial dispossession, educational systems designed to divide families and eradicate Native languages and knowledge traditions.[15] Education enables the colonial land grab to expand into a broad project of cultural erasure. As author and

---

[12] Sayet, 17. The concept of Ariel as a flock of blackbirds alludes to the meaning of Sayet's Mohegan name, Acokayis, and extends the play's thematic pattern of exploring the contrast of staying at home or leaving home through the figures of the wolf and the bird.

[13] Sayet, 37.

[14] Sayet, 38.

[15] As the Mexican-born writer Valeria Luiselli points out in *Tell Me How It Ends: An Essay in Forty Questions* (Coffee House, 2017), 'removal' is also a common term in reference to the deportation of undocumented immigrants, marking the continuity of settler projects to erase Indigenous cultures and expel certain migrant groups (17).

Wisdom and Welcome in *Where We Belong* [291

member of the Citizen Potawatomi Nation Robin Wall Kimmerer writes, Indian Removal succeeded in displacing countless people from their homelands but failed to 'extinguish identity', so the government placed Indigenous children in distant schools 'to make them forget who they were'.[16] Both Kimmerer and Sayet illustrate how this colonial attempt at assimilation through forgetting depends on education as violence and theft—the play points out that both Harvard and Dartmouth were founded to educate Indigenous students—but also that the settler effort to eradicate Native identity was a failure. Settler disavowal refuses to recognise Indigenous identity in the present, preferring a world, as Sayet puts it, with a '*last* of the Mohegans' (emphasis in original).[17] The play depicts the continuity of Indigenous cultures despite colonial attempts to eradicate and replace them with an Anglocentric inheritance that perpetuates white supremacy through territorial and material relations as well as ways of knowledge and collective life.

Sayet highlights the failures of that inheritance by addressing Shakespearean—and, by extension, settler colonial—ignorance of Indigenous cultural identity in relation to geography and language. She says:

> He never met us. Never heard our stories. Our language. He didn't know we didn't use curses . . . then. And wouldn't have claimed the island 'mine' . . . We have our own way of seeing the world they can't define . . . But could open their minds.[18]

The reference to seeing *the world* is more than shorthand for a specific perspective, as it suggests an attentive relation to the earth, modelling forms of wisdom and care in which the non-human world is not viewed in extractive, exploitative terms, but where culture and ecology are entwined in service of the health of both the land and the community. Just as lack of cursing marks a concept of language that Shakespeare would not have understood, Sayet implies that Caliban would not have thought of the island in terms

---

[16] Robin Wall Kimmerer, *Braiding Sweetgrass: Indigenous Wisdom, Scientific Knowledge, and the Teachings of Plants* (Milkweed, 2013, 2015), 16–17.

[17] Sayet, *Where We Belong*, 50.

[18] Sayet, 36.

of ownership because that would conflict with traditional relations with the earth. Kimmerer writes:

> In the settler mind, land was property, real estate, capital, or natural resources. But to our people, it was everything: identity, the connection to our ancestors, the home of our nonhuman kinfolk, our pharmacy, our library, the source of all that sustained us. Our lands were where our responsibility to the world was enacted, sacred ground. It belonged to itself; it was a gift, not a commodity, so it could never be bought or sold.[19]

While it is crucial not to assume that all Native perspectives and ways of knowing are identical—there are always key distinctions and wide variations both within and between cultures—Sayet suggests a similar ethic of interrelation to the non-human world as Kimmerer. In a scene that takes place at TED Global, where her character is characteristically barraged with clumsy and offensive questions about both Shakespeare and Indigeneity, she responds to a talk on the shared nature of the global commons with 'Ask literally any Native person ever and they coulda told you this'.[20] *Where We Belong* emphasises that land as private property is inimical to inclusive and reciprocal Mohegan conceptions of geography as communal and political space, further dramatising white settler disavowal as the speaker's imagined epiphany depends on the refusal to acknowledge the existence of alternatives to European colonial traditions. Only a mind that presupposes that land exists as a commodity to be exploited can be surprised or enlightened by a perspective that emphasises the commons; only the mind that already assumes a radical separation between the human and non-human worlds can be awakened to an alternative relation to the earth.

The inquiry into land in the play suggests human/non-human interdependence and forms of nationhood that, in the words of Michi Saagiig Nishnaabeg scholar Leanne Betasamosake Simpson, are founded on 'a series of radiating responsibilities' rather than ownership and resource extraction.[21] Similar views are explored

---

[19] Kimmerer, *Braiding Sweetgrass*, 17.
[20] Sayet, *Where We Belong*, 30.
[21] Leanne Betasamosake Simpson, *As We Have Always Done: Indigenous Freedom through Radical Resistance* (U of Minnesota P, 2017), 8–9.

Wisdom and Welcome in *Where We Belong*   [293

elsewhere in this volume in the context of Pythagorean Oneness and ecognosis (Borlik), Stoic cosmopolitanism (Parris), Buddhist interbeing (Tassi) and the commons (Sale). Those radiating responsibilities Simpson mentions promote a vision that extends beyond a critique of the European settler colonial relation to the earth and its legacy in modern forms of global political organisation, ultimately problematising the concept of the nation-state itself. Just as Simpson's *radiating responsibilities* extend outward, crossing the artificial borders of the earth rather than hermetically sealing land into discrete political identities, Sayet's personal journeys and ancestral Mohegan narratives ultimately denaturalise the border itself as a form of political organisation. As she is handed her passport by another border guard on returning to the US, she says: 'You'd think they can't keep Native Americans out. But try telling that to the Indigenous nations whose territories fall on both sides of the border to Mexico. They predate the US constitution.'[22] Referencing the lands of North America before European contact serves to remind Sayet's audience, especially white descendants of settlers, of histories they would often prefer to forget—as Sayet notes in the play, they would rather talk about Shakespeare than colonialism, after all. While the Shakespeare-talk of popular culture does not engage deeply with the plays themselves, the persistence of Shakespeare in collective cultural memory provides an opportunity to interrogate what we claim and what we disavow from the past, which is especially crucial when considering the Indigenous nations that precede settler colonialism. Mohawk scholar Audra Simpson writes of the Iroquois across the US/Canada border:

> [T]hey remind nation states such as the United States and Canada that they possess this very history [of territorial dispossession], and within that history and seized space, they possess a precarious assumption that their boundaries are permanent, uncontestable, and entrenched. They possess a precarious assumption about their own (just) origins. And by extension, they possess a precarious assumption about themselves.[23]

---

[22] Sayet, *Where We Belong*, 47.
[23] Audra Simpson, *Mohawk Interruptus: Political Life across the Borders of Settler States* (Duke UP, 2014), 22.

294]   *Robin Alfriend Kello*

Sayet performs what Simpson argues—that the presence of Indigenous nations troubles the presumed legitimacy of the settler nation-state. If the border regimes of the modern nation-state depend upon exclusion, the play asks what form of communal life might arise from the wisdom of welcome. Whether through Sayet's performance or Simpson's anthropological research, that reminder of Indigenous nationhood troubles not only specific borders but larger, exclusionary statist political formations. As in the common axiom in migrant justice movements that remind us of the 1848 Treaty of Guadalupe Hidalgo—'We didn't cross the border; the border crossed us'—Indigenous nationhood articulates the historical contingency of political geography. Centring an ethic of welcome, the play poses an implicit demand to reimagine sovereign nationhood beyond the frame of borders that cross, cut and divide communities.

While not proposing a specific alternative to the modern nation-state or programmatic outline of language restoration, *Where We Belong* presents a contrast between spaces of belonging and unbelonging through two different museums, gesturing toward a vision of communities of care. In the section 'Indians in Boxes', Sayet narrates a visit to the British Museum, where a chipper British academic tells her that their collection includes the remains of 12,000 people.[24] The refusal to repatriate them and allow a proper burial marks the proprietary nature of colonial logic, where even the bodies of the dead are viewed as possessions that the colonisers have the right to hold in perpetuity. By contrast, Sayet shares with the audience her memories of the Tantaquidgeon Indian Museum, where Gladys Tantaquidgeon and her brother 'protected [Mohegan] stories and other sacred relations, like pipes and baskets' and 'it was warm and dusty and always smelled like good medicine'.[25] The British Museum refuses to treat even the stolen bones of the dead with reverence, while the Tantaquidgeon Museum extends an appreciation of the sacred nature of cultural artefacts to pipes and baskets. Where the British Museum expropriates, the Tantaquidgeon Museum protects. The 'good medicine' of the museum is that of home, of belonging, and a communal ethic of care.

---

[24] Sayet, *Where We Belong*, 42.
[25] Sayet, 11.

Wisdom and Welcome in *Where We Belong* [295

In its final sections, *Where We Belong* articulates forms of language reclamation, repair and welcome that structure the theatre itself, much like that museum, as a space of communal healing. Madeline Fielding Sayet was given her English name for Fidelia Fielding/Flying Bird/Jeets Bodernasha, the last fluent speaker of Mohegan. While the epilogue varies slightly depending on the time and place of performance, in the published version of the work, Sayet returns in the end to language, moving from ancestral inheritance to future generations. Noting that Fielding's journals, long held by Cornell University, had been repatriated to the Mohegan Tribe, Sayet says: 'Our language came home / To teach our children / Our grandchildren / So that one day / My descendants will write plays, / tell stories / Carry their names / Speak to the ancestors / In our language once more.'[26] Language and homeland, past and future, and narrative art and communal life here coalesce in a vision of repair after the ongoing trauma of settler colonialism.[27]

That gesture of restoration serves as a broader metaphor for decolonial and non-proprietary possibilities through an ethic of communal responsibility. With Cornell standing in for continued legacies of colonialism in settler states, Sayet writes:

The institution let her come home.
They always can.
You just have to decide it's okay to let go.
To hold on less tightly, release what isn't yours
To listen
To care
Our planet is so small.
When will we learn that we're all responsible for each other?[28]

This ethical vision suggests Simpson's *radiating responsibilities* to human and non-human alike, and past and future lives, that imagine alternatives to the prevailing structures of domination.[29] What

---

[26] Sayet, 58.

[27] Sayet's rider for the play calls also for theatres to collaborate with local Indigenous communities to support local Native languages and donate to language revitalisation projects.

[28] Sayet, *Where We Belong*, 58.

[29] Simpson, *As We Have Always Done*, 8–10.

those alternatives may be is uncertain, and the decolonial work of the imagination must extend to material change in the world, but the last moments of *Where We Belong* offer radical collective possibility. Sayet sings the final words of the play in Mohegan: 'Wigwomun, wigwomun wami skeetôpák, oh hai, oh hai, heyuh, heyuh, weyuh hey'.[30] In that Welcoming Song, which voices 'welcome to all the people' in Mohegan, Sayet enacts the power of language and the collective experience of theatre to forge communal bonds. Against the many and varied legacies of settler colonialism, the present dispossessions enabled by the nation-state, and the centring of English at the expense of Indigenous tongues, Sayet's play fosters community and articulates an active hope for a future beyond the colonial frame.

That ethic responds to the dual nationalisms illustrated by the rise of Trump and the success of Brexit at the time of the play's composition. As I draft this chapter, the UK has instated Prime Minister Liz Truss, who is afflicted with a nostalgia for empire; hundreds of Trumpian candidates are running in the US mid-terms; and a leading figure of the anti-migrant right has tricked Venezuelan asylum seekers into boarding planes in service of a cynical political stunt. European nationalists—most recently Giorgia Meloni, who has proposed a naval blockade to keep Mediterranean asylum seekers from Italian shores—are thriving. Imperialism through territorial expansion likewise survives in Vladimir Putin's attempt to annex Ukraine, a war effort that adds daily to the tens of millions of globally displaced people. The tools of the dominant cartographers are weaponry and capital; the former restricts the mobility of human beings, while the latter is free to cross borders. Such is our modern union of empire, nationalism and global capitalism, which descends from the European imperial project and an ensuing global order based on sovereign nation-states, border controls and the free transnational flow of wealth between those states. Goeman asks,

> What might the poet say when she sees the detriments of colonial and imperial mapping—containment, restriction, restructuring, and erasure of cultures—continue and live in the buzz of a city or stream

---

[30] Sayet, *Where We Belong*, 58. The Mohegan Welcoming Song was created by the Unity of Nations drum group.

of nightly news in short sound bites ordering the people of the world through language and metaphors, the very tools of poets?[31]

Sayet responds to that legacy by reminding audiences that we might imagine language and relation in other ways than the failed models inherited from violent campaigns of empire, an inheritance that replaces the varied spiritual and knowledge traditions of the world with the modes of extraction, accumulation and the privileging of wealth and power over community. Dramatising an alternative, expansive ethic of collective reclamation and repair, *Where We Belong* transforms theatrical space into a cartography of possibility, a site of necessary wisdom and radical welcome.

[31] Goeman, *Mark My Words*, 119.

CHAPTER 12

WÉTOS, VITUS, VECCHIA, VITA

Jos Charles

In the winter of 2020, in the midst of a global pandemic and sub-sequent lockdown, following the death of a friend, and alongside a long-standing and worsening mental illness—which had been developing both newer as well as forgotten symptoms of auditory and visual hallucinations, involuntary movements, and a disordering of thought that made speech some days difficult to impossible—my attention, or my interest, dwindled, and, as a poet, the sonnet proved, for me, of a length, of a certain portability, to read and write my way through the time. The sonnet became a little heart-book, a tablet, an aphoristic and carriable thing to grieve with, opening up a posture toward the sonnet, wisdom and a certain lyric.

I both read and wrote sonnets.[1] I began work on a cycle that I tentatively called 'A Little Night Cycle'. Personally, I've found it a bit regrettable how form in poetry tends to be taught in school—from the idea that a haiku is its syllable count rather than a network of varying assemblages of association across time, place, perception. Certainly, the most striking thing about, say, the works of Issa is not strictly or even mostly syllabic economy. Likewise, I felt the sonnet, at least in my education, had been rather short-changed. Line length and syllable count dominated classroom discussions as 'formal', while things like which metaphorics tended to be available to sonnets, the formal resolutions possible from its inner mechanics, were often swept under 'individual expression' rather than considered within generic convention, reference and history.

With this cycle, I wanted to precisely engage the formal gestures common to the sonnet cycles of early modernity, the letter of the

---

[1] The sonnet cycle has since grown into a nearly completed, unpublished book-length manuscript.

wétos, vitus, vecchia, vita   [299

spirit we might say, even to the exclusion of line consistency, the law. The cycle took as a reference point an image I had written years before in my first poetry collection, *Safe Space*.[2] I wrote the poem when I was closest to my friend whose later passing appears as a kind of ballast in that book, a penultimate cut: 'things / were so peaceful then underneath / the californian sun which is the same / sun really for everyone on this planet'. At the time, it had been a reworking of *there is nothing new under the sun*: we were parting ways but together, at least for a time, then. An image of triangulation and situation. We also had a similar childhood beset with similar woundings—the continuing and excessive cruelties that at least one articulation of Christendom can inflict. This image, I had thought, was also a moment of reprieve. The sun functioned as an external referent as well as condition of future possibility.

I didn't know it then, but it, prophecy-like, was quite a sonnet-like line. However, as the world and myself grew older, and as I returned to the image, I turned toward images of the place we grew up in, in particular, the coldness of light, as a counterbalance, a refiguring of the prior image as grief:

Why should there be burning beneath
the sun? Why should we have walked
among arnica, the rich hill road behind
where we grew? Should there have
been homes where such figures stood
alit in the americana windows of night?
Should we have likened it to
a curtain beneath which, silhouetted,
greater bodies move? I saw
a neighbor maintain a Judith statuette
the same day the lizards came back.
The sun has been really very
bright since. The waves loud
in the hollows of sea caves.[3]

---

[2] Jos Charles, 'The World Is Flat', in *Safe Space* (Ahsahta, 2016), 53–64.
[3] Unpublished, 2020. I include my own work less to establish a lineage—I stand far behind, after, following, those cited here—than to acknowledge what has enabled its possibility, what histories seem loudest in the silent framing of this, of any, hermeneutic.

The sonnet, in one sense, is hardly a sonnet. In another sense, the gestures throughout seemed extremely sonnet-like—nearly sonata-like, actually—with just under four lines of 'why' questions, followed by just over four lines of 'should' questions, then three lines describing the place the opening 'why' questions begin, with, lastly, a turn in the final three lines, with the scene now having to hold the weight of the questions we have just passed through. We might even describe the progression as A-B-A′—that most baroque of resolutions. I wanted the sonnet both to carry something gentle and old while simultaneously 'hardly' being there. As if the form of the sonnet lies beneath the reader's feet, only sounding up and under like a wailing ghost. See, I was too much in the sun. I was in California, in Long Beach, the city I was born, and the land was burning, the wildernesses burning, the people again and rightfully starting fires in the street, my mind misfiring, the burning of a heart in mourning. And that suddenness of loss, or of a vision, or a delusion, striking like a flare, like a face lit up, on a final day, or on a road, or down or up a mountain.

I had delusions and visions concerning eyes then. I have a scar on my right eye from an instance of self-harm as a child, a bright and brilliant orb, which began shifting into all manner of shapes. One night I awoke to it having changed into the outline of a bull's head staring at me through my window. I also began seeing persons without eyes at times when walking in public. Occasionally, I'd see some ash or smoke billowing out. The visions were Dantean and the sonnets I read and wrote were often too concerned with eyes—and light, burning, the sun. In other words, I was both calling to the sonnet and it was calling to me. It was the form I was in: full of repetitions, obstructions, possible worlds, *voltas*, returns. It was not the poems I wrote, but the world, as my mind took it in, or put it out, that leapt and turned toward this type of closure. The sonnet form seemed at once to posit the problem of its own closure even as it, ultimately, denies it. The promise of closure became its closure. Or, more practically, it's the promise of closure which made those sonnets ripe for denial, the withholding and delay of resolution that feels, as it felt for me then, so immediate in grief.

Shakespeare's sonnets seemed, at every turn, to prove the path I was on: the cold and enlivening, revealing light of grief. Even in the first sonnet of Shakespeare's cycle, images of light pervade. Notably, the 'bright eyes' of the beloved appear and feed 'light's flame'. These

wétos, vitus, vecchia, vita [301

are also offset by, within the first line, images of death, burial and, in the last couplet, consumption: that 'beauty's Rose might never die', to 'within thine own bud buriest thy content' and 'Pity the world, or else this glutton be, / To eat the world's due, by the grave and thee'.[4] A sketch, immediately, of the stakes at play throughout the cycle— that pining courtly or post-courtly love theatric, but also death and loss, light as equally revelatory and obscuring. A shadow-erotics. We also have the intermingling of light with light, anticipating forthcoming images of consumption, reflection and artistic creation. To this, Sonnet 24 develops at length:

> Mine eye hath play'd the painter and hath stell'd
> Thy beauty's form in table of my heart;
> My body is the frame wherein 'tis held,
> And perspective it is the painter's art.
> For through the painter must you see his skill,
> To find where your true image pictured lies;
> Which in my bosom's shop is hanging still,
> That hath his windows glazed with thine eyes.
> Now see what good turns eyes for eyes have done:
> Mine eyes have drawn thy shape, and thine for me
> Are windows to my breast, where-through the sun
> Delights to peep, to gaze therein on thee;
> Yet eyes this cunning want to grace their art;
> They draw but what they see, know not the heart.

The eye applies its light outward, the way a painter does paint, taking the beloved's image to tablet, the tiny book, the heart-book, as it reflects to the eye, illuminating a play of visions there.[5] As a painting, this image is shown in the poem itself. Really, the poem *is* the image. To look upon the poem is to look through 'the window' of the poem directly. The viewer, both poet and reader, is likened to the sun peeping delightfully through the window of the poem at the poet's own open heart. The sun, rather than illuminating the image—the

---

[4] William Shakespeare, *The Sonnets*, in *The Complete Works of William Shakespeare* (MIT, 1993). https://shakespeare.mit.edu/Poetry/sonnets.html

[5] For more on classical and medieval optical theory, see Suzanne Conklin Akbari, *Seeing through the Veil: Optical Theory and Medieval Allegory* (U of Toronto P, 2015).

coloured glass illuminated by the light of the divine or self—gazes 'unknowingly' in upon the image of the beloved's eyes, reflecting the beloved, but also the self's representation of the beloved.[6] The poem is a dark glass; it obstructs as well as reflects. The final couplet, like the first sonnet, fulfils, justifies, inaugurating the reasoning for the poem which precedes it. For all this image-production, for all the beams the eye sends forth to grasp the beloved, we remain on the side of unknowing.

But, like the beloved's eyes glazing the glass, one might mark, draw upon, the glass: an aphoristic sketch, of necessity requiring the poem that promised it, yet also marked by a separability from 'the poem'. We can't call what lies upon the heart unto us, but we might recall what marked the window, the frame, the reflection. There is also our series of three quatrains and turn—A-B-A'. The poem lays out its metaphorics in the first four lines—the painter is the frame, the poem the painting or window—only to move toward a contrasting image of eyes—no, it is the reader/beloved who glazes the mirrour—to return to the opening image, updated now with the prior contrast, through a triangulation with the sun. The reader follows that sun—first source—rather than the poet, even as it's the poet's mark which directs the reader to look past it. Poet and reader follow the same source. The volta then pushes us through to pronouncement and reflection. The final couplet is like that writing that might appear on the glass ('mene, mene . . .'), the glass we anticipated seeing through but confront instead. The couplet is a proverb, whose context, life of production, is the poem itself. The poem's conclusion—the unknowability of the heart—stands quite apart from the poem whose very unfolding undresses the eyes from the heart. What gets taken out, carried past or handed out and down, is neither the volta nor the poem it leaves but the effect of reading across the two.

Or perhaps—not even as analogue, a co-occurrent happening—like a *kharja*, the final refrain of the *muwashshah*, whose history of independence from text is historically pronounced. A lyric genre of Al-Andalus, the muwashshah is a strophic form like the sonnet, unique to the region, a result of the 'multiethnic and multilingual fabric of Andalusian society'. Whereas the muwashshah is strophic and

---

[6] Both Chaucer's *House of Fame* and John Lydgate's *The Temple of Glas* come to mind.

utilises a classical idiom, the kharja is direct and frequently a quotation from a character introduced in the last, preceding strophe.[7] The kharja was often composed independently, however, whether before or after the poem, or even by another author: 'sometimes it seems [the poet] wrote the kharja himself, but many times the kharja existed separately before he [sic] wrote'.[8] Regardless of the timeline of composition, historically or with respect to the author, the kharja was to surpass and leave the muwashshah historically behind, becoming the more popular genre throughout the Muslim world. The kharja, which translates to 'final', is separable and portable much like the sonnet's volta or turn. Both point to the poem that produces it, which the poem abandons, justifies and reinscribes as its promise.

As early as Peter Dronke's *Medieval Latin and the Rise of European Love-Lyric* (1968), this very connection between the kharja and European lyric, and the sonnet in particular, has been made, in reference to their mutual portability. Writing of the similarity of kharjas to many of the refrains developed within the fourteenth-century Middle English, Latin and Anglo-Norman Harley lyrics, Dronke writes of how their length, 'highly charged' emotional similarity and use of common vernacular made them both apt for memorisation and repetition.[9] One might argue a lineage from Iberia to Provence to London, though historiography is less the point here than their common horizon.[10] The kharja and volta share in iterability, separability and instruction—even as they may butt heads with the certainty and stability of these categories—the proverbial as hermeneutic.

Consider one of the oldest known kharjas, from the eleventh century, by the songwriter-poet Yosef al-Katib:

---

[7] María Rosa Menocal, Raymond P. Scheindlin and Michael Sells, eds., *The Literature of Al-Andalus* (Cambridge UP, 2000, 2006), 165–89.

[8] Peter Dronke, *Medieval Latin and the Rise of European Love-Lyric*, 2nd ed. (Clarendon, 1999), 23.

[9] Dronke, 113.

[10] Though, were one to trace such a historiography, it would still need to be justified how, by whom, toward what end, and so on. For more, see María Rosa Menocal, 'Close Encounters in Medieval Provence: Spain's Role in the Birth of Troubadour Poetry', *Hispanic Review* 49.1 (Winter 1981): 43–64.

304] *Jos Charles*

> I love you so much, so much,
> so much, my love,
> that my eyes are red with weeping
> and always burn.[11]

The preceding muwashshah, which culminates in this kharja, praises two brothers, Ishaq and Abu Ibrahim Semuel, with the kharja presented as a song from within the text, a song the poet presents to the brothers as exemplary of his excellence as a writer-performer. There is not only portability—brief, easy to memorise, applicable in a variety of contexts (at least sans muwashshah)—but a resonance of sound, register and repetition (the first line, for instance, transliterates to 'tnt 'm'ry tnt 'm'ry hbyb tnt 'm'ry'). The Hebraicisation, too, of both Arabic and Romance words is commented on by James DenBoer, the translator of the above kharja, as reflecting 'the Arab, Hebrew, and Christian religious and social divisions in Al-Andalus, while highlight[ing] the code-switching between each group'. There's a linguistic mobility to the poem, a feature of wisdom literatures, Shakespeare.

The muwashshah serves here, as elsewhere, to set up a context which the kharja fulfils. Yet the kharja remains detachable from it—centring parted loves however conceived (characters, self, allegory and so on). The detachability of text opens the reading to another space rather than simply truncating or consolidating the preceding text. That gap anticipates a performative albeit readerly response, then, from the audience, as readers or listeners.[12] The reader must

---

[11] Yosef al-Katib, [no. 1, untitled] from 'Some Kharjas', trans. and comm. James DenBoer, in *Poems for the Millennium, Volume 4: The University of California Book of North African Literature*, ed. Pierre Joris and Habib Tengour (U of California P, 2012), 46–9.

[12] We might think of Bakhtin's speech genre wherein 'the utterance' is finalised only by *the possibility of responding to it* or, more precisely, broadly, of assuming a responsive attitude toward it. Further, though, these gaps, between the sonnet and turn as well as muwashshah and kharja, formalise the responsive attitude to genre completely. We might say a reader's capacity to sever the text is as constitutional a generic response as their capacity to unite the two. Or rather, these are, ultimately, the same receptive, anticipatory response. For more, see Mikhail Mikhaĭlovich Bakhtin, 'The Problem of Speech Genres', in *Speech Genres and Other Late Essays*, trans. Vern W. McGee, ed. Caryl Emerson and Michael Holquist (U of Texas P, 1986), 60–102 (76).

wétos, vitus, vecchia, vita   [305

suture the gap, hear the song as at once a conclusion to the preceding text as well as an 'individual' 'lyric'. The aphoristic quality, alongside the relationship to the preceding text, allows for a particular groundedness, an occasion for its composition, while also gesturing to a universality beyond it. The kharja separates and unites, divides and sutures, even as, denotatively, the speaker and beloved are eternally separated and united across muwashshah and kharja.

I point to the kharja and its relation to wisdom literature to sketch the position I see the sonnet having in relation to wisdom literature. Like Shakespeare's sun, the reader is what defines, peeks in and illuminates: she triangulates, supplies the meaning or resonance of the kharja and its relation to the muwashshah.[13] The portability, the aphoristic split, within the al-Katib kharja—a cut and suturing of self to lover, poem to text, kharja to muwashshah, the slip between proverb and text, couplet and strophe—simultaneously testifies, fixed and stilled in text, to the wound it enacts as well as the promise of its suturing through this third thing, the reader, who triangulates the two through a temporally in-flux act of reading or listening. The reader testifies to the burning eyes of the poet-lover. For us on the side of readership, then, to read is to mourn. She carries the possible, the only, unification of lover with beloved, volta with sonnet, text with text—that view—not in but of the window, out of the text and into the (other) world.

I used to say, from time to time, to friends, during readings, 'wisdom is proximity to death'. I don't know what wisdom is, really, but I do know I was wrong. Proximity to death—whether by age, illness, identity or position—can bring about with it a sense of scope,

---

[13] To continue to think with Paul Celan, I also think of the quasi-Heideggerian distinction he made upon abandoning his translation of Rilke and Gide's French letters—the project being too labour intensive as he had to not only translate (*übersetzt*) the text, but transport, or, literally, ferry meaning across (*übergesetzt*) to the reader. Perhaps this account of translation is the simplest way of marking the performative role of the reader or listener with respect to the gap of the sonnet and volta, muwashshah and kharja. The reader not only 'reads' the two together, but ferries meaning, Charon-like, despite and in the face of death, across the two. The reader supplying their Lethe. See John Felstiner, '"Ziv, That Light": Translation and Tradition in Paul Celan', *New Literary History* 18.3 (Spring 1987): 611–31 (611).

306] *Jos Charles*

perhaps, but scope only. Proximity to death requires a reconceptualisation of knowledge in relation to that obvious and utter commonality of individual finitude. That relationship—of taking, limerent-like, every action and holding it up to death—is also the structure of grief. So, wisdom, perhaps not, or not necessarily so, but the gap between certainty and its absence enables a new scale in relation to both. Absolute cut. A gap that won't leave you alone—a turn—the poetics of a turn.

Not poetry per se but a poetic relation. I see that same relation, for instance, in the impossible knowledge of the heart in Sonnet 24, and also in 'sonnet-like' moments throughout the plays, particularly as a technique to call attention to some separation, denial, grief. In *Hamlet*, it's a hastiness of reunification of text with text, through mourning, that separates Claudius and Hamlet's differences in how they speak of mourning in Act 1, scene 2. The play itself contains a diverse set of references to formalised mourning practices ranging from references to heraldic mourning attire to the Vanities aesthetic of the Yorick scene.[14] When Claudius speaks of the not-even-two-months since the King's passing as still 'green', there is little reason to doubt him—the play has begun, as we are told, mid-mourning. Yet Claudius presents himself as having already overcome grief, as bearing loss 'with equanimity' (to borrow a phrase from Seneca).[15] He portrays 'discretion' as having 'fought with nature', mourning being on the side of the natural world, sure, common, and discretion being a kingly and wise virtue which ascends above it. Claudius would be the wise king *against* Hamlet's grief, to make a foil of himself and his position by speaking thus to the court, publicly. Unlike the Senecan claim above, Claudius has had no interim, no break, no wound, from which to mourn, but rather portrays himself as sacrificial, swallowing his grief, for the sake of his rule. He disavows any 'hastiness' to his mourning, presenting a continuity, masking over, where a clear patrilineal rupture lies, by displacing the rupture on to Hamlet. Rather than a later strain of reading Hamlet as melancholic,

---

[14] María Isabel Romero Ruiz, 'The Ritual of the Early Modern Death, 1550–1650', *Analecta Malacitana (AnMal) Electrónica* 17 (June 2005). http://www.anmal. uma.es/numero17/Romero.htm

[15] From the ninth letter. Lucius Annaeus Seneca, *Letters from a Stoic: Epistulae morales ad Lucilium*, trans. and intro. Robin Campbell (Penguin, 1969, 1974).

wétos, vitus, vecchia, vita　　　　　　　[307

the audience is presented with a Claudius who, at best, is melancholic, who, as melancholics do, projects his own suppressed grief on to Hamlet as fault.

That Claudius diagnoses Hamlet as having an improper relation to grief so that he might appear as the wise king is summed up in Claudius's initial address to Hamlet: 'How is it that the clouds still hang on you?' To which Hamlet replies, 'I am too much i'th'sun'. Whereas Claudius sees grief as something lingering, Hamlet cannot see past the condition, the all-pervasiveness of the sun of grief. To read along Sonnet 24's imagery, Hamlet is like the heart lit up. For Hamlet, or so he claims, has, in this sonnet-like moment—a nine-line list of appositives followed by volta, couplet, rhyme—a show of outward mourning that reflects poorly the inward: 'But I have that within which passes show. / These but the trappings and the suits of woe.'[16] The sun of grief shines inward, yet, unlike the sonnet, no lover, mother, father, court, gazes on. Where the sonnet takes the body as an operative movement to lead us to the volta, particularly the eye as forever reaching toward the unreachable, so here the 'seems' of grief—with clothing pun, weeping, a mourning cloak, sighs and so on—operates to lead us to the quasi-volta of its apposite: the untestifiable grief of Hamlet's heart. Hamlet has no witness other than the audience, including us, the viewers, who lean in, to see Hamlet's grieving, his reading, suturing, of the two parts of the sonnet internal to the text.

This Shakespearean sonnet-like turn elicits much. Hamlet has an awareness of propriety—as royal, son, friend and so on—with

---

[16] In full:

> Seems, madam! Nay, it is! I know not 'seems.'
> 'Tis not alone my inky cloak, good mother,
> Nor customary suits of solemn black,
> Nor windy suspiration of forced breath,
> No, nor the fruitful river in the eye,
> Nor the dejected 'havior of the visage,
> Together with all forms, moods, shows of grief,
> That can denote me truly. These indeed seem,
> For they are actions that a man might play.
> But I have that within which passes show.
> These but the trappings and the suits of woe. (1.2.76–86)

308]   *Jos Charles*

respect to mourning, 'the suits of woe', as well as that which surpasses any showing, the woe 'itself'. Hamlet is balanced with such
a reading; he has the posture of wisdom literature, the posture of
virtue. Claudius's response echoes this, referring to Hamlet's very
'nature' as 'commendable' even as he disavows such grief from
within himself. Claudius's scolding, against Hamlet's wisdom, reads
as dismissive and childish: ''tis sweet [. . .] to give these mourning
duties to your father', though it is an 'unmanly grief', 'a fault against
the dead', 'a fault to nature'. Claudius denies any 'withinness' to his
own grief while searching out Hamlet's unreachable heart and woe.
And while we—the court, the audience—know where the play is to
lead Hamlet—the drama the ghost unfolds both within and without
for our Hamlet, in visions, word, deed—for now, Hamlet is all wisdom. There is a Hamlet, perhaps, who leaves court to write or sing
his elegies—an Orlando, Shakespeare, Orpheus, singing the world of
the gone rather than vocalising, possessed by it, where what 'passes
show' might be rhymed and read and shared, memorised, written
into its own heart-book like the one Polonius carries throughout the
play.
    There is haunting though and ways to reach—oh, we know—
it. The stakes of the play sit, inactive but capable, latent, before us
in the exchange. Mourning is a way of containing the uncontain-
ability of woe while, simultaneously and contradictorily, testifying
to its incommunicability. Hamlet stands in the raw sun of it. We,
all sun, viewers and readers, must supply our own woe, anterior to
the reading, which in reading becomes articulable, much like the
gap between sonnet and volta. It is only then we peek through the
window. This is how we exchange with the text, how, in operation,
Hamlet might enable mourning from (upon?) an audience. Reading or listening cues the reader to activate instruction like the proverb. Once, however, Hamlet begins to believe in an exchange of this
world and that one, once he hears the father, believes his charge of
revenge, and vows to it—I mean once one no longer contents oneself
with incommunicability, but must actualise, communicate incommunicability—madness ensues. The reader does not gaze in on the vow,
but hears it, and knows she cannot follow. Hamlet shifts from virtue
to cathexis, comedy to tragedy, wisdom to folly.
    While the unreachable—whether ghost, sun, heart—reaches into
the world, it remains unreachable to those of us above the floorboards,

wétos, vitus, vecchia, vita [309

under the sun. We take the promise out. In Shakespeare's sonnet, the image, rather than revealing the heart, knows it not, and stands in a dumbstruck awe before its withdrawal. It is a public suturing: the image testifies to the split by the very unification it promises. Which is what a heart-book is, what a leaflet is, what an aphorism is—an unreachable fulfilment whose utterance ushers in its own possibility. One must remember what one will not, keep close what one cannot. Or, the volta is like a charm, the promise of healing, even as the poem it appears in is the detailing of the wound. Waves pound loudly beneath a bright sun. We remain too seen, in sight. But of whom. Lying silent before the heart.

Despite the heat, we step outside.[17] The joint is tiny and you eat a chocolate-coated ice cream on a stick. There's this place on my porch I like to sit, a perch, shaded, that overlooks a few neighbouring apartments, a few homes—you can tell because they have political signs in their lawns—and a storage complex. There's a man who sits and smokes a cigar there frequently whose leg I can see from beyond the wall, beyond the ivy and other greenery. He often wears shirts with text like MAN AND WOMAN ONLY and verses from the Christian Bible with the word 'devil' on them. It does not feel dusk-like at all. You tell me the stronger a person becomes the easier it is to carry heavy things. You've been feeling the weight of what you're carrying lately, what you've been made to carry, though you're speaking with a nonchalance and curiosity about it that's generous and light. You're wearing hiking sandals in a chic way and a black dress, and you belong here, leaning about as you do, improvisatory, though with all the severity of rehearsal. You face the sun. It's about structure, you tell me, that's what it comes down to, what it all comes down to, and I bring up the thing you said earlier at Vine after I started talking about sonnets and sonatas and A-B-A′ form, which really was just a reworking of another conversation we had about the ballad and ballade, when you said you saw my relationship to the sonnet like a vision the other day—me, sitting in a castle

---

[17] All my thanks to my best friend, Bernadette, for her contributions here and throughout, to my thought, the fallow times of thought, the unknowing, the joy, laughter, television and all involvement here. She provided, importantly, narrative recall of these closing events and edits from here onward. Bernadette Bautista (teacher, pianist) in discussion with the author, August 2022.

looking out one small and chiselled window at two petrified tablets on top of a hill of sand. A great albeit traversable distance between. A shirtless biker passes us down the street on his way to the sea. I've been writing about that conversation, I say. It's about distance too, and I mention the András Schiff quote you brought up about Bach creating a problem before you that he might solve it, the promise of an impossible closure that is itself the closure.[18] You turn the ice cream to its side, avoiding a drip. Huh, that's what you're doing now. And, I say, that's the so-called didacticism of confession too, teaching the reader how to solve it—and that the sonnet teaches you it's enough to accept the promise without fulfilment, to have the faith of fulfilment be enough fulfilment to do it yourself, that it be a charge to live up to rather than solution. And mourning. It teaches you how to solve it, and you take it with you. And that's like the sonnets and the grieving and neurodivergence and psychosis and this time of sickness and madness and oversaturation of our own representations. Our inevitable failure to ever amount to our spectacular loudness. I take the joint and realise that's the form, really, too, of the paper— Shakespeare's sonnet to al-Katib to Hamlet, health to psychosis to recovery—and, excitedly, I exclaim, ah, that's what I've been doing, and, at this—the gold on your wrist, from your ear, your skin, that shines in your hair—I already said that! you say—you come to my land and steal my ideas! Oh no, I say. You're not gloating or grandiose but revelling in a confidence you have now, knowing how agile your mind, and the care and way with language you have, that those in your life once and still don't afford you. You describe yourself as a jester, stick in hand. To me, you are the peacock and his fan, the seal and her head through the wave, the lion and his mane. From the back corner to the upstairs neighbour's door a dark flash and rustle through the bushes. You're right, I say, I cede to you. The shadows like blue ink beneath our feet. It is not mirror-like at all. The cat lifts her eyes to yours.

---

[18] András Schiff, 'Lecture on the Bach Partitas', filmed June 2018 at the Pierre Boulez Saal, YouTube, posted May 11, 2022. https://www.youtube.com/watch?v=JVjBIKNed_Q

CHAPTER 13

THE BUDDHA AND THE BARD:
ON SHAKESPEARE AND MINDFULNESS

Lauren Shufran

All things are ready, if our minds be so.

Henry V, IV.iii

For the last decade, I've regarded Shakespeare as one of my mindfulness teachers. It's a rather curious claim, one that demands an essay-sized explanation. And lucky me, I've been offered that space. I discovered meditation and mindfulness while in the doctoral programme in the Literature Department at the University of California, Santa Cruz. Or, to be faithful to chronology, I discovered yoga—a moving meditation—first. At the time, I was ecstatically immersed in seventeenth-century devotional poetry for my coursework: John Donne, George Herbert, Richard Crashaw—poets who were Shakespeare's near-contemporaries but who were also priests, and who wrote some of the most gorgeous poetries of piety, and of reverence, I'd encountered. These were poems steeped in the wonder—and the despair—of God's simultaneous intimacy and His unapproachable majesty. They expressed the soul's turbulent journey in navigating the paradoxical waters of separation from, and sheer proximity to, the divine. I can still hear Herbert's speaker dejectedly craving God's ear— 'O that Thou shouldst give dust a tongue / To cry to Thee, / And then not hear it crying!'—in 'The Denial'. In exploring the English sonnet sequence in the context of the Protestant Reformation, I was interested in the fact that the sonnet (as poetic form) and the Reformation (as formal principle) came to England at the same time, and I argued that this lent a theological infrastructure to the sonnet sequence. The amatory sequences of Shakespeare's period, it seemed to me, were sites for writers to work through the doctrinal matters most pressing for them. I saw the relationship between works and grace, the assurance of predestination, the Pauline struggle of spirit-versus-flesh in the

312]   *Lauren Shufran*

Elizabethan sonnet sequence. These were poems, but they were also salvational inquiries.

What my foray demanded of me was a return to biblical scripture in a wholly different context from my evangelical upbringing: when I came out as queer in my teens, I was rejected by the church I'd begun to come of age in. There was conversion therapy. There were years of tears from my mother, who agonised over my imminent fire-and-brimstone afterlife. These things occasioned a counter-rejection: I wanted nothing to do with either religion or a prevailing spiritual realm. But the dissertation was an invitation to approach the Scriptures—indeed, *all* scriptures—differently. *Not* to wrest the text into preconceived meaning as denominational thinking often does, but rather to meet it with open inquiry as good scholarship does. To let what acted upon me *as itself* move me. And so the possibility of spiritual life—a connection to unmediated divinity as *I* experienced it—opened up again as I wrote with the 1599 Geneva Bible by my side.

Earnest scholarship is hard on the body, and I knew I needed to find ways to honour mine while doing that work. I'd also come to see my dissertation as a devotional practice, and I wanted a physical practice that echoed its reverential spirit. It so happened that my dissertation chair at the time was also a yoga instructor—its own serendipitous invitation. So I spent those years as a doctoral candidate moving between 'daily practices' at the desk, on the mat, and in the classroom teaching Shakespeare. I studied with a yoga teacher who said: 'the practice is to put yourself in uncomfortable positions (*asanas*) and follow the breath until you're no longer uncomfortable. Then transfer that practice to life *off* the mat, which is also a series of discomforts.' Buddhism's *dukkha*—suffering—would one day resonate in her instruction. In the meantime, I was learning not to take my body personally. Between the mat and Shakespeare's plays, I was beginning to perceive how both yoga and the theatre use the body to *transcend* it. My yoga practice led to a meditation practice, since 'let's sit together' was the invitation at the beginning of every class. And the more I practised seated meditation, the more I found myself in mindfulness—a traditional Buddhist practice—*off* the cushion.

I loved how these practices aligned with the life of inquiry I'd already chosen. They never pressed me to conclusions but rather challenged me *not* to conclude. They challenged me to be curious about what arose in me in a moment-to-moment way. While I was

The Buddha and the Bard [313

teaching undergraduate courses on Shakespeare, something new surfaced in the space between literature and spiritual work. I realised that the subtle attention I asked my students to cultivate for Shakespeare's language transferred to a perceptive consideration—let's call it mindfulness—of other things: how carefully they listened to their classmates, the ways they chose their own words more deliberately in speaking, how they paused between phrases as though authenticating with themselves that what they were about to speak was most true. I had already experienced this transformation in myself: the rigour and ritual of close reading cultivated broader forms of attention and aliveness for me. Beholding this change communally in my students was remarkable. Attention is transformative; it's a form of love. It's ultimately what spiritualises any experience. In time, I observed a shift in the question our classroom discussions hinged on: from 'What is Shakespeare doing with language here?' to 'What might Shakespeare be proposing about the ways we *are*, as human "players", here?'

Is it a question the Humanities Department would've frowned upon? Would it have disapproved of the fact that I'd become more invested in my students'—and my own—self-cultivation than in whether they could write a 'proper essay', or whether Shakespeare 'got it wrong' in *The Merchant of Venice* when Bassanio invites Shylock to dine with him, since a Jew in Venice would've been under curfew? I witnessed my students' sufferings—some routine and modest, others grave. I was a listening ear for these during office hours—always shortly after observing my *own* sufferings arise in *asana* practice, in morning meditation. They bore striking resemblances. Self-cultivation is one thing, but as the Mahāyāna tradition stresses, compassion for others and the desire for them to be relieved of suffering is an even nobler aspiration. Historical facts and figures, scholarly formalities, took a distant second place to the ways Shakespeare could answer students' questions about the nature of being, and could a little relieve their particular sufferings—and our common one.

There's always been a compelling if inarticulable sense among readers, critics, directors and playgoers that Shakespeare taught us to understand ourselves by reading us so definitively—that he displays us *to* ourselves through characters that reflect us and show us what's possible in us. For myself, I'll never forget the day that close-reading Antonio's remarks to his friend Bassanio in *The Merchant* revealed

314] *Lauren Shufran*

to me my own passive-aggressive tendencies. In retrospect, this day proffered the seeds of a much larger project—one I'm still at work on—because it was the day I began to think of Shakespeare as a kind of mindfulness teacher for vigilant readers. My students and I were engaged in a close reading of the men's exchange in Act 1, scene 1, when Bassanio asks Antonio, yet again, to borrow money—this time so he can suitably woo Portia. Antonio's response to his friend's petition is this:

> Thou know'st that all my fortunes are at sea;
> Neither have I money nor commodity
> To raise a present sum: therefore go forth;
> Try what my credit can in Venice do:
> That shall be rack'd, even to the uttermost,
> To furnish thee to Belmont, to fair Portia.

Two things struck us in this passage as we sifted it slowly. One was that first line. Antonio tells Bassanio that 'all [his] fortunes are at sea' when he's just painted a very different picture of his financial state to two other friends—one in which he's wisely distributed his wealth and hasn't risked everything at once; not all his investments depend on the outcome of this year ('My ventures are not in one bottom [ship] trusted . . . nor is my whole estate / Upon the fortune of this present year'). So why lie to Bassanio except to engender guilt in his friend that the request will demand even more of Antonio than Bassanio could've imagined? The second was the word 'rack'd'. A rack was a torture device: *I will stretch my credit thin for you*, Antonio is saying. Yet what he seems to hope Bassanio will envision isn't Antonio's 'credit' being stretched on the rack (an inconceivable visual, credit being immaterial), but Antonio himself. The merchant is semantically making himself a martyr for his friend.

As we observed Antonio's self-martyrdom in these lines, we started flipping through the text and detected it elsewhere: 'my ships have all miscarried,' he writes to Bassanio, though the rumour is that only one has; 'Grieve not that I am fallen to this for you'. Does Antonio ultimately believe his friend's suit will fail, since 'the four winds blow in from every coast / Renowned suitors', and Bassanio is but one of Portia's wooers? How we each answered the question that

The Buddha and the Bard [315

day determined the degree to which we believed Antonio had taken up the mantle of the martyr.

What was Shakespeare showing us here about the subtle ways we emotionally manipulate those we love? My students began registering moments in their own lives in which they'd been passive-aggressive with parents, or partners, or friends. It was a gorgeous unfolding. The room turned tender as students embraced vulnerability, offering up difficult examples of their own Antonio-like behaviour. Shakespeare had invited a conversation about linguistic nuance that evolved into a conversation about how to be better with each other.

After class that day, I got in my car and made the seventy-five-mile drive from Santa Cruz to San Francisco to be with my lover. And it was upon arriving at her house that I was able to clearly see one of the small manipulations I'd been using with her for years: one of the first things I recounted after walking in the door was the traffic I'd endured to get there. It took some hard but honest reflection—buoyed by that close reading of Shakespeare—to realise I wanted my lover to feel indebted to me for all the time I spent in the car so that we could be together. Behind a complaint about traffic on the 280, I was hiding a secret grievance that I was driving to *her* more than she was to *me*. I watched it all play out like a movie in front of me: I was inhabiting Antonio after meditating on Antonio all morning.

To date, of all the characters in Shakespeare's plays, Antonio has taught me the most about my own manipulations. He's helped me understand how indelicate and heavy-handed passive aggressiveness can feel from the other side, as Antonio's reader. He's helped me recognise how emotional manipulation—that unwillingness, and often the fear, of speaking one's truth courageously aloud—is the breeding ground for our personal sadness. Remarkably, Shakespeare seems to have recognised this correlation. He has Antonio tell Gratiano—in the same scene in which he's imaginatively 'rack'd' for Bassanio—'I hold the world but as the world . . . A stage where every man must play his part, / And mine a sad one'.

* * *

I left academia shortly after finishing my PhD. I had a great deal of clarity that my time there was up. But Shakespeare is magnetic and bewitching, habit-forming in the most wholesome of ways. As salvific inertia would have it, I could neither stop reading nor writing—particularly about Bardic matters. I started a book project that I initially called '"Who's There?": What Shakespeare Can Teach Us About Mindfulness'. ('Who's There?' is *Hamlet*'s opening line—an underappreciated one, I think, planted in a remarkable context.) Still struck by Antonio's mirroring-of-myself-to-myself, I approached it as a project in what the yogic tradition calls *svādhyāya*, self-study. *Svādhyāya* ultimately encourages these questions: what are our patterns of attraction and repulsion, like and dislike? What phenomena trigger our anger, our agitation, our jealousy, our joy, our fear? What is the source and the nature of our suffering? What are we ignorant of, and what's that ignorance causing us to miss—or convincing us exists when it doesn't? How can we be our most open-hearted, equanimous selves in the roles we've been handed—judges, doctors, merchants, soldiers, tradespeople? How, on the other hand, do we remember that we're ultimately *not* those roles after all? That book traced what Brutus had to teach me about fear, Antony and Cleopatra about clinging, Hamlet about grief and, ultimately, forgiveness.

Svādhyāya takes the self as its focus. But the longer I self-reflected and self-refracted through Shakespeare, the more compelled I felt to make those reflections public in an Instagram profile called 'Shakespeare and Mindfulness'. Unhae Langis, co-editor of this volume, has perceived in this effort what she calls 'bodhisattvic aims': the spontaneous wish and compassionate mind to benefit all sentient beings. Most days, that feels like an overly generous description of a social media profile. The reality is that I'm writing about what I love, and about what *I* need to contemplate and digest for self-cultivation and self-growth. But looking back over the six years since the inception of @shakespeare_and_mindfulness, the messages I've received from followers indicate a ripple-effect I couldn't have imagined when I published my first post in May of 2018.

The posts share an architecture, confined to 2,200 characters each: some context on the quote I've chosen, a commentary on its language, an illumination of how the quote has become a mantra for my own self-realisation or an invitation to readers to use it as their own. Here are two examples:

The Buddha and the Bard

Figure 13.1 Quotation from *The Two Noble Kinsmen* II.ii by William Shakespeare. Created by Lauren Shufran.

This is all our world.
We shall know nothing here but one another. (*The Two Noble Kinsmen*, II.ii)

Two 'noble' cousins—Arcite and Palamon—have been imprisoned as war captives. This scene traces the arc of the intimates' dialogue from grief ('we are prisoners, / I fear, forever') to acceptance—and then pleasure—in their changed circumstances. As the friends exhaust the catalogue of things they'll never experience as free men (to 'feel our fiery horses / Like proud seas under us' or 'the sweet embraces of a loving wife / Loaden with kisses'), they begin to perceive something remarkable in the fact that 'This is all our world. / We shall know nothing here but one another.' Even as the cousins' world materially shrinks, it imaginatively swells with this abundant vision, emerging as a cosmos rather than a cell.

In the context of their conversation, Arcite's metaphor is initially one of despair—occurring just moments before his recognition that out of their captivity actually arise 'two comforts', two 'blessings': the cousins have been invited to practise a 'brave patience' and to 'enjoy' their griefs together. As the lens through which the men view their captivity is revised, the prison becomes a 'holy sanctuary' and the cousins 'endless mine[s]' for one another: abundant sources of supply for the most precious materials of this life—not gold, but the 'other' who sees us, reflects us, tenderly challenges us, and joys us . . . but only if we're paying attention.

For me, these lines constitute an exquisite moment-to-moment mantra. Indeed, there *is* nothing but this world—the one that belongs to this very second, and no more. And all we can harness as fodder for being in it is our best selves, as we can conjure them, now. 'This is all our world' is a call to radical presence in each next fleeting instant. If the world is but here—no longer a microcosm or a metaphor, but truly the entirety of what is—the impulse is all at once to be gentle, and generous, and tender-hearted, and affectionate with all beings who inhabit it with us, because there's nowhere else to go. If 'all we know' is whom we're in this moment with, we will truly want to know them as the precious materials they are.

What changes in our encounters this week if we bring this mantra to each one?

Figure 13.2 Quotation from *The Winter's Tale* III.ii by William Shakespeare. Created by Lauren Shufran.

> Look down
> And see what death is doing (*The Winter's Tale*, III.ii)

The Buddha and the Bard [319

When Leontes, King of Sicily, accuses his wife Hermione of infidelity, the story he's concocted is so self-convincing that, when a message arrives from the Oracle at Delphi that the queen is innocent, the paranoid king pronounces even the oracle false. With no evidence against her but his own suspicions—the gods are certainly not on his side—Leontes will persist in 'justice'. When news arrives that the royal couple's son has died of distress for his mother, Hermione, who's been present for her own indictment, falls into a swoon. 'This news is mortal to the queen,' her lady-in-waiting says to Leontes. 'Look down / And see what death is doing.'

It's here that the enormity of Leontes's *in*justice comes crashing down on him—the tragic consequences of not listening, of not living with every sense open to the world. The king's awful illumination—coupled with Paulina's command to 'look down'—is a recipe for our own instruction. Most of us have what Buddhist scholar George Bond calls an 'unexamined assumption of our own immortality'. We prefer not to acknowledge the death we're hastening toward. It's an understandable by-product of duality, of being-two: we carry a vague awareness of our splendid infinitude, yet the only form of 'ourselves' we know goes back into the ground—'something' vanishing into 'nothing'.

There's a very real sense in which the entire Buddhist path begins with a recognition of death, and it's still a form of meditation at some monasteries to observe the progressive rotting of a corpse ('Look down / And see . . .'). Far from morbid, these meditations on the scarcity of time are opportunities for joy. Mindfulness-of-death spurs us into diligent practice. It diminishes our attachment to what causes short-sighted suffering. It softens our urge to engage in escapist activities, because there's no longer a terror to escape. It aligns our lives with our values because it raises the urgency of every-moment-counting. Every breath becomes infinitely precious, and wondrous, and light.

Recognising that death is happening in every moment and kept at bay only by the fragility of living, we discover the awe of 'the meantime'. Loving you in this, our interim, my friends.

* * *

@shakespeare_and_mindfulness has grown into a tender community of over 13,000. On occasion its exchanges have travelled

320]   *Lauren Shufran*

offline—someone I've sporadically engaged with on the platform for years will tell me they're passing through the Bay Area, and we'll meet for coffee and express awe at the connection. The most frequent comment I receive in response to a post is some version of 'Thank you; I needed this today'. But often those who comment teach me things. They unguardedly share what they're working through in this shared space. They articulate lessons they've learned and ways they've grown that resonate with the quote at hand. Some of them have directed or performed in Shakespeare's plays and tell me how they approached that line. We are a cosmos of revelling, aching and inquiring together.

Given the nature of our inquiries—and given that precisely what we're cultivating together is an awareness to relieve our collective suffering—the Instagram community often feels like a *sangha* (a spiritual family, 'good company'). Over the years it's kept me committed—if not always to the practice of routinely posting, then always to the practices and inquiries those posts concern. What does it look like in my own life to 'utter sweet breath' (IV.ii), as Bottom instructs the rude mechanicals to do in *A Midsummer Night's Dream*? How does the Second Servant's observation that 'We cannot be here and there too' (I.v) in *Romeo and Juliet* become a mantra that calls me back to each exquisite present moment? Can I experience a renewed sense of contentment and enoughness in my life when I take up Gonzalo's claim in *The Tempest* that 'Here is everything advantageous to life' (II.i)? What tenacious grips and inflexible beliefs does Volumnia's remark to Coriolanus—'You are too absolute' (III.i)—expose in my own mind? What transforms when I arrive to each new encounter with Pericles' observation in mind—'thou look'st / Like one I loved indeed' (V.i)—remembering that each of you has been my mother, my liberator, my lover in some life; remembering our interbeing?

Ultimately, a book called *The Buddha and the Bard* (Mandala Publishing, 2022) spun out of this social media project. When I approached Mandala with the idea, I characterised it as a project about mindfulness, broadly speaking. But the prosaic truth about the book's origin is that Mandala was drawn to the alliteration of what became the title; and the parameters of the project—Buddhism rather than, or alongside, mindfulness—simultaneously contracted and swelled. I should say that, until writing this book—and indeed, even now—I'd describe myself as agnostic but Buddhist-leaning. But

The Buddha and the Bard [321

agreeing to the title became a commitment to undertake a profound and self-directed course of study on Buddhism. Along with this shift from the Instagram project, which centred on mindfulness, to the book project, which centred on Buddhism, came another remarkable transformation: Shakespeare was no longer only a guide in learning how to be a better human. He also became a guide in learning to transcend my humanness, in not taking my own made-manifestness too seriously.

I could point you to plenty of reasons why I think this is so. I could propose that Shakespeare's having been an actor (a 'shadow', a 'player') before he was a dramatist endowed him with a mind vast as space—one that could enter into another's subjectivity and share their interiority, one that made room for all forms of experience. That in the practice of emptying-himself-of-himself, night after night, surely Shakespeare began to perceive what Buddhism understands as the root of our suffering (*dukkha*): that we are persons and personas (temporary individuals and transient players) who earnestly believe we're permanent selves. I could point to the long history of the theatre being used as a metaphor for human incarnation and spiritual practice—as when American spiritual teacher Ram Dass describes spiritual work as coming to 'understand that you are a soul passing through a life in which the entire drama is a script for your awakening and that you are more than just the drama'. 'All the world's a stage,' Jaques marvellously claims in *As You Like It*, 'And all the men and women merely players'.

As I placed Shakespeare and the Buddha side by side, day after day, listening for their resonances, this connection became clear: one had the ability to represent inwardness and suffering better than any writer of his time; the other discerned how to liberate us from that suffering. It's a connection, and a union, I've come to think of as 'the Dharma of Shakespeare'. And it's hardly to say that Shakespeare was Buddhist. It's to say that, in all the becoming and *un*becoming he 'performed' as an actor and a conceiver-of-actors, Shakespeare seems to have understood something about *inter*being and *non*being, a truth about our vaster selves: our lives and interests are actually deeply, inextricably interdependent—a truth we forget when we become accustomed to playing only a single persona, a word referring to both the mask worn by an actor and the part one plays in a drama.

Perhaps there *is* after all something fundamentally bodhisattvic about modelling *svādhyāya*, or spiritual inquiry, in public. 'Bodhisattva' is still a term that sits strangely with me; and maybe this has to do with how fresh, and how messy, and how fumbling I often feel on this path. But what I know is that mindfulness—even in its convoluted, commodified, despiritualised forms—is as important as ever; and I'm up for the ongoing humility of expressing out loud what I'm discovering in those listening spaces. 'All things are ready', says Shakespeare's Henry V, 'if our minds be so' (IV.iii). It's a line that conjures the Buddha's claim, in the *Dhammapada*, I.2, that

> All that we are arises with our thoughts.
> With our thoughts we make the world.
> Speak or act with a pure mind
> And happiness will follow you
> As your shadow, unshakable.

What's outside the mind is but a reflection of what's in it. So how can I cultivate through a steady mindfulness practice a mind that conceives the world I most want to live in—equanimous, compassionate, unguarded, in awe, at peace? And in what ways can Shakespeare's characters—even his most villainous ones—meet me with mantras along that path?

The answers are still unfolding.

AFTERWORD: SHAKESPEARE'S OPEN O: SOUNDING GLOBAL WISDOMS INTO THE FUTURE

Joan Pong Linton

In 'Wisdom Ecology', Unhae Park Langis proposes 'mapping the ancient wisdom world into the future', an activity that is, by implication, open-ended across times and cultures. The title turns out to hold space for a collective endeavour that is less *telos*-driven than guided by the shared goal of coexistence and belonging with nature. In mapping their own journeys, contributors mark the sites where they travel/travail (variant spellings in early modern usage) with Shakespeare, engaging with wisdom sources in their generative and regenerative potentials in exploring questions relevant to his time and ours. Open-ended, then, also describes a collective mapping with multiple points of entry, to which readers are invited as fellow travellers. And I, for one, am grateful to encounter anew Shakespeare's works in their diverse wisdom connections.

The most direct of these connections cohere around characters whose embodiments of wisdom figures from textual traditions transform our perceptions of them and our access to the plays. Thus Cleopatra, associated with Sophia from the Judeo-Egyptian legacy of Alexandria, emerges as a wise ruler whose use of erotic power belies the critical commonplace of her as one ruled by passion, the perfect Egyptian foil to Rome. What strikes me about Julia Reinhard Lupton's description of Cleopatra are the motif of fragrance ('sweet smells', 'pleasant odours', 'perfume') and images of iridescence and 'play of light'. These details, so resonant with our senses, register her lively presence, even as her textual assemblage places the character beyond the familiar terms of identification or disidentification we encounter in reader response and character criticisms. In *King Lear*, Cordelia embodies the 'transcendent value of the Mother', the 'light of wisdom' *Heart Sūtra* in Mahāyāna Buddhism, that cuts through illusion in its compassion for all suffering life. With Margaret Tassi, we appreciate the 'radical nature of Shakespeare's ethical and aesthetic vision' that prepares us to encounter the self-emptying that is not nothing but rather potential for spiritual wisdom. In imagining Othello as the Sufi traveller seeking the 'perfect soul' and Desdemona as the 'Sophianic Feminine', Langis explores their potential for theo-erotic union, albeit thwarted by Iago. In this light, we see the divinity of eros in Sufi wisdom—and why Iago should weaponise the erotic in reducing Othello to a criminal fulfilling the 'turning Turk' trope.

Besides characters, wisdom's erotic energy also infuses formal and generic resources with new ethical possibilities in Shakespeare's works. In *The Winter's Tale*, as Benjamin Parris observes, human *poiesis* and literary *poiesis* cooperate, creating the 'dramatic mixture' of 'tragi-comic romance' in connection with the practice of Stoic wisdom: Perdita embodies a virtue 'that resonates with Stoic accounts of goodness and cosmic harmony', while Paulina performs a 'therapeutic' role in Leontes's virtue-based healing. Pivotal to the tragi-comic turn, I would suggest, is the return of the absent mother that heals the broken family, an event with implications for Shakespeare's other plays. Unlike the comedies and tragedies in which the mother's absence is simply given, *The Winter's Tale* stages the physical removal of the mother, Hermione being presumed dead, as the result of a wrong for which the Oracle judges Leontes a 'jealous tyrant' (3.2.132).[1] In Audre Lorde's terms this wrong is a 'suppression of the erotic', the source of creative energy that births and holds together the family.[2] The generic turn in *The Winter's Tale* thus provides a vantage point from which to map wisdom's erotic orientations of Shakespeare's fictive worlds. In choosing suicide, Cleopatra is 'fire and air', liberated from 'baser life' (5.2.280–1). Dying by the asp—'my baby at my breast / That sucks the nurse asleep' (5.2.368–9)—she asserts her symbolic role as mother in an erotic gesture at once ethical and political. When Cordelia assumes the 'salvific' role through the inverted trope of

---

[1] All quotations from Shakespeare's plays in this Afterword are from *The Norton Shakespeare*, 3rd ed., ed. Stephen Greenblatt et al. (Norton, 2016).

[2] Audre Lorde, 'Uses of the Erotic: The Erotic as Power', in *Sister Outsider: Essays and Speeches* (Crossing, 2012), 53–9 (53).

Afterword

[325

'daughter-as-mother', tragedy is not averted but it makes room for 'illumination of the human potential to transform suffering into wisdom'. Such are the manifold emanations of Woman Wisdom.

Beyond the family, the erotic is, for Lorde, a 'source of power within the culture of the oppressed that can provide energy for change'.[3] This may in part explain why wisdom travels/travails with the oppressed in Shakespeare, including Caliban, 'one of only two characters who exhibit any kind of wisdom' in *The Tempest*,[4] Lear's fool whipped for his truth-telling riddles, and Emilia, late-wakening. Where Iago's bad-faith emplotment of tragedy holds open the possibility for 'divine comedy', it is Emilia who exposes his crime, protesting Desdemona's innocence. The play's transhistorical value emerges in exposing the false dichotomy 'between the spiritual and the political' underwriting racial injustice today,[5] which criminalises persons of colour while overlooking structural violence in education, health and judicial systems. The Lordean harmonising of the spiritual and the political would instead direct life-giving eros toward care-centred activisms that enact social change.[6] If genres are, as Bakhtin suggests, projections of worldviews, then wisdom's erotic energy aspires to a world in which individuals, in life or in death, fulfil their potentials.

This is the case with Shakespeare's sonnets which, Sean Keilen observes, quicken Christian morality with pleasure in confronting the 'sad mortality'. Keilen identifies pronoun patterns as indices to relationships between speaker and addressee, and changes therein, in presenting 'forms of life' with which readers might examine their own lives, whether in relationships of love (#108) and forgiveness (#120), or in exploring Christian and Pythagorean relational attitudes regarding death (#60). The poetic modelling of wisdom pertains to the entire sequence, as Keilen also finds a pattern in the 'I–you' address by which the speaker 'engrafts' 'once and future readers' into a collective 'vitality of reading', a performative vitality 'where breath most breathes, even in the mouths of men'. Inhabiting the performative 'first-person pronoun' connects readers to

---

[3] Lorde, 53.
[4] Sale, Chapter 9 in this volume.
[5] Lorde, 'Uses of the Erotic', 56.
[6] Lorde, 53.

'*pneuma* ("breath"): the name Stoic philosophers gave to the life-giving spirit of individual souls and the cosmos itself'. Inspiring, how wisdom works in verse.

And Jos Charles is so inspired, thinking and co-creating with Shakespeare, working through a COVID year of loss, grief and mental illness. She explores the Sonnets' formal resources, especially #24, and finds that even as the heart's unknowability makes for a 'promised yet impossible closure', the poem holds out for readerly recovery. The final couplet offers wisdom for which the poem provides context. It is detachable wisdom, a proverb that readers or listeners can relate to their own life experiences, thereby suturing 'the gap' between poem and couplet. For Charles, sonnet wisdom heals by purging the tragic vision of grief in Hamlet that ultimately destroys him. In theorising the sonnet, she works through tragedy, couplet/kharja, proverb and autoethnography in storytelling, bringing into play the relational hospitality of forms.

In its orientation toward change, wisdom's creative eros solicits audience engagement also in public performances that individuals can shape to their own needs and interests. In discussing the morality play and those written by Fabio Glissenti for the seventeenth-century Venetian stage, Eugenio Refini finds in the staging of morality 'experiential wisdom' involving free will and moral conscience one can apply to the performance of everyday life. While claims for the efficacy of such staging may be 'exaggerated', Refini notes, several highly successful modern moralities in different media—theatre, opera and animation—point to 'an ongoing fascination with a kind of moral discourse that merges moral knowledge and behaviour'. Besides discourse, wisdom also communicates through dance, synaesthetically and kinaesthetically engaging the mind, heart and eye. Identifying in *The Tempest* a view of Indigenous people as the 'epitome of gentle-kindness', Carolyn Sale focuses on the islanders' dance as a source of wisdom available in performance to playgoers through 'kinaesthetic resonance'. This happens when we experience 'our own bodies as instruments of attention', alert to the 'transfer of feeling' in the movements of dancers and the kindness they model. Just how this wisdom participates in 'theatrical space as the site of a possible transformation' remains an open question, since so much depends on individual capacities to learn and grow wise in 'kinaesthetic response' to entertainment, beginning, as the play suggests, with freeing our own docile bodies and enslaved senses.

Afterword [327

Perhaps the question maps a broader energy field, where Indigenous dancers have long connected with Mother Earth, and the hoop dance heals by harmonising with nature's circles;[7] or where Sufi dervishes whirl, in meditation orbiting the sun; or where William Butler Yeats sees 'among school children' a 'daughter of the swan', cosmically attuned, who 'stands before me as a living child'. Rhetorically, he asks: 'How can we know the dancer from the dance?'[8] When the whole person is attuned to the cosmic dance, theatre, regardless of where and how it happens, becomes the dancer even as audiences come into attention as the 'site of a possible transformation'. For Lauren Shufran, 'attention is transformative; it's a form of love'. The practice of attention is central to her pedagogy in the Shakespeare classroom, and one suspects it is likewise at work in the 'architecture' of her Instagram postings. Her considerable internet following and readership of *The Buddha and the Bard* suggest the power of self-organising through existing technologies, even as her mindful community, 'cultivating together . . . an awareness to relieve our collective suffering', is a resistant force to social media sites that sow hate and fear in order to incite mindless violence. Aligned with Sale and Refini, Shufran's interest in transformation invites future mappings around questions of how attention practices across media may serve to deepen individual engagements with wisdom among public audiences; how wisdom transforms theatrical, classroom, internet and community spaces; how wisdom travailers can make constructive use of existing and new technologies enabling individuals in exercising free will to enter collective endeavours for the greater good.

Love's transformation is urgently needed in our neoliberal societies today where money corrupts ethics and politics, and authoritarian forces threaten democratic institutions by stoking self-centred hate, using the power of social media algorithms to personalise consumers' addiction to hate, whether in the early modern sense of giving over one's will to a higher power, or as a learning disorder in which

---

7   Dallas Arcand, 'Living a Circular Life', TEDxYYC, YouTube, posted September 8, 2014. https://www.youtube.com/watch?v=niRs_VIqzYU

8   William Butler Yeats, 'Among School Children', Poetry Foundation, accessed September 25, 2023. https://www.poetryfoundation.org/poems/43293/among-school-children

one fixates on destructive behaviours in chasing after the elusive high and illusion of belonging that hate promises.[9] Amidst these dangers, wisdom travailers 'mapping [the present] into the future' could draw from the many insights developed in this volume, the most profoundly encompassing of which is the way wisdom reshapes our understanding of what 'inclusive' means and entails. Beyond institutional buzzwords and policy benchmarks, wisdom is the erotic energy in and around us that reorients those who so choose from 'ego- to ecology'. It is inclusive in promoting a 'shared humanity' in voicing global concerns for 'thriving and healing'. This broadly shared value/goal of thriving and healing brings together social and environmental ethics through respect for all sentient beings as members of a 'natural democracy'. In offering a fresh view of Jaques as a Pythagorean, Todd Borlik finds in *As You Like It* a comic idiom from which Pythagorean wisdom speaks anew to 'ecognostic' concerns relevant to both Shakespeare's world and our own. In doing so, Borlik draws on Timothy Morton's description of ecognosis as 'weird knowing', a humbling awareness of oneself amidst 'the strangeness of a non-anthropocentric universe' that remains strange, not to be familiarised or appropriated.[10] Borlik finds facilitation for this transhistorical connection in works familiar to Shakespeare and to readers today: Ovid's *Metamorphoses*, 'relay[ing]' the 'encounter with strangeness' through 'poetic estrangement'; and Montaigne's wry expression of 'humble knowingness'.

For Indigenous artists and scholars, however, any relationship to Shakespeare would be deeply vexed, given the legacy of colonial violence and dual dispossession of land and language. Even so, in speaking of wisdom, Madeline Sayet points to Shakespeare's 'ability to hold space for many voices', which entails 'being able to hold space for difference, hold space for many meanings, and hold space for questions'. The same can be said of Sayet herself, and this shared ability to 'hold space for possibility' suggests wisdom's power of traversing differences and vexed histories. To this company we might add Gloria Anzaldúa, whose 'new mestiza consciousness' calls upon 'women and men of

---

[9] Rebecca Lemon, *Addiction and Devotion in Early Modern England* (U of Pennsylvania P, 2018); Maia Szalavitz, *Unbroken Brain: A Revolutionary New Way of Understanding Addiction* (St. Martin's, 2016).

[10] Timothy Morton, qtd. in Borlik, Chapter 5 in this volume.

Afterword [329

color' to go beyond the 'us-versus-them' logic: 'I, for one, choose to use some of my energy to serve as mediator' in helping whites 'rid themselves of race hatred and fear' because 'we need to allow whites to become our allies'.[11] Wisdom tests our limits and means of inclusion. In 'Now Let Us Shift' and elsewhere, Anzaldúa presents *la naguala*, mythic shapeshifter and symbol of one's capacity for change. Her proposal for an inclusive *us* shifting together thus weaves individual change with collective self-organising.[12] And there is Joy Harjo who 'this morning', in praying for her enemies, says 'the door to the mind should only open from the heart. / An enemy who gets in, risks the danger of becoming a friend.'[13] Wisdom is inclusive as the heart is forgiving. What, then, might we say of Shakaliban our wise hybrid—that the world is their 'scammel'?

Sayet further acknowledges learning from Shakespeare the art of posing questions that characters 'grapple with' but do not answer. As Robin Kello notes, in *Where We Belong*, Sayet poses the question of 'how communities might form a place, anticolonial and deeply welcoming, where we all belong'. Admitting no ready-made answer, the question engages audiences in thinking it throughout—and beyond—the play, which ends on the word 'Welcome'. This welcome is an invitation that is also a challenge to assume communal responsibility. Remarkably, Borlik the Pythagorean connects with Sayet's question, in his appeal to shared ecological responsibility, through the image he brings forth of Jaques's 'jacent grovelling in the earth'. The pun on Jaques's name—'the Latin *jaces*, to lie recumbent', in his lament of the stag wounded and left to die by humans—registers as an act of 'eco-piety' that 'enables him to feel how profoundly connected human beings are to other life forms and the humusy earth that sustains us'. Grovelling, a spatial description of one's relation to the earth, internalises a posture by which *where* one belongs is effectively *how* one belongs.

---

[11] Gloria Anzaldúa, *Borderlands/La Frontera: The New Mestiza*, 2nd ed. (Aunt Lute, 1999), 107.

[12] Gloria Anzaldúa, 'now let us shift: inner work ... public acts', in *Light in the Dark/Luz en lo Oscuro: Rewriting Identity, Spirituality, Reality*, ed. AnaLouise Keating (Duke UP, 2015), 117–59.

[13] Joy Harjo, 'This Morning I Pray for My Enemies', poets.org, accessed September 25, 2023. https://poets.org/poem/morning-i-pray-my-enemies

Borlik further suggests harnessing Shakespeare's 'cultural prestige to broadcast non-Western wisdom traditions and Indigenous knowing systems, overcome Nimbyism, and foster collective solutions to environmental problems'. His own renewal of Pythagorean wisdom for our times puts me in mind of Robin Kimmerer's painstaking 'learning the grammar of animacy', a grammar of relational belonging that voices Indigenous ecognosis. I think as well of Langis's patient tracking of the international transmission of wisdom traditions East and West, traditions that have survived the vicissitudes of commerce and war, often beyond the attestation of written record. In this context, holding space for possibility is the positive structure of inclusion one practises in everyday life, often unacknowledged, as the wisdom of welcome. It is the antidote to critique, the centrepiece in what Sayet calls the 'negative structure' of exclusion—the exclusion of Indigenous and other kinds of unwanted knowledge and modes of inquiry—by which the academy maintains its 'false assumption' of wisdom. What, then, might holding space *for possibility* mean and entail for the inclusive education of new generations? How might eros enable self-organising among new travellers in wisdom's open-ended travels? On a very small scale, mappers of this journey have self-organised around Shakespeare and wisdom in addressing challenges and cultivating possibilities for the present and future, so that broadly casting is also *where* and *how* we belong.

NOTES ON CONTRIBUTORS

Todd Andrew Borlik is Professor of Shakespeare Studies and Renaissance Literature at the University of Huddersfield. He is the author of *Shakespeare Beyond the Green World* (2023), *Literature and Nature in the English Renaissance: An Ecocritical Anthology* (2019), *Ecocriticism and Early Modern English Literature* (2011), and over a dozen articles in academic journals such as *Shakespeare Bulletin, Shakespeare Quarterly, Shakespeare Survey* and *English Literary Renaissance*. His research and teaching interests include early environmental literature, Renaissance drama and Global Shakespeares. Recent publications have explored topics such as the enchanted entomology of *A Midsummer Night's Dream, The Winter's Tale* and the fur trade, and cyber-punk Hamlets. His study of *The Tempest* and the fens ranks among the 'most read articles' of the *Shakespeare* journal.

Jos Charles is author of the poetry collection *feeld*, a Pulitzer-finalist and winner of the 2017 National Poetry Series, *Safe Space* and *A Year & Other Poems*. She received the 2016 Ruth Lilly & Dorothy Sargent Rosenberg Fellowship through the Poetry Foundation and the 2015 Monique Wittig Scholarship through the University of Arizona. Charles is a 2024 Guggenheim Fellow. She has presented at the Sewanee Medieval Colloquium and Concordia University. Charles holds an MFA from the University of Arizona and currently resides in Long Beach, CA.

Sean Keilen is Professor of Literature and Founding Director of Shakespeare Workshop at UC Santa Cruz. He is the author of *Vulgar Eloquence: On the Renaissance Invention of English Literature* and,

332] *Shakespeare and Wisdom*

with Nick Moschovakis, the editor of *The Routledge Research Companion to Shakespeare and Classical Literature*.

Robin Alfriend Kello has received his PhD in English from the University of California, Los Angeles, where he focuses on Shakespeare, the theatre of migration, and early modern literature in English and Spanish. His other interests in teaching, research and community outreach include bilingual theatre, adaptation and appropriation, translation, abolitionist and prison education initiatives, and Shakespeare and social justice on the stage and in the classroom.

Unhae Park Langis is a humanist-activist, a stitcher of text and textile, and a volunteer for Citizens' Climate Lobby. A former teacher of twenty years, she is the author of *Passion, Prudence, and Virtue in Shakespearean Drama* (2011) and numerous essays in ethical criticism in collections and journals including *Shakespeare Studies*, *EMLS*, *Upstart Crow* and *Literature Compass*. As a research fellow at the New Swan Shakespeare Center, University of California, Irvine, Langis has evolved from virtue ethics to a multi-perspectival wisdom hermeneutic through Stoic, Buddhist and Sufi readings of Shakespeare in several collections including this present volume.

Joan Pong Linton is an Associate Professor Emerita of English at Indiana University. She is the author of *The Romance of the New World: Gender and the Literary Formations of English Colonialism* (1998), and co-editor of two critical anthologies, *The Age of Thomas Nashe: Elizabethan London, Print Culture, and Authorship in Early Modern England* (2013) and *Go-Figure: Energies, Forms, and Institutions in the Early Modern World* (2011).

Julia Reinhard Lupton is Professor of English at the University of California, Irvine. She is the author or co-author of five books, including *Shakespeare Dwelling: Designs for the Theater of Life* (2018), *Thinking with Shakespeare* (2015) and *Citizen-Saints* (2012). She has edited or co-edited many volumes and special issues, including *Shakespeare and Virtue: A Handbook* (with Donovan Sherman), *Shakespeare and Hospitality* (with David Goldstein), and *Face to Face with Shakespeare* (with Matthew

Notes on Contributors

[333

Smith). She is a former Guggenheim Fellow and a former Trustee of the Shakespeare Association of America.

Benjamin Parris is Assistant Professor of English at Rice University, where he teaches courses on Shakespeare, Milton, classical and early modern poetry and drama, and the histories of philosophy and science. He is the author of *Vital Strife: Sleep, Insomnia, and the Early Modern Ethics of Care* (2022). His essays on sleep and early modern drama and poetry have appeared in *Shakespeare Studies, Modern Philology, SEL: Studies in English Literature*, and an edited collection from Penn State University Press. His current book project, 'Endless Goods: Virtue and Political Economy in Early Modern England', argues that early modern literature grapples with the transition from feudalism into capitalism through figures of endlessness that respond to crises in the understanding and social distribution of ethical, spiritual and economic forms of value.

Eugenio Refini (PhD, Scuola Normale Superiore di Pisa) is Professor of Italian Studies at New York University. Prior to joining NYU, he was a postdoctoral research fellow at the University of Warwick (2010–13) and he taught at Johns Hopkins University (2014–19). His work focuses on reception, translation, early modern drama, and the intersections of music and literature. His recent publications include the monograph *The Vernacular Aristotle: Translation as Reception in Medieval and Renaissance Italy* (2020), *Staging the Soul: Allegorical Drama as Spiritual Practice in Baroque Italy* (2023) and articles in *Renaissance Quarterly, The Italianist* and *Romance Quarterly*. With Jessica Goethals, he co-edited a special issue of *The Italianist* (40.3) on 'Genre-Bending in Early Modern Performative Cultures'. A recipient of fellowships from Harvard University's Villa I Tatti, the Bodleian Library and the Warburg Institute, he has recently been awarded the Rome Prize for the academic year 2021–22.

Carolyn Sale is an Associate Professor at the University of Alberta (Canada). Her primary research interests are in early modern literature and the law; Shakespeare and performance theory; and early modern political theory, including the history and theory of the common. Her work has been published in *Shakespeare Quarterly, Renaissance*

334] *Shakespeare and Wisdom*

Drama, *ELH* and various collections including *The Law in Shakespeare* (2006); *The History of British Women's Writing, Volume 2: 1500–1610* (2013); *Shakespeare and Judgment* (2016); *The Oxford Handbook of English Law and Literature, 1500–1700* (2017); and *The Oxford Handbook of Shakespearean Comedy* (2018). She is completing the book manuscript 'The Literary Commons: The Common Law and the Writer in Early Modern England, 1528–1628' and has co-edited with Julia Lupton and Kent Lehnhof the collection *Shakespeare's Virtuous Theatre* (2023).

Madeline Sayet is a Mohegan theatre maker and Assistant Professor at Arizona State University with the Arizona Center for Medieval and Renaissance Studies (ACMRS). A national tour of her play *Where We Belong* (2022), produced by Woolly Mammoth Theatre Company in association with the Folger Shakespeare Library, included notable venues such as The Public Theater, The Goodman Theater, Seattle Rep, Oregon Shakespeare Festival, Hudson Valley Shakespeare and Portland Center Stage, after its initial performance at Shakespeare's Globe in London. Recognition for her work as a director, writer and performer include Forbes 30 Under 30, TED Fellowship and The White House Champion of Change Award from President Barack Obama.

Lauren Shufran is a ghostwriter and content strategist in the Bay Area (laurenshufran.com) and a practitioner of yoga and mindfulness. A former teacher of creative writing, Renaissance poetics and Shakespeare, they hold an MFA in Creative Writing/Poetry from San Francisco State University and a PhD in Early Modern British Literature from University of California, Santa Cruz. They are the author of a collection of poetry called *Inter Arma* (2013), which won the Motherwell Prize. Their poetry has appeared in *Best American Experimental Writing*, *Postmodern Culture*, *The Los Angeles Review of Books*, *Emerge: An Anthology of Writing by Lambda Fellows* and elsewhere. Their scholarly essays have been published in a handful of peer-reviewed journals.

Marguerite A. Tassi is Professor of English Literature at the University of Nebraska at Kearney. She is the author of two books, *The Scandal of Images: Iconoclasm, Eroticism, and Painting in*

Notes on Contributors [335

Early Modern English Drama (2005) and *Women and Revenge in Shakespeare: Gender, Genre, and Ethics* (2011). Her articles have appeared in journals such as *Comparative Drama, Explorations in Renaissance Culture* and *The Ben Jonson Journal,* as well as essay collections published by presses such as Classiques Garnier, Edinburgh and Routledge. She is co-editor of the series New Interdisciplinary Approaches to Early Modern Culture and editor of *Poetry for Kids: William Shakespeare.*

WORKS CITED

'15 Black Environmental Leaders to Follow'. *Yale Sustainability*. February 13, 2023. https://sustainability.yale.edu/blog/15-black-environmental-leaders-follow

Abram, David. *Becoming Animal: An Earthly Cosmology*. Pantheon, 2010.

Adelman, Janet. *The Common Liar: An Essay on Antony and Cleopatra*. Yale UP, 1973.

——. *Suffocating Mothers: Fantasies of Maternal Origin in Shakespeare's Plays, 'Hamlet' to 'The Tempest'*. Routledge, 1992.

Agamben, Giorgio. *State of Exception*. Trans. Kevin Attell. U of Chicago P, 2005.

Agricola, Georgius. *De Re Metallica*. Trans. from the first Latin edition of 1556 by Herbert Clark Hoover and Lou Henry Hoover. Dover, 1950. Project Gutenberg. https://www.gutenberg.org/files/38015/38015-h/38015-h.htm

Aitken, James K. 'Apocalyptic, Revelation and Early Jewish Wisdom Literature'. In *New Heaven and New Earth: Prophecy and the Millennium, Essays in Honour of Anthony Gelston*. Ed. Peter J. Harland and Robert Hayward. Supplements to Vetus Testamentum. Vol. 77. Brill, 1999. 181–93.

Akbari, Suzanne Conklin. *Seeing through the Veil: Optical Theory and Medieval Allegory*. U of Toronto P, 2015.

Akhimie, Patricia. 'Performance in the Periphery: Colonial Encounters and Entertainments'. In *Acoustemologies in Contact: Sounding Subjects and Modes of Listening in Early Modernity*. Ed. Emily Wilbourne and Suzanne G. Cusick. Open Book, 2021. 65–82.

Akuno, Kali, and Ajamu Nangwaya, eds. *Jackson Rising: The Struggle for Economic Democracy and Black Self-Determination in Jackson, Mississippi*. Daraja, 2017.

Al-Dabbagh, Abdulla. 'The Oriental Sources of Courtly Love'. *International Journal of English-Arabic Studies* 3.1 (2002): 21–32.

Allen, Michael J. B. 'Marsilio Ficino on Plato's Pythagorean Eye'. *Modern Language Notes* 97.1 (January 1982): 171–82.

Works Cited

[337

Allen, Nick. 'The Common Origin Approach to Comparing Indian and Greek Philosophy'. In *Universe and Inner Self in Early Indian and Early Greek Thought*. Ed. Richard Seaford. Edinburgh UP, 2016. 12–27.

Allot, Robert. *Wits theater of the little world*. Nicholas Ling, 1599.

Alster, Bendt. *Wisdom of Ancient Sumer*. CDL, 2005.

Al-Sulami, Muhammad ibn al-Husayn, and Tosun Bayrak. *The Way of Sufi Chivalry: When the Light of the heart is reflected in the beauty of the face, that beauty is Futuwwah*. Inner Traditions, 1991.

Alter, Robert. *The Art of Biblical Poetry*. Revised and updated edition. Basic Books, 2011.

Andrews, Richard. *Scripts and Scenarios: The Performance of Comedy in Renaissance Italy*. Cambridge UP, 1993.

Andrus, Marc. *Brothers in the Beloved Community: The Friendship of Thich Nhat Hanh and Martin Luther King Jr*. Parallax, 2021. PDF.

Anzaldúa, Gloria. *Borderlands/La Frontera: The New Mestiza*. 2nd ed. Aunt Lute, 1999.

——. *Light in the Dark/Luz en lo Oscuro: Rewriting Identity, Spirituality, Reality*. Ed. AnaLouise Keating. Duke UP, 2015.

Apuleius (Lucius Apuleius Madaurensis 'Africanus'). *The Apologia and Florida*. Trans. Harold Edgeworth Butler. Clarendon, 1909.

——. *The Golden Asse*. Trans. William Adlington. H. Wykes, 1566. Kindle. Rpt. from the 1639 edition.

——. *Metamorphoses, Book XI: The Isis Book*. Ed. Wytse Hette Keulen and Ulrike Egelhaaf-Gaiser. Brill, 2015.

Arai, Yoshio. 'Shakespeare in Japan's Zen Philosophy: The Plays of Nothing at the Theatre of Nothing'. *Ilha do Desterro: A Journal of English Language, Literatures in English and Cultural Studies* 49 (July–December 2005): 143–57.

Arcand, Dallas. 'Living a Circular Life'. TEDxYYC. YouTube. Posted September 8, 2014. https://www.youtube.com/watch?v=niRs_VIqzYU

Aristotle. *Ethica Nicomachea* (*Nicomachean Ethics*). In *The Basic Works of Aristotle*. Ed. Richard McKeon. Modern Library, 2001.

Armstrong, Karen. *Buddha*. Viking Penguin, 2001.

Arnold, David. 'Unsettling the Harmony Stereotype in Buddhist American Poetry'. *ANQ: A Quarterly Journal of Short Articles, Notes and Reviews* 33.4 (2020): 293–305.

Athanasius. *On the Incarnation: New Edition*. Trans. and ed. Penelope Lawson. St Vladimir's Seminary, 1998.

Austin, Naomi, Stephen Cooter and Alice Jones, dirs. *Our Universe*. Netflix Documentary Series. Narr. Morgan Freeman. BBC Studios, 2022.

Bakhtin, Mikhail Mikhaïlovich. 'The Problem of Speech Genres'. In *Speech Genres and Other Late Essays*. Trans. Vern W. McGee. Ed. Caryl Emerson and Michael Holquist. U of Texas P, 1986. 60–102.

Baldwin, T. W. *William Shakespeare's Small Latine & Lesse Greeke*. 2 vols. U of Illinois P, 1944.

Baldwin, William. *A treatise of Morall Phylosophie, contayning the sayinges of the wyse*. Edward Whitchurch, 1547. Ed. Robert Hood Bowers. Scholars' Facsimiles and Reprints, 1967.

Barber, William. 'Racist Shootings "Don't Happen in a Vacuum": Bishop Barber on DeSantis, Trump & Those Who Spread Hate'. Interviewed by Amy Goodman. *Democracy Now!* September 5, 2023. https://www.democracynow.org/2023/9/5/rev_william_barber_jacksonville_florida_shooting

Barker, Francis, and Peter Hulme. 'Nymphs and Reapers Heavily Vanish: The Discursive Con-texts of *The Tempest*'. In *Alternative Shakespeares*. Ed. John Drakakis. Methuen, 1985. 194–208.

Bärnthaler, Richard. 'Towards Eco-Social Politics: A Case Study of Transformative Strategies to Overcome Forms-of-Life Crises'. *Environmental Politics* (2023): 1–22. PDF. https://www.tandfonline.com/doi/full/10.1080/09644016.2023.2180910

Batchelor, Stephen. 'Greek Buddha: Pyrrho's Encounter with Early Buddhism in Central Asia'. Review of *Greek Buddha: Pyrrho's Encounter with Early Buddhism in Central Asia*, by Christopher I. Beckwith. *Contemporary Buddhism* 17.1 (2016): 195–215.

Beal, Rebecca S. 'Bonaventure, Dante and the Apocalyptic Woman Clothed with the Sun'. *Dante Studies, with the Annual Report of the Dante Society* 114 (1996): 209–28.

Beckwith, Christopher I. *Greek Buddha: Pyrrho's Encounter with Early Buddhism in Central Asia*. Princeton UP, 2015.

Behrendt, Kurt A. *The Art of Gandhara in the Metropolitan Museum of Art*. Metropolitan Museum of Art, 2007.

Bellah, Robert N., and Hans Joas, eds. *The Axial Age and its Consequences*. Harvard UP, 2012.

Bennett, Robert B. 'The Reform of a Malcontent: Jaques and the Meaning of *As You Like It*'. *Shakespeare Studies* 9 (1976): 183–204.

Bernabé, Alberto, and Julia Mendoza. 'Pythagorean Cosmogony and Vedic Cosmogony (RV 10.129). Analogies and Differences'. *Phronesis* 58.1 (2013): 32–51.

Bernheimer, Richard. 'Theatrum Mundi'. *The Art Bulletin* 38.4 (December 1956): 225–47.

Berzin, Alexander. 'Historical Survey of the Buddhist and Muslim Worlds' Knowledge of Each Other's Customs and Teachings'. *The Muslim World* 100.2–3 (2010): 187–203.

Works Cited

[339

Bett, Richard. 'Beauty and its Relation to Goodness in Stoicism'. In *Ancient Models of Mind: Studies in Human and Divine Rationality*. Ed. Andrea Nightingale and David Sedley. Cambridge UP, 2010. 130–52.

Bevington, David M. *Action Is Eloquence: Shakespeare's Language of Gesture*. Harvard UP, 1984.

——. *From Mankind to Marlowe: Growth of Structure in the Popular Drama of Tudor England*. Harvard UP, 1962.

Blackhawk, Ned. *The Rediscovery of America: Native Peoples and the Unmaking of U.S. History*. Yale UP, 2023.

Boggs, Grace Lee, and Scott Kurashige. *The Next American Revolution: Sustainable Activism for the Twenty-First Century*. U of California P, 2012.

The bokes of Salomon namely. Prouerbia Ecclesiastes Cantica canticorum Sapientia Ecclesiasticus or Iesus the sonne of Syrach. Wylliam Bonham, 1546. STC 2755.

Bonneuil, Christophe, and Jean-Baptiste Fressoz. *The Shock of the Anthropocene: The Earth, History and Us*. Trans. David Fernbach. Verso, 2016.

Bono, Barbara J. *Literary Transvaluation: From Vergilian Epic to Shakespearean Tragicomedy*. U of California P, 1984.

Booty, John E., ed. *The Book of Common Prayer, 1559: The Elizabethan Prayer Book*. U of Virginia P, 2005.

Borlik, Todd A. *Ecocriticism and Early Modern English Literature: Green Pastures*. Routledge, 2011.

Bourgeault, Cynthia. 'Centering Prayer and Attention of the Heart'. *CrossCurrents* 59.1 (March 2009): 15–27.

——. *The Heart of Centering Prayer: Nondual Christianity in Theory and Practice*. Shambhala, 2016.

——. *The Meaning of Mary Magdalene: Discovering the Woman at the Heart of Christianity*. Shambhala, 2010.

——. 'The Way of the Heart'. *Parabola*, January 31, 2017. https://parabola. org/2017/01/31/the-way-of-the-heart-cynthia-bourgeault/

——. *The Wisdom Way of Knowing: Reclaiming an Ancient Tradition to Awaken the Heart*. Wiley, 2003.

Bowerbank, Sylvia. *Speaking for Nature: Women and Ecologies of Early Modern England*. Johns Hopkins UP, 2004.

Breitenberg, Mark. 'Anxious Masculinity: Sexual Jealousy in Early Modern England'. *Feminist Studies* 19.2 (Summer 1993): 377–98.

Brenk, Frederick E., SJ. 'Antony-Osiris, Cleopatra-Isis: The End of Plutarch's Antony'. In *Plutarch and the Historical Tradition*. Ed. Philip A. Stadter. Routledge, 1992. 159–82.

Bricault, Laurent. *Isis Pelagia: Images, Names and Cults of a Goddess of the Seas*. Religions in the Graeco-Roman World. Vol. 190. Trans. Gil H. Renberg. Brill, 2020.

Broek, Roelof van den. *Gnostic Religion in Antiquity*. Trans. Anthony Runia. Cambridge UP, 2013.

Brotton, Jerry. *This Orient Isle: Elizabethan England and the Islamic World*. Penguin, 2016. PDF.

brown, adrienne maree. *Emergent Strategy: Shaping Change, Changing Worlds*. AK, 2017. PDF.

Brown, William P. 'Virtue and its Limits in the Wisdom Corpus: Character Formation, Disruption, and Transformation'. In *The Oxford Handbook of Wisdom and the Bible*. Ed. Will Kynes. Oxford UP, 2021. 45–64.

Brunnhölzl, Karl. *The Heart Attack Sūtra: A New Commentary on the 'Heart Sūtra'*. Shambhala, 2012.

Bruyneel, Kevin. *Settler Memory: The Disavowal of Indigeneity and the Politics of Race in the United States*. U of North Carolina P, 2021.

Bry, Theodor de. *Magus goggled and tracking Nature through the night with staff and lamp*. 1618. Woodcut. In *Atalanta fugiens, hoc est, Emblemata nova de secretis naturae chymica* [. . .], by Michael Maier. Oppenheim, Germany: Hieronymus Galler for Johann Theodor de Bry, 1618.

——. *Their danses vvhich they vse at their highe feastes*. 1590. Woodcut. In *A briefe and true report of the new found land of Virginia* [. . .], by Thomas Hariot. Francoforti ad Moenum: Typis Ioannis Wecheli, sumtibus vero Theodori de Bry, 1590.

Burkert, Walter. *Greek Religion*. Trans. John Raffan. Harvard UP, 1985.

——. *Lore and Science in Ancient Pythagoreanism*. Trans. Edwin L. Minar Jr. Harvard UP, 1972.

Burnet, John. 'Sceptics'. In *Encyclopædia of Religion and Ethics*. Ed. James Hastings et al. Vol. 11. T. & T. Clark, 1921. 228–31.

Bushnell, Rebecca W. *A Culture of Teaching: Early Modern Humanism in Theory and Practice*. Cornell UP, 1996.

Bussanich, John. 'Plato and Yoga'. In *Universe and Inner Self in Early Indian and Early Greek Thought*. Ed. Richard Seaford. Edinburgh UP, 2016. 87–103.

Cajete, Gregory. *Native Science: Natural Laws of Interdependence*. Clear Light, 2000.

——. 'Philosophy of Native Science'. In *American Indian Thought: Philosophical Essays*. Ed. Anne Waters. Blackwell, 2004. 45–57.

Calvin, Jean. *The Psalmes of Dauid and others, with M. Iohn Caluins commentaries*. Trans. Arthur Golding. Printed by Thomas East and Henry Middelton for Lucas Harison and George Byshop, 1571. STC 4395.

Calvo, Ana Manzanas. 'Conversion Narratives: Othello and Other Black Characters in Shakespeare's and Lope de Vega's Plays'. *SEDERI* 7 (1996): 231–6.

Works Cited

[341

Camus, Albert. *The Myth of Sisyphus and Other Essays*. Trans. Justin O'Brien. Vintage, 1955.

Caporicci, Camilla. 'Black But Yet Fair: The *Topos* of the Black Beloved from Song of Songs in Shakespeare's Work'. *Shakespeare* 14.4 (2018): 360–73.

Carlyle, Thomas. *On Heroes, Hero-Worship, and the Heroic in History*. Ed. David R. Sorensen and Brent E. Kinser. Yale UP, 2013.

Carruthers, Mary. '"Sweet Jesus"'. In *Mindful Spirit in Late Medieval Literature: Essays in Honor of Elizabeth D. Kirk*. Ed. Bonnie Wheeler. Palgrave Macmillan, 2006. 9–19.

Casares, Aurelia Martín. *La esclavitud en la Granada del siglo XVI: Género, raza y religión*. Editorial Universidad de Granada, 2000.

Castiglione, Baldassare. *The Book of the Courtier*. Trans. and ed. George Bull. Penguin, 1976. PDF.

Caygill, Howard. 'The Alexandrian Aesthetic'. In *The New Aestheticism*. Ed. John J. Joughin and Simon Malpas. Manchester UP, 2003. 99–118.

Celenza, Christopher S. 'Pythagoras in the Renaissance: The Case of Marsilio Ficino'. *Renaissance Quarterly* 52.3 (Autumn 1999): 667–711.

Chakrabarty, Dipesh. 'The Climate of History: Four Theses'. *Critical Inquiry* 35.2 (Winter 2009): 197–222.

Chapman, George. *A pleasant comedy entituled: An humerous dayes myrth*. Valentine Syms, 1599.

Charbonnier, Pierre. *Affluence and Freedom: An Environmental History of Political Ideas*. Trans. Andrew Brown. Polity, 2021.

Charles, Jos. 'The World Is Flat'. In *Safe Space*. Ahsahta, 2016. 53–64.

Cheney, Liana de Girolami. 'Lavinia Fontana's *Cleopatra the Alchemist*'. *Journal of Literature and Art Studies* 8.8 (August 2018): 1,159–80.

Chew, Samuel C. *The Crescent and the Rose: Islam and England during the Renaissance*. Oxford UP, 1937; Octagon Books, 1965.

Christian, Lynda Gregorian. *Theatrum Mundi: The History of an Idea*. Garland, 1987.

Cleland, Katharine. *Irregular Unions: Clandestine Marriage in Early Modern English Literature*. Cornell UP, 2021.

Coates, Ta-Nehisi. 'Ta-Nehisi Coates Speaks Out against Israel's "Segregationist Apartheid Regime" after West Bank Visit'. Interviewed by Amy Goodman and Nermeen Shaikh. *Democracy Now!* November 2, 2023. https://www.democracynow.org/2023/11/2/ta_nehisi_coates

Cohen, D. M. 'The Jew and Shylock'. *Shakespeare Quarterly* 31.1 (Spring 1980): 53–63.

Cohen, Yoram. *Wisdom from the Late Bronze Age*. Writings from the Ancient World. Vol. 34. Society of Biblical Literature, 2013.

342] *Shakespeare and Wisdom*

—— and Nathan Wasserman. 'Mesopotamian Wisdom Literature'. In *The Oxford Handbook of Wisdom and the Bible*. Ed. Will Kynes. Oxford UP, 2021. 121–40.

Coke, Edward. *La sept part des reports Sr. Edw. Coke Chiualer*. Societie of Stationers, 1608.

Coleridge, Samuel Taylor. *Biographia Literaria; or, Biographical Sketches of my Literary Life and Opinions*. Leavitt, Lord and Company, 1834.

Colie, Rosalie Littell. *Shakespeare's Living Art*. Princeton UP, 1974.

Considine, John. 'Wisdom-Literature in Early Modern England'. *Renaissance Studies* 13.3 (September 1999): 325–42.

Cook, Francis H. *Hua-yen Buddhism: The Jewel Net of Indra*. Penn State UP, 2010.

Cook, Johann. *The Septuagint of Proverbs—Jewish and/or Hellenistic Proverbs? Concerning the Hellenistic Colouring of LXX Proverbs*. Supplements to Vetus Testamentum. Vol. 69. Brill, 1997.

Cormack, Bradin. *A Power to Do Justice: Jurisdiction, English Literature, and the Rise of Common Law, 1509–1625*. U of Chicago P, 2007.

——. 'Shakespeare's Other Sovereignty: On Particularity and Violence in *The Winter's Tale* and the Sonnets'. *Shakespeare Quarterly* 62.4 (Winter 2011): 485–513.

Cortes, Mayra. 'Acousmatic Noise: Racialization and Resistance in *The Tempest*'s "New World" Soundscape'. *Early Theatre* 25.1 (2022): 79–106.

Cousins, A. D. 'Shakespeare's Sonnets'. In *The Cambridge Companion to the Sonnet*. Ed. A. D. Cousins and Peter Howarth. Cambridge UP, 2011. 125–44.

Coverdale, Myles. *Goostly psalmes and spirituall songes drawen out of the holy Scripture*. John Gough, 1535. STC 5892.

——. *The Psalter or Boke of Psalmes both in Latyn and Englyshe*. Richard Grafton, 1540. STC 2368.

Crane, Mary Thomas. *Framing Authority: Sayings, Self, and Society in Sixteenth-Century England*. Princeton UP, 1993.

Crenshaw, James L. *Old Testament Wisdom: An Introduction*. 3rd ed. Westminster John Knox, 2010.

Cresti, Federico. 'Il Manoscritto della Cosmographia de l'Affrica di Giovanni Leone Africano. Note in Margine all'Edizione Critica del Testo'. *Mediterranea: Ricerche Storiche* 31 (August 2014): 383–96.

Čulík-Baird, Hannah. 'Ipse dixit: Citation and Authority'. *Sententiae Antiquae*. April 23, 2019. https://sententiaeantiquae.com/2019/04/23/ipse-dixit-citation-and-authority/

Cunsolo, Ashlee, and Neville R. Ellis. 'Ecological Grief as a Mental Health Response to Climate Change-Related Loss'. *Nature Climate Change* 8 (2018): 275–81.

Works Cited

[343

Dakake, Maria Massi. '"Walking upon the Path of God like Men"? Women and the Feminine in the Islamic Mystical Tradition'. In *Sufism: Love and Wisdom*. Ed. Jean-Louis Michon and Roger Gaetani. World Wisdom, 2006. 131–51.

Daniélou, Alain. *Gods of Love and Ecstasy: The Traditions of Shiva and Dionysus*. Inner Traditions, 1992. EPUB.

Davie, Emma, and Peter Mettler, dirs. *Becoming Animal*. With David Abram, Peter Mettler. Maximage and SDI Productions. 2018.

Davies, John. *Le primer report des cases & matters en ley resolues & adiudges en les courts del Roy en Ireland*. John Franckton, 1615.

Davis, Natalie Zemon. *Trickster Travels: A Sixteenth-Century Muslim between Worlds*. Hill & Wang, 2006.

Dawson, Anthony B. *Watching Shakespeare: A Playgoers' Guide*. St. Martin's, 1988.

Deats, Sara Munson. '"Truly, an obedient lady": Desdemona, Emilia, and the Doctrine of Obedience in *Othello*'. In *Othello: New Critical Essays*. Ed. Philip C. Kolin. Routledge, 2002. 233–54.

Degenhardt, Jane Hwang. 'Globability: The Virtue of Worlding'. In *Shakespeare and Virtue: A Handbook*. Ed. Julia Reinhard Lupton and Donovan Sherman. Cambridge UP, 2023. 334–46.

Dessen, Alan C. 'The Morall as an Elizabethan Dramatic Kind: An Exploratory Essay'. *Comparative Drama* 5.2 (Summer 1971): 138–59.

——. 'On-Stage Allegory and its Legacy: *The Three Ladies of London*'. In *Locating the Queen's Men, 1583–1603: Material Practices and Conditions of Playing*. Ed. Helen Ostovich, Holger Schott Syme and Andrew Griffin. Ashgate, 2009. 147–58.

De Vos, Paula. 'Rosewater and Philosophers' Oil: Thermo-Chemical Processing in Medieval and Early Modern Spanish Pharmacy'. *Centaurus* 60.3 (August 2018): 159–72.

Diogenes Laertius. *Lives of Eminent Philosophers*. Trans. R. D. Hicks. 2 vols. Loeb Classical Library. Harvard UP, 1925, 1972. Perseus Digital Library. Accessed October 3, 2023. https://www.perseus.tufts.edu/hopper/

Donaldson, Brianne. 'Bioethics and Jainism: From *Ahiṃsā* to an Applied Ethics of Carefulness'. *Religions* 10.4 (2019): 1–19. https://doi.org/10.3390/rel10040243

Donkin, R. A. *Beyond Price: Pearls and Pearl Fishing: Origins to the Age of Discoveries*. American Philosophical Society, 1998.

Donne, John. *John Donne's Sermons on the Psalms and Gospels, with a Selection of Prayers and Meditations*. Ed. Evelyn M. Simpson. U of California P, 1963.

Dowden, Edward. *Shakespeare: A Critical Study of his Mind and Art*. Henry S. King, 1875.

344] *Shakespeare and Wisdom*

Dronke, Peter. *Medieval Latin and the Rise of European Love-Lyric*. 2nd ed. Clarendon, 1999.

Dunbar-Ortiz, Roxanne. *An Indigenous Peoples' History of the United States*. Beacon, 2014.

Duncan-Jones, Katherine. *Ungentle Shakespeare: Scenes from his Life*. Thomson Learning, 2001.

Dyer, Wayne W. *Change Your Thoughts—Change Your Life: Living the Wisdom of the Tao*. Hay House, 2009.

Dysinger, Luke. 'Wisdom in the Christian Tradition'. In *The World's Great Wisdom: Timeless Teachings from Religions and Philosophies*. Ed. Roger Walsh. SUNY, 2014. 29–54.

Eden, Kathy. *Friends Hold All Things in Common: Tradition, Intellectual Property, and the 'Adages' of Erasmus*. Yale UP, 2001.

Eden, Richard. *The decades of the newe worlde or West India*. Guilhelmi Powell, 1555.

Edmondson, Paul. *Shakespeare: Ideas in Profile*. Profile Books, 2015.

Edwards, Richard. *The Works of Richard Edwards: Politics, Poetry, and Performance in Sixteenth-Century England*. Ed. Rosalind King. Manchester UP, 2001.

Egan, Gabriel. *Green Shakespeare: From Ecopolitics to Ecocriticism*. Routledge, 2006.

El Daly, Okasha. *Egyptology: The Missing Millennium: Ancient Egypt in Medieval Arabic Writings*. UCL, 2005; Routledge, 2016.

Eliot, Sir Charles. *Japanese Buddhism*. Routledge & Kegan Paul, 1935, 2018. EPUB.

Elverskog, Johan. *Buddhism and Islam on the Silk Road*. U of Pennsylvania P, 2010.

Epictetus. *Discourses, Fragments, Handbook*. Trans. Robin Hard. Intro. Christopher Gill. Oxford UP, 2014.

Erasmus, Desiderius. *The Adages of Erasmus*. Ed. William Barker. U of Toronto P, 2001.

Estes, Nick. Foreword to *Becoming Kin: An Indigenous Call to Unforgetting the Past and Reimagining our Future*, by Patty Krawec. Broadleaf Books, 2022. xiii–xiv.

Feerick, Jean E. 'Groveling with Earth in Kyd and Shakespeare's Historical Tragedies'. In *The Indistinct Human in Renaissance Literature'*. Ed. Jean E. Feerick and Vin Nardizzi. Palgrave Macmillan, 2012. 229–52.

Feldman, Christina. *Boundless Heart: The Buddha's Path of Kindness, Compassion, Joy, and Equanimity*. Shambhala, 2017. EPUB.

Felstiner, John. '"Ziv, That Light": Translation and Tradition in Paul Celan'. *New Literary History* 18.3 (Spring 1987): 611–31.

Works Cited

[345

Ferber, Ilit, and Paula Schwebel, eds. *Lament in Jewish Thought: Philosophical, Theological, and Literary Perspectives*. De Gruyter, 2014.

Ferguson, Gaylon. 'Awakening Loving-Kindness and Compassion'. Talk presented at The Wisdom of Pema Chödrön: A Summit of Timeless Teachings to Awaken the Heart. April 7–11, 2022. https://learn.lionsroar.com/p/the-wisdom-of-pema-chodron-summit-upgrade

Ficino, Marsilio. *Marsilio Ficino's Commentary on Plato's Symposium*. Trans. and ed. Sears Reynolds Jayne. U of Missouri P, 1944.

Fink, Z. S. 'Jaques and the Malcontent Traveler'. *Philological Quarterly* 14 (1935): 237–52.

Fitzpatrick, Joan. *Food in Shakespeare: Early Modern Dietaries and the Plays*. Ashgate, 2007.

Flesch, William. 'Personal Identity and Vicarious Experience in Shakespeare's Sonnets'. In *A Companion to Shakespeare's Sonnets*. Ed. Michael Schoenfeldt. Blackwell, 2007. 383–401.

Fletcher, Richard. 'Prosthetic Origins: Apuleius the Afro-Platonist'. In *Apuleius and Africa*. Ed. Benjamin Todd Lee, Ellen Finkelpearl and Luca Graverini. Routledge, 2014. 297–312.

Flintoff, Everard. 'Pyrrho and India'. *Phronesis* 25.1 (1980): 88–108.

Florek, Stan. 'Book and Sutra'. *Australian Museum*, June 14, 2023. https://australian.museum/learn/cultures/international-collection/african/book-and-sutra/

Ford, James Ishmael, and Melissa Myozen Blacker, ed. and intro. *The Book of Mu: Essential Writings on Zen's Most Important Koan*. Wisdom, 2011.

Fox, Michael V. *Proverbs 1–9: A New Translation with Introduction and Commentary*. Anchor Bible 18A. Doubleday, 2000.

Franz, Margaret. 'Legal Rhetoric and the Ambiguous Shape of the King's Two Bodies in *Calvin's Case* (1608)'. *Advances in the History of Rhetoric* 20.3 (September 2017): 262–84.

Fraser, Nancy. *Cannibal Capitalism: How our System Is Devouring Democracy, Care, and the Planet—and What We Can Do about It*. Verso, 2022.

Freinkel, Lisa. 'The Name of the Rose: Christian Figurality and Shakespeare's Sonnets'. In *Shakespeare's Sonnets: Critical Essays*. Ed. James Schiffer. Garland, 2000. 241–61.

Freinkel, Lisa Myōbun. 'Doing Time: Shakespeare's Weasel, Chao-Chou's Dog, and the Melancholy Lyric'. *The Yearbook of Comparative Literature* 57 (2011): 213–29.

——. 'Empson's Dog: Emptiness and Divinity in *Timon of Athens*'. In *Shakespeare and Religion: Early Modern and Postmodern Perspectives*. Ed. Ken Jackson and Arthur F. Marotti. U of Notre Dame P, 2011. 188–204.

346]   *Shakespeare and Wisdom*

Frye, Northrop. *Fables of Identity: Studies in Poetic Mythology*. Harcourt, Brace, 1963.

Frye, Susan. *Pens and Needles: Women's Textualities in Early Modern England*. U of Pennsylvania P, 2011.

Fuchs, Barbara. 'Conquering Islands: Contextualizing *The Tempest*'. *Shakespeare Quarterly* 48.1 (Spring 1997): 45–62.

Fulbecke, William. *A Direction, or Preparative to the Study of the Lawe*. Thomas Wight, 1600.

Garner, Stanton B., Jr. *Kinesthetic Spectatorship in the Theatre: Phenomenology, Cognition, Movement*. Palgrave Macmillan, 2018.

Geary, David C. 'Coevolution of Paternal Investment and Cuckoldry in Humans'. In *Female Infidelity and Paternal Uncertainty: Evolutionary Perspectives on Male Anti-Cuckoldry Tactics*. Ed. Steven M. Platek and Todd K. Shackelford. Cambridge UP, 2006. 14–34.

The Geneva Bible: A Facsimile of the 1560 Edition. Intro. Lloyd E. Berry. Hendrickson, 2007.

Gesner, Konrad. *The newe iewell of health wherein is contayned the most excellent secretes of phisicke and philosophie*. Henrie Denham, 1576.

Geus, Klaus. 'Oikoumene/Orbis Terrarum'. In *Oxford Classical Dictionary*. Published online December 22, 2016. https://doi.org/10.1093/acrefore/9780199381135.013.8008

Ghosh, Amitav. *The Great Derangement: Climate Change and the Unthinkable*. U of Chicago P, 2016.

——. *The Nutmeg's Curse: Parables for a Planet in Crisis*. U of Chicago P, 2021.

Glissenti, Fabio. *Discorsi morali dell'eccellente S. Fabio Glissenti contra il dispiacer del morire*. Domenico Farri, 1596.

——. *L'Andrio cioè l'huomo virile favola morale dell'eccellentiss*. Giovanni Alberti, 1607.

——. *L'Androtoo cioè l'huomo innocente, favola morale*. Marco Ginammi, 1616.

——. *La Morte innamorata* (1607). Biblioteca Nazionale Marciana, Venice. MS. Ital. IX.316.

——. *La Morte innamorata, favola morali*. Giovanni Alberti, 1608.

——. *La Ragione sprezzata, favola tragica morale*. Marco Claseri, 1606.

Goeman, Mishuana. *Mark My Words: Native Women Mapping Our Nations*. U of Minnesota P, 2013.

Goldtooth, Tom, and Eriel Deranger. 'Indigenous Activists Tom Goldtooth & Eriel Deranger on the Link between Colonialism & Climate Crisis'. Interviewed by Amy Goodman. *Democracy Now!* November 17, 2022. https://www.democracynow.org/2022/11/17/eriel_deranger_tom_goldtooth_at_cop27

Works Cited

Goodrich, Peter. 'The New Casuistry'. *Critical Inquiry* 33.4 (Summer 2007): 673–709.

——. 'The Pure Theory of Law Is a Hole in the Ozone Layer'. *University of Colorado Law Review* 92.4 (Fall 2021): 985–1,012.

Gordley, Matthew E. *The Colossian Hymn in Context: An Exegesis in Light of Jewish and Greco-Roman Hymnic and Epistolary Conventions.* Mohr Siebeck, 2007.

Gordon, Colby. 'Candied Cleopatra: The Cute Aesthetics of Shakespeare's Political Theology'. *Journal for Early Modern Cultural Studies* 16.3 (Summer 2016): 30–45.

Goswami, Amit. *Quantum Creativity: Think Quantum, Be Creative.* Hay House, 2014.

Grady, Hugh. *Shakespeare's Dialectic of Hope: From the Political to the Utopian.* Cambridge UP, 2022.

Grove, Jairus Victor. *Savage Ecology: War and Geopolitics at the End of the World.* Duke UP, 2019.

Groves, Beatrice. 'Shakespeare's Sonnets and the Genevan Marginalia'. *Essays in Criticism* 57.2 (April 2007): 114–28.

Gurr, Andrew. *Playgoing in Shakespeare's London.* 2nd ed. Cambridge UP, 1996.

Gutas, Dimitri. 'Classical Arabic Wisdom Literature: Nature and Scope'. *Journal of the American Oriental Society* 101.1 (January–March 1981): 49–86.

Guthrie, Kenneth Sylvan, trans. and comp., and David R. Fideler, ed. *The Pythagorean Sourcebook and Library: An Anthology of Ancient Writings Which Relate to Pythagoras and Pythagorean Philosophy.* Phanes, 1987.

Habib, Imtiaz. 'The Black Alien in *Othello*: Beyond the European Immigrant'. In *Shakespeare and Immigration.* Ed. Ruben Espinosa and David Ruiter. Ashgate, 2014. EPUB.

Haddad, G. F. 'Sufism in Islam'. Living Islam: Islamic Tradition. Accessed October 6, 2023. https://www.livingislam.org/k/si_e.html

Hadid, Diaa. 'In Pakistan, residents are returning to ancient practices to deal with melting glaciers'. *Weekend Edition Sunday*, NPR, September 3, 2023. https://www.npr.org/2023/09/03/1197461145/in-pakistan-residents-are-returning-to-ancient-practices-to-deal-with-melting-gl

Halkias, Georgios T. 'When the Greeks Converted the Buddha: Asymmetrical Transfers of Knowledge in Indo-Greek Cultures'. In *Religions and Trade: Religious Formation, Transformation and Cross-Cultural Exchange between East and West.* Ed. Peter Wick and Volker Rabens. Brill, 2014. 65–116.

Halliwell, Stephen. *Between Ecstasy and Truth: Interpretations of Greek Poetics from Homer to Longinus.* Oxford UP, 2012.

348] *Shakespeare and Wisdom*

Halpern, Richard. *Leibnizing: A Philosopher in Motion*. Columbia UP, 2023.

Hamlin, Hannibal. *The Bible in Shakespeare*. Oxford UP, 2013.

——. *Psalm Culture and Early Modern English Literature*. Cambridge UP, 2004.

Hariot, Thomas. *A briefe and true report of the new found land of Virginia*. 1590.

Harjo, Joy. 'This Morning I Pray for My Enemies'. Poets.org. Accessed September 25, 2023. https://poets.org/poem/morning-i-pray-my-enemies

Haupt, Lyanda Lynn. *Rooted: Life at the Crossroads of Science, Nature, and Spirit*. Little, Brown Spark, 2021.

Hawken, Paul. *Blessed Unrest: How the Largest Movement in the World Came into Being, and Why No One Saw It Coming*. Penguin, 2007.

Hazrat, Florence. '"The Wisdom of Your Feet": Dance and Rhetoric on the Shakespearean Stage'. In *The Oxford Handbook of Shakespeare and Dance*. Ed. Lynsey McCulloch and Brandon Shaw. Oxford UP, 2019. 217–36.

Heckscher, W. S. 'The "Anadyomene" in the Mediaeval Tradition: (Pelagia–Cleopatra–Aphrodite) A Prelude to Botticelli's "Birth of Venus"'. *Nederlands Kunsthistorisch Jaarboek (NKJ)/Netherlands Yearbook for History of Art* 7 (1956): 1–38.

Heise, Ursula K. *Sense of Place and Sense of Planet: The Environmental Imagination of the Global*. Oxford UP, 2008.

Helminski, Camille Adams. *Women of Sufism: A Hidden Treasure—Writings and Stories of Mystic Poets, Scholars and Saints*. Shambhala, 2003.

Helminski, Kabir. *The Knowing Heart: A Sufi Path of Transformation*. Shambhala, 2000.

Helou, Ariane. 'Sibylline Voices: Prophecy and Power at the Medici Theater'. *The Sixteenth Century Journal* 50.3 (Autumn 2019): 679–704.

Heninger, S. K., Jr. *Touches of Sweet Harmony: Pythagorean Cosmology and Renaissance Poetics*. Huntington Library, 1974.

Henke, Robert. *Performance and Literature in the Commedia dell'Arte*. Cambridge UP, 2002.

Henslowe, Philip. *Henslowe's Diary*. Ed. R. A. Foakes. 2nd ed. Cambridge UP, 2002.

Hesiod. *Theogony*. In *Homeric Hymns, Epic Cycle, Homerica*. Trans. H. G. Evelyn-White. Vol. 57 of Loeb Classical Library. William Heinemann, 1914. https://www.theoi.com/Text/HesiodTheogony.html

Hixon, Lex. *Mother of the Buddhas: Meditation on the Prajnaparamita Sutra*. Quest Books, 1993.

Höchst, Solveig. '*Son scellerato perché son uomo*'. *Das Motiv des Bösen in Arrigo Boitos Libretto 'Otello'*. GRIN Verlag, 2013.

Works Cited

[349

Hodgen, Margaret T. 'Montaigne and Shakespeare Again'. *Huntington Library Quarterly* 16.1 (November 1952): 23–42.

Homer. *The Iliad*. Trans. Richmond Lattimore. U of Chicago P, 1951.

Horky, Phillip Sidney. 'Cosmic Spiritualism among the Pythagoreans, Stoics, Jews and Early Christians'. In *Cosmos in the Ancient World*. Ed. Phillip Sidney Horky. Cambridge UP, 2019. 270–94.

——. 'Italic Pythagoreanism in the Hellenistic Age'. In *The Oxford Handbook of Roman Philosophy*. Ed. Myrto Garani, David Konstan and Gretchen Reydams-Schils. Oxford UP, 2023. 3–26.

——. 'Our Common Breath: "Conspiration" from the Stoics to the Church Fathers'. In *The Life of Breath in Literature, Culture and Medicine: Classical to Contemporary*. Ed. David Fuller, Corinne Saunders and Jane Macnaughton. Springer Nature, 2021. 55–68.

Hughes, Paul L., and James F. Larkin, eds. *Tudor Royal Proclamations*. 3 vols. Yale UP, 1964.

Hugo, Victor. *William Shakespeare*. Trans. Melville B. Anderson. McClurg, 1899.

Hulsebosch, Daniel J. 'The Ancient Constitution and the Expanding Empire: Sir Edward Coke's British Jurisprudence'. *Law and History Review* 21.3 (Fall 2003): 439–82.

Hutson, Lorna. *The Invention of Suspicion: Law and Mimesis in Shakespeare and Renaissance Drama*. Oxford UP, 2008.

'Hymn of the Pearl'. Trans. G. R. S. Mead. In *Echoes from the Gnosis*. Vol. 10. Theosophical Publishing Society, 1908. Accessed October 6, 2023. http://gnosis.org/library/hymnpearl.htm

Iamblichus. *Iamblichus' Life of Pythagoras*. Trans. Thomas Taylor. Inner Traditions, 1986.

Ingenito, Domenico. *Beholding Beauty: Sa'di of Shiraz and the Aesthetics of Desire in Medieval Persian Poetry*. Brill, 2020.

Jackson, Ken, and Arthur F. Marotti, eds. *Shakespeare and Religion: Early Modern and Postmodern Perspectives*. U of Notre Dame P, 2011.

James I, King of England (VI of Scotland). *Basilikon dōron: Devided into three bookes*. Robert Walde-graue, 1599.

——. *The Political Works of James I*. Rpt. from the 1616 edition. Ed. Charles Howard McIlwain. Harvard UP, 1918.

——. *The true lawe of free monarchies*. Robert Walde-graue, 1598.

Jenkinson, Stephen. *Come of Age: The Case for Elderhood in a Time of Trouble*. North Atlantic Books, 2018.

Jenzen, Roy. 'Thoughts on the Relevance of Qigong to the Understanding and Practice of Chinese Medicine'. *The Journal of Chinese Medicine* 87 (June 2008): 10–13.

Johnson, Eleanor. *Staging Contemplation: Participatory Theology in Middle English Prose, Verse, and Drama*. U of Chicago P, 2018.

Johnson, Samuel. 'Preface to the Plays of William Shakespeare'. In *Samuel Johnson: Selected Poetry and Prose*. Ed. Frank Brady and W. K. Wimsatt. U of California P, 1977. 299–336.

Jones, Myrddin. 'Gray, Jaques, and the Man of Feeling'. *The Review of English Studies* 25.97 (February 1974): 39–48.

Jonson, Ben. *The Masque of Blackness* (1605). In *The Works of Ben Jonson*. Ed. William Gifford. Phillips, Sampson, 1853. 660–3. Luminarium Editions Online. Accessed December 20, 2023. https://www.luminarium. org/editions/maskblack.htm

Jordan, Peter. *The Venetian Origins of the Commedia dell'Arte*. Routledge, 2014.

Junker, William. 'The Image of Both Theaters: Empire and Revelation in Shakespeare's "Antony and Cleopatra"'. *Shakespeare Quarterly* 66.2 (Summer 2015): 167–87.

Just, Michal. 'Neoplatonism and Paramadvaita'. *Comparative Philosophy* 4.2 (2013): 1–28. https://doi.org/10.31979/2151-6014(2013).040206

Kabir, Ananya Jahanara. 'Deep Topographies in the Fiction of Uzma Aslam Khan'. *Journal of Postcolonial Writing* 47.2 (May 2011): 173–85.

Kahn, Charles H. *Pythagoras and the Pythagoreans: A Brief History*. Hackett, 2001.

Kahn, Coppélia. 'The Absent Mother in *King Lear*'. In *Rewriting the Renaissance: The Discourses of Sexual Difference in Early Modern Europe*. Ed. Margaret W. Ferguson, Maureen Quilligan and Nancy J. Vickers. U of Chicago P, 1986. 33–49.

——. *Man's Estate: Masculine Identity in Shakespeare*. U of California P, 1981.

Kajtár-Pinjung, Olga. 'Finding a Tribe in a Hopeless Place: Mansoor Adayfi and Guantánamo Bay'. In *Off Campus: Seggau School of Thought*. Vol. 8 of *Stability, Security, and Happiness*. Ed. Maureen Daly Goggin and Ursa Marinsek. Leykam, 2022. 57–70.

Kantorowicz, Ernst. *The King's Two Bodies: A Study in Medieval Political Theology*. Princeton UP, 1957.

Katib, Yosef al-. 'I love you so much, so much, [. . .]', [no. 1, untitled] from 'Some Kharjas'. Trans. and comm. James DenBoer. In *Poems for the Millennium, Volume 4: The University of California Book of North African Literature*. Ed. Pierre Joris and Habib Tengour. U of California P, 2012. 46–9.

Kaufman, Sheiba Kian. 'Persian Virtues: Hospitality, Tolerance, and Peacebuilding in the Age of Shakespeare'. In *Shakespeare and Virtue: A Handbook*. Ed. Julia Reinhard Lupton and Donovan Sherman. Cambridge UP, 2023. 300–5.

Works Cited

Kavusa, Kivatsi Jonathan. 'The Torah Likened with Nurturing Water of Rivers in Sirach 24:23–34: Eco-Theological Significance'. *Pharos Journal of Theology* 99 (2018): 1–12. PDF. https://www.pharosjot.com/uploads/7/1/6/3/7163688/article_23_vol_99_2018_-_kivatsi_up.pdf

Keats, John. *The Letters of John Keats, 1814–1821*. Ed. Hyder Edward Rollins. 2nd ed. 2 vols. Harvard UP, 1965.

Keepin, William. *Belonging to God: Spirituality, Science and a Universal Path of Divine Love*. SkyLight Paths, 2016.

Keller, Catherine. *Political Theology of the Earth: Our Planetary Emergency and the Struggle for a New Public*. Columbia UP, 2018.

Kelsey, Rachel M. 'Indian Dances in "The Tempest"'. *The Journal of English and Germanic Philology* 13.1 (January 1914): 98–103.

Keltner, Dacher. 'The Compassionate Instinct'. *Greater Good Magazine*, March 1, 2004. https://greatergood.berkeley.edu/article/item/the_compassionate_instinct

Kempton, Sally. *Meditation for the Love of It: Enjoying Your Own Deepest Experience*. Sounds True, 2011.

Kimmerer, Robin Wall. *Braiding Sweetgrass: Indigenous Wisdom, Scientific Knowledge, and the Teachings of Plants*. Milkweed, 2013, 2015.

King, Pamela M. 'Morality Plays'. In *The Cambridge Companion to Medieval English Theatre*. Ed. Richard Beadle and Alan J. Fletcher. Cambridge UP, 1994. 240–64.

Klein, Jacob. 'The Stoic Argument from Oikeiōsis'. In *Oxford Studies in Ancient Philosophy*. Ed. Victor Caston. Vol. 50. Oxford UP, 2016. 143–200.

Kleinhempel, U. R. 'Traces of Buddhist Presence in Alexandria: Philo and the "Therapeutae"'. *Aliter* 11 (2019): 3–31. https://ub01.uni-tuebingen.de/xmlui/bitstream/handle/10900/110361/Kleinhempel_016.pdf?sequence=1&isAllowed=y

Klett, Elizabeth. 'Dreaming of Orientalism in Kenneth Branagh's *As You Like It*'. *Borrowers and Lenders: The Journal of Shakespeare and Appropriation* 3.2 (Fall/Winter 2008): 1–6. https://borrowers-ojs-azsu.tdl.org/borrowers/article/view/66/131

Kloppenborg, John S. 'Isis and Sophia in the Book of Wisdom'. *Harvard Theological Review* 75.1 (January 1982): 57–84.

Knight, G. Wilson. *The Imperial Theme: Further Interpretations of Shakespeare's Tragedies, Including the Roman Plays*. 3rd ed. Methuen, 1951.

Kohn, Livia. *Daoism: A Contemporary Philosophical Investigation*. Routledge, 2019.

Kolbet, Paul R. 'Athanasius, the Psalms, and the Reformation of the Self'. *Harvard Theological Review* 99.1 (January 2006): 85–101.

Kolbrener, William. 'The Hermeneutics of Mourning: Multiplicity and Authority in Jewish Law'. *College Literature* 30.4 (Fall 2003): 114–39.

Korsgaard, Christine M. 'Natural Goodness, Rightness, and the Intersubjectivity of Reason: Reply to Arroyo, Cummiskey, Moland, and Bird-Pollan'. *Metaphilosophy* 42.4 (July 2011): 381–94.

Kott, Jan. *Shakespeare Our Contemporary*. Trans. Boleslaw Taborski. Norton, 1974.

Kottman, Paul A. 'Defying the Stars: Tragic Love as the Struggle for Freedom in "Romeo and Juliet"'. *Shakespeare Quarterly* 63.1 (Spring 2012): 1–38.

Krawec, Patty. *Becoming Kin: An Indigenous Call to Unforgetting the Past and Reimagining our Future*. Broadleaf Books, 2022.

Kubica, Olga. *Greco-Buddhist Relations in the Hellenistic Far East: Sources and Contexts*. Routledge, 2023.

Kutluer, İlhan. 'Hikmet'. In *Türkiye Diyanet Vakfı İslâm Ansiklopedisi*. Vol. 17. Türkiye Diyanet Vakfı, İslâm Ansiklopedisi Genel Müdürlüğü, 1998. 503–11.

Kuzminski, Adrian. 'Pyrrhonism and the Mādhyamaka'. *Philosophy East and West* 57.4 (October 2007): 482–511.

Kynes, Will, ed. *The Oxford Handbook of Wisdom and the Bible*. Oxford UP, 2021.

Langis, Unhae Park. 'Buddhist Virtues: Equanimity, Mindfulness, and Compassion in *Hamlet*'. In *Shakespeare and Virtue: A Handbook*. Ed. Julia Reinhard Lupton and Donovan Sherman. Cambridge UP, 2023. 306–16.

——. 'Humankindness: *King Lear* and the Suffering, Wisdom, and Compassion within Buddhist Interbeing'. In *Literature and Religious Experience: Beyond Belief and Unbelief*. Ed. Matthew J. Smith and Caleb D. Spencer. Bloomsbury, 2022. 209–26.

——. *Passion, Prudence, and Virtue in Shakespearean Drama*. Continuum, 2011.

——. 'Sufi Theoeroticism, the Sophianic Feminine, and Desdemona's Tragic Heroism'. In *Shakespeare's Virtuous Theatre: Power, Capacity and the Good*. Ed. Kent Lehnhof, Julia Reinhard Lupton and Carolyn Sale. Edinburgh UP, 2023. 205–27.

Lanyer, Aemilia. *The Poems of Aemilia Lanyer: Salve Deus Rex Judaeorum*. Ed. Susanne Woods. Oxford UP, 1993.

Laskowska-Hinz, Sabina. '*Jaques and the Wounded Stag* by William Hodges, Sawrey Gilpin and George Romney: (Re)Painting Shakespeare's Melancholic Figure'. *Anglica: An International Journal of English Studies* 25.3 (2016): 37–50.

Lee, Benjamin Todd, Ellen Finkelpearl and Luca Graverini, eds. *Apuleius and Africa*. Routledge, 2014.

Works Cited

[353

Lee, H. D. P., trans. and ed. *Zeno of Elea: A Text, with Translation and Notes*. Cambridge UP, 1936.

Legaspi, Michael C. 'Wisdom in Dialogue with Greek Civilization'. In *The Oxford Handbook of Wisdom and the Bible*. Ed. Will Kynes. Oxford UP, 2021. 155–72.

Lehnhof, Kent, Julia Reinhard Lupton and Carolyn Sale, eds. *Shakespeare's Virtuous Theatre: Power, Capacity and the Good*. Edinburgh UP, 2023.

Leibniz, Gottfried Wilhelm. *New Essays on Human Understanding*. Trans. and ed. Peter Remnant and Jonathan Bennett. Cambridge UP, 1996.

Leishman, J. B. *Themes and Variations in Shakespeare's Sonnets*. Hutchinson, 1961.

Lemon, Rebecca. *Addiction and Devotion in Early Modern England*. U of Pennsylvania P, 2018.

Leo Africanus. *Description de l'Afrique*. Trans. Alexis Épaulard. Adrien-Maisonneuve, 1956, 1981.

——. *A geographical historie of Africa, written in Arabicke and Italian by Iohn Leo a More, borne in Granada, and brought vp in Barbarie [. . .]*. Trans. John Pory. Georg. Bishop, 1600.

——. *Libro de la cosmogrophia et Geographia de Affrica*, 1526. National Central Library of Rome. Accessed October 6, 2023. http://digitale. bnc.roma.sbn.it/tecadigitale/manoscrittoantico/BNCR_V_E_953/ BNCR_V_E_953/92

Levi, Doro. 'Aion'. *Hesperia* 13.4 (1944): 269–314.

Levi, Renee A. 'Holographic Theory and Groups'. *Collective Wisdom Initiative*. December 16, 2001.

Lewis, Murshid Samuel L. 'The Perfection of the Heart: An Original Sangatha'. PDF. Sufi Ruhaniat International, Murshid Samuel Lewis Archives. Accessed October 6, 2023. https://www.ruhaniat.org/index. php/major-papers/sufi-practices-ryazat/2247-the-perfection-of-the-heart--an-original-sangatha

Lings, Martin. *Shakespeare's Window into the Soul: The Mystical Wisdom in Shakespeare's Characters*. Inner Traditions, 2006.

Lloyd, Michael. 'Cleopatra as Isis'. *Shakespeare Survey* 12 (1959): 88–94.

Lockhart, Douglas. 'The McEvilley Bombshell'. Accessed October 3, 2023. https://www.douglaslockhart.com/wp-content/uploads/The-McEvilley-Bombshell.pdf

Lorde, Audre. 'Uses of the Erotic: The Erotic as Power'. In *Sister Outsider: Essays and Speeches*. Crossing, 2012. 53–9.

Loughton, Gavin. 'Calvin's Case and the Origins of the Rule Governing "Conquest" in English Law'. *Australian Journal of Legal History* 8.2 (January 2004): 143–80.

Luchte, James. *Pythagoras and the Doctrine of Transmigration: Wandering Souls*. Continuum, 2009.

Luiselli, Valeria. *Tell Me How It Ends: An Essay in Forty Questions*. Coffee House, 2017.

Lumbard, Joseph E. B. 'From *Ḥubb* to *'Ishq*: The Development of Love in Early Sufism'. *Journal of Islamic Studies* 18.3 (September 2007): 345–85.

——. 'Love and Beauty in Sufism'. In *Routledge Handbook on Sufism*. Ed. Lloyd Ridgeon. Routledge, 2020. 172–86.

Lupić, Ivan. *Subjects of Advice: Drama and Counsel from More to Shakespeare*. U of Pennsylvania P, 2019.

Lupton, Julia Reinhard. 'Creature Caliban'. *Shakespeare Quarterly* 51.1 (Spring 2000): 1–23.

——. '"Good in Every Thing": Erasmus and Communal Virtue in *As You Like It*'. *Journal of Medieval and Early Modern Studies* 52.3 (2022): 567–91.

——. '*The Tempest* and Black Natural Law'. *Religions* 10.2 (February 2019): 1–15. https://doi.org/10.3390/rel10020091

——. *Thinking with Shakespeare: Essays on Politics and Life*. U of Chicago P, 2011.

——. 'The Titania Translation: *A Midsummer Night's Dream* and the Two Metamorphoses'. In *Ovid's 'Metamorphoses' and the Environmental Imagination*. Ed. Francesca Martelli and Giulia Sissa. Bloomsbury, 2023. 145–62.

—— and Donovan Sherman, eds. *Shakespeare and Virtue: A Handbook*. Cambridge UP, 2023.

Maalouf, Amin. *Léon, l'Africain*. Lattès, 1986.

MacGillivray, Erlend D. 'Reassessing Epictetus' Opinion of Divination'. *Apeiron: A Journal for Ancient Philosophy and Science* 53.2 (2020): 147–60.

Macy, Joanna. *World as Lover, World as Self: Courage for Global Justice and Ecological Renewal*. 30th Anniversary Edition. Ed. Stephanie Kaza. Parallax, 2021.

Magnone, Paolo. 'Soul Chariots in Indian and Greek Thought: Polygenesis or Diffusion?' In *Universe and Inner Self in Early Indian and Early Greek Thought*. Ed. Richard Seaford. Edinburgh UP, 2016. 149–67.

Mahyuddin, Muhammad Khairi, Dato' Zakaria Stapa and Faudzinaim Badaruddin. 'The Relationship between the Shari'ah, Tariqah, Haqiqah and Ma'rifah by Wan Sulaiman b Wan Siddik, a 19th Malay Sufi Scholar in the Malay World'. *Journal of Islamic Studies and Culture* 1.1 (2013): 1–11.

Works Cited

Majorana, Bernadette. 'Commedia dell'Arte and the Church'. In *Commedia dell'Arte in Context*. Ed. Christopher B. Balme, Piermario Vescovo and Daniele Vianello. Cambridge UP, 2018. 133–48.

Mann, Jenny C. *The Trials of Orpheus: Poetry, Science, and the Early Modern Sublime*. Princeton UP, 2021.

Marcus Aurelius. *Meditations*. Trans. and intro. Gregory Hays. Modern Library, 2003.

——. *Meditations, Books 1–6*. Trans. with intro. and comm. by Christopher Gill. Oxford UP, 2013.

——. *The Meditations of the Emperor Marcus Antoninus, Volume 1: Text and Translation*. Trans. A. S. L. Farquharson. Oxford UP, 1944.

Marcus, Leah S. *How Shakespeare Became Colonial: Editorial Tradition and the British Empire*. Routledge, 2017.

Marshall, Cynthia. 'The Doubled Jaques and Constructions of Negation in *As You Like It*'. *Shakespeare Quarterly* 49.4 (Winter 1998): 375–92.

Martzavou, Paraskevi. 'Isis Aretalogies, Initiations, and Emotions: The Isis Aretalogies as a Source for the Study of Emotions'. In *Unveiling Emotions: Sources and Methods for the Study of Emotions in the Greek World*. Ed. Angelos Chaniotis. Franz Steiner, 2012. 267–91.

Matar, Nabil. *Europe through Arab Eyes, 1578–1727*. Columbia UP, 2008.

Maus, Katharine Eisaman. *Inwardness and Theater in the English Renaissance*. U of Chicago P, 1995.

Maxwell, Julie, and Kate Rumbold, eds. *Shakespeare and Quotation*. Cambridge UP, 2018.

McClure, George W. 'The *Artes* and the *Ars moriendi* in Late Renaissance Venice: The Professions in Fabio Glissenti's *Discorsi morali contra il dispiacer del morire, detto Athanatophilia* (1596)'. *Renaissance Quarterly* 51.1 (Spring 1998): 92–127.

McEvilley, Thomas. *The Shape of Ancient Thought: Comparative Studies in Greek and Indian Philosophies*. Allworth, 2002. PDF.

McKirahan, Richard D. *Philosophy Before Socrates: An Introduction with Texts and Commentary*. Hackett, 1994.

McMullen, Ejo. 'Your Whole Body Is Hands and Eyes'. *Lion's Roar*. May 16, 2022. https://www.lionsroar.com/your-whole-body-is-hands-and-eyes/

McPeek, James A. S. 'The Psyche Myth and *A Midsummer Night's Dream*'. *Shakespeare Quarterly* 23.1 (Winter 1972): 69–79.

Menocal, María Rosa. 'Close Encounters in Medieval Provence: Spain's Role in the Birth of Troubadour Poetry'. *Hispanic Review* 49.1 (Winter 1981): 43–64.

——, Raymond P. Scheindlin and Michael Sells, eds. *The Literature of Al-Andalus*. Cambridge UP, 2000, 2006.

Merchant, Carolyn. *The Death of Nature: Women, Ecology, and the Scientific Revolution.* Harper & Row, 1980.

Meres, Francis. *Palladis Tamia. Wits Treasury Being the Second part of Wits Common wealth.* Cuthbert Burbie, 1598. STC 17834.

Merrell-Wolff, Franklin. *The Philosophy of Consciousness without an Object: Reflections on the Nature of Transcendental Consciousness.* Julian, 1973.

Mills, Ethan. 'Skepticism and Religious Practice in Sextus and Nāgārjuna'. In *Ethics without Self, Dharma without Atman: Western and Buddhist Philosophical Traditions in Dialogue.* Ed. Gordon F. Davis. Springer, 2018. 91–106.

Milton, John. *Areopagitica and Other Writings.* Ed. William Poole. Penguin, 2014.

Mitova, Veli. 'The Duty of Inquiry, or Why Othello Was a Fool'. In *The Routledge Companion to Shakespeare and Philosophy.* Ed. Craig Bourne and Emily Caddick Bourne. Routledge, 2018. EPUB. 461–78.

Modrzejewski, Joseph Meleze. 'How to Be a Jew in Hellenistic Egypt?' In *Diasporas in Antiquity.* Ed. Shaye J. D. Cohen and Ernest S. Frerichs. Brown Judaic Studies. Vol. 288. Scholars, 2020. 65–92.

Montaigne, Michel de. *The Complete Essays of Montaigne.* Trans. Donald M. Frame. Stanford UP, 1958.

——. *The essayes or morall, politike and millitarie discourses of Lo: Michaell de Montaigne.* Trans. John Florio. Edward Blount, 1603.

——. *Essays vvritten in French by Michael Lord of Montaigne.* Trans. John Florio. Edward Blount and William Barret, 1613.

Moore, Jason W. 'The Capitalocene, Part I: On the Nature and Origins of our Ecological Crisis'. *The Journal of Peasant Studies* 44.3 (April 2017): 594–630.

More, Thomas. *The Essential Works of Thomas More.* Ed. Gerard B. Wegemer and Stephen W. Smith. Yale UP, 2020.

Morelli-White, Nan. 'The Evolution of the Vice Character from Medieval Through Restoration Drama'. PhD diss. Florida State U, 1990.

Morley, Thomas. *A plaine and easie introdvction to practicall mvsicke.* Peter Short, 1597.

Morton, Timothy. *Dark Ecology: For a Logic of Future Coexistence.* Columbia UP, 2016.

Müller, F. Max, trans. *The Upanishads*, Part 1. The Sacred Books of the East, vol. 1. Clarendon, 1879.

Munday, Anthony, and Henry Chettle. *Sir Thomas More.* Rev. by Henry Chettle, Thomas Dekker, Thomas Heywood and William Shakespeare. Ed. John Jowett. Arden Shakespeare, 2011.

Works Cited

Munk, Linda. 'His Dazzling Absence: The Shekinah in Jonathan Edwards'. *Early American Literature* 27.1 (1992): 1–30.

Munroe, Jennifer. 'It's all about the gillyvors: Engendering Art and Nature in *The Winter's Tale*'. In *Ecocritical Shakespeare*. Ed. Lynne Bruckner and Dan Brayton. Routledge, 2016. 139–54.

Murakami, Ineke. *Moral Play and Counterpublic: Transformations in Moral Drama, 1465–1599*. Routledge, 2011.

Murdoch, Iris. *The Sovereignty of Good*. Routledge, 2013.

Nagel, Thomas. 'Moral Luck'. In *Mortal Questions*. Cambridge UP, 1979. 24–38.

Nail, Thomas. *Being and Motion*. Oxford UP, 2019.

Namgyel, Elizabeth Mattis. *The Logic of Faith: A Buddhist Approach to Finding Certainty beyond Belief and Doubt*. Shambhala, 2018.

—— and Greg Seton. 'Unlocking the Meaning of Prajnaparamita'. Open Question Conversations, The Middle Way Initiative, June 18, 2022.

Nasr, Seyyed Hossein. *Knowledge and the Sacred*. SUNY, 1989.

Newman, Judith H. 'Hybridity, Hydrology, and Hidden Transcript: Sirach 24 and the Judean Encounter with Ptolemaic Isis Worship'. In *Jewish Cultural Encounters in the Ancient Mediterranean and Near Eastern World*. Ed. Mladen Popović, Myles Schoonover and Marijn Vandenberghe. Brill, 2017. 157–76.

Nielsen, Melinda E. '"Nothing almost sees miracles / But misery": Lucretian Philosophy and Ascetic Experience in *King Lear*'. *Logos: A Journal of Catholic Thought and Culture* 19.4 (Fall 2016): 101–16.

Norman, Joanne S. *Metamorphoses of an Allegory: The Iconography of the Psychomachia in Medieval Art*. Peter Lang, 1988.

'One Epic Story, Many Epic Storytellers'. *Epic of Evolution*. Accessed October 2, 2023. https://epicofevolution.com/one-epic-story-many-epic-storytellers

Orgel, Stephen. 'Shakespeare and the Cannibals'. In *Cannibals, Witches, and Divorce: Estranging the Renaissance*. Ed. Marjorie Garber. Johns Hopkins UP, 1987. 40–66.

Ovid (Publius Ovidius Naso). *Metamorphoses*. Trans. Arthur Golding. Ed. Madeleine Forey. Penguin, 2002.

——. *Metamorphoses*. Trans. Frank Justus Miller. Rev. by G. P. Goold. Loeb Classical Library. 2nd ed. Harvard UP, 1994.

——. *Ovid's Metamorphoses: The Arthur Golding Translation of 1567*. Ed. John Frederick Nims. Paul Dry Books, 2000.

Pal, Dipanwita. 'Forest of Arden Revisited: Re-assessing the Role of Jaques in Shakespeare's *As You Like It* from an Ecocritical Perspective'. *RAIS Journal for Social Sciences* 4.2 (2020): 5–13. https://journal.rais.education/index.php/raiss/article/view/127/96

358] *Shakespeare and Wisdom*

'Parallel Reading (paragraph granularity) of The Buddha's Path of Wisdom—Dhammapada (Dhp.)—Fulltext'. Fucheng Buddhism Network. Updated October 9, 2016. https://nanda.online-dhamma.net/tipitaka/sutta/khuddaka/dhammapada/dhp-contrast-reading/dhp-contrast-reading-en/

Parker, Matthew. *The Whole Psalter Translated into English Metre, Which Contayneth an Hundreth and Fifty Psalmes.* John Daye, 1567. STC 2729.

Parmenides (of Elea). *Parmenidean Fragments*, 1–19. Trans. John Burnet. In *Early Greek Philosophy*, 2nd ed. Adam and Charles Black, 1908. 196–203. Lexundria: A Digital Library of Classical Antiquity. https://www.lexundria.com/parm_frag/1-19/b

Parris, Benjamin. *Vital Strife: Sleep, Insomnia, and the Early Modern Ethics of Care.* Cornell UP, 2022.

Paulson, Julie. *Theater of the Word: Selfhood in the English Morality Play.* U of Notre Dame P, 2019.

Peele, George. *The honour of the garter Displaied in a poeme gratulatorie.* Iohn Busbie, 1593.

Peet, Christopher. *Practicing Transcendence: Axial Age Spiritualities for a World in Crisis.* Palgrave Macmillan, 2019.

Perdue, Leo G. *Wisdom Literature: A Theological History.* Westminster John Knox, 2007.

The Perfection of Wisdom in Eight Thousand Lines and its Verse Summary. Trans. Edward Conze. Sri Satguru Publications, 1973.

Philostratus. *The Life of Apollonius of Tyana.* Vol. I: Books 1–5. Trans. F. C. Conybeare. Loeb Classical Library. Heinemann, 1912.

Plato. *Apology.* In *Plato: Complete Works.* Ed. John M. Cooper and D. S. Hutchinson. Hackett, 1997. 17–36.

———. *Phaedo.* In *Plato: Complete Works.* Ed. Cooper and Hutchinson. Hackett, 1997. 49–100.

———. *Symposium.* In *Plato: Complete Works.* Ed. Cooper and Hutchinson. Hackett, 1997. 457–505.

Plotinus. *Ennead IV.8: On the Descent of the Soul into Bodies.* Trans. with intro. and comm. by Barrie Fleet. Parmenides, 2012.

Plutarch. 'The Life of Marcus Antonius'. From *The Lives of the Noble Grecians and Romans.* Trans. Sir Thomas North. Abraham Miller, 1657. In Appendix A to *Antony and Cleopatra.* Ed. Michael Neill. Oxford UP, 1994. 327–62.

———. 'Of Isis and Osiris'. In *The philosophie, commonlie called, the morals.* Trans. Philemon Holland. Arnold Hatfield, 1603.

Pope, Marvin H., ed. *Job: A New Translation with Introduction and Commentary.* Anchor Bible 15. Doubleday, 1965.

Works Cited

[359

Prasetya, Mochammad Dwi Teguh, and Muhammad Arif Rokhman. 'A Journey to Ethical Life: A Moral Reading of Shakespeare's *Othello* through the Nasirean Ethics of Naṣir Al-Din Al-Ṭuṣi'. *Lexicon* 6.2 (October 2019): 139–55.

Pritchard, James B., ed. *Ancient Near Eastern Texts Relating to the Old Testament*. 3rd ed. Princeton UP, 1969.

Prudentius. *The Psychomachia of Prudentius: Text, Commentary, and Glossary*. Ed. Aaron Pelttari. U of Oklahoma P, 2019.

Purchas, Samuel. *Purchas his Pilgrimes, In Five Bookes*. Henrie Fetherstone, 1625.

Quispel, Gilles. *Gnostica, Judaica, Catholica: Collected Essays of Gilles Quispel*. Ed. Johannes van Oort. Brill, 2008.

Rahman, Jamal. 'Sufi Stories of Laughter'. Interview with Farah Nazarali. Banyen Books. YouTube. January 22, 2020. https://www.youtube.com/watch?v=BuY1ajuvXY8

Raju, Poolla Tirupati. *Structural Depths of Indian Thought*. SUNY, 1985.

Rancière, Jacques. *The Emancipated Spectator*. Trans. Gregory Elliott. Verso, 2009.

Rappenglück, Michael A. 'The World as a Living Entity: Essentials of a Cosmic Metaphor'. *Mediterranean Archaeology and Archaeometry* 18.4 (2018): 323–31.

Refini, Eugenio. '"*Quasi una tragedia delle attioni humane*": le tragique entre allégorie et édification morale dans l'œuvre de Fabio Glissenti (1542–1615)'. *Cahiers d'études italiennes* 19 (2014): 185–98.

——. 'Reforming Drama: Theater as Spiritual Practice in the Works of Fabio Glissenti'. In *Innovation in the Italian Counter-Reformation*. Ed. Shannon McHugh and Anna Wainwright. U of Delaware P, 2020. 169–89.

——. *Staging the Soul: Allegorical Drama as Spiritual Practice in Baroque Italy*. Legenda, 2023.

——. '"*Sufficienti e fedeli*": Aristotelian and Biblical Patterns in *The Prince*, Chapter XXII'. In *Machiavelli's 'Prince': Traditions, Text and Translations*. Ed. Nicola Gardini and Martin McLaughlin. Viella, 2017. 153–64.

Richardson, Kristina. 'Blue and Green Eyes in the Islamicate Middle Ages'. *Annales islamologiques* 48.1 (2014): 13–29. https://doi.org/10.4000/anisl.3051

Riedweg, Christoph. *Pythagoras: His Life, Teaching, and Influence*. Trans. Steven Rendall. Cornell UP, 2008.

Rollins, Hyder Edward, ed. *The Keats Circle: Letters and Papers, and More Letters and Poems of the Keats Circle*. 2 vols. 2nd ed. Harvard UP, 1965.

Rosenthal, Margaret F. *The Honest Courtesan: Veronica Franco, Citizen and Writer in Sixteenth-Century Venice*. U of Chicago P, 2012.

Rowan, Jamin C. 'Ideas About Nature: An Ecocentric Look at *As You Like It*'. *The Upstart Crow* 21 (2001): 15–26.

Rowlandson, Jane, and Ryosuke Takahashi. 'Brother-Sister Marriage and Inheritance Strategies in Greco-Roman Egypt'. *The Journal of Roman Studies* 99 (2009): 104–39.

Ruiz, María Isabel Romero. 'The Ritual of the Early Modern Death, 1550–1650'. *Analecta Malacitana (AnMal) Electrónica* 17 (June 2005). http://www.anmal.uma.es/numero17/Romero.htm

Rūmī (Jalāl al-Dīn Rūmī). 'A Basket of Fresh Bread'. In *The Essential Rumi*. Trans. Coleman Barks. Castle, 1997. 256.

——. *Spiritual Verses: The First Book of the Masnavi-ye Ma'navi*. Trans. Alan Williams. Penguin, 2006.

——. 'Where the Light Enters You'. Trans. Omid Safi. On Being Project. May 7, 2015. https://onbeing.org/blog/where-the-light-enters-you/

Ryrie, Alec. *Being Protestant in Reformation Britain*. Oxford UP, 2013.

Ryuta, Minami. '"What, has this thing appear'd again tonight?" Re-playing Shakespeares on the Japanese Stage'. In *Re-playing Shakespeare in Asia*. Ed. Poonam Trivedi and Minami Ryuta. Routledge, 2010. 76–96.

Sacerdoti, Gilberto. *Nuovo cielo, nuova terra: la rivelazione copernicana di 'Antonio e Cleopatra' di Shakespeare*. Il Mulino, 1990.

——. 'Three Kings, Herod of Jewry, and a Child: Apocalypse and Infinity of the World in *Antony and Cleopatra*'. In *Italian Studies in Shakespeare and his Contemporaries*. Ed. Michele Marrapodi and Giorgio Melchiori. U of Delaware P, 1999. 165–84.

Sadiq. 'A Sufi Parable of Sea'. *Technology of the Heart*, January 24, 2012. https://www.techofheart.com/2012/01/parable-of-sea-niffari-travel.html

Saito, Kohei. *Karl Marx's Ecosocialism: Capital, Nature, and the Unfinished Critique of Political Economy*. Monthly Review, 2017.

Sale, Carolyn. 'Black Aeneas: Race, English Literary History, and the "Barbarous" Poetics of *Titus Andronicus*'. *Shakespeare Quarterly* 62.1 (Spring 2011): 25–52.

——. 'Cordelia's Fire'. In *Shakespeare's Virtuous Theatre: Power, Capacity and the Good*. Ed. Kent Lehnhof, Julia Reinhard Lupton and Carolyn Sale. Edinburgh UP, 2023. 25–48.

——. 'Eating Air, Feeling Smells: *Hamlet*'s Theory of Performance'. *Renaissance Drama* 35 (2006): 145–68.

Samuk, Tristan. 'Satire and the Aesthetic in *As You Like It*'. *Renaissance Drama* 43.2 (Fall 2015): 117–42.

Saval, Peter Kishore. *Shakespeare in Hate: Emotions, Passions, Selfhood*. Routledge, 2015.

Works Cited

[361

Sayet, Madeline. 'Interrogating the Shakespeare System'. *HowlRound*, August 31, 2020. https://howlround.com/interrogating-shakespeare-system

——. *Where We Belong*. Methuen, 2022.

Schäfer, Peter. 'Mirror of His Beauty: The Femininity of God in Jewish Mysticism and in Christianity'. *Irish Theological Quarterly* 70.1 (March 2005): 45–59.

Schiff, András. 'Lecture on the Bach Partitas'. Filmed June 2018 at the Pierre Boulez Saal. YouTube. Posted May 11, 2022. https://www.youtube.com/watch?v=JVjBIKNed_Q

Schiff, Stacey. *Cleopatra: A Life*. Little, Brown, 2011.

Schimmel, Annemarie. *I Am Wind, You Are Fire: The Life and Work of Rumi*. Shambhala, 1992.

——. *My Soul Is a Woman: The Feminine in Islam*. Trans. Susan H. Ray. Continuum, 1997.

——. *Mystical Dimensions of Islam*. U of North Carolina P, 1975.

——. 'Rumi and the Symbols Used by Him'. *Ilm* 7.3 (December 1981–February 1982): 29–31. https://www.iis.ac.uk/media/nlhdbdrn/rumi-symbols-3-470185473.pdf

——. *A Two-Colored Brocade: The Imagery of Persian Poetry*. U of North Carolina P, 1992, 2014.

Schofer, Jonathan. 'Wisdom in Jewish Theology'. In *The Oxford Handbook of Wisdom and the Bible*. Ed. Will Kynes. Oxford UP, 2021. 241–54.

Schulz, William F. *Reversing the Rivers: A Memoir of History, Hope, and Human Rights*. U of Pennsylvania P, 2023.

Schuon, Frithjof. *The Essential Writings of Frithjof Schuon*. Ed. Seyyed Hossein Nasr. Amity House, 1986.

Scofield, Bruce. 'Gaia: The Living Earth—2,500 Years of Precedents in Natural Science and Philosophy'. In *Scientists Debate Gaia: The Next Century*. Ed. Stephen H. Scheider, James R. Miller, Eileen Crist and Penelope J. Boston. MIT, 2004. 151–60.

Scott, R. B. Y. 'Wisdom in Creation: The āmôn of Proverbs VIII 30'. *Vetus Testamentum* 10.2 (April 1960): 213–23.

Seaford, Richard. *The Origins of Philosophy in Ancient Greece and Ancient India: A Historical Comparison*. Cambridge UP, 2019.

Seipp, David J. 'The Concept of Property in the Early Common Law'. *Law and History Review* 12.1 (Spring 1994): 29–91.

Selbie, Joseph. *The Physics of God: Unifying Quantum Physics, Consciousness, M-Theory, Heaven, Neuroscience and Transcendence*. New Page, 2017.

Seneca, Lucius Annaeus. *Letters from a Stoic: Epistulae morales ad Lucilium*. Trans. and intro. Robin Campbell. Penguin, 1969, 1974.

——. *Letters on Ethics* [to Lucilius]. Trans. with intro. and comm. by Margaret Graver and A. A. Long. U of Chicago P, 2015.

362] *Shakespeare and Wisdom*

——. *Natural Questions*. Trans. Harry M. Hine. U of Chicago P, 2010.

Serjeantson, Deirdre. 'The Book of Psalms and the Early Modern Sonnet'. *Renaissance Studies* 29.4 (September 2015): 632–49.

Shah-Kazemi, Reza. *Common Ground between Islam and Buddhism: Spiritual and Ethical Affinities*. Fons Vitae, 2010.

Shakespeare, William. *Antony and Cleopatra*. Ed. Michael Neill. Oxford UP, 1994.

——. *As You Like It*. Ed. Alan Brissenden. Oxford UP, 1993.

——. *As You Like It*. Ed. Juliet Dusinberre. Thomson Learning, 2006.

——. *As You Like It*. Ed. Richard Knowles. New Variorum Edition of Shakespeare. MLAA, 1977.

——. *The Complete Sonnets and Poems*. Ed. Colin Burrow. Oxford UP, 2002.

——. *The Complete Works*. Ed. Stephen Orgel and A. R. Braunmuller. Penguin, 2002.

——. *Hamlet*. Ed. A. R. Braunmuller. Penguin, 2001.

——. *Hamlet*. Ed. G. R. Hibbard. Oxford UP, 1987.

——. *Hamlet*. Ed. Ann Thompson and Neil Taylor. Arden Shakespeare, 2006.

——. *The Merchant of Venice*. Ed. A. R. Braunmuller. Penguin, 2000.

——. *The New Oxford Shakespeare: The Complete Works, Modern Critical Edition*. Ed. Gary Taylor, John Jowett, Terri Bourus and Gabriel Egan. Oxford UP, 2016. Oxford Scholarly Editions Online. doi:10.1093/actrade/9780199591152.book.1

——. *The Norton Shakespeare*. 3rd ed. Ed. Stephen Greenblatt, Walter Cohen, Jean E. Howard and Katharine Eisaman Maus. Norton, 2016.

——. *Shakespeare's Sonnets*. Ed. Stephen Booth. Yale UP, 1977.

——. *Shakespeare's Sonnets and Poems*. Ed. Barbara A. Mowat and Paul Werstine. Simon & Schuster, 2009.

——. *The Sonnets*. In *The Complete Works of William Shakespeare*. MIT, 1993. https://shakespeare.mit.edu/Poetry/sonnets.html

——. *The Tempest*. Ed. Virginia Mason Vaughan and Alden T. Vaughan. Arden Shakespeare, 1999, 2017.

——. *The Tempest*. In *The Complete Works of William Shakespeare*. MIT, 1993. https://shakespeare.mit.edu/tempest/full.html

——. *The Tragedy of Othello, the Moor of Venice*. Ed. Barbara A. Mowat and Paul Werstine. Simon & Schuster, 2017.

——. *The Winter's Tale*. Ed. Stephen Orgel. Oxford Shakespeare. Clarendon, 1996.

Shankman, Steven. '(m)Other Power: Shin Buddhism, Levinas, *King Lear*'. In *From Ritual to Romance and Beyond: Comparative Literature and Comparative Religious Studies*. Ed. Manfred Schmeling and Hans-Joachim Backe. Königshausen & Neumann, 2011. 229–37.

Works Cited

[363

Shannon, Laurie. *Sovereign Amity: Figures of Friendship in Shakespearean Contexts*. U of Chicago P, 2002.

——, Vin Nardizzi, Ken Hiltner, Saree Makdisi, Michael Ziser, Imre Szeman and Patricia Yaeger. 'Editor's Column: Literature in the Ages of Wood, Tallow, Coal, Whale Oil, Gasoline, Atomic Power, and Other Energy Sources'. *PMLA* 126.2 (2011): 305–26.

Shapiro, James. *1599: A Year in the Life of William Shakespeare*. Harper-Collins, 2005.

Shaw, George Bernard. *Shaw on Shakespeare: An Anthology of Bernard Shaw's Writings on the Plays and Production of Shakespeare*. Ed. and intro. Edwin Wilson. Applause Books, 1961.

Shaw, Miranda. *Buddhist Goddesses of India*. Princeton UP, 2006.

Shibayama, Zenkei. 'Joshu's Mu'. Trans. Sumiko Kudo. In *The Book of Mu: Essential Writings on Zen's Most Important Koan*. Ed. James Ishmael Ford and Melissa Myozen Blacker. Wisdom, 2011. 83–93.

Shufran, Lauren. *The Buddha and the Bard: Where Shakespeare's Stage Meets Buddhist Scriptures*. Mandala, 2022.

Sick, David H. 'When Socrates Met the Buddha: Greek and Indian Dialectic in Hellenistic Bactria and India'. *Journal of the Royal Asiatic Society* 17.3 (July 2007): 253–78.

Siddiqui, Mona. *Hospitality and Islam: Welcoming in God's Name*. Yale UP, 2015.

Simmer-Brown, Judith. *Dakini's Warm Breath: The Feminine Principle in Tibetan Buddhism*. Shambhala, 2001.

Simonds, Peggy Muñoz. *Myth, Emblem, and Music in Shakespeare's 'Cymbeline': An Iconographic Reconstruction*. U of Delaware P, 1992.

Simpson, Audra. *Mohawk Interruptus: Political Life across the Borders of Settler States*. Duke UP, 2014.

Simpson, Leanne Betasamosake. *As We Have Always Done: Indigenous Freedom through Radical Resistance*. U of Minnesota P, 2017.

Simpson, William. 'The Buddhist Praying Wheel'. *The Journal of the Royal Asiatic Society of Great Britain and Ireland* 30.4 (October 1898): 873–5.

Singh, Anand. 'Buddhist Environmentalism: Narratives from the Jātakas'. *Journal of the Royal Asiatic Society of Sri Lanka* 60.2 (2015): 59–79.

Sissa, Giulia, and Francesca Martelli, eds. *Ovid's 'Metamorphoses' and the Environmental Imagination*. Bloomsbury, 2023.

Skelley, Geoffrey, and Mary Radcliffe. 'Florida Started a Race to Reshape Conservatism. Now It Has Some Catching Up to Do.' *FiveThirtyEight*, May 19, 2023. https://fivethirtyeight.com/features/desantis-florida-conservatism-2024/

Skura, Meredith Anne. 'Discourse and the Individual: The Case of Colonialism in *The Tempest*'. *Shakespeare Quarterly* 40.1 (Spring 1989): 42–69.

Sloan, Kim. *A New World: England's First View of America*. U of North Carolina P, 2007.

Smith, Ian. 'Othello's Black Handkerchief'. *Shakespeare Quarterly* 64.1 (Spring 2013): 1–25.

Soen, Shaku. 'Teisho on Joshu's Dog'. Trans. Victor Hori. In *The Book of Mu: Essential Writings on Zen's Most Important Koan*. Ed. James Ishmael Ford and Melissa Myozen Blacker. Wisdom, 2011. 35–43.

Soeng, Mu. *The Heart of the Universe: Exploring the Heart Sutra*. Wisdom, 2010.

Song, Chorong, Harumi Ikei and Yoshifumi Miyazaki. 'Physiological Effects of Nature Therapy: A Review of the Research in Japan'. *International Journal of Environmental Research and Public Health* 13.8 (2016): 781–98. https://doi.org/10.3390/ijerph13080781

Spade, Dean. *Mutual Aid: Building Solidarity during This Crisis (and the Next)*. Verso, 2020.

Spenser, Edmund. *Edmund Spenser's 'Amoretti' and 'Epithalamion': A Critical Edition*. Ed. Kenneth J. Larsen. Vol. 146. Medieval & Renaissance Texts & Studies, 1997.

——. 'An Hymne of Heavenly Beautie'. In *Select Poetry, Chiefly Devotional, of the Reign of Queen Elizabeth*. Ed. Edward Farr. Cambridge UP, 1845. Bartleby. Accessed December 20, 2023. https://www.bartleby.com/261/5.html

Spivack, Bernard. *Shakespeare and the Allegory of Evil: The History of a Metaphor in Relation to his Major Villains*. Columbia UP, 1964.

Staudinger, Ursula M., and Judith Glück. 'Intelligence and Wisdom'. In *The Cambridge Handbook of Intelligence*. Ed. Robert J. Sternberg and Scott Barry Kaufman. Cambridge UP, 2011. 827–46.

Stefaniak, Regina. 'Isis Rising: The Ancient Theology of Donatello's "Virgin" in the Santo'. *Artibus et Historiae* 27.53 (2006): 89–110.

Sternberg, Robert J., and Jennifer Jordan, eds. *A Handbook of Wisdom: Psychological Perspectives*. Cambridge UP, 2005.

Sterne, Melvin. 'Shakespeare, Buddha, and King Lear'. *Journal of Buddhist Ethics* 14 (2007): 129–52.

Strabo. *The Geography of Strabo*. Trans. H. C. Hamilton and W. Falconer. 3 vols. George Bell, 1903. Perseus Digital Library. Accessed October 3, 2023. https://www.perseus.tufts.edu/hopper/

Strier, Richard. *The Unrepentant Renaissance: From Petrarch to Shakespeare to Milton*. U of Chicago P, 2011.

Strong, Roy. 'The Elizabethan Malady: Melancholy in Elizabethan and Jacobean Portraiture'. *Apollo* 79 (1964): 264–9.

Suzuki, Daisetz Teitaro. *Zen Buddhism: Selected Writings of D. T. Suzuki*. Ed. William Barrett. Doubleday, 1956.

Works Cited

[365

Swetnam, Joseph. *The arraignment of lewde, idle, froward and unconstant women, or the vanitie of them, choose you whether: with a commendacion of wise, vertuous, and honest women: pleasant for married men, profitable for young men, and hurtfull to none.* Thomas Archer, 1615.

Swift, Daniel. *Shakespeare's Common Prayers: The Book of Common Prayer and the Elizabethan Age.* Oxford UP, 2012.

Szalavitz, Maia. *Unbroken Brain: A Revolutionary New Way of Understanding Addiction.* St. Martin's, 2016.

Szeman, Imre, and Jennifer Wenzel. 'What Do We Talk About When We Talk About Extractivism?' *Textual Practice* 35.3 (2021): 505–23.

Tarn, William Woodthorpe. *The Greeks in Bactria and India.* Cambridge UP, 1938, 2010.

Tassi, Marguerite A. 'The Way of the *Bodhisattva*: A Buddhist Understanding of *King Lear*'. *Critical Survey* 35.2 (2023): 80–91.

Tate, William. 'King James I and the Queen of Sheba'. *English Literary Renaissance* 26.3 (Autumn 1996): 561–85.

Tay, Louis, and James O. Pawelski, eds. *The Oxford Handbook of the Positive Humanities.* Oxford UP, 2021.

Tevdovski, Ljuben. 'The Beauty of the *Oikumene* Has Two Edges: Nurturing Roman Imperialism in the "Glocalizing" Traditions of the East'. In *Community and Identity at the Edges of the Classical World.* Ed. Aaron W. Irvin. Wiley Blackwell, 2021. 7–28.

Theis, Jeffrey S. *Writing the Forest in Early Modern England: A Sylvan Pastoral Nation.* Duquesne UP, 2009.

Thom, Johan C. 'Sophia as Second Principle in Wisdom of Solomon'. In *Toward a Theology of the Septuagint: Stellenbosch Congress on the Septuagint, 2018.* Ed. Johann Cook and Martin Rösel. Society of Biblical Literature, 2020. 263–76.

Thoreau, Henry David. *Walden; or, Life in the Woods.* In *Walden, The Maine Woods, Collected Essays and Poems.* Ed. Robert F. Sayre and Elizabeth Hall Witherell. Library of America, 2007.

Thubten, Anam. *The Fragrance of Emptiness: A Commentary on the Heart Sutra.* Dharmata, 2018.

——. *No Self, No Problem: Awakening to our True Nature.* Snow Lion, 2009.

Thurman, Robert. *Wisdom Is Bliss: Four Friendly Fun Facts That Can Change Your Life.* Hay House, 2021. PDF.

Toscano, Alberto. '"By contraries execute all things": Figures of the Savage in European Philosophy'. *Radical Philosophy* 2.04 (Spring 2019): 9–22.

Touati, Houari. *Islam et Voyage au Moyen Âge: Histoire et anthropologie d'une pratique lettrée.* Éditions du Seuil, 2000.

Trowbridge, Richard Hawley. 'Waiting for Sophia: 30 Years of Conceptualizing Wisdom in Empirical Psychology'. *Research in Human Development* 8.2 (2011): 149–64.

A true declaration of the estate of the colonie in Virginia. William Barret, 1610.

Trungpa, Chögyam. *Shambhala: The Sacred Path of the Warrior*. Ed. Carolyn Rose Gimian. Shambhala, 2009.

Tryon, Thomas. *The way to health, long life, and happiness, or, a discourse of temperance*. Andrew Sowle, 1683.

Tymme, Thomas. *A dialogue philosophicall. Wherein natures secret closet is opened*. Clement Knight, 1612.

Uhlig, Claus. '"The Sobbing Deer": *As You Like It*, II.i.21–66 and the Historical Context'. *Renaissance Drama* 3 (1970): 79–109.

Uždavinys, Algis. 'At-Tasawwuf and Neoplatonic Philosophy'. *Acta Orientalia Vilnensia* 2 (2001): 73–83.

Vaughan, Alden T. '"Expulsion of the Salvages": English Policy and the Virginia Massacre of 1622'. *The William and Mary Quarterly* 35.1 (January 1978): 57–84.

——. 'William Strachey's "True Reportory" and Shakespeare: A Closer Look at the Evidence'. *Shakespeare Quarterly* 59.3 (Fall 2008): 245–73.

Vaughan-Lee, Llewellyn. 'Adab—Sufi Etiquette in the Outer and Inner Worlds'. *SUFI: Journal of Mystical Philosophy and Practice* 86 (December 2013). Rpt. by The Golden Sufi Center. Accessed October 6, 2023. https://goldensufi.org/adab-sufi-etiquette-in-the-outer-and-inner-worlds/

Vendler, Helen. *The Art of Shakespeare's Sonnets*. Harvard UP, 1997.

Verde, Tom. 'A Man of Two Worlds'. *AramcoWorld* 59.1 (January/February 2008). https://archive.aramcoworld.com/issue/200801/a.man.of.two.worlds.htm

Vergil. *The Aeneid*. Trans. Shadi Bartsch. Modern Library, 2021.

Viret, Pierre. *The schoole of beastes; intituled, the good housholder, or the oeconomickes. Made dialogue-wise, by M. Peter Viret, translated out of French into English, by I. R.* Printed by Robert VValde-graue, 1585.

Vitkus, Daniel J. *Turning Turk: English Theater and the Multicultural Mediterranean, 1570–1630*. Palgrave Macmillan, 2003, 2016.

Vives, Juan Luis. *The Education of a Christian Woman: A Sixteenth-Century Manual*. Trans. and ed. Charles Fantazzi. U of Chicago P, 2000.

Vogt, Katja Maria. *Law, Reason, and the Cosmic City: Political Philosophy in the Early Stoa*. Oxford UP, 2008.

——. 'The Stoics on Virtue and Happiness'. In *The Cambridge Companion to Ancient Ethics*. Ed. Christopher Bobonich. Cambridge UP, 2017. 183–99.

Works Cited

[367

Walker, Katherine. 'Shakespeare and the Magic of Mummy: *Julius Caesar*'s Consumed/Consuming Bodies'. *Preternature: Critical and Historical Studies on the Preternatural* 7.2 (2018): 215–38.

Walsh, Roger. 'What Is Wisdom? Cross-Cultural and Cross-Disciplinary Syntheses'. *Review of General Psychology* 19.3 (2015): 278–93.

——. 'The World's Great Wisdom: An Integral Overview'. In *The World's Great Wisdom: Timeless Teachings from Religions and Philosophies*. Ed. Roger Walsh. SUNY, 2014. 213–42.

——, ed. *The World's Great Wisdom: Timeless Teachings from Religions and Philosophies*. SUNY, 2014.

Waters, Anne, ed. and intro. *American Indian Thought: Philosophical Essays*. Blackwell, 2004.

Watson, Alasdair. 'From Qays to Majnun: The Evolution of a Legend from 'Udhri Roots to Sufi Allegory'. *La Trobe Journal* 91 (June 2013): 35–45.

Watson, Robert N. *Back to Nature: The Green and the Real in the Late Renaissance*. U of Pennsylvania P, 2006.

Watts, Alan. *Nature, Man and Woman*. Thames & Hudson, 1958.

——. *The Way of Zen*. Vintage, 1999. PDF.

Weemes, John. *The pourtraiture of the image of God in man*. Iohn Bellamie, 1627.

Wehrs, Donald. 'Cognitive Virtue and Global Ecosociability'. In *Shakespeare and Virtue: A Handbook*. Ed. Julia Reinhard Lupton and Donovan Sherman. Cambridge UP, 2023. 244–56.

——. 'Touching Words: Embodying Ethics in Erasmus, Shakespearean Comedy, and Contemporary Theory'. *Modern Philology* 104.1 (August 2006): 1–33.

Weissbourd, Emily. '"I Have Done the State Some Service": Reading Slavery in *Othello* through *Juan Latino*'. *Comparative Drama* 47.4 (Winter 2013): 529–51.

Wenham, Gordon J. *Psalms as Torah: Reading Biblical Song Ethically*. Baker Academic, 2012.

West, M. L. *Early Greek Philosophy and the Orient*. Oxford UP, 1971.

West, William N. *As If: Essays in 'As You Like It'*. Punctum, 2016.

Wheatley, Margaret J. *Leadership and the New Science: Discovering Order in a Chaotic World*. 2nd ed. Berrett-Koehler, 1999.

Wied, Hermann von. *A briefe and a plaine declaration of the duety of maried folks*. Trans. Haunce Dekin. H. Singleton, 1588.

——. *The Glasse of Godly Love*. Trans. Haunce Dekin. J. Charlewood, 1588.

Williams, Bernard. *Moral Luck: Philosophical Papers 1973–1980*. Cambridge UP, 1981.

Shakespeare and Wisdom

Wilson, Harold S. '"Nature and Art" in *Winter's Tale* IV, iv, 86 ff'. *The Shakespeare Association Bulletin* 18.3 (July 1943): 114–20.

Wind, Edgar. *Pagan Mysteries in the Renaissance*. Rev. ed. Norton, 1968.

Witmore, Michael. 'Shakespeare and Wisdom Literature'. In *Shakespeare and Early Modern Religion*. Ed. David Loewenstein and Michael Witmore. Cambridge UP, 2015. 191–213.

Yates, Frances A. *Giordano Bruno and the Hermetic Tradition*. Routledge & Kegan Paul, 1964.

——. *The Occult Philosophy in the Elizabethan Age*. Routledge & Kegan Paul, 1979.

——. *Theatre of the World*. U of Chicago P, 1969.

Yazicioglu, U. Isra. 'Wisdom in the Qur'an and the Islamic Tradition'. In *The Oxford Handbook of Wisdom and the Bible*. Ed. Will Kynes. Oxford UP, 2021. 221–40.

Yeats, William Butler. 'Among School Children'. Poetry Foundation. Accessed September 25, 2023. https://www.poetryfoundation.org/poems/43293/among-school-children

Yoo, Dosung. *Thunderous Silence: A Formula for Ending Suffering*. Wisdom, 2013.

Yunkaporta, Tyson. *Sand Talk: How Indigenous Thinking Can Save the World*. HarperCollins, 2019.

Zanlonghi, Giovanna. *Teatri di formazione: Actio, parola e immagine nella scena gesuitica del Sei-Settecento a Milano*. Vita e Pensiero, 2002.

Zhmud, Leonid. *Pythagoras and the Early Pythagoreans*. Trans. Kevin Windle and Rosh Ireland. Oxford UP, 2012.

Zysk, Kenneth G. 'The Science of Respiration and the Doctrine of the Bodily Winds in Ancient India'. *Journal of the American Oriental Society* 113.2 (April–June 1993): 198–213.

INDEX

Page numbers in italics refer to illustrations, those followed by n are notes and those followed by t are tables

Abram, David, 26n, 37, 42
academia, 271, 281–2
adab, 213–14, 225, 229
Advaita Vedantism, 34
  Afro-Eurasian *oikumene*, 23, 27–35
Afro-Eurasian thoughtworld, 233
Afro-Platonism, 9, 56, 60
Agamben, Giorgio, 240–1
Agricola, Georgius, *De Re Metallica*, 247
ahimsā, 8
Al-Andalus, 302–4
al-Asad, Yūḥannā, 213–14, 224n
  Cosmographia and Geographia de Africa, 223–4
  Description of Africa, 223
  Geographiocal historie of Africa, 212–13
  see also Leo Africanus
alchemy, 246–7
Alexandria, 32–3, 210
Alexandrian aesthetics, 9, 60–1
al-Ghazālī, Abu Ḥamid, *Alchemy of Happiness*, 215–16
al-Ghazālī, Ahmad, 208, 214
Algonquians, 237–8, 241, 243, 245, 257, 260–4

Al-Hujwiri, 220
allegorical drama, 95–6
Allen, Nick, 36
Allot, Robert, *Wits theater of the little world*, 132, 133n
All's Well That Ends Well, 7–8, 10, 214, 220
Al-Masudi, 64
al-Rudhabari, 207
al-Yamāma, Zarqā', 248
al-Zamakhshari, al-Harizmi, 230
Americas, 237–67
anthropomorphism, 135–6
anti-Muslim racism, 211–15, 234–5
Antony and Cleopatra, 9
  as wisdom literature, 46–72
aphorisms, 7–8, 31
Apocalyptic Woman, 66, 67
apophasis, 43
apophatic theology, 172n, 177, 199, 203; *see also via negativa*
Apuleius, 56, 59, 128n
  The Golden Ass, 50–1
Arabic-Aristotelian confluence, 214
Arabic poetry, 298–310
areté, 148

370] *Shakespeare and Wisdom*

Aristotle, 12, 25, 36, 129, 134n, 239
  Nicomachean Ethics, 148
Armstrong, Karen, 183
ars moriendi, 105
As You Like It, 119–45
  dukkha in, 321
  sapiential pluralism in, 26
As You Like It (2007, dir Kenneth Branagh), 119, 144
ascension, 64–9
Ashoka, 31–2
astronomy, 123n
Athanasius, Saint, 75
attunement, 26, 38–9, 119, 136–7, 150, 153–6, 214, 228, 262, 327
Augustine, 49, 208
Avalokiteśvara, 181, 184–5, 193
Axial Age of sages, 40n, 45, 122, 143
Ayurveda, 11

Bacon, Francis, 244–5
Baghdad's 'House of Wisdom', 32
Bakhtin, Mikhail Mikhailovich, 304n
Baldwin, William
  Sayings of the Wise . . ., 124, 130–1
  A Treatise of Morall Philosophie, 7, 27
Band, Tonawanda, 285
Barker, Francis, 264
Basil, Saint, 75
beauty and love, 207–8
'becoming animal', 26n
belonging, 149, 160, 165, 274, 285, 287
Ben Sira (Ecclesiasticus), 55
Bennett, Robert, 139n
Berenice, bride of Vespasian, 71

Bermuda, 242–3
Bible
  Colossians, 52
  Corinthians, 140
  Deuteronomy, 67
  'dominion' in, 281
  Ecclesiastes, 68, 76
  Exodus, 27, 49, 69
  Geneva Bible, 92, 93, 312
  Hebrew Bible, 33, 60–1
  Job, 68
  Kings, 54, 61
  metempsychosis in, 85–6
  New Testament, 57
  Proverbs, 6–7, 48–9, 51, 53–5, 66, 71, 76, 92–3
  Psalm 51, 76
  Psalm 90, 86
  Psalm 103, 86, 93
  Psalms, 66, 68, 74–6
  Psalms 104, 52–3, 66
  Psalms 119, 73
  Revelation, 65–6
  Song of Songs, 60–1, 66, 67
bodhisattva, 25, 127n, 178, 178n, 181, 182n, 194, 316, 322
bodhisattvadevi, 193–5, 197
Boggs, Grace Lee, 205
Bond, George, 319
Bono, Barbara J., 60
Book of Common Prayer, 76, 85–6
borders, 278–9, 288–9, 293–4
Bourgeault, Cynthia, 6, 25, 218
Brahmins, 30–1, 57, 128n
Brazil, 245–6
breath of life, 37–42, 81–2;
  see also conspiration
Breitenberg, Mark, 220
Brenk, Frederick E., 59
Brexit, 278, 287, 289, 296
Brissenden, Alan, 134n

Index

[371

British Museum, 294
Brotton, Jerry, 212
Brunnhölzl, Karl, 179n, 185
Bruyneel, Kevin, 287
Bry, Theodor de, 260, 261
  Atalanta fugiens, 248, 249
  Magus goggled and tracking
    Nature through the night with
    staff and lamp, 249
  Their danses vvhich they vse at
    their highe feastes, 261
Buddha
  and the Bard, 311–22
  in non-human form, 136n
Buddhism
  anthropomorphism and ecology,
    136–7
  arhat, 34n
  bodhisattva, 172, 178–81
  clown figure, 192n
  Dhammapada, 30–2
  dukkha [suffering], 182–3,
    188, 312, 321
  'four noble truths', 178n,
    193n
  Greco-Buddhism, 28, 127–8
  human heartedness, 11–12
  impermanence, 126–8, 144
  Indra's Net, 42–5
  interbeing, 2, 11, 43–5, 293,
    320–1
  and Islam, 32n
  Mahāyāna, 172, 172n, 313
  Mahāyāna Bodhisattva ideal,
    178–82
  path of wisdom, 171–99
  Pythagoras, 128n
  tantra, 13
  As You Like It (2007, dir
    Kenneth Branagh), 119–20
Burkert, Walter, 125n
Burrow, Colin, 80

Cajete, Greg, 35
Calvin, Jean, 75
Calvin's Case, 238–41
Caporicci, Camilla, 61, 67
care, ethic of, 2, 9, 14, 16, 17, 35,
  39, 44, 186, 191–2, 194, 199,
  204, 294
  communities of, 294
  of self and for others, 149–56
  sovereign, 146–69
  theatre of, 286
Carlyle, Thomas, 93–4
Castiglione, Baldassare, 214
  The Book of the Courtier, 224–5
Caygill, Howard, 9
Celan, Paul, 305n
change, 73–94
Chapman, George, *A pleasant*
  comedy entituled: An
  humerous dayes myrth, 137
Charles, Jos, 'A Little Night Cycle',
  298–300
Chinese shamanic wisdom, 41–2
Chokmah [allegorised Wisdom],
  49, 51–5, 56n, 173
chokmah [wisdom], 24
Christian humanism, 27, 49,
  68, 69
Christianity, 25, 93, 103–14, 172n,
  216
  Greco-Christian, 129, 207, 218;
    see also Neoplatonism
  Sufi-Christian path, 201, 208–10,
    215, 217, 219
Chrysippus, 40
Cicero, 141
Citizen Potawatomi Nation, 291
Cleopatra [character], Egyptian
  gold, 69–72
Cleopatra [historical person],
  63–4, 70–1
  'Dialogue of the Philosophers', 64

372] *Shakespeare and Wisdom*

clown figure, 140, 192n; *see also* fools

Coccia, Emanuele, 252–3

Cohen, Yoram, 35–6

Coke, Edward, 238, 240–1

Colie, Rosalie Littell, 149, 159

colonial erasure, 283–4

colonialism, 234–5, 277–80, 285–97

  and climate crisis ['Co$_2$lonialism'], 235

  English language and, 283, 285–97

  settler, 234–5, 272, 285–97

  and Shakespeare, 285–97

commonplace books, 7, 27

compassion, xiii, 16, 19, 93, 119, 127, 171–99, 216, 313, 323

conscience [archaic], 40, 105, 108–9, 114, 326

consciousness [as unitive awareness], 26–7, 34, 40, 44, 63, 72, 173, 188–9, 199, 274, 328–9; *see also* Oneness

'seeing the world', Sayet, 291

conspiration, 40–1

contemplation as exercise of stillness, 37–8

conversion narrative, 215

conviviality, 38–9

Copernicus, Nicolaus, 123n

Cordelia [character]

  kind nursery, 193–9

  Nothing koan, 182–93

Coriolanus, Instagram, 320

Cormack, Bradin, 147, 159

Cortes, Mayra, 255

cosmology

  holistic, 143

  pneumatic, 56, 244, 258

cosmopolitanism, 154–5

counsel, 95–117

  self-serving, 97–100

courtesy, 224–5; *see also adab*

courtly love, 218

Cousins, A. D., 77n

Coverdale, Myles, 80–1

  Goostly psalmes and spirituall songes, 74–6

creative wisdom, 268–330

cultural cross-fertilisation, 23

cultural erasure, 290–1

Cymbeline, Cleopatra [historical person], 46, 61

Cyprus, 200–1, 217, 220, 221

daimon, 12, 153, 160

Dakake, Maria Massi, 208–9

dance, 139, 165, 256n, 259–65, 326–7

Dass, Ram, 321

Davies, John, 238

Davis, Natalie Zemon, 210, 214–15

death, 73–94, 305–8, 318–19

De Vos, Paula, 247

DenBoer, James, 304

Desdemona [character], as a divine ocean, 217–20

desert, 57–64

Dhammapada, 30–1, 322

dharma, 32, 43, 177–8, 321

Digges, Thomas, 123n

Diogenes Laertius, 27, 30

diversity, 27, 48

divination, 164n

Divine courtship, 215–17

Divine Love, 207–8, 225

Divine ocean, 217–20

Donne, John, 75, 76

Dronke, Peter, *Medieval Latin and the Rise of European Love-Lyric*, 303

dualism, 26n, 143, 180, 188, 204, 215

Index

[373

dukkha [suffering], 182–3, 188, 312, 321

East-West transmission, 12, 23–45, 330
Eastern spirituality, 119–20
ecocosmopolitanism, 142–5
ecognosis, 125–8, 134, 136–7, 140–5, 280–1
  melancholy as symptom of, 136–9
ecological Shakespeare, 1–5
ecology, 2, 8, 23–45, 62, 137, 205, 291, 328
ecosophy, 44
ecumenical pluralism, 71
ecumenism, 1–5, 23, 27, 34, 37, 44, 143
Eden, Richard, 242
Edmondson, Paul, 82
Edwards, Richard, *Damon and Pythias*, 131–2, 133n, 143
ego-logic vs ecologic, 2, 8, 14, 17, 38, 62, 205, 236, 328
Egypt
  Alexandria, 32–3, 47
  Cleopatra [character] and, 69–72
  and metempsychosis, 128n
  and Woman Wisdom, 48–57
  women in, 47n
Empedocles, 36
'engines', 247–50, 263, 266
English language, and colonialism, 283, 285–97
environmental activism, 39, 43–5, 204–5, 325
'epochic' philosophy, 31
Erasmian humanism, 130
Erasmus, Desiderius
  Adagia, 7, 124
  Praise of Folly, 140

erasure
  colonial, 283–4
  cultural, 290–1
  language, 285–97
eros, 16, 67, 201–4, 228–9, 324–6, 330
erōs, 8, 201–2, 215
erotic knowledge, 201–4
erotic love, 228–9
ethical karma, 30–1
eudaimonia, 12, 153, 167, 217
experiential wisdom, 229–36
extractivism, 249–50

false Wisdom figure, 98
feminism, 174n, 201, 218;
  see also Woman Wisdom, Sophia, *sophia*
Ficino, Marsilio, 124
'filth', 250–4, 265
Fletcher, Richard, 56
Flintoff, Everard, 31
Florio, John, 241, 245–6
folly of human wisdom, 140–2
fools, 7, 192n; *see also* clown figure
forgiveness, 87–93
'four noble truths', 178n, 193n
Fox, Michael V., 49, 52–3
free will, 107–14
Freud, Sigmund, 137
Frye, Northrop, 161, 163
Fulbecke, William, 242

Garner, Stanton B., 252, 255
Gateless Gate (Mumonkan), 188–90
generosity, 39, 44, 143, 182, 187, 192, 196, 214
genocide, 235, 241, 245, 257n, 287

374] *Shakespeare and Wisdom*

Gesner, Konrad, *The newe iewell of health wherein is contayned the most excellent secretes of phisicke and philosophie*, 246
ghazal poetry, 207–15
Ghosh, Amitav, 245, 247
Gill, Christopher, 153–4
Glissenti, Fabio, 98
  Discorsi morali contra il dispiacer del morire, 104–7, 115
  La Morte innamorata, 115
  La Ragione sprezzata, 107–10, 114–15
  L'Andrio, 110–11
  L'Androtoo, 110–11
  morality plays, 103–14
Global Shakespeare, 121, 142–5
Globe theatre, 270, 279
gnosis, 11, 11n, 25
Gnosticism, 11n
Goeman, Mishuana, 285, 296–7
gold, 69–72
Golding, Arthur, 84–5, 125–6, 129
Goodrich, Peter, 258–9
goodness, 146–167
Goswami, Amit, 228
Greco-Buddhism, 28, 127–8;
  see also East-West transmission
Greco-Christian, 207
Greek philosophy, 33
Greek ethics, 2, 12, 18, 148, 150
Grove, Jairus Victor, 264
Guadeloupe, 242

Habib, Imtiaz, 214
hadith, 208–10, 219
Hamlet
  aphorisms in, 7–8
  attunement in, 26–7
  forgiveness in, 92

  melancholy as symptom of ecognosis in, 137
  mourning in, 306–8
  Pythagoras in, 132
  scepticism in, 31
  time in, 13
Hamlin, Hannibal, 57
haraam [sacred space], 222–9
haram [women's quarters], 222
Hariot, Thomas, *A briefe and true report of the new found land of Virginia*, 260, 261
Harjo, Joy, 285
harmony
  ecognosis, 143
  Leibniz, G. W. F., 162–3
  in *Othello*, 200–2
  Pythagoras, 4, 121, 123–5, 132–4
  Shakespeare and scripture, 93–4
  in Sonnet 60, 86
  Stoicism, 41, 150–4, 324
  in *The Tempest*, 256, 260, 263–4
  see also conviviality, *koinonia*
Hawken, Paul, *Blessed Unrest*, 44
healing arts, 10
  capacity to heal and be healed, 282–3, 324, 328
  Hinduism, 11
Heart Sūtra, 178–82, 184, 191, 196
heart-mind, 170–267
heart-mind-body experience, 35
Hebrew Bible, 33, 60–1
Hebrew wisdom, 47–8
Heckscher, W. S., 59
hêgemonikon, 152, 154
I *Henry IV*, wisdom, 6–7
Henry V, mindfulness, 311, 322
Henry VIII, Queen of Sheba (Bilqis), 54
Henslowe, Philip, 130n
  'Diary', 129

Index

[375

Herbert, George, 76, 311
Hesiod, *Theogony*, 200–1
hikma, 229–30
Hinduism
 healing arts, 11
 Indra, 232–3
 Pythagoras and, 127
 tantra, 13
Hixon, Lex, 177, 193
holographic wisdom, 35–6, 44
Horky, Phillip Sidney, 56
Hudson Valley Shakespeare,
 274–5
Hugo, Victor, 171
Hulme, Peter, 264
humanism
 Christian, 49, 68, 69
 Erasmian, 130
 transcendental, 59–60
 Hymn of the Pearl, Apostle
 Thomas, 233

Iago [character], 96–108,
 115–16
Iamblichus' Life of Pythagoras,
 122n, 133n
Ibn Jubayr, 210
imperialism, 279, 296–7
inclusion, 15, 148, 195, 329–30;
 see also welcome
India, 256n
Indian Removal Act, 290
Indian Vedantic teaching, 11
'Indians in Boxes', 294
Indigenous audience, 275–6
Indigenous kinship, 44, 269–97
Indigenous languages, reclamation
 of, 285–97
Indigenous people, 269–97
 of 'Virginia', 237–8
Indigenous science, 269–97
Indigenous understandings, 23

Indo-European thoughtworld,
 30, 64, 144, 200; see also
 oikumene
Indo-Greek interaction, 29–30
Indra's Net, 42–5
Ingenito, Domenico, 215
Instagram, 320
 'Shakespeare and Mindfulness',
 316
interbeing, 2, 11, 43–5, 293,
 320–1
interconnection, 6, 42, 105, 108,
 149, 163, 259
interdependence, 2, 12, 34, 43,
 46–7, 58, 69, 292–3
interspirituality, 222–6
'ishq, 206, 231
Isis, 49–51, 59
Islam
 anti-Muslim racism, 211–13,
 227, 234–5
 beauty and love in, 207–8
 and Buddhism, 32, 233n
 Muslims, 303
 and Neoplatonism, 208
 Sufism as mysticism of the One,
 208
 Sufism and Othello, 206–7
 travel as path to discovery, 210
 see also Sufism, 'turning Turk',
 'Turk'
Islamophobia, 211–13, 227, 234–5
Israel, 49n

Jacques [character], the
 Pythagorean, 128–40
James I, King of England (VI of
 Scotland), 54, 60
 True Law of Free Monarchies,
 239
jealousy, 222–9
 zealous to jealous love, 224, 226

376]   *Shakespeare and Wisdom*

Jews, 57
  of Alexandria, 8–9
jhana, 11
Johnson, Samuel, 76
Jonson, Ben, *Masque of Blackness*,
  258
Julius Caesar, self-counsel, 116
Junker, William, 57, 67
jurisprudence, 237–67
Just, Michal, 34

Kahn, Coppélia, 227
kalon, 157, 160, 162, 164–5, 167
karma, ethical, 30–1
Katib, Yosef al-, 303–5
Keats, John, 6
Keilen, Sean, 63
Keller, Catherine, 252, 265–6
  Political Theology of the Earth,
  258
Kello, Robin, 269–84
Kelsey, Rachel M., 256n
kenosis, 6, 25, 177, 203, 214
kharja, 302–5
Kimmerer, Robin Wall, 39–40,
  262, 291–2
kinaesthetic
  ethics, 170–267
  experience, 255
  power, 252–3
  resonance, 262–6
  wisdom, 237–67
kind
  gentle-, 256–9
  nursery, 193–9
King Lear
  heart-mind-body experience in, 7
  and the path of wisdom, 171–99
kinship, 134, 137, 142, 149, 235
  Indigenous, 18, 44
  Krawec, Patty, 235
Kleinhempel, U. R., 33

Kloppenborg, John S., 56
Knight, G. Wilson, 59–60
knowing-with, 23
knowledge, erotic, 201–4
koan, 16, 177–82, 188–92, 195–7
  nothing, 193–9
koímaō, 153–4
Kottman, Paul A., 63
Krawec, Patty, 235–6

Langis, Unhae Park, 191, 316, 323
language erasure, 285–97
'law of nature', 238–41, 265
Layla-Majnūn story, 207
Leibniz, Gottfried Wilhelm, 150,
  161–3, 166
Leishman, J. B., 77
Leo Africanus, *see also* al-Asad,
  Yūḥannā
  Cosmographia and Geographia
  de Africa, 223–4
  Description of Africa, 223, 223n
  Geographiocal historie of Africa,
  212–13
Leviathan, 52–3
leviathans, 66
'ligeance', 238–40, 253–4, 265
Lloyd, Michael, 63
Locke, Anne, 76
Lorde, Audre, 204
  'Uses of the Erotic: The Erotic as
  Power', 201–2
Lord's Prayer, 79–80
Love's Labour's Lost, courtly love,
  218
Lumbard, Joseph E. B., 205–8
Lupić, Ivan, 96
Lupton, Julia Reinhard, 130, 151,
  258

Macbeth (dir. Yukio Ninagawa), 144
McMullen, Ejo, 181

Index

Macy, Joanna, 190
Magnone, Paolo, 29
Mahāyāna Bodhisattva ideal, 178–82
Mahāyāna Buddhism, 172, 172n, 313
Mandala, 320–1
Manetho, 33
Mann, Jenny C., 159–60
Mansur, Caliph, 32
mapping
  into the future, 23–45
  historical, 27–35
Marcus, Leah S., 288
Marcus Aurelius, 157, 164n
  Meditations, 153–4
Matar, Nabil, 207, 222–3
Measure for Measure
  intellectual and experiential knowledge in, 7
  noetic wisdom in, 36
meditation, 7, 11, 25, 38, 76, 87, 91–3, 176, 180, 311–13, 319, 327
Megathenes, 30
melancholy as symptom of ecognosis, 136–9
Meloni, Giorgia, 296
Merchant, Carolyn, 244–5
The Merchant of Venice
  mercy in, 93
  metempsychosis in, 128
  self-martyrdom in, 313–15
  wisdom in, 7
Meres, Francis, 73
meta-theatricality, 98
metempsychosis, 128n, 129
  as ecognosis, 125–8
Mexico, 278, 293
A Midsummer Night's Dream, 320
  Isis in, 50

migration, 32, 235, 269, 290n, 294
Milton, John, *Areopagitica*, 68–9
mind and character, 25–6
mind and wind, 37–8
mindfulness, and Shakespeare, 311–22
mindfulness-of-death, 319
Mind-World relation, 26n, 41
mirror, 42, 52n, 75, 105, 115, 136, 173, 177, 185, 188, 259, 262, 263, 265
Mitova, Veli, 231
Mohegans, 269–97
Montaigne, Michel de, 128n, 142
  Essais, 241, 245–6
  'That to Philosophise Is to Learn to Die', 38
'Moor' *see* 'Turk'
Moore, Jason W., 247
morality, 95–117
morality plays, 95–6
Morley, Thomas, 134, 134n
Morton, Timothy, 121, 125–6, 136–7
Mother, 173–7
  Prajñāpāramitā, 178–82
mourning, 67–9, 138, 198, 300, 305–10
'Mu', 188–90, 195
Muhammad, 10
mutual aid, 39, 44
muwashshah, 302–5
'Myne and Thine', 242, 252
mysticism, 34, 208

nafs, 206, 232–3
Nasr, Seyyed Hossein, 10–11
Native American wisdom, 39–40
Native audience, 275–6
Native land, 275
Native people/person, 269–84
nativity, 57–64

378] *Shakespeare and Wisdom*

natural goodness, 146–69
natural reciprocity, 39–40
Nāṭya-śāstra, 233
negative capability, 6, 142n
negative wisdom, 23–4
Neoplatonism, 34, 53, 201n,
    208–9, 218, 229
'new world', 238, 240–1, 243,
    251–3
Newman, Judith H., 55
Nhat Hanh, Thich, 43
Niccholes, Alexander, 220
Nielson, Melinda E., 172n
nihilism, 97–8
noble and sensual love, 201n
noetic wisdom, 10, 25, 36, 49, 55,
    203, 208–9, 214, 226, 228
nondualism, 72, 126–7, 143
Nonnus, *Dionysiaca*, 13
norms, 10, 43, 149–50, 156–7,
    159, 235
'Nothing', 177–80, 197
Nothing koan, 182–93
'nursery', 186–7

oikeiôsis, 12, 40, 148–9, 151–2,
    154–5, 157
  and care of self and for others,
    149–56
  and ecology, 118–69
oikos, 2–3, 26–7
oikumene, 1, 10–11, 46–7, 58,
    70–1
  Afro-Eurasian, 23, 27–35
  see also Indo-European
    thoughtworld
oil, 245–50, 257, 263
Oneness [as unitive awareness], 18,
    123, 134, 139–40, 234, 293;
    see also consciousness, wisdom
    ecology
Orgel, Stephen, 155–6, 158

'oriental cults', 71
Orientalism, 119
Othello, 200–36
  Afro-Platonism in, 9
  cistern in, 53–4
  Divine ocean in, 217–20
  'perfect soul', 201, 202, 213–15,
    219, 224, 229
  race in, 200–36
  religion in, 200–36
  self-serving counsel in, 97–100
  as Sufi traveller, 206–15
Ovid, 73–4
  Fasti, 161
  Metamorphoses, 83–7, 123–9,
    134–5

Parker, Matthew, Archbishop of
    Canterbury, 74–5
Path of Love, 203, 205–6, 209–10,
    216
path of negation (*via negativa*),
    172, 172n, 178–9
pearl, viii, ix, 42, 193, 210, 229,
    231–3, 254
Pequots, 245
Percy, George, 257, 260
Perdue, Leo G., 9, 67
*The Perfection of Wisdom in Eight
    Thousand Lines*, 176, 178–9,
    194–5, 197
performance
  actors' embodied art, 237–67
  meta-theatricality, 98
  as moral and spiritual practice,
    103–14
  open O, 323–30
  play in, 237–67
  wooden O, 6, 179
Pericles, 320
Persianate School of Love, 205–6
Persian Empire, 27–8

Index

[379

personal essay, 311–22
Peter Matyr d'Anghiera, 'Decades',
242
'Pethagores' play, 130n
Philo, 56–7
phronesis, 10
'pilgrimage', 209–11, 215
Plato
Symposium, 8, 202
Timaeus, 36
Plotinus, 66, 218–19
pluralism
ecumenical, 71
sapiential, 32–3
Plutarch, 56, 59, 60, 70
pneuma, 9, 37, 40, 67, 82, 151–3,
221, 326
'pneumatic cosmology', 15, 56,
244, 258
pneumatics, 220
political theology, 70, 239
Pory, John, 223–4
positive wisdom, 23–4
Potawatomi, 262
prajñā 173–4, 177, 184–5,
196–7
Prajñāpāramitā 171–99
prajñāpāramitā, 174n, 177n,
178n
prisca sapienta, 71
prisca theologia, 34, 36, 49, 124
pronouns, 88–91
property, 47, 183, 187, 238, 242–3,
246, 248, 253, 292
prophecy, 164n, 299
proverbs, 7, 12, 86
Psalms, 74–6, 79–80, 85–7, 179
psychoanalysis, 174n
psychosis, 151, 310
The Public Theater, 275
Purchas, Samuel, 243, 244
purity, 9, 214–15

inner, as *adab*, 213–14, 225, 229
man of, 213–14, 224
Sufism, 207
Putin, Vladimir, 296
Pyrrho, 31–2, 34n
Pythagoras
and Buddhism, 128n
and edification of others, 127n
and harmony of the spheres, 65,
134n
and Orient and Occident, 29–30
and Sonnet 60, 83–7, 94
travels of, 133n
Pythagoras [lost play], 129–30
Pythagoreanism, 119–45
astronomy, 123n
attunement, 38
koinonia, 44, 221
monadism, 137
Orphic and Eleusinian mysteries,
125n
and Platonism, 39
sensus communis, 36–7
wisdom literature, 119–45
wisdom tradition, 121–5
in *As You Like It*, 128–40

Qur'an, 217–18, 221, 224, 230

racism, 222, 226–7, 245, 254,
258–9, 277
anti-Muslim, 9, 211–13, 227,
234–5
radiating responsibilities, 292–5
Rahman, Jamal, 207
Ramusio, Giovanni Battista,
*Cosmographia and
Geographioa de Africa*, 223n
Rancière, Jacques, 266
reader engagement, 300–10,
313–15
reciprocity, 39

reconciliation, 87–93
repetitions, 78–80, 83
responsibility, 111, 259, 281, 292, 295, 329
Richardson, Kristina, 248
Romeo and Juliet
  in relation to Instagram, 320
  relatedness in, 43
  theoerotic courtship in, 215
Rumi, 7, 221, 228, 232
Ryuta, Minami, 144

Sacerdoti, Gilberto, 57
St Paul, 10, 52, 140
Sale, Caroline, 195
Sanskrit, 8, 11, 12–13
Santner, Eric, 151
sapienta, 10–11
sapiential pluralism, 32–3
satisfying nature, 241–5
Sayet, Madeline, 235
  conversation with, 269–84
  Where We Belong, 269–97
scepticism, 28n, 30–2, 135–6, 140–2
Schimmel, Annemarie, 218
science, 18, 32, 35–6, 40, 122, 247, 262
Scots, 238–9
Sea Venture, 242–3
'sea-change', 254–5
Seaford, Richard, 128n
Seipp, David J., 242
self-counsel, 103–14
self-reflexive knowing, 125–6
Seneca, Lucius Annaeus, 37–8, 160, 244n
  circle of gifts, 39–40
sensus communis, 3–4, 23, 35–42
Septuagint, 33, 56–7, 60–1, 67
settler colonialism, 272, 285–97
'settler memory', 287–8

Shakespeare
  and colonialism, 285–97
  and mindfulness, 311–22
  and wisdom literature, 5–13
@shakespeare_and_mindfulness, 316–17, 319–20
Shakespearean legacy, 28
Shankman, Steven, 183, 183n
Shannon, Laurie, 156–7, 250
'Shakespeare and Mindfulness' [Instagram profile], 316
'shapes', 256–60
Shapiro, James, 134
Shaw, George Bernard, 76
Sheba, Queen of (Bilqis), 52, 54, 60–2
Shekinah, 52
Shibayama, Zenkei, 188
Shufran, Lauren, 176
  The Buddha and the Bard, 320–1
Sick, David H., 128n
Simpson, Audra, 293–4
Simpson, Leanne Betasamosake, 292–3
Sir Thomas More, The Marriage of Wit and Wisdom, 100–3
Sirach (Ecclesiasticus), 76
Skura, Meredith Anne, 243–4, 258
social media, 311–22
Socrates, 38, 42–3, 140
Solomon, 54–6, 62
Sonnet 11, wisdom in, 78
Sonnet 15, time in, 81–2
Sonnet 18, time in, 82
Sonnet 24
  knowledge of the heart in, 306–9
  shadow-erotics in, 301–2
Sonnet 34, forgiveness in, 91–2
Sonnet 35, fallibility in, 93
Sonnet 60, time in, 82–7, 94
Sonnet 81, time in, 81

Index

[381

Sonnet 108, good life in, 78–9, 87, 94
Sonnet 120
    position of the pronouns in, *90*
    reconciliation in, 87–94
    time in, 89t
sonnets, 298–300, 304n, 305n, 311–12
Sonnets
    light in, 300–2
    love in, 63
    as spiritual exercise, 73–94
    use of language in, 82–5
    as worldly, 77n
Sophia, 8–9, 46–72
sophia, 10, 25–7
Sophianic Feminine, 216–18
sound, 161n, 255, 256, 264
sovereign care, 146–69
sovereignty, 25, 62, 66, 147, 151, 159, 186–7, 243, 258
Spade, Dean, 44
'speak Shakespeare', 285–97
Spenser, Edmund, 66
    Amoretti, 76
    'An Hymn of Heavenly Beauty', 57
spirit, 2, 11, 37, 41–2, 80–2, 188, 196, 205, 219, 228, 299, 311–12, 326
spiritual exercise, 27, 38
    Sonnets as, 73–94
    see also contemplation
spiritual journey, 194, 203, 206, 209–13, 217; *see also* travels
spiritual practice, xiii, 27, 38–9, 95–118, 171–236, 311–22; *see also* meditation, mindfulness
spirituality, 2, 18, 25–6, 34, 119, 224
    as radical, 216–17

stillness, 37–8
Stoic cosmopolitanism, 2, 25–6, 44, 154, 293
Stoic wisdom, 146–69
Stoicism, 40–1, 164n
Strachey, William, 'True Reportory', 243
Strange Woman (*ishah zarah*), 9, 53–4, 71
Stranger [as God], 210, 216, 219, 229
stranger, xiii, 206–15, 219, 227, 229
Strier, Richard, 66
'subditus natus' 'subject born', 238–41
suffering, 6, 87, 91–3, 136, 171–99, 236, 312–27
Sufism
    adab, 213–14, 225, 229
    fanā' [annihilation], 207
    'isha, 206, 231
    as Islamic mysticism, 206–7
    nafs, 206, 232–3
    in *Othello*, 203–15, 218, 220, 222–3, 233–4
    Sufi-Christian path, 201
    tarīqah [path], 203
    tawhīd [Reality], 207
    theoeroticism, 200–36
    universalism, 207, 215, 234
sumpatheia, 154, 162–3
sūtra, 12–13, 42–5, 178n
    Heart Sūtra, 178–82, 184, 191, 196
svādhyāyā, 316, 322
Swetnam, Joseph, 220–1
Szeman, Imre, 249

Tantaquidgeon Indian Museum, 294
tantra, 13

Tao Sheng, 142–3
taqiyya, 212–15
Tate, Nahum, *King Lear*, 171–2
The Tempest, 237–67
  in relation to Instagram, 320
  Sayet and, 271–2, 285, 289–90
Teo, Mei Ann, 273
Tevdovski, Ljuben, 58, 70–1
theatre, 95–117, 237–67,
  269–97
theatrum mundi, 104–5, 132,
  143, 173
theoeroticism, 200–36
Thom, Johan C., 9
Thoreau, Henry David, 81
Thubten, Anam, 178
thunderbolt, 191
  as *vairā*, 215, 218, 232–3
time
  Aion, 13
  authority of, 80–1
  in *Hamlet*, 13
  in Sonnet 15, 81–2
  in Sonnet 18, 82
  in Sonnet 60, 82–7, 94
  in Sonnet 81, 81
  in Sonnet 120, 89t
Timon of Athens, Pythagoras in,
  129
Toscano, Alberto, 243, 250
'transcendental humanism', 59–60
transhistorical, 3, 13, 15, 173,
  204, 325, 328
transmarinis, 238–41
travels, 133n, 206–15
Tree of Life, 36–7
Troilus and Cressida
  ethics of welcome in, 235
  harmony with nature in, 41
  travels in, 210
Trowbridge, Richard Hawley,
  25–6

*A true declaration of the estate of
  the colonie in Virginia*, 243
Trump, Donald, 289, 296
Trungpa, Chögyam, 226
Truss, Liz, 296
Tryon, Thomas, 127
Tupinamba people, 245–6
'Turk'
  as barbaric, 204
  as Muslim, 204, 206
  and xenophobia, 211
'turning Turk'
  purification, 233–4
  Sufi theoeroticism, 205–6, 221–2
  zealous to jealous love, 224, 226
Twelfth Night
  fools in, 7
  good life in, 73
  Pythagoras in, 129
The Two Gentlemen of Verona
  leviathans in, 66
  'peevish', 74–5n
  sapiential pluralism in, 53
The Two Noble Kinsmen,
  mindfulness in, 317–18, *317*
Tymme, Thomas, 254
  *A dialogue philosophicall.
  Wherein natures secret closet
  is opened*, 246

unforgetting, 14, 235
universal wisdom, 280–1
universe of oppositions, 62–3
unmantling, 265–6

Valentinus, 219–20
Vedānta, 38
vegetarianism, 121, 123, 127, 143
veil, 177, 232–3, 233n
Vendler, Helen, 79, 80n
Venetian-Cypriot world, 204,
  224–5

Index [383

Venice, 103–14, 200–1, 222, 227
Venus, 58–9, 200–1, 220
  and Isis iconography, 47–8
Verde, Tom, 223n
via negativa, 172, 178–9
vice figures, 97–100, 115–16
Virginia, 204, 240–44, 252
  Indigenous people of, 237–8
  Their danses vvhich they vse at their highe feastes, 261
virtue, 7–8, 31, 46, 54, 71, 95–117, 130, 306, 308, 324
  as ability or power, 99
  as *aretē*, 39
  Buddhism in, 171–99
  ethics, 3
  Stoic, 40–1, 146–68
  Sufism in, 200–36
Vitkus, Daniel J., 211, 232–4
Vogt, Katja Maria, 153, 154
volta, 300–9

Wasserman, Nathan, 35–6
water, 57–64
Waters, Anne, 39
Watson, Robert N., 135, 142
'weird knowing', 126
welcome, ethics of, 235, 272–3, 283, 285–97
Wenzel, Jennifer, 249
West, William N., 136n
whiteness, 258
Whitmore, Michael, 1
Whitney, Isabella, *A Sweet Nosegay*, 7
Wilson, Harold S., 163
wind, 37, 59, 66
The Winter's Tale, 318–19
  mindfulness-of-death in, 318–19, 318
  stoic wisdom in, 146–69

wisdom
  capabilities, 24
  Chinese shamanic, 41–2
  ecology [as virtue ecology], 2, 8, 23–45, 62, 323
  experiential, 229–36
  false Wisdom figure, 98
  folly of human, 140–2
  and good counsel, 100–3
  Hebrew, 47–8
  holographic, 35–6, 44
  Indo-European traditions, 144
  kinaesthetic, 237–67
  as maternal, 173–7
  motifs of, 14, 42, 57, 67, 173, 233
  Native American, 39–40
  negative, 23–4
  noetic, 10, 25, 36, 49, 55, 203, 208–9, 214, 226, 228
  passed down, 12–13
  positive, 23–4
  as practical advice, 23
  and proximity to death, 305–8
  as revealed, 23
  Sayet, Madeline, 279–84
  sensus communis, 35–42
  stoic, 146–69
  transmission of through writing, 12–13
  universal, 280–1
  and welcome, 285–97
  wit and, 100–3
  and women, 8–10
wisdom literature
  Antony and Cleopatra as, 46–72
  in *As You Like It*, 119–45
  contemporary, 142–5
  Hebrew, 27
  kharja as, 305–8
  in *King Lear*, 199
  morality plays and, 96–7

384] *Shakespeare and Wisdom*

wisdom literature (*cont.*)
  and oral tradition, 12, 31, 178n
  Pythagorean, 119–45
  and Shakespeare, 5–13
  sonnet as, 305–8
Wisdom of Sirach, 66
Wisdom of Solomon (Book of
    Wisdom), 56
Woman Wisdom (*chokmah*), 8–9,
    48–57, 71
women
  in Egypt, 47n
  feminism, 174n, 201, 218
  and wisdom, 8–10
  wise women, 8–9

world as living organism, 36
  self-organising, 35, 41, 327,
    329–30

xenophobia, 211–12; *see also*
  racism

Yazicioglu, U. Isra, 32,
  229–30
yoga, 311–12, 316
Yunkaporta, Tyson, 250, 253

zealousness, 222–9
Zeno of Elea, 161n
Zhmud, Leonid, 125n